African American Voices

Uncovering the Past: Documentary Readers in American History

Series Editors: Steven Lawson and Nancy Hewitt

The books in this series introduce students in American history courses to two important dimensions of historical analysis. They enable students to engage actively in historical interpretation, and they further students' understanding of the interplay between social and political forces in historical developments.

Consisting of primary sources and an introductory essay, these readers are aimed at the major courses in the American history curriculum, as outlined further below. Each book in the series will be approximately 225–250 pages, including a 25–30 page introduction addressing key issues and questions about the subject under consideration, a discussion of sources and methodology, and a bibliography of suggested secondary readings.

Published

Paul G. E. Clemens
The Colonial Era: A Documentary Reader

Sean Patrick Adams
The Early American Republic: A Documentary Reader

Stanley Harrold
The Civil War and Reconstruction: A Documentary Reader

Steven Mintz
African American Voices: A Documentary Reader, 1619–1877

Robert P. Ingalls and David K. Johnson
The United States Since 1945: A Documentary Reader

Camilla Townsend
American Indian History: A Documentary Reader

Steven Mintz
Mexican American Voices: A Documentary Reader

Brian Ward
The 1960s: A Documentary Reader

Nancy Rosenbloom
Women in American History Since 1880: A Documentary Reader

Jeremi Suri
American Foreign Relations Since 1898: A Documentary Reader

Carol Faulkner
Women in American History to 1880: A Documentary Reader

David Welky
America Between the Wars, 1919–1941: A Documentary Reader

William A. Link and Susannah J. Link
The Gilded Age and Progressive Era: A Documentary Reader

G. Kurt Piehler
The United States in World War II: A Documentary Reader

Leslie Brown
African American Voices: A Documentary Reader from Emancipation to the Present

In preparation

Edward Miller
The Vietnam War: A Documentary Reader

Joseph Cullon
The Era of the American Revolution: A Documentary Reader

David Freund
The Modern American Metropolis: A Documentary Reader

African American Voices

A Documentary Reader from Emancipation to the Present

Edited by Leslie Brown

WILEY Blackwell

This edition first published 2014
© 2014 John Wiley & Sons, Inc.

Registered Office
John Wiley & Sons, Ltd, The Atrium, Southern Gate, Chichester, West Sussex, PO19 8SQ, UK

Editorial Offices
350 Main Street, Malden, MA 02148-5020, USA
9600 Garsington Road, Oxford, OX4 2DQ, UK
The Atrium, Southern Gate, Chichester, West Sussex, PO19 8SQ, UK

For details of our global editorial offices, for customer services, and for information about how
to apply for permission to reuse the copyright material in this book please see our website at
www.wiley.com/wiley-blackwell.

The right of Leslie Brown to be identified as the author of the editorial material in this work has
been asserted in accordance with the UK Copyright, Designs and Patents Act 1988.

Library of Congress Cataloging-in-Publication Data

African American Voices: A Documentary Reader from Emancipation to the Present / edited by
Leslie Brown. –1.
      pages   cm.   (Uncovering the past: documentary readers in American history)
   Includes bibliographical references and index.
   ISBN 978-1-4443-3940-6 (hardback) – ISBN 978-1-4443-3941-3 (paper)
1. African Americans–History–Sources.   I. Brown, Leslie, 1954–
   E184.6A346 2014
   973'.0496073–dc23

                                                            2013028187

A catalogue record for this book is available from the British Library.

Cover image: Crowd at the Lincoln Memorial, Civil Rights March on Washington D.C., 28 August
1963. Source: U.S. National Archives and Records Administration / Wikimedia Commons
Cover design by Simon Levy

Set in 10/12.5pt Sabon by SPi Publisher Services, Pondicherry, India

1   2014

Contents

List of Illustrations

Series Editors' Preface

Primary sources have become an essential component in the teaching of history to undergraduates. They engage students in the process of historical interpretation and analysis and help them understand that facts do not speak for themselves. Rather, students see how historians construct narratives that recreate the past. Most students assume that the pursuit of knowledge is a solitary endeavor; yet historians constantly interact with their peers, building upon previous research and arguing among themselves over the interpretation of documents and their larger meaning. The documentary readers in this series highlight the value of this collaborative creative process and encourage students to participate in it.

Each book in the series introduces students in American history courses to two important dimensions of historical analysis. They enable students to engage actively in historical interpretation, and they further students' understanding of the interplay among social, cultural, economic, and political forces in historical developments. In pursuit of these goals, the documents in each text embrace a broad range of sources, including such items as illustrations of material artifacts, letters and diaries, sermons, maps, photographs, song lyrics, selections from fiction and memoirs, legal statutes, court decisions, presidential orders, speeches, and political cartoons.

Each volume in the series is edited by a specialist in the field who is concerned with undergraduate teaching. The goal is not to offer a comprehensive selection of material but to provide items that reflect major themes and debates; that illustrate significant social, cultural, political, and economic dimensions of an era or subject; and that inform, intrigue, and inspire undergraduate students. The editor of each volume has written an introduction that discusses the central questions that have occupied historians in this field and the ways historians have used primary sources to answer them.

In addition, each introductory essay contains an explanation of the kinds of materials available to investigate a particular subject, the methods by which scholars analyze them, and the considerations that go into interpreting them. Each source selection is introduced by a short headnote that gives students the necessary information and a context for understanding the document. Also, each section of the volume includes questions to guide student reading and stimulate classroom discussion.

Leslie Brown's *African American Voices: A Documentary Reader from Emancipation to the Present* takes readers on a journey from the abolition of slavery in 1865 through the election of Barack Obama as the first African American president of the United States. Events unfold chronologically, but Brown organizes them in ways that offer new perspectives. "Freedom," "Upbuilding," and "Migration" recount the early years after emancipation and the reconstruction of black communities in the South and the North. "Determination," "Resistance," and "Resolve" take us through the Jim Crow era and the efforts of African Americans to marshal economic, political, and cultural resources within their communities and challenge the white racism limiting equal opportunity and citizenship. "Discontent," "Revolt," "Power," and "Revolution" document the extraordinary efforts to obtain full equality, overthrow segregation and disfranchisement, and empower black citizens to shape their own destinies. Finally, "Crosscurrents" and "Paradox" bring the story past the post-civil rights years during which, despite considerable progress, African Americans continue to face and attempt to overcome implicit or structural racial discrimination. Thus, as *African American Voices* vividly shows, in Brown's words, "African American history is the story of black people's struggle for freedom, fought on their own terms on the front lines of American culture, politics, and economics, and sustained by a deep belief (and arguably faith) in core American principles: democracy and equality."

The primary sources Brown includes in this volume underscore the long arc of the black freedom struggle from the end of the Civil War to the present. Her documents allow African Americans to speak on their own behalf by drawing on speeches, essays, photographs, posters, letters, articles, narratives, poetry, lyrics, raps, and petitions. With striking diversity, domestic workers, miners, sharecroppers, and migrants offer their voices alongside scholars, politicians, organizers, and activists to provide their own testimonies of race and racism. An experienced and dedicated teacher, Leslie Brown guides students toward a better understanding of the complexities and subtleties of modern African American history.

Steven F. Lawson and Nancy A. Hewitt,
Series Editors

Acknowledgments

The work on this collection began as an independent study project with an energetic group of Williams College students. We gathered weekly to think and talk about primary sources in African American history, then we set about finding multiple voices and interesting pieces that we thought should appear in the book. For their contributions, hard work, and enthusiasm I thank Shenai Williams, Anne Kerth, Lydia Carmichael, Lorenzo Patrick, Chris Edmonds, Lauren Zachary, Chris Hickel, Quaneece Calhoun, and Jade Carter.

Thanks also to my friends Emilye Crosby, Leslie Harris, and Alex Byrd who made many helpful suggestions; Maria Quintero, who did the herculean work of creating order from a tangle of folders, notes, and photocopies; and Rhon Manigault-Bryant and James Manigault-Bryant who read and commented on various sections and drafts. Special appreciation goes to the Dean of the Faculty at Williams College and my colleagues in the Department of History who made it possible for me to take time away from teaching to focus on this project. The staff of the John Nicholas Brown Center for Public Humanities and American Heritage at Brown University—especially Jenna Legault— welcomed me as a visiting scholar. Special gratitude goes to Martha Powers for listening to me drone on.

Series editors Nancy Hewitt and Steven Lawson sustained their faith that the collection would get done. I am indebted to my readers for their careful reviews, but especially the editorial staff of Wiley-Blackwell, including Julia Kirk, Peter Coveney, Georgina Coleby, Sue Leigh and others for bringing this thing home at last. Finally, to my partner Annie Valk, I owe special appreciation for her encouragement, support, and everlasting love.

The editor and publisher gratefully acknowledge the permission granted to reproduce the copyright material in this book:

1.7   "The Washerwoman's Strike" and "Letter to Mr. James English" reproduced with permission from "Black Laundresses Demand Higher Wages," *Atlanta Constitution*, July–August 1881, in Tera W. Hunter, "African-American Women Workers' Protest in the New South," *The OAH Magazine of History*, 13 (Summer 1999). Courtesy of OAH and T. Hunter.

4.2   Claude McKay, "If We Must Die," in *Harlem Shadows: The Poems of Claude McKay* (New York: Harcourt, Brace and Co., 1922). Courtesy of the Literary Representative for the works of Claude McKay, Schomurg Center for Research in Black Culture, The New York Public Library, Astor, Lenox and Tilden Foundation.

5.0   Epigraph reproduced from Bessie Smith, "Backwater Blues," 1927. © Hal Leonard. Reprinted with permission.

5.3   "The Bronx Slave Market," by Ella Baker and Marvel Cooke, *The Crisis*, 42 (November 1935). We wish to thank the Crisis Publishing Co., Inc., the publisher of the magazine of the National Association for the Advancement of Colored People, for the use of the material first published in the November 1935 issue of *The Crisis*.

5.5   "Proclamation of Southern Negro Youth: For Freedom, Equality, and Opportunity," reproduced with permission from Herbert Aptheker (ed.), *A Documentary History of the Negro People in the United States*, Vol. 4 (reprint, New York: Carroll Publishing, 1992), pp. 258–261. Courtesy of B. Aptheker.

5.6   Reproduced with permission from Adam Clayton Powell, Jr., "Soap Box: The Fight For Jobs," New York *Amsterdam News*, May 7 and 14, 1938.

6.3   Grant Reynolds, "What the Negro Soldier Thinks About This War," *The Crisis*, 51 (September, October, and November 1944). We wish to thank the Crisis Publishing Co., Inc., the publisher of the magazine of the National Association for the Advancement of Colored People, for the use of the material first published in the September, October, and November 1944 issue of *The Crisis*.

6.4   Pauli Murray, "A Blueprint for First Class Citizenship," *The Crisis*, 51 (November 1944), pp. 359–359. We wish to thank the Crisis Publishing Co., Inc., the publisher of the magazine of the National Association for the Advancement of Colored People, for the use of the material first published in the November 1944 issue of *The Crisis*.

6.5 Civil Rights Congress, *We Charge Genocide: The Historic Petition to the United Nations for Relief From a Crime of The United States Government Against the Negro People* (New York: Civil Rights Congress, 1951), pp. xi–xiii, 3–10. Reproduced with permission from Civil Rights Congress, 1951. © 1970 International Publishers.

6.6 "A Petition to the President of the United States and the U.S. Delegation to the United Nations," reproduced with permission from Herbert Aptheker (ed.), *A Documentary History of the Negro People in the United States*, Volume 6 (reprint, New York: Citadel Press, 1993), pp. 98–105. Courtesy of B. Aptheker.

7.1 Appellant Brief in *Brown v. Board of Education*, reargued December 8, 1953, from *Brown v. Board of Education*, in Gerhard Casper and Kathleen Sullivan (eds.), *Landmark Briefs and Arguments of the Supreme Court of the United States: Constitutional Law* (UPA Collections, Lexis-Nexis). Reprinted by permission of ProQuest LLC. Further reproduction prohibited. www.proquest.com.

7.2 Reproduced from Jo Ann Gibson Robinson with David Garrow, *The Montgomery Bus Boycott and the Women Who Started It: The Memoir of Jo Ann Gibson Robinson* (Knoxville: University of Tennessee Press, 1987).

7.3 Rev. Dr. Martin Luther King, Jr., "Nonviolence and Racial Justice," *Christian Century*, 74 (February 6, 1957), pp. 165–167. Reprinted by arrangement with The Heirs to the Estate of Martin Luther King, Jr., c/o Writers House as agent for the proprietor New York, NY. Copyright 1957 Dr. Martin Luther King, Jr.; copyright renewed 1995 Coretta Scott King.

7.4 Reproduced with permission from Robert F. Williams, "Can Negroes Afford to Be Pacifists?" *Liberation*, 4 (September 1959), pp. 4–7.

8.2 Reproduced from "Bigger Than a Hamburger" by Ella Baker, *The Southern Patriot*, May 1960.

8.3 Reproduced from Robert Moses, Letter from Magnolia County Jail to Tom Hayden (1961). Courtesy of R. Moses.

8.5   Reproduced with permission from interview with Diane Nash, November 12, 1985, Chicago, Illinois, for Blackside, Inc., *Eyes on the Prize: America's Civil Rights Years (1954–1965)*, edited transcript. Henry Hampton Collection, Film & Media Archive, Washington University Libraries.

8.6   Rev. Dr. Martin Luther King, Jr., "Letter from Birmingham Jail." Reprinted by arrangement with The Heirs to the Estate of Martin Luther King, Jr., c/o Writers House as agent for the proprietor New York, NY. Copyright 1963 Dr. Martin Luther King, Jr.; copyright renewed 1991 Coretta Scott King.

8.7   Reprinted with the permission of the author and Simon & Schuster Publishing Group from *Walking With The Wind: A Memoir of the Movement* by John Lewis with Michael D'Orso. Copyright © 1998 by John Lewis. All rights reserved.

9.1   Reproduced from "The Ballot or the Bullet," in George Breitman (ed.), *Malcolm X Speaks: Selected Speeches and Statements* (Grove Weidenfeld, 1969). Copyright © 1965, 1989 by Betty Shabazz and Pathfinder Press. Reprinted by permission.

10.1   Reproduced from *War Against the Panthers* by Huey P. Newton, by Writers & Readers Publishing, Inc. (now For Beginners LLC), 1996. Reprinted with permission.

10.2   Rev. Dr. Martin Luther King, Jr., "Beyond Vietnam – A Time to Break Silence." Reprinted by arrangement with The Heirs to the Estate of Martin Luther King, Jr., c/o Writers House as agent for the proprietor New York, NY. Copyright 1957 Dr. Martin Luther King, Jr.; copyright renewed 1995 Coretta Scott King.

10.5   Gil Scott-Heron, "The Revolution Will Not Be Televised" (New York: RCA Records, 1971). Courtesy of the estate of Gil Scott-Heron.

11.2   Reproduced from *Toxic Wastes and Race in the United States: A National Report on the Racial and Socio-Economic Characteristics of Communities with Hazardous Waste Sites*. Preface, pp. ix–x; Executive Summary, pp. xi–xvi; and Chapter 1, "A Context for Examining Toxic Wastes and Race," pp. 1–8. Copyright © 1987 United Church of Christ. All rights reserved. Reprinted with permission.

11.4   Joy James, "African American Women in Defense of Ourselves," published in *The Black Scholar*, 22, Nos. 1 & 2 (1992): 155. Reprinted with permission.

11.6   Text of the pledge that Minister Louis Farrakhan asked black men to take on October 16, 1995, during the Million Man March on Washington, DC.

11.7   Angela Y. Davis, "Masked Racism: Reflections on the Prison Industrial Complex," *ColorLines*, Fall 1998. Reprinted with permission.

Every effort has been made to trace copyright holders and to obtain their permission for the use of copyright material. The publisher apologizes for any errors or omissions in the above list and would be grateful if notified of any corrections that should be incorporated in future reprints or editions of this book.

Introduction

This 1862 photograph depicts a family residing on Smith's Plantation, named for James Joyner Smith, a secessionist who fled before the Union troops arrived. The Confederate Smith considered these people his possessions, his slaves, and at the time the United States government also considered them property, contraband to be confiscated under the auspices of the Union Army for the cause of war. Timothy O'Sullivan, who took the picture, worked for the famous Civil War photographer Matthew Brady, who wanted to bring to the public images it had never seen. The photograph went on exhibit at a Washington, DC, gallery in 1863, and with little information viewers could draw their own conclusions. O'Sullivan put a face on a deeply troubling topic, but he did not record the names of the people in the photograph.

What can we know about the black residents of Smith's Plantation, or what they represented? To understand what they thought and did, we must seek out their voices. A reporter from *The New York Times*, present when O'Sullivan made the photograph, wrote that the residents already considered themselves free. As far as they were concerned, the only thing that had held them in slavery was the power of – and the power behind – the slaveowner, and he had run away. In fact, their frozen pose presents an antithesis of the momentum generating beyond the camera lens, where freedpeople had begun the work of freedom. No young men appear in the photo, for instance, but other documents reveal that they had gone to join

African American Voices: A Documentary Reader from Emancipation to the Present, First Edition. Edited by Leslie Brown.
© 2014 John Wiley & Sons, Inc. Published 2014 by John Wiley & Sons, Inc.

Figure 0.1   Timothy O'Sullivan, "Five Generations on Smith's Plantation, Beaufort, South Carolina," photograph, 1862.

Source: Library of Congress, Prints and Photographs Division.

the 1st South Carolina Volunteers, a Beaufort-based military unit comprised of black men from surrounding plantations. For African Americans, ending slavery was the course of the war. They viewed their support of the Union as a requisite exercise in self-liberation as well as an act of citizenship.

Indeed, a national debate about African Americans unfolded in response to black initiatives in places like the Smith Plantation. A Union general freed them in the spring of 1862 by a field order, which Lincoln promptly rescinded. They were freed again as the slaves of "persons adjudged guilty of treason," when Congress passed the Second Confiscation Act in the summer of 1862. By the time the photograph appeared on exhibit, the Smith Plantation residents were considered "persons held as slaves within any State or designated part of a State, the people whereof shall then be in rebellion against the United States." In accordance with the Emancipation Proclamation, they were "thenceforward, and forever free."

Abraham Lincoln's Proclamation provided some legal clarity, but the document neither affected the view of African Americans who, like those in this photo, considered themselves already free, nor did it free the slaves in any larger sense, as is commonly believed. Slavery in the United States did not end until enough individual States ratified the Thirteenth Amendment that Secretary of State William Seward could declare the measure adopted, December 1865, eight months after the Civil War ended, some three years after this photograph was taken. Only then were the last of 4 million black Americans – those held in the Confederacy, the Union, and the territories – free by law from the bonds that had held them enslaved for more generations than five.

Primary Sources

The "Five Generations" photograph encourages us to explore the process of Emancipation, and that exploration leads us to consider the thoughts and experiences of its subject. The photo is evidence of history – a *primary source* – one of many visual, written, or spoken materials produced by persons with first-hand knowledge of a particular historical moment. Primary sources include letters, diaries, government reports, newspaper articles, accounting books, memoirs, autobiographies, poetry, songs, treaties, essays, manifestos, memorials, petitions, speeches, interviews, and more. Produced at the time or in retrospect, these records require interpretation and analysis. Historians must "read" for clues and ask not only "What is the document?" "What does it say?" and "What does it mean?" but also, "Who created it?" "Under what conditions?" "With what intention?" and "For what audience?"

Primary sources comprise the bones of history that, pieced together, give shape to the past. But one bone does not make a skeleton. Historians consult, compare, and assess multiple sources to flesh out the stories they wish to tell. For more details about the freedpeople on Smith's Plantation, one could consult the owner's account books for the names or the extensive collections of diaries, letters, and reports of observers – officials, missionaries, and travelers – who discussed them at length. A singular document cannot stand alone, however, because sources usually reflect their creators' viewpoint. A memoir provides one individual's interpretation of events; one by another person from the same era may provide a completely different take on the same issue. Most obviously, the reflections of James Joyner Smith would differ significantly from the people he owned. Thus, the photograph compels us to ask about the people it depicts. What did freedom mean to them? And what happened to the five generations that followed?

African American History and Primary Sources

To garner African Americans' perspectives we must turn to materials – primary sources – that capture their words, tell of their lives, offer their analyses, explain their demands, provide their remembrances. This book is a collection of primary sources by and about African Americans, speaking on their own behalf. It includes speeches, essays, photographs, posters, letters, articles, narratives, poetry, lyrics, raps, petitions, and more. Although sometimes mediated by an interrogator or documentarian – a journalist, photographer, or oral historian – the materials here mostly were produced by and made available through African American sources. Drawing on the questions introduced by the Five Generations photograph, the documents make it clear that African Americans have struggled for freedom and its essential rights and protections usually by themselves, and that the struggle has been as persistent as it has been strong and long.

Accessing black voices from black sources enables us to read African American perspectives and to connect them across time and place. We can ask about consistency and change, discern their similarities and differences. For example, how did African Americans experience or discuss race and racism in the 1890s versus the 1930s? They deployed similar tactics in the 1940s as in the early 1960s, but did they have the same effect? Also, by bringing together black perspectives we can view the diversity of Afro-America and examine the influence not only of race, but also of class, generation, gender, or region. Speaking from within the veil, to use the scholar W. E. B. Du Bois' term for the black side of the color line, some of the documents here reflect internal discourses among African Americans, intended to engender unity or marshal resources, to convey praise or admonishments, or to generate action. Other documents speak across the color line to local, national, or international audiences detailing grievances, providing analyses, persuading allies, building coalitions, and demanding redress.

African Americans documented themselves through their media. For example, journals like *The Crisis* provided a platform to debate and disseminate ideas and information. Newspapers like *The Chicago Defender* and *The Amsterdam News* carried information about black folk and communities from one location to another. As copies traveled hand to hand the actual circulation far exceeded the number of subscribers. In a similar vein organizations like the National Association of Colored Women, the Universal Negro Improvement Association, the National Negro Congress, or the Hip-Hop Summit Action Network linked participants across the nation, and issued posters, newsletters, mission statements, and reports. With greater access to mainstream media – books, periodicals, political conventions, and most recently the blogosphere – African Americans conveyed their perspectives to more diverse audiences.

Primary sources produced by African Americans can help us to transcend received knowledge or assumptions, even to reconsider the basics – chronology, context, cause, contingencies, and consequences – of important historical events. Materials by Women's Political Council of Montgomery, Alabama, provide a *chronology* that places plans for the 1955 bus boycott well ahead of Martin Luther King, Jr.'s emergence as a leader. The call to the March on Washington in 1941 offers a *context* for World War II about how carefully the United States crafted its international image before entering the conflict. Angelo Herndon's autobiography explains the *cause* for black and white workers' embrace of communism in the 1930s. The Niagara Movement's 1905 statement provides a *contingency*, an alternative to Booker T. Washington's dominance. Robert F. Williams' description of events in 1950s Monroe, North Carolina, describes the *consequences*, a positive outcome, of his community's decision to use armed self defense.

About the Book

This volume introduces some of the most profound and affective documents of African American history, from 1865 to the present. These pieces of evidence invite students to enrich their understanding of the black past and to begin their own explorations of the issues the documents raise. Not all of the sources presented here are written or spoken. Usually, the author's point, intent, or perspective comes across with startling clarity, but sometimes the materials call upon readers' imaginations to find descriptive words or analytical phrasings to explain or interpret their meaning. It is impossible to capture in book form the plunk of blues chords, the sound of marching feet, the pride evoked by Dorie Miller, or the thump of a bass riff from a passing car.

Certain entities appear often. For instance, the NAACP put publishing to work as activism through *The Crisis*, in addition to sponsoring myriad events that generated speeches, pamphlets, photos, and news coverage, and arguing court cases that produced briefs and testimony. In a similar vein, certain persons appear often because those who have had access to media tended to leave the most impressionable legacy. The widely covered speeches of Martin Luther King, Jr., demonstrate that his ideas and rhetoric changed over time, despite the tendency to freeze his image on the National Mall in Washington, DC. Clearly many others – from Frederick Douglass to Angela Y. Davis – could have been included similarly.

The prominence of particular organizations, speakers, and writers should not overshadow the lesser-known ones. In this volume, domestic workers, miners, sharecroppers, and migrants stand alongside scholars, politicians, organizers, and activists to provide their own analyses of race and racism. Nor should prominent speakers and prolific authors be taken as representative of the masses of black women and men. Instead, readers are encouraged to consider who, in a given historical context, *could* speak for "the race"? who could speak the loudest? and who listened?

The task of this volume is to present a range of black voices that look from the inside out, not just at African Americans' status or condition, but also at their aspirations, expectations, interpretations, and actions. Given the limited framework of a book designed for classroom use, the execution is necessarily inadequate. For reasons of space, some texts are edited down to focus on essential ideas. The objective of this collection, then, is not to provide a comprehensive overview of African American history since 1865, but to encourage students to pursue additional research and study.

That said, the book contains several themes. Primarily, it demonstrates that African American history is the story of black people's struggle for freedom, fought on their own terms on the front lines of American culture, politics, and economics, and sustained by a deep belief (and arguably faith) in core American principles: democracy and equality. Characterized by connections and tensions – individual/organizational; gender/race; local/national; youth/elder; personal/political; innovation/tradition – the black freedom struggle encompassed diverse participants, ideas, and strategies, not always in agreement. But those frictions also generated energies that sparked new initiatives. As a crusade for social, political, and economic justice, the black freedom struggle transformed the nation to the benefit of all. The opposition was fierce, but struggle was persistent because the oppression was unrelenting and it has yet to fully abate. Each of the voices rendered here would agree that there is still work to be done.

Organization

African American Voices: A Documentary Reader from Emancipation to the Present follows a chronological format that channels the evolution of black freedom initiatives in the United States from 1865 to the beginning of the twenty-first century. Chapter introductions lay out summary analyses and themes. Headnotes for individual documents provide background and comment on significance, while questions at the end of each segment encourage students to think comparatively. The bibliography at the end of each chapter provides a list of secondary sources, but recognizes that in the writing of history, eras cross from one to another. Thus, some selections reflect broader periods than the time frame of the chapter.

In order to place events in broad context, the volume avoids the tendency to lock into classical terms or chronologies. For example, rather than point to the Harlem Renaissance as the defining event of the 1920s, it appears here as part of a larger New Negro movement, which proffered a range of black political and intellectual thought. Similarly, the book avoids the limiting phrase "the civil rights movement" as applied to a specific set of years, and instead highlights how African Americans have engaged and used "civil rights" language and issues continuously. Thus, the Supreme Court decision in *Brown v. Board of Education* marks an important shift – a watershed, if you will – but it also came about in the flow of cases brought before and after 1954. And, yes, something different happened in the 1960s, when young people launched "the Movement." But we also must acknowledge that movements for civil rights occurred before and after "the 60s," albeit not on the same scale, and that "the Movement" as such evolved as it unfolded. In this way, the book encourages students and teachers to bring some of their own historical analyses to bear on the readings.

Finally, a note about terminology: this book uses the term black freedom (e.g., black freedom struggles or black freedom initiatives) to capture the core of African American history since Emancipation, writ large. Readers will find that authors of various documents used terms like "colored" and "Negro" as appropriate to their times. While these phrases appear within primary sources, materials outside of the documents use "African American," "black American," or "black" to refer to the participants in or descendants of African diasporas who reside in the United States, and "Afro-America" or "Africana" to refer to their world.

Chapter 1   Freedom, 1865–1881

For African Americans freedom meant more than the end of bondage and required more than the Confederacy's defeat. It entailed self-determination, the ability to act in their own interests, and by extension, the rights, privileges, and protections of citizenship that historically whites had held as racial license. With a very clear understanding for what slavery had wrought, freedpeople linked their futures together and pursued aspirations for family, community, and capital. Through institutions and organizations, they forged networks of associations that stretched outward into national affiliations, and that articulated an astute set of politics.

The transition from slavery to freedom fundamentally altered African Americans' relationship to the state, and held implications not only for persons enslaved in the South, but also for blacks – enslaved, freed, or free – in all regions of the United States. Yet, to acknowledge black people as political beings undermined whites' ability to claim absolute power on the basis of race. Reconstruction provided the constitutional basis for black citizenship – an end to slavery, federally guaranteed citizenship rights and, finally, suffrage – but as white resistance strengthened, federal resolve weakened. Disillusioned, African Americans nonetheless expanded their struggles. Writing petitions, filing reports, and testifying on their own behalf, they took their concerns directly to local, state, and federal officials. And they proved willing to take their labor and their resources, and leave oppressive conditions behind.

African American Voices: A Documentary Reader from Emancipation to the Present,
First Edition. Edited by Leslie Brown.
© 2014 John Wiley & Sons, Inc. Published 2014 by John Wiley & Sons, Inc.

1 Black Ministers Meet with Representatives of the Federal Government, January 1865

"where we could reap the fruit of our own labor"

In January of 1865, two years after Lincoln issued the Emancipation Proclamation, twenty "persons of African descent," as the New-York Daily Tribune termed the group, convened at the request of General William Tecumseh Sherman, "to have a conference upon matters relating to the freedmen of the State of Georgia." Mostly church officials representing black communities near Savannah, they articulated their understanding of slavery, of emancipation as it related to Lincoln's Proclamation, and of freedom as African Americans interpreted it. The document below is the Tribune's *report of the meeting.*

Minutes of an Interview between the Colored Ministers and Church Officers at Savannah with the Secretary of War and Major-Gen. Sherman

Headquarters of Maj.-Gen. Sherman,

City of Savannah, Ga., Jan., 12, 1865—8 P.M.

...

Garrison Frazier being chosen by the persons present to express their common sentiments upon the matters of inquiry, makes answers to inquiries as follows:

First: State what your understanding is in regard to the acts of Congress and President Lincoln's proclamation, touching the condition of the colored people in the Rebel States.

Answer: So far as I understand President Lincoln's proclamation to the Rebellious States, it is, that if they would lay down their arms and submit to the laws of the United States before the first of January, 1863, all should be well; but if they did not, then all the slaves in the Rebel States should be free henceforth and forever. That is what I understood.

Second: State what you understand by Slavery and the freedom that was to be given by the President's proclamation.

Answer: Slavery is, receiving by irresistible power the work of another man, and not by his consent. The freedom, as I understand it, promised by the proclamation, is taking us from under the yoke of bondage, and placing us where we could reap the fruit of our own labor, take care of ourselves and assist the Government in maintaining our freedom.

Third: State in what manner you think you can take care of yourselves, and how can you best assist the Government in maintaining your freedom.

Answer: The way we can best take care of ourselves is to have land, and turn it and till it by our own labor – that is, by the labor of the women and children and old men; and we can soon maintain ourselves and have something to spare. And to assist the Government, the young men should enlist in the service of the Government, and serve in such manner as they may be wanted. (The Rebels told us that they piled them up and made batteries of them, and sold them to Cuba; but we don't believe that.) We want to be placed on land until we are able to buy it and make it our own.

Fourth: State in what manner you would rather live – whether scattered among the whites or in colonies by yourselves.

Answer: I would prefer to live by ourselves, for there is a prejudice against us in the South that will take years to get over; but I do not know that I can answer for my brethren. [Mr. Lynch says he thinks they should not be separated, but live together. All the other persons present, being questioned one by one, answer that they agree with Brother Frazier.]

Fifth: Do you think that there is intelligence enough among the slaves of the South to maintain themselves under the Government of the United States and the equal protection of its laws, and maintain good and peaceable relations among yourselves and with your neighbors?

Answer: I think there is sufficient intelligence among us to do so.

Sixth: State what is the feeling of the black population of the South toward the Government of the United States; what is the understanding in respect to the present war – its causes and object, and their disposition to aid either side. State fully your views.

Answer: I think you will find there are thousands that are willing to make any sacrifice to assist the Government of the United States, while there are also many that are not willing to take up arms. I do not suppose there are a dozen men that are opposed to the Government. I understand, as to the war, that the South is the aggressor. President Lincoln was elected President by a majority of the United States, which guaranteed him the right of holding the office and exercising that right over the whole United States. The South, without knowing what he would do, rebelled. The war was commenced by the Rebels before he came into office. The object of the war was not at first to give the slaves their freedom, but the sole object of the war was at first to bring the rebellious States back into the Union and their loyalty to the laws of the United States. Afterward, knowing the value set on the slaves by the Rebels, the President thought that his proclamation would stimulate them to lay down their arms, reduce them to obedience, and help to bring back the Rebel States; and their not doing so has now made the freedom of the slaves a part of the war. It is my opinion that there is not a man in this city that could be started to help the Rebels one inch, for that would be suicide. There were two black men left with the Rebels because they had taken an active part for the Rebels, and thought something might befall them if they stayed behind; but there is not another man. If the prayers that have gone up for the Union army could be read out, you would not get through them these two weeks.

Seventh: State whether the sentiments you now express are those only of the colored people in the city; or do they extend to the colored population through the country? and what are your means of knowing the sentiments of those living in the country?

Answer: I think the sentiments are the same among the colored people of the State. My opinion is formed by personal communication in the course of my ministry, and also from the thousands that followed the Union army, leaving their homes and undergoing suffering. I did not think there would be so many; the number surpassed my expectation.

Eighth: If the Rebel leaders were to arm the slaves, what would be its effect?

Answer: I think they would fight as long as they were before the bayonet, and just as soon as they could get away, they would desert, in my opinion.

Ninth: What, in your opinion, is the feeling of the colored people about enlisting and serving as soldiers of the United States? and what kind of military service do they prefer?

Answer: A large number have gone as soldiers to Port Royal [SC] to be drilled and put in the service; and I think there are thousands of the young men that would enlist. There is something about them that perhaps is wrong. They have suffered so long from the Rebels that they want to shoulder the musket. Others want to go into the Quartermaster's or Commissary's service.

Tenth: Do you understand the mode of enlistments of colored persons in the Rebel States by State agents under the Act of Congress? If yea, state what your understanding is.

Answer: My understanding is, that colored persons enlisted by State agents are enlisted as substitutes, and give credit to the States, and do not swell the army, because every black man enlisted by a State agent leaves a white man at home; and, also, that larger bounties are given or promised by State agents than are given by the States. The great object should be to push through this Rebellion the shortest way, and there seems to be something wanting in the enlistment by State agents, for it don't strengthen the army, but takes one away for every colored man enlisted.

Eleventh: State what, in your opinion, is the best way to enlist colored men for soldiers.

Answer: I think, sir, that all compulsory operations should be put a stop to. The ministers would talk to them, and the young men would enlist. It is my opinion that it would be far better for the State agents to stay at home, and the enlistments to be made for the United States under the direction of Gen. Sherman.

Source: Minutes of an Interview between the Colored Ministers and Church Officers at Savannah with the Secretary of War and Major-Gen. Sherman (January 12, 1865), "Negroes of Savannah," clipping from *New-York Daily Tribune* (February 13, 1865), Consolidated Correspondence File, ser. 225, Central Records, Quartermaster General, Record Group 92, National Archives.

2 Frederick Douglass Argues for Black Suffrage, April 1865

"We want it because it is our right"

Frederick Douglass (1818–1895) escaped bondage in 1838 and made his way to New Bedford, Massachusetts, and then to Rochester, New York, where he settled into his career as an abolitionist. A renowned speaker, Douglass also wrote extensively, publishing influential biographies and several prominent newspapers. With a Confederate defeat imminent in April 1865, anti-slavery activists wondered if the work of abolition was complete. Douglass disagreed, and in the speech excerpted below, he recommended an agenda on rights that informed black politics for generations to come.

"What the Black Man Wants"

...

I have had but one idea for the last three years to present to the American people, and the phraseology in which I clothe it is the old abolition phraseology. I am for the "immediate, unconditional, and universal" enfranchisement of the black man, in every State in the Union. [Loud applause.] Without this, his liberty is a mockery; without this, you might as well almost retain the old name of slavery for his condition; for in fact, if he is not the slave of the individual master, he is the slave of society, and holds his liberty as a privilege, not as a right. He is at the mercy of the mob, and has no means of protecting himself.

It may be objected, however, that this pressing of the Negro's right to suffrage is premature. Let us have slavery abolished, it may be said, let us have labor organized, and then, in the natural course of events, the right of suffrage will be extended to the Negro. I do not agree with this. The constitution of the human mind is such, that if it once disregards the conviction forced upon it by a revelation of truth, it requires the exercise of a higher power to produce the same conviction afterwards. ... I fear that if we fail to do it now, if abolitionists fail to press it now, we may not see, for centuries to come, the same disposition that exists at this moment. [Applause.] Hence, I say, now is the time to press this right.

It may be asked, "Why do you want it? Some men have got along very well without it. Women have not this right." Shall we justify one wrong by another? This is the sufficient answer. Shall we at this moment justify the deprivation of the Negro of the right to vote, because some one else is deprived of that privilege? I hold that women, as well as men, have the right to vote [Applause.], and my heart and voice go with the movement to extend suffrage to woman; but that question rests upon another basis than which our right rests. We may be asked, I say, why we want it. I will tell you why we want it. We want it because it is our right, first of all. No class of men can, without insulting their own nature, be content with any deprivation of their rights. We want it again, as a means for educating our race. Men are so constituted that they derive their conviction of their own possibilities largely by the estimate formed of them by others. If nothing is expected of a people, that people will find it difficult to contradict that expectation. By depriving us of suffrage, you affirm our incapacity to form an intelligent judgment respecting public men and public measures; you declare before the world that we are unfit to exercise the elective franchise, and by this means lead us to undervalue ourselves, to put a low estimate upon ourselves, and to feel that we have no possibilities like other men. Again, I want the elective franchise, for one, as a colored man, because ours is a peculiar government, based upon a peculiar idea, and that idea is universal suffrage. ... [H]ere where universal suffrage is the rule, where that is the fundamental idea of the Government, to rule us out is to make us an exception, to brand us with the stigma of inferiority, and to invite to our heads the missiles of those about us; therefore, I want the franchise for the black man.

There are, however, other reasons, not derived from any consideration merely of our rights, but arising out of the conditions of the South, and of the country. ... [When] this Rebellion shall have been swept down ... there will be this rank undergrowth of treason, to which reference has been made, growing up there, and interfering with, and thwarting the quiet operation of the Federal Government in those states. You will see those traitors, handing down, from sire to son, the same malignant spirit which they have manifested and which they are now exhibiting, with malicious hearts, broad blades, and bloody hands in the field, against our sons and brothers. That spirit will still remain; and whoever sees the Federal Government extended over those Southern States will see that Government in a strange land, and not only in a strange land, but in an enemy's land. ... That enmity will not die out in a year, will not die out in an age. The Federal Government will be looked upon in those States precisely as the Governments of Austria and France are looked upon in Italy at the present moment. They will endeavor to circumvent, they will endeavor to destroy, the peaceful operation of this Government. Now, where will you find the strength to counterbalance this spirit, if you do not find it in the Negroes of the South? They are your friends, and have always been your friends. They were your friends even when the Government did not regard them as such. They comprehended the genius of this war before you did. ... [T]he Negro, apparently endowed with wisdom from on high, saw more clearly the end from the beginning than we did. ... They are our only friends in the South, and we should be true to them in this their trial hour, and see to it that they have the elective franchise. ...

[T]he Negro, when he is to be robbed of any right which is justly his, is an "inferior man." It is said that we are ignorant; I admit it. But if we know enough to be hung, we know enough to vote. If the Negro knows enough to pay taxes to support the government, he knows enough to vote; taxation and representation should go together. If he knows enough to shoulder a musket and fight for the flag, fight for the government, he knows enough to vote....

... I hold that the American people are bound, not only in self-defense, to extend this right to the freedmen of the South, but they are bound by their love of country, and by all their regard for the future safety of those Southern States, to do this – to do it as a measure essential to the preservation of peace there. ... I hold that the American government has taken upon itself a solemn obligation of honor, to see that this war – let it be long or short, let it cost much or let it cost little – that this war shall not cease until every freedman at the South has the right to vote. ... Why, you have asked them to incur the enmity of their masters, in order to befriend you and to befriend this Government. You have asked us to call down, not only upon ourselves, but upon our children's children, the deadly hate of the entire Southern people. You have called upon us to turn our backs upon our masters, to abandon their cause and espouse yours; to turn against the South and in favor of the North; to shoot down the Confederacy and uphold the flag – the American flag. You have called upon us to expose ourselves to all the subtle machinations of their malignity for all time. And now, what do you propose to do when you come to make peace? To reward your enemies, and trample in the dust your friends? Do you intend to sacrifice the very men who have come to the rescue of your banner in the South, and incurred the lasting displeasure of their masters thereby? Do you intend to sacrifice them and reward your enemies? Do you mean to give your enemies the right to vote, and take it away from your friends? Is that wise policy? Is that honorable? ... There is something too mean in looking upon the Negro, when you are in trouble, as a citizen, and when you are free from trouble, as an alien. ...

... What I ask for the Negro is not benevolence, not pity, not sympathy, but simply justice. [Applause.] The American people have always been anxious to know what they shall do with us. ... "What shall we do with the Negro?" I have had but one answer from the beginning. Do nothing with us! Your doing with us has already played the mischief with us. Do nothing with us! ... All I ask is, give him a chance to stand on his own legs! Let him alone! If you see him on his way to school, let him alone, don't disturb him! If you see him going to the dinner table at a hotel, let him go! If you see him going to the ballot-box, let him alone, don't disturb him! ... – your interference is doing him a positive injury ...

... If you will only untie his hands, and give him a chance, I think he will live. ...

Source: Frederick Douglass, "What the Black Man Wants: Speech at the Annual Meeting of the Massachusetts Anti-Slavery Society at Boston," April 1865. See University of Rochester Frederick Douglass Project.

3 Jourdon Anderson Writes to His Old Master, 1865

"we have concluded to test your sincerity"

Jourdon Anderson had been enslaved on a Tennessee plantation owned by Col. Patrick H. Anderson. Freed by the Union Army in 1864, Anderson made his way to Nashville, and then on to Ohio where he lived for the rest of his life.

The letter below was reprinted widely (misspelling his name Jordon Anderson) in the mid-1860s by anti-slavery presses, and it has been cited through the years by scholars as a superb example of what African Americans thought about slavery and freedom. Until recently, questions lingered about its authenticity. But recent research by journalists and historians has revealed that, indeed, the words and ideas belong to Jourdon Anderson, dictated to an acquaintance, banker and abolitionist Valentine Winters of Dayton, Ohio.

Dayton, Ohio, August 7, 1865

To My Old Master, Colonel P. H. Anderson
Big Spring, Tennessee

Sir: I got your letter and was glad to find you had not forgotten Jourdon, and that you wanted me to come back and live with you again, promising to do better for me than anybody else can. I have often felt uneasy about you. I thought the Yankees would have hung you long before this for harboring Rebs they found at your house. I suppose they never heard about your going to Col. Martin's to kill the Union soldier that was left by his company in their stable. Although you shot at me twice before I left you, I did not want to hear of your being hurt, and am glad you are still living. It would do me good to go back to the dear old home again and see Miss Mary and Miss Martha and Allen, Esther, Green, and Lee. Give my love to them all, and tell them I hope we will meet in the better world, if not in this. I would have come back to see you all when I was working in Nashville, but one of the neighbors told me Henry intended to shoot me if he ever got a chance.

I want to know particularly what the good chance is you propose to give me. I am doing tolerably well here; I get $25 a month, with victuals and clothing; have a comfortable home for Mandy (the folks here call her Mrs. Anderson), and the children, Milly, Jane and Grundy, go to school and are learning well; the teacher says Grundy has a head for a preacher. They go to Sunday-School, and Mandy and me attend church regularly. We are kindly treated; sometimes we overhear others saying, "Them colored people were slaves" down in Tennessee. The children feel hurt when they hear such remarks, but I tell them it was no disgrace in Tennessee to belong to Col. Anderson. Many darkies would have been proud, as I used to was, to call you master. Now, if you will write and say what wages you will give me,

I will be better able to decide whether it would be to my advantage to move back again.

As to my freedom, which you say I can have, there is nothing to be gained on that score, as I got my free-papers in 1864 from the Provost-Marshal-General of the Department at Nashville. Mandy says she would be afraid to go back without some proof that you are sincerely disposed to treat us justly and kindly – and we have concluded to test your sincerity by asking you to send us our wages for the time we served you. This will make us forget and forgive old scores, and rely on your justice and friendship in the future. I served you faithfully for thirty-two years and Mandy twenty years. At $25 a month for me, and $2 a week for Mandy, our earnings would amount to $11,680. Add to this the interest for the time our wages has been kept back and deduct what you paid for our clothing and three doctor's visits to me, and pulling a tooth for Mandy, and the balance will show what we are in justice entitled to. Please send the money by Adams Express, in care of V. Winters, esq., Dayton, Ohio. If you fail to pay us for faithful labors in the past we can have little faith in your promises in the future. We trust the good Maker has opened your eyes to the wrongs which you and your fathers have done to me and my fathers, in making us toil for you for generations without recompense. Here I draw my wages every Saturday night, but in Tennessee there was never any payday for the negroes any more than for the horses and cows. Surely there will be a day of reckoning for those who defraud the laborer of his hire.

In answering this letter please state if there would be any safety for my Milly and Jane, who are now grown up and both good-looking girls. You know how it was with poor Matilda and Catherine. I would rather stay here and starve and die if it comes to that than have my girls brought to shame by the violence and wickedness of their young masters. You will also please state if there has been any schools opened for the colored children in your neighborhood, the great desire of my life now is to give my children an education, and have them form virtuous habits.

P.S. – Say howdy to George Carter, and thank him for taking the pistol from you when you were shooting at me.

From your old servant,
Jourdon Anderson

Source: Jourdon Anderson to Col. Patrick H. Anderson, August 7, 1864; reprinted in Lydia Maria Child, *The Freedmen's Book* (Boston: Tickenor and Fields, 1865).

4 Harriet Simril Testifies Before a Congressional Committee, South Carolina, 1871

"they wanted him to join this democratic ticket"

Black freedom met violent resistance from whites. In 1866 in Pulaski, Tennessee, a group of veteran Confederate officers founded the Ku Klux Klan intending to use terrorism – beatings, hangings, burnings, and rapes – as a means of control. In 1871–1872 as the violence grew, Congress held hearings to investigate "The Condition of Affairs in the Late Insurrectionary States." Thousands of pages of testimony provided by blacks, whites, Union Army officials, ex-Confederates, and Freedmen's Bureau agents detailed persistent assaults. Here Harriet Simril, a freedwoman from Clay Hill, South Carolina, describes theft, assault, rape, and arson committed by the Klan.

Testimony of Harriet Simril

Harriet Simril (colored) was called as a witness for the prosecution, and, being duly sworn, testified as follows:

Question: Who is your husband?
Answer: Sam Simmons.

Question: Where do you live?
Answer: At Clay Hill, in York county.

Question: How long have you lived there?
Answer: A good many years.

Question: Has your husband lived there a good many years?
Answer: Yes, sir.

Question: Did he vote at the last election?
Answer: Yes, sir.

Question: Do you know what politics he is?
Answer: He is a radical [republican].

Question: Did the Ku-Klux ever visit your house?
Answer: Yes, sir; I think along in the spring.

Question: About what time in the spring?
Answer: I cannot tell you exactly.

Question: Have they been there more than once?
Answer: Yes, sir, they came on him three times.

Question: Now tell the jury what they did each time.

Answer: The first time they came my old man was at home. They hollered out "open the door," and he got up and opened the door. They asked him what he had in his hand he told them the door-pin. They told him to come out, and he came out. These two men that came in, they came in and wanted me to make up a light the light wasn't made up very good, and they struck matches to a pine stick and looked about to see if they could see anything. They never said anything, and these young men walked up and they took my old man out after so long and they wanted him to join this democratic ticket and after that they went a piece above the house and hit him about five cuts with the cowhide.

Question: Do you know whether he promised to be a democrat or not?

Answer: He told them he would rather quit all politics, if that was the way they was going to do to him.

Question: What did they do to you?

Answer: That is the second time they came. They came back after the first time on Sunday night after my old man again, and this second time the crowd was bigger.

Question: Did they call for your old man?

Answer: Yes, sir; they called for him, and I told them he wasn't here; then argued me down, and told me he was here. I told them they no, sir, he wasn't here. They asked me where was my old man? I told them I couldn't tell, when he went away he didn't tell me where he was going. They searched about in the house a long time, and staid with me an hour that time; searched about a long time, and made me make up a light; and after I got the light made up, then they began to search again, and question me again about the old man, and I told them I didn't know where my old man had gone.

Question: What did they do to you?

Answer: Well, they were spitting in my face and throwing dirt in my eyes; and when they made me blind they bursted open my cupboard. I had five pies in my cupboard, and they eat all my pies up, and then took two pieces of meat; then they made me blow up the light again, cursing me; and after awhile they took me out of doors and told me all they wanted was my old man to join the democratic ticket; if he joined the democratic ticket they would have no more to do with him; and after they had got me out of doors, they dragged me into the big road, and they ravished me out there.

Question: How many of them?

Answer: There was three.

Question: One right after the other?

Answer: Yes, sir.

Question: Threw you down on the ground?
Answer: Yes, sir, they throwed me down.

Question: Do you know who the men were who ravished you?
Answer: Yes, sir, [I] can tell who the men were; there were Ches McCollum, Tom McCollum, and this big Jim Harper.

Question: Who ravished you first?
Answer. Tom McCollum grabbed me first by the arm.

Question: What next?
Answer: All nasty talk they put out of their mouths. (Witness here detailed the conversation on the part of her tormentors, but it was of too obscene a nature to permit of publication.)

Question: What was your condition when they left you? How did you feel?
Answer: After they got done with me I had no sense for a long time. I laid there, I don't know how long.

Question: Did you get up that night?
Answer: Yes, sir, and walked back to the house again.

Question: Have the Ku-Klux ever come to you again?
Answer: ... [T]hey came back, too, but I was never inside the house.

Question: Did your husband lay out at night?
Answer: Yes, sir; and I did too – took my children, and it rained, thunder and lightning.

Question: When they came back what did they do? ... Did they burn your house down?
Answer: Yes, sir; I don't know who burnt it down, but the next morning I went to my house and it was in ashes.

Question: Why did you lay out? ... To get out of the way of the Ku-Klux?
Answer: Yes, sir; I got out of the way of them ... I think we laid out for four nights. Yes, we lay out four nights; I cannot exactly tell how many nights, but he lay out a long time before I lay out.

Question: Did these Ku-Klux have on masks and gowns?
Answer: Yes, sir; they had on gowns, and they had on false caps on their faces.

(The defense waived cross-examination.)

Source: Harriet Simril Testimony (December 19, 1871), *Testimony taken by the Joint Select Committee to Inquire into the Condition of Affairs in the Late Insurrectionary States, South Carolina, Volume III* (Washington, DC: GPO, 1872), pp. 1861–1862.

5 Resolutions of the National Civil Rights Convention, 1873

"still laboring under certain disabilities on account of color"

Even before Emancipation national black congresses and conventions provided settings where African Americans from various places could plan action together. When the National Civil Rights Convention met in Washington, DC, in 1873, representatives met with the President and participants sent a statement to Congress arguing for federal attention to race issues and calling for passage of civil rights legislation. The Convention's summary Resolutions are printed below.

"Memorial of the National Convention of Colored Persons, Praying to be Protected in their Civil Rights"

December 19, 1873

Washington, DC

...

Honorable Senate and House of Representatives in Congress assembled:
We regret the necessity which compels us to again come before you and say "we are aggrieved." We are authorized to say to those in authority, to Congress, to the people whom it represents, that there are nearly five millions of American citizens who are shamefully outraged; who are thus treated without cause. The recognition made within a few years respecting in part our rights, make us more sensitive as to the denial of the rest.

...

Resolutions unanimously adopted by the convention:

Whereas a large class of citizens of the United States of America, numbering nearly five million of souls, are still laboring under certain disabilities on account of color, as is generally admitted throughout the country, namely, a non-recognition of their equal rights to all the public privileges properly attaching to American citizenship, among which we number the right to enjoy upon equal terms with other citizens the benefits of the public schools, common carriers, public places of amusement or resort; and

Whereas these disabilities under which we labor can only be removed effectually by national law, to be made as far-reaching as the jurisdiction of the National Government itself; and

Whereas the whole people of the country, more than a year since, speaking through the conventions of both great political parties made solemn declaration, at Philadelphia, that "complete liberty and exact equality in the enjoyment of all civil, political, and public rights should be established and effectually maintained throughout the Union by efficient and appropriate State and Federal legislation;" and that "neither law nor its administration should admit of any discrimination in respect to the citizen by reason of race, creed, color, or previous condition of servitude;" and, at Cincinnati and Baltimore, "that we recognize the equality of all men before the law, and hold that the Government in its dealings with the people should mete out equal and exact justice to all, of whatever nativity, race, color or persuasion, religious or political:"

Therefore,

Resolved, That the protection of civil rights in the persons of every inhabitant of the country is the first and most imperative duty of the Government, in order that freedom in this country and American citizenship may be made valuable to us.

Resolved, That no people can aid in sustaining and upholding either themselves or the nation unless they are fully protected in their pursuit of happiness.

Resolved, That we earnestly petition the Congress of the United States, representing, as it does, the two great political parties above referred to, being committed, as they are, to the doctrine of civil rights, to pass at the earliest practical moment, in the interest of justice and humanity, the civil-rights bill now pending in the United States Senate, and known as Senate bill No. 1, or some equally comprehensive and just measure.

Source: "Memorial of the National Convention of Colored Persons Praying to Be Protected In Their Civil Rights, December 19, 1873," National Civil-Rights Convention, Washington, DC, December, 1873. 43rd Congress, 1st Session, Senate, mis. doc. no. 21 (Washington, DC: [s.n.], 1873), pp. 1–5.

6 The Exodusters, 1878

"Brethren, Friends, & Fellow Citizens"

African Americans sought self-segregation to meet their aspirations for peace and prosperity. The poster below encouraged "the colored people of Lexington KY" to move to Kansas to homestead. The movement from Lexington, led by Pap Singleton, was only one of many organized migrations of African Americans determined to escape the difficulties of black life in the South and to establish their own communities.

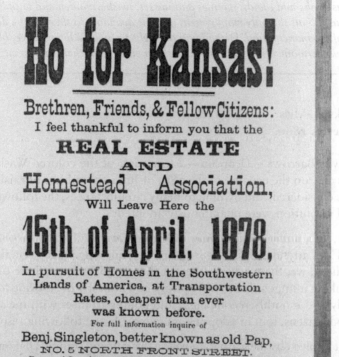

Figure 1.1   "Ho for Kansas!" Nashville, Tennessee, March 18, 1878. Copyprint of broadside.

Source: The Exodusters, 1878–1879, Library of Congress, Prints and Photographs Division.

7 Black Washerwomen Demand a Living Wage, 1866 and 1881

"the fruits of our labor"

*If freedom meant independence, then it also required all members of the
black family – women, elders, and children included – to continue to work.
As they had done during slavery, African American women provided most
of the South's household labor in addition to working the fields. Indeed, jobs
as cooks and maids, nannies and nurses, washerwomen and laundresses were
just about the only employment options available to them in the decades
after emancipation. Demanding the right to make a living wage, black
washerwomen in at least two southern cities took their case to city officials.*

Jackson, Miss.
June 20, 1866.

Mayor Barrows – Dear Sir: – At meeting of the colored Washerwomen of
this city, on the evening of the 18th of June, the subject of raising the wages
was considered, and owning to many circumstances, the following preamble
and resolution were unanimously adopted:

Whereas, under the influence of high prices of all of the necessaries of life,
and the attendant high rates of rent, while our wages remain very much
reduced, we, the washerwomen of the city of Jackson, State of Mississippi,
thinking it impossible to live upright and honestly in laboring for the present
daily and monthly recompense, and hoping to meet with the support of all
good citizens, join in adopting unanimously the following resolution:

Be it resolved by the washerwomen of this city and county, That on and after the
foregoing date, we join in charging a uniform rate for our labor, that rate being
an advance over the original price by the month or day[,] the statement of said
price to be made public by printing the same, and any one belonging to the class
of washerwomen, violating this, shall be liable to a fine regulated by the class.

We do not wish in the least to charge exorbitant prices, but desire to be able
to live comfortably if possible from the fruits of our labor.

We present the matter to your Honor, and hope that you will not reject it as
the condition of prices call on us to raise our wages. The prices charged as:
    $1.50 per day for washing
    $15.00 per month for family washing
    $10.00 per month for single individuals

We ask you to consider the matter in our behalf, and should you deem it just and right, your sanction of the movement will be greatly received.

Yours, very truly,
The Washerwomen of Jackson

Source: "Petition of the Washerwomen, 20 June 1866," Jackson (Mississippi) *Daily Clarion*, June 24, 1866; reprinted in Philip H. Foner and Ronald L. Lewis (eds.), *Black Workers: A Documentary History from Colonial Times to the Present* (Philadelphia: Temple University Press, 1989), p. 142.

July 21, 1881
"The Washerwoman's Strike" (from the *Atlanta Constitution*)

The laundry ladies' efforts to control the prices for washing are still prevalent and no small amount of talk is occasioned thereby. The women have a thoroughly organized association and additions to the membership are being made each day…. During the day the house of every colored woman who is not a member of the association is visited and a regular siege begun, and in nearly every instance an addition to the membership is the result. In this way the meetings, which are had every night, are largely attended and generally very demonstrative…. Speeches advocating their rights and exhorting the members to remain firm are numerous and frequent. To several families whose washing left home Monday morning the clothing has been returned [w]ringing wet, the woman having become a member of the association after taking the washing away. It is rumored that house help is also on the eve of a strike.

August 1, 1881
Letter to Mr. James English (from black washerwomen)

Mr. Jim English, Mayor of Atlanta

Atlanta Georgia, August 1 [1881]

Dear Sir:
We the members of our society, are determined to stand to our pledge and make extra charges for washing, and we have agreed, and are willing to pay $25 or $50 for licenses as a protection, so we can control the washing for the city. We can afford to pay these licenses, and will do it before we will be defeated, and then we will have full control of the city's washing at our own prices, as the city has control of our husbands' work at their prices. Don't

forget this. We hope to hear from your council Tuesday morning. We mean business this week or no washing. Yours respectfully,

From 5 Societies, 486 Members

Source: "The Washerwoman's Strike" and "Letter to Mr. James English" reproduced with permission from "Black Laundresses Demand Higher Wages," *Atlanta Constitution*, July–August 1881, in Tera W. Hunter, "African-American Women Workers' Protest in the New South," *The OAH Magazine of History*, 13 (Summer 1999). Courtesy of OAH and T. Hunter. Also see "African-American Laundry Women Go on Strike in Atlanta," on HERB by the American Social History Project, Item 897.

Questions for Consideration

How did Emancipation differ from freedom?
What was the meaning of the vote to African Americans? Why did whites question this right?
In the period 1865–1881, how do African Americans perceive the role of government in relation to their aspirations? How did they define justice?
How did the meaning of black freedom differ for women and men? How did the tools of self-determination differ for women than for men? In what ways did opportunities for self-determination change for African Americans during this period?

Bibliography

Berlin, Ira, et al. *Free at Last: A Documentary History of Slavery, Freedom, and the Civil War*. New York: New Press, 1993.
Foner, Eric. *Reconstruction: America's Unfinished Revolution*. Reprint. New York: Harper Perennial Modern Classics, 2002.
Glymph, Thavolia. *Out of the House of Bondage: The Transformation of the Plantation Household*. New York: Cambridge University Press, 2008.
Hahn, Steven. *A Nation Under Our Feet: Black Political Struggles in the Rural South from Slavery to the Great Migration*. Cambridge, MA: Belknap Press of Harvard University, 2005.
Hunter, Tera W. *To 'Joy My Freedom: Southern Black Women's Lives and Labors After the Civil War*. Cambridge, MA: Harvard University Press, 1998.
Litwack, Leon F. *Been in the Storm So Long: The Aftermath of Slavery*. New York: Vintage Publishing, 1980.

Masur, Kate. An *Example for All the Land: Emancipation and the Struggle over Equality in Washington, D.C.* Chapel Hill: University of North Carolina Press, 2010.

Painter, Nell Irvin. *Exodusters: Black Migration to Kansas after Reconstruction.* New York: W. W. Norton, 1992.

Rose, Willie Lee. *Rehearsal for Reconstruction: The Port Royal Experiment.* Reprint. University of Georgia Press, 1999.

Williams, Heather Andrea. *Help Me to Find My People: The African American Search for Family Lost in Slavery.* Chapel Hill: University of North Carolina Press, 2012.

Chapter 2   Upbuilding, 1893–1910

We wear the mask that grins and lies,
It hides our cheeks and shades our eyes, –
This debt we pay to human guile;
With torn and bleeding hearts we smile,
And mouth with myriad subtleties.

Why should the world be otherwise,
In counting all our tears and sighs?
Nay, let them only see us, while
          We wear the mask.

We smile, but, O great Christ, our cries
To thee from tortured souls arise.
We sing, but oh the clay is vile
Beneath our feet, and long the mile;
But let the world dream otherwise,
          We wear the mask!

Paul Laurence Dunbar, "We Wear the Mask," in *Lyrics of Lowly Life*
(New York: Dodd, Mead, and Company, 1896)

The poem "We Wear the Mask" by Paul Laurence Dunbar (1872–1906)
intones the resentment African Americans expressed regarding the racial
tensions at the end of the nineteenth century. These well-known words assert

African American Voices: A Documentary Reader from Emancipation to the Present,
First Edition. Edited by Leslie Brown.
© 2014 John Wiley & Sons, Inc. Published 2014 by John Wiley & Sons, Inc.

the wearer's inability or unwillingness to reveal a true self to white observers. William Edward Burghardt Du Bois (1868–1963) used a different term, "double-consciousness," to describe similar positioning: "looking at one's self through the eyes of others." Essentially outsiders in their own nation, black people lived two existences, he wrote in *The Souls of Black Folk*: "One ever feels his two-ness, – an American, a Negro…."

In response to black aspirations, white southerners imposed a contentious system of racial codes known as Jim Crow: harsh racial segregation and exclusion, severely limited educational options, gross employment restrictions, and absurd laws and customs. Reinforced by racial violence and validated by the Supreme Court in *Plessy v. Ferguson* (1896), Jim Crow undermined the Fourteenth Amendment and sanctioned whites' power to discriminate for the cause of racial supremacy. The Court confirmed what African Americans already realized, that the justice system would provide no relief. Nor would the electoral system. State by state across the South the movement for black disenfranchisement escalated, barring black male suffrage (women could not vote in most places in the United States) – in clear violation of the Fifteenth Amendment. Yet, the duplicitous tactics that whites employed – literacy and residential requirements, poll taxes, outright fraud, organized violence, and more – garnered no government intervention or public outcry.

Excluded from juries, barred from the voting booth, and curbed from practicing law in a courtroom, blacks found the official venues for recourse closed. They sought redress for rights and protections where they could, attempting negotiations with white authorities, building alliances with white liberals, and posing direct challenges. While continuing the fight for civil rights, they also pursued upbuilding. Defined by Du Bois as the "social and economic development" of black communities, upbuilding entailed African Americans' creating from scratch the foundations and structures of their own society, including their own churches, schools, voluntary associations, learned societies, and businesses. These spaces provided the physical and psychic distance from whites and from oppression. Here, black progress could be crafted and future initiatives could be launched. And they engaged in racial uplift, generating projects specifically designed to improve African Americans' quality of life.

Thus interlocking struggles characterized black activism in the Jim Crow era. In fact, the same individuals and organizations that led crusades for civil rights and against Jim Crow also engineered upbuilding and piloted racial uplift. Black folk worked together *and* separately on this freedom project, and they sometimes disagreed. But internal tensions and differences also operated as critical forces that generated new ideas, new forms of resistance and protest, and new strategies of survival and achievement. Meanwhile, racial violence worsened.

1   Ida B. Wells Speaks Out Against Lynching in the South, 1893

"lawlessness prevails"

Civil and human rights activist Ida B. Wells (1862–1931) began her career as a journalist in Memphis, Tennessee, using her newspaper to speak African Americans' frustrations with the injustices of Jim Crow. She is best known, however, for her crusade against lynching. A demonstration of white supremacy – and of the ends to which whites would go to sustain their position – lynchings were extra-legal, ritualized, public murders, where a victim, shot or stabbed, often was hanged, burned alive, and then torn apart. Wells' research exposed region-wide violence, committed for nothing more than black assertions of their humanity or rights. She wrote and spoke extensively, reaching European as well as American audiences. The following document is excerpted from an 1893 speech in Boston.

"Lynch Law in All its Phases"

I am before the American people today through no inclination of my own, but because of a deep-seated conviction that the country at large does not know the extent to which lynch law prevails in parts of the Republic nor the conditions which force into exile those who speak the truth. I cannot believe that the apathy and indifference which so largely obtains regarding mob rule is other than the result of ignorance of the true situation. And yet, the observing and thoughtful must know that in one section, at least, of our common country, a government of the people, by the people, and for the people, means a government by the mob; where the land of the free and home of the brave means a land of lawlessness, murder and outrage; and where liberty of speech means the license of might to destroy the business and drive from home those who exercise this privilege contrary to the will of the mob. Repeated attacks on the life, liberty and happiness of any citizen or class of citizens are attacks on distinctive American institutions; such attacks imperiling as they do the foundation of government, law and order, merit the thoughtful consideration of far-sighted Americans; not from a standpoint of sentiment, not even so much from a standpoint of justice to a weak race, as from a desire to preserve our institutions.

... Times without number, since invested with citizenship, the race has been indicted for ignorance, immorality and general worthlessness declared guilty and executed by its self-constituted judges. The operations of law do not dispose of negroes fast enough, and lynching bees have become the favorite pastime of the South. As excuse for the same, a new cry, as false as it is foul, is raised in an effort to blast race character, a cry which has proclaimed to the world that virtue and innocence are violated by Afro-Americans who must be killed like wild beasts to protect womanhood and childhood.

...

In the past ten years over a thousand colored men, women and children have been butchered, murdered and burnt in all parts of the South. The details of these terrible outrages seldom reach beyond the narrow world where they occur. Those who commit the murders write the reports, and hence these blots upon the honor of a nation cause but a faint ripple on the outside world. They arouse no great indignation and call forth no adequate demand for justice. The victims were black, and the reports are so written as to make it appear that the helpless creatures deserved the fate which overtook them ...

... In the past ten years three instances, at least, have been furnished where men have literally been roasted to death to appease the fury of Southern mobs. The Texarkana instance of last year and Paris, Texas, case of this month are the most recent as they are the most shocking and repulsive. Both were charged with crimes from which the laws provide adequate punishment. The Texarkana man, Ed Coy, was charged with assaulting a white woman. A mob pronounced him guilty, strapped him to a tree, chipped the flesh from his body, poured coal oil over him and the woman in the case set fire to him. The country looked on and in many cases applauded, because it was published that this man had violated the honor of the white woman, although he protested his innocence to the last....

The Paris, Texas, burning of Henry Smith, February 1st, has exceeded the others in its horrible details. The man was drawn through the streets on a float, as the Roman generals used to parade their trophies of war, while scaffold ten feet high, was being built, and irons were heated in the fire. He was bound on it, and red-hot irons began at his feet and slowly branded his body while the mob howled with delight at his shrieks. Red hot irons were run down his throat and cooked his tongue; his eyes were burned out, when he was at last unconscious, cotton seed hulls were placed under him, coal oil poured all over him, and a torch applied to the mass. When the flames burned away the ropes which bound Smith and scorched his flesh he was brought back to sensibility and burned and maimed and as he was, he rolled off the platform and away from the fire. His half-cooked body was seized and trampled and thrown back into the flames while a mob of twenty thousand persons who came from all over the country howled with delight, and gathered up some buttons and ashes after all was over to preserve for relics. The man was charged with outraging and murdering a four-year-old white child, covering her body with brush, sleeping beside the body through the night, then making his escape. If true, it was the deed of a mad-man, and should have been clearly proven so. The fact that no time for verification of the newspaper reports was given, is suspicious, especially when I remember that a negro was lynched in Indianola, Sharkey Co., Miss., last summer. The dispatches said it was because he had assaulted the sheriff's eight-year-old daughter. The girl was more than eighteen years old and was found by her father in this man's room, who was a servant on the place.

Of these 728 black men who were murdered [between 1882 and 1892], 269 were charged with rape, 253 with murder, 44 with robbery, 37 with incendiarism, 32 with reasons unstated (it was not necessary to have a reason), 27 with race prejudice, 13 with quarreling with white men, 10 with making threats, 7 with rioting, 5 with miscegenation, 4 with burglary. One of the men lynched in 1891 was Will Lewis, who was lynched because "he was drunk and saucy to white folks." A woman who was one of the 73 victims in 1886, was hung in Jackson, Tenn., because the white woman for whom she cooked, died suddenly of poisoning. An examination showed arsenical poisoning. A search in the cook's room found rat poison. She was thrown into jail, and when the mob had worked itself up to the lynching pitch, she was dragged out, every stitch of clothing torn from her body, and was hung in the public court house square in sight of everybody. That white woman's husband has since died in the insane asylum, a raving maniac, and his ravings have led to the conclusion that he and not the cook, was the poisoner of his wife. A fifteen-year-old colored girl was lynched last spring, at Rayville, La., on the same charge of poisoning. A woman was also lynched at Hollendale, Miss., last spring, charged with being an accomplice in the murder of her paramour who had abused her. These were only two of the 159 persons lynched in the South from January 1, 1892, to January 1, 1893. Over a dozen black men have been lynched already since this new year set in, not yet two months old.

It will thus be seen that neither age, sex nor decency are spared. Although the impression has gone abroad that most of the lynchings take place because of assaults on white women only one third of the number lynched in the past ten years have been charged with that offense, to say nothing of those who were not guilty of the charge. And according to law none of them until proven so. But the unsupported word of any white person for any cause is sufficient to cause a lynching. So bold have the lynchers become masks are laid aside, the temples of justice and strongholds of law are invaded in broad daylight and prisoners taken out and lynched, while governors of states and officers of law stand by and see the work well done.

And yet this Christian nation, the flower of the nineteenth century civilization, says it can do nothing to stop this inhuman slaughter. The general government is willingly powerless to send troops to protect the lives of its black citizens, but the state governments are free to use state troops to shoot them down like cattle, when in desperation the black men attempt to defend themselves, and then tell the world that it was necessary to put down a "race war."

...

The lawlessness which has been here described is like unto that which prevailed under slavery. The very same forces are at work now as then. The attempt is being made to subject to a condition of civil and industrial dependence, those whom the Constitution declares to be free men.... The right of the Afro-American to vote and hold office remains in the Federal Constitution, but is destroyed in the constitution of the Southern states. Having destroyed the citizenship of the man, they are now trying to destroy the manhood of the citizen. All their laws are shaped to this end, school laws, railroad car regulations, those governing labor liens on crops, every device is adopted to make slaves of free men and rob them of their wages. Whenever a malicious law is violated in any of its parts, any farmer, any railroad conductor, or merchant can call together a posse of his neighbors and punish even with death the black man who resists and the legal authorities sanction what is done by failing to prosecute and punish the murders. The Repeal of the Civil Rights Law removed their last barrier and the black man's last bulwark and refuge. The rule of the mob is absolute.

Those who know this recital to be true, say there is nothing they can do, they cannot interfere and vainly hope by further concession to placate the imperious and dominating part of our country in which this lawlessness prevails. Because this country has been almost rent in twain by internal dissension, the other sections seem virtually to have agreed that the best way to heal the breach is to permit the taking away of civil, political, and even human rights, to stand by in silence and utter indifference while the South continues to wreak fiendish vengeance on the irresponsible cause. They pretend to believe that with all the machinery of law and government in its hands; with the jails and penitentiaries and convict farms filled with petty race criminals; with the well-known fact that no negro has ever been known to escape conviction and punishment for any crime in the South. Still there are those who try to justify and condone the lynching of over a thousand black men in less than ten years an average of one hundred a year. The public sentiment of the country, by its silence in press, pulpit and in public meetings has encouraged this state of affairs, and public sentiment is stronger than law. With all this country's disposition to condone and temporize with the South and its methods; with its many instances of sacrificing principles to prejudice for the sake of making friends and healing the breach made by the late war; of going into the lawless country with capital to build up its waste places and remaining silent in the presence of outrage and wrong, the South is as vindictive and bitter as ever. She is willing to make friends as long as she is permitted to pursue unmolested and uncensored, her course of proscription, injustice, outrage and vituperation ...

Do you ask the remedy? A public sentiment strong against lawlessness must be aroused. Every individual can contribute to this awakening. When a sentiment against lynch law as strong, deep and mighty as that roused by slavery prevails, I have no fear of the result. It should be already established as a fact and not as a theory, that every human being must have a fair trial for his life and liberty, no matter what the charge against him. When a demand goes up from fearless and persistent reformers from press and pulpit, from industrial and moral associations that this shall be so from Maine to Texas and from ocean to ocean, a way will be found to make it so ...

Source: Ida B. Wells, "Lynch Law in All its Phases," an Address at Tremont Temple in the Boston Monday Lectureship, February 13, 1893, reprinted in *Our Day* (Boston: Our Day Publishing Co., 1893), pp. 333–347.

2 Booker T. Washington Speaks on Race at Atlanta, 1895

"The laws of changeless justice bind Oppressor with oppressed"

Booker T. Washington (1856–1915) had built Tuskegee Institute against great odds, including dearth of public support for black education and the resistance of local whites. He managed to grow his school by maintaining the delicate balance between staying white animosity and supporting black aspirations. In 1895 he was invited to give a speech at the Cotton States and International Exposition, held in Atlanta. The fair was an opportunity, white organizers believed, to demonstrate southern progress since the Civil War, not only in terms of economics, but also in terms of race relations. Washington faced a difficult task, the least of which was to tender a significant statement about race relations and the South economically, and to do so before an audience of thousands of whites at the height of racial violence.

Washington may have intended to use the moment to mediate the racial pressure on African Americans. His speech, printed below, encouraged black people to seek opportunities where they could, but he also recommended

limiting their ambitions. He offered nothing on civil rights, except a rebuke
of black politics altogether. And in deploying the metaphor of "separate
fingers on a hand," he appeared accepting of segregation. In the final
analysis, the Tuskegeean suggested a one-sided compromise: that African
Americans would give up some of their greatest ambitions in exchange for
what was supposed to be theirs already: security.

Mr. President and Gentlemen of the Board of Directors and Citizens:

One-third of the population of the South is of the Negro race. No enterprise
seeking the material, civil, or moral welfare of this section can disregard this
element of our population and reach the highest success. I but convey to
you, Mr. President and Directors, the sentiment of the masses of my race
when I say that in no way have the value and manhood of the American
Negro been more fittingly and generously recognized than by the managers
of this magnificent Exposition at every stage of its progress. It is a recognition that will do more to cement the friendship of the two races than any
occurrence since the dawn of our freedom.

Not only this, but the opportunity here afforded will awaken among us
a new era of industrial progress. Ignorant and inexperienced, it is not strange
that in the first years of our new life we began at the top instead of at the bottom; that a seat in Congress or the state legislature was more sought than real
estate or industrial skill; that the political convention or stump speaking had
more attractions than starting a dairy farm or truck garden.

A ship lost at sea for many days suddenly sighted a friendly vessel. From
the mast of the unfortunate vessel was seen a signal, "Water, water; we die
of thirst!" The answer from the friendly vessel at once came back, "Cast
down your bucket where you are." A second time the signal, "Water, water;
send us water!" ran up from the distressed vessel, and was answered, "Cast
down your bucket where you are." And a third and fourth signal for water
was answered, "Cast down your bucket where you are." The captain of the
distressed vessel, at last heeding the injunction, cast down his bucket, and it
came up full of fresh, sparkling water from the mouth of the Amazon River.
To those of my race who depend on bettering their condition in a foreign
land or who underestimate the importance of cultivating friendly relations
with the Southern white man, who is their next-door neighbor, I would say:
"Cast down your bucket where you are" – cast it down in making friends in
every manly way of the people of all races by whom we are surrounded.

Cast it down in agriculture, mechanics, in commerce, in domestic service,
and in the professions. And in this connection it is well to bear in mind that

whatever other sins the South may be called to bear, when it comes to business, pure and simple, it is in the South that the Negro is given a man's chance in the commercial world, and in nothing is this Exposition more eloquent than in emphasizing this chance. Our greatest danger is that in the great leap from slavery to freedom we may overlook the fact that the masses of us are to live by the productions of our hands, and fail to keep in mind that we shall prosper in proportion as we learn to dignify and glorify common labour, and put brains and skill into the common occupations of life; shall prosper in proportion as we learn to draw the line between the superficial and the substantial, the ornamental gewgaws of life and the useful. No race can prosper till it learns that there is as much dignity in tilling a field as in writing a poem. It is at the bottom of life we must begin, and not at the top. Nor should we permit our grievances to overshadow our opportunities.

To those of the white race who look to the incoming of those of foreign birth and strange tongue and habits for the prosperity of the South, were I permitted I would repeat what I say to my own race, "Cast down your bucket where you are." Cast it down among the eight millions of Negroes whose habits you know, whose fidelity and love you have tested in days when to have proved treacherous meant the ruin of your firesides. Cast down your bucket among these people who have, without strikes and labour wars, tilled your fields, cleared your forests, builded your railroads and cities, and brought forth treasures from the bowels of the earth, and helped make possible this magnificent representation of the progress of the South. Casting down your bucket among my people, helping and encouraging them as you are doing on these grounds, and to education of head, hand, and heart, you will find that they will buy your surplus land, make blossom the waste places in your fields, and run your factories. While doing this, you can be sure in the future, as in the past, that you and your families will be surrounded by the most patient, faithful, law-abiding, and unresentful people that the world has seen. As we have proved our loyalty to you in the past, in nursing your children, watching by the sick-bed of your mothers and fathers, and often following them with tear-dimmed eyes to their graves, so in the future, in our humble way, we shall stand by you with a devotion that no foreigner can approach, ready to lay down our lives, if need be, in defense of yours, interlacing our industrial, commercial, civil, and religious life with yours in a way that shall make the interests of both races one. In all things that are purely social we can be as separate as the fingers, yet one as the hand in all things essential to mutual progress.

There is no defense or security for any of us except in the highest intelligence and development of all. If anywhere there are efforts tending to curtail the fullest growth of the Negro, let these efforts be turned into stimulating, encouraging, and making him the most useful and intelligent citizen. Effort or means so invested will pay a thousand per cent interest. These efforts will be twice blessed – blessing him that gives and him that takes. There is no escape through law of man or God from the inevitable:

> The laws of changeless justice bind
> Oppressor with oppressed;
> And close as sin and suffering joined
> We march to fate abreast ...

Nearly sixteen millions of hands will aid you in pulling the load upward, or they will pull against you the load downward. We shall constitute one-third and more of the ignorance and crime of the South, or one-third [of] its intelligence and progress; we shall contribute one-third to the business and industrial prosperity of the South, or we shall prove a veritable body of death, stagnating, depressing, retarding every effort to advance the body politic.

Gentlemen of the Exposition, as we present to you our humble effort at an exhibition of our progress, you must not expect overmuch. Starting thirty years ago with ownership here and there in a few quilts and pumpkins and chickens (gathered from miscellaneous sources), remember the path that has led from these to the inventions and production of agricultural implements, buggies, steam-engines, newspapers, books, statuary, carving, paintings, the management of drug stores and banks, has not been trodden without contact with thorns and thistles. While we take pride in what we exhibit as a result of our independent efforts, we do not for a moment forget that our part in this exhibition would fall far short of your expectations but for the constant help that has come to our educational life, not only from the Southern states, but especially from Northern philanthropists, who have made their gifts a constant stream of blessing and encouragement.

The wisest among my race understand that the agitation of questions of social equality is the extremest folly, and that progress in the enjoyment of all the privileges that will come to us must be the result of severe and constant struggle rather than of artificial forcing. No race that has anything to contribute to the markets of the world is long in any degree ostracized. It is important and right that all privileges of the law be ours, but it is vastly more important that we be prepared for the exercise of these privileges. The opportunity to earn a dollar in a factory just now is worth infinitely more than the opportunity to spend a dollar in an opera-house.

In conclusion, may I repeat that nothing in thirty years has given us more hope and encouragement, and drawn us so near to you of the white race, as this opportunity offered by the Exposition; and here bending, as it were, over the altar that represents the results of the struggles of your race and mine, both starting practically empty-handed three decades ago, I pledge that in your effort to work out the great and intricate problem which God has laid at the doors of the South, you shall have at all times the patient, sympathetic help of my race; only let this be constantly in mind, that, while from representations in these buildings of the product of field, of forest, of mine, of factory, letters, and art, much good will come, yet far above and beyond material benefits will be that higher good, that, let us pray God, will come, in a blotting out of sectional differences and racial animosities and suspicions, in a determination to administer absolute justice, in a willing obedience among all classes to the mandates of law. This, coupled with our material prosperity, will bring into our beloved South a new heaven and a new earth.

Source: Booker T. Washington, *Up From Slavery: An Autobiography* (Garden City, NY: Doubleday & Company, Inc., 1901), pp. 218–225.

3 The National Association of Colored Women, 1897 and 1898

"lifting as we climb"

Mary Eliza Church Terrell (1863–1954) was of the same generation as Ida B. Wells. Devoted to race work, in addition to family and community, they both balked at any suggestion that women's place should be limited. Like feminists of their day, they viewed gender and race as inseparable parts of their identities, which also combined to complicate discriminations that black women confronted under Jim Crow. Consequently, they argued that race progress was inextricably bound to that of its women, and that women had a particular role to play in the quest for black freedom. Thus they supported equal rights, including access to full educational and employment opportunities, and woman suffrage.

Terrell was elected the first president of the National Association of Colored Women (NACW), founded in 1896 to respond to vicious attacks on black women's character, false and demoralizing accusations that also damaged their economic and educational prospects. "In Union There is Strength," Terrell's address to the first meeting of the NACW, excerpted below, intended to inspire her sisters to take up the work uplift, of community service focused especially on the lives of women and children among the black poor. Also excerpted below, "The Progress of Colored Women," addressed to the (mostly white) National American Woman Suffrage Association, describes NACW accomplishments that stretched far beyond its initial scope.

"In Union There is Strength" (1897)

In Union there is strength is a truism that has been acted upon by Jew and Gentile, by Greek and Barbarian, by all classes and conditions alike from the creation of the universe to the present day. It did not take long for men to learn that by combining their strength, a greater amount of work could be accomplished with less effort in a shorter time. Upon this principle of union, governments have been founded and states built.... Acting upon this principle of concentration and union have the colored women of the United States banded themselves together to fulfill a mission to which they feel peculiarly adapted and especially called.

We have become National, because from the Atlantic to the Pacific, from Maine to the Gulf, we wish to set in motion influences that shall stop the ravages made by practices that sap our strength and preclude the possibility of advancement which under other circumstances could easily be made. We call ourselves an Association to signify that we have joined hands one with the other to work together in a common cause. We proclaim to the world that the women of our race have become partners in the great firm of progress and reform. We denominate ourselves colored, not because we are narrow, and wish to lay special emphasis on the color of the skin, for which no one is responsible, which of itself is no proof of an individual's virtue nor of his vice, which neither is a stamp, neither of one's intelligence nor of ignorance, but we refer to the fact that this is an association of colored women, because our peculiar status in this country at the present time seems to demand that we stand by ourselves in the special work for which we have organized.

For this reason it was thought best to invite the attention of the world to the fact that colored women feel their responsibility as a unit, and together have clasped hands to assume it. Special stress has been laid upon the fact that our association is composed of women, not because we wish to deny rights and privileges to our brothers in imitation of the example they have set for us so many years, but because the work which we hope to accomplish can be done better, by the mothers, wives, daughters, and sisters of our race than by the fathers, husbands, brothers, and sons. The crying need of our organization of colored women is questioned by no one conversant with our peculiar trials and perplexities, and acquainted with the almost insurmountable obstacles in our path to those attainments and acquisitions to which it is the right and privilege of every member of every race to aspire.

It is not because we are discouraged at the progress made by our people that we have uttered the cry of alarm which has called together this band of earnest women assembled here tonight. In the unprecedented advancement made by the Negro since his emancipation, we take great pride and extract therefore both courage and hope. From a condition of dense ignorance, but thirty years ago, we have advanced so far in the realm of knowledge and letters as to have produced scholars and authors of repute. Though penniless as a race a short while ago, we have among us today a few men of wealth and multitudes who own their homes and make comfortable livings. We therefore challenge any other race to present a record more creditable and show a progress more wonderful than that made by the ex-slaves of the United States and that too in the face of prejudice, proscription, and persecution against which no other people has ever had to contend in the history of the world.

And yet while rejoicing in our steady march, onward and upward, to the best and highest things of life, we are nevertheless painfully mindful of our weaknesses and defects which we know [in] the Negro is no worse than other races equally poor, equally ignorant, and equally oppressed, we would nevertheless see him lay aside the sins that do so easily beset him, and come forth clothed in all these attributes of mind and grace of character that claims the real man.

To accomplish this end through the simplest, swiftest, surest methods, the colored women have organized themselves into this Association, whose power for good, let us hope, will be as enduring as it is unlimited. Believing that it is only through the home that a people can become really good and truly great, the N.A.C.W. shall enter that sacred domain to inculcate right principles of living and correct false views of life. Homes, more homes, purer homes, better homes, is the text upon which our sermons to the masses must be preached. So long as the majority of people call that place home in which the air is foul, the manners bad, and the morals worse, just so long is this so called home a menace to health, a breeder of vice, and the abode of crime.

Not alone upon the inmates of these hovels are the awful consequences of their filth and immorality visited, but upon the heads of those who sit calmly by and make no effort to stem the tide of disease and vice will vengeance as surely fall. The colored youth is vicious we are told, and statistics showing the multitudes of our boys and girls who fill the penitentiaries and crowd the jails appall and discourage us. Side by side with these facts and figures of crime, I would have presented and pictured the miserable hovels from which these youthful criminals come. Crowded into alleys, many of them the haunts of vice, few if any of them in a proper sanitary condition, most of them fatal to mental and moral growth, and destructive of healthful physical development as well, thousands of our children have a wretched heritage indeed.

It is, therefore, into the home, sisters of the Association, that we must go, filled with all the zeal and charity which such a mission demands. To the children of the race we owe, as women, a debt which can never be paid, until Herculean efforts are made to rescue them from evil and shame for which they are in no way responsible.

...

That we have no money to help the needy and poor, I reply, that having hearts, generous natures, willing feet, and helpful hands can without the token of a single penny work miracles in the name of humanity and right. Money we need, money we must have to accomplish much which we ache to effect. But it is not by powerful armies and the outlays of vast fortunes that the greatest revolutions are wrought and the most enduring reforms inaugurated. It is by the silent, though powerful force of individual influences thrown on the side of right, it is by arduous persistence and effort keep those with whom we come in daily contact, to enlighten the heathen at our door, to create wholesome public sentiment in the communities in which we live, that the heaviest blows are struck for virtue and right. Let us not only preach, but practice race unity, race pride, reverence, and respect for those capable of leading and advising us. Let the youth of the race be impressed about the dignity of labor and inspired with a desire to work. Let us do nothing to handicap children in the desperate struggle for existence in which their unfortunate condition in this country forces them to engage. Let us purify the atmosphere of our homes till it become so sweet that those who dwell in them will have a heritage more precious than ... silver or gold.

"The Progress of Colored Women" (1898)

Fifty years ago a meeting such as this, planned, conducted and addressed by women would have been an impossibility. Less than forty years ago, few sane men would have predicted that either a slave or one of his descendants would in this century at least, address such an audience in the Nation's Capital at the invitation of women representing the highest, broadest, best type of womanhood, that can be found anywhere in the world. Thus to me this semi-centennial of the National American Woman Suffrage Association is a double jubilee, rejoicing as I do, not only in the prospective enfranchisement of my sex but in the emancipation of my race. When Ernestine Rose, Lucretia Mott, Elizabeth Cady Stanton, Lucy Stone and Susan B. Anthony began that agitation by which colleges were opened to women and the numerous reforms inaugurated for the amelioration of their condition along all lines, their sisters who groaned in bondage had little reason to hope that these blessings would ever brighten their crushed and blighted lives, for during those days of oppression and despair, colored women were not only refused admittance to institutions of learning, but the law of the States in which the majority lived made it a crime to teach them to read. Not only could they possess no property, but even their bodies were not their own.

Nothing, in short, that could degrade or brutalize the womanhood of the race was lacking in that system from which colored women then had little hope of escape. So gloomy were their prospects, so fatal the laws, so pernicious the customs, only fifty years ago. But, from the day their fetters were broken and their minds released from the darkness of ignorance to which for more than two hundred years they had been doomed, from the day they could stand erect in the dignity of womanhood, no longer bond but free, till tonight, colored women have forged steadily ahead in the acquisition of knowledge and in the cultivation of those virtues which make for good. To use a thought of the illustrious Frederick Douglass, if judged by the depths from which they have come, rather than by the heights to which those blessed with centuries of opportunities have attained, colored women need not hang their heads in shame.

Consider if you will, the almost insurmountable obstacles which have confronted colored women in their efforts to educate and cultivate themselves since their emancipation, and I dare assert, not boastfully, but with pardonable pride, I hope, that the progress they have made and the work they have accomplished, will bear a favorable comparison at least with that of their more fortunate sisters, from the opportunity of acquiring knowledge and the means of self-culture have never been entirely withheld. For, not only are colored women with ambition and aspiration handicapped on account of their sex, but they are everywhere baffled and mocked on account of their race. Desperately and continuously they are forced to fight that opposition, born of a cruel, unreasonable prejudice which neither their merit nor their necessity seems able to subdue. Not only because they are women, but because they are colored women, are discouragement and disappointment meeting them at every turn. Avocations opened and opportunities offered to their more favored sisters have been and are tonight closed and barred against them. While those of the dominant race have a variety of trades and pursuits from which they may choose, the woman through whose veins one drop of African blood is known to flow is limited to a pitiful few. So overcrowded are the avocations in which colored women may engage and so poor is the pay in consequence, that only the barest livelihood can be eked out by the rank and file.

And yet, in spite of the opposition encountered, the obstacles opposed to their acquisition of knowledge and their accumulation of property, the progress made by colored women along these lines has never been surpassed by that of any people in the history of the world. Though the slaves were liberated less than forty years ago, penniless, and ignorant, with neither shelter nor food, so great was their thirst for knowledge and so herculean were their efforts to secure it, that there are today hundreds of negroes, many of them women, who are graduates, some of them having taken degrees from the best institutions of the land....

With this increase of wisdom there has sprung up in the hearts of colored women an ardent desire to do good in the world. No sooner had the favored few availed themselves of such advantages as they could secure than they hastened to dispense these blessings to the less fortunate of their race. With tireless energy and eager zeal, colored women have, since their emancipation, been continuously prosecuting the work of educating and elevating their race, as though upon themselves alone devolved the accomplishment of this great task. Of the teachers engaged in instructing colored youth, it is perhaps no exaggeration to say that fully ninety per cent are women. In the back-woods, remote from the civilization and comforts of the city and town, on the plantations reeking with ignorance and vice, our colored women may be found battling with evils which such conditions always entail. Many a heroine, of whom the world will never hear, has thus sacrificed her life to her race, amid surroundings and in the face of privations which only martyrs can tolerate and bear.

Shirking responsibility has never been a fault with which colored women might be truthfully charged. Indefatigably and conscientiously, in public work of all kinds they engage, that they may benefit and elevate their race. The result of this labor has been prodigious indeed. By banding themselves together in the interest of education and morality, by adopting the most practical and useful means to this end, colored women have in thirty short years become a great power for good ...

... Questions affecting our legal status as a race are also constantly agitated by our women. In Louisiana and Tennessee, colored women have several times petitioned the legislatures of their respective States to repeal the obnoxious "Jim Crow Car" laws, nor will any stone be left unturned until this iniquitous and unjust enactment against respectable American citizens be forever wiped from the statutes of the South. Against the barbarous Convict Lease System of Georgia, of which negroes, especially the female prisoners, are the principal victims, colored women are waging a ceaseless war. By two lecturers, each of whom, under the Woman's Christian Temperance Union has been National Superintendent of work among colored people, the cause of temperance has for many years been eloquently espoused. In business, colored women have had signal success. There is in Alabama a large milling and cotton business belonging to and controlled entirely by a colored woman who has sometimes as many as seventy-five men in her employ. In Halifax, Nova Scotia, the principal ice plant of the city is owned and managed by one of our women. In the professions we have dentists and doctors, whose practice is lucrative and large ...

... And, finally, as an organization of women nothing lies nearer the heart of the National Association than the children, many of whose lives, so sad and dark, we might brighten and bless. It is the kindergarten we need. Free kindergartens in every city and hamlet of this broad land we must have, if the children are to receive from us what it is our duty to give. Already during the past year kindergartens have been established and successfully maintained by several organizations, from which most encouraging reports have come. May their worthy example be emulated, till in no branch of the Association shall the children of the poor, at least, be deprived of the blessings which flow from the kindergarten alone. The more unfavorable the environments of children, the more necessary is it that steps be taken to counteract baleful influences on innocent victims ...

And so, lifting as we climb, onward and upward we go, struggling and striving, and hoping that the buds and blossoms of our desires will burst into glorious fruition ere long. With courage, born of success achieved in the past, with a keen sense of the responsibility which we shall continue to assume, we look forward to a future large with promise and hope. Seeking no favors because of our color, nor patronage because of our needs, we knock at the bar of justice, asking an equal chance.

Source: Mary Church Terrell, "In Union There is Strength" (1897) and "The Progress of Colored Women" (1898), African American Perspectives: Selections from the Daniel P. Murray Collection, Library of Congress.

4 The Negro National Anthem, 1900 and 1905

"Stony the road we trod"

The poem "Lift Every Voice and Sing" was written by James Weldon Johnson and performed in 1900 to honor Booker T. Washington. In musical form, arranged by his brother John Johnson in 1905, it was adopted by the National Association for the Advancement of Colored People (NAACP) as "The Negro National Anthem." A staple of black gatherings, the song affects fierce pride, faith, and optimism, while acknowledging the struggle inherent to black life in America. In 1999 "Lift Every Voice and Sing" was entered into the Record of the 106th Congress as the "African American National Anthem."

Lift Every Voice and Sing (The Negro National Anthem)

Lift every voice and sing,
'Til earth and heaven ring,
Ring with the harmonies of Liberty;
Let our rejoicing rise
High as the listening skies,
Let it resound loud as the rolling sea.
Sing a song full of the faith that the dark past has taught us,
Sing a song full of the hope that the present has brought us;
Facing the rising sun of our new day begun,
Let us march on 'til victory is won.

Stony the road we trod,
Bitter the chast'ning rod,
Felt in the days when hope unborn had died;
Yet with a steady beat,
Have not our weary feet
Come to the place for which our fathers sighed?
We have come over a way that with tears has been watered,
We have come, treading our path through the blood of the slaughtered,
Out from the gloomy past
'Til now we stand at last
Where the white gleam of our bright star is cast.

God of our weary years,
God of our silent tears,
Thou who has brought us thus far on the way;
Thou who has by Thy might
Led us into the light,
Keep us forever in the path, we pray.
Lest our feet stray from the places, our God, where we met Thee,
Lest, our hearts drunk with the wine of the world, we forget Thee;
Shadowed beneath Thy hand,
May we forever stand,
True to our God,
True to our native land.

Source: James Weldon Johnson, "Lift Every Voice and Sing," in *The Complete Poems of Weldon Johnson* (New York: Penguin Classics, 2000).

5 Photographs from the Paris Exposition, 1900

An exhibit documenting the history and life of African Americans in the United States appeared at the International Exposition at Paris, France, in 1900. Curated by W. E. B. Du Bois, it included charts describing "present conditions," compendia of segregation laws, and a photographic collection entitled "A Small Nation of People." Selected to counter vicious stereotypes of African Americans that pervaded popular culture, the images depicted pride and progress.

Figure 2.1   Officers of Tobacco Trade Union, Petersburg, Virginia, *c.* 1900.

Source: Library of Congress, Prints and Photographs Division, Du Bois Collection of Visual Materials about African Americans Assembled for the Paris Exposition of 1900.

Figure 2.2   Four African American women seated on steps of building at Atlanta University, Georgia.

Source: Library of Congress, Prints and Photographs Division, Du Bois Collection of Visual Materials about African Americans Assembled for the Paris Exposition of 1900.

6 From W. E. B. Du Bois, *The Souls of Black Folk*, 1903

"One ever feels his two-ness"

The differences between W. E. B. Du Bois and Booker T. Washington are well known, published in the renowned essay "Of Mr. Booker T. Washington and Others" in Du Bois' treatise on black history, The Souls of Black Folk. *Du Bois directly criticized Washington's politics, asking: "Is it possible, and probable, that nine millions of men can make effective progress in economic lines if they are deprived of political rights, made a servile caste, and allowed only the most meager chance for developing their exceptional men?" He answered, "an emphatic No." Indeed, he argued, the three things that African Americans needed to survive and thrive – the vote, civil rights, and access to higher education – were the three issues where Washington equivocated.*

But Souls was a remarkable literary achievement for more reasons than its criticism of the Tuskegeean. It was a political statement. Here, Du Bois penned his famous words: "[T]he problem of the Twentieth Century is the problem of the color line." The essay "Of Our Spiritual Strivings," excerpted below, tells the story of emancipation, focusing on the irony of black life in the United

Figure 2.3   Summit Avenue ensemble, Atlanta, Georgia.

Source: Library of Congress, Prints and Photographs Division, Du Bois Collection
of Visual Materials about African Americans Assembled for the Paris Exposition
of 1900.

> *States: unfree in a nation that valued freedom, black Americans were the true*
> *exponents of the principles expressed in the Declaration of Independence.*
> *Like all fourteen essays in* Souls, *this one draws on the black cultural tradition*
> *of call and response in its opening, matching a riff from a "sorrow song" – a*
> *slave melody (in this case "Nobody Knows the Trouble I've Seen") – with the*
> *words of a European poet to capture the commonality of human struggle.*

"Of Our Spiritual Strivings"

O water, voice of my heart, crying in the sand,
All night long crying with a mournful cry,
As I lie and listen, and cannot understand
The voice of my heart in my side or the voice of the sea,
O water, crying for rest, is it I, is it I?
All night long the water is crying to me.

Unresting water, there shall never be rest
Till the last moon droop and the last tide fail,
And the fire of the end begin to burn in the west;
And the heart shall be weary and wonder and cry like the sea,
All life long crying without avail,
As the water all night long is crying to me.

Arthur Symons

BETWEEN me and the other world there is ever an unasked question: unasked by some through feelings of delicacy; by others through the difficulty of rightly framing it. All, nevertheless, flutter round it. They approach me in a half-hesitant sort of way, eye me curiously or compassionately, and then, instead of saying directly, How does it feel to be a problem? they say, I know an excellent colored man in my town; or, I fought at Mechanicsville; or, Do not these Southern outrages make your blood boil? At these I smile, or am interested, or reduce the boiling to a simmer, as the occasion may require. To the real question, How does it feel to be a problem? I answer seldom a word.

...

After the Egyptian and Indian, the Greek and Roman, the Teuton and Mongolian the Negro is a sort of seventh son, born with a veil, and gifted with second-sight in this American world, – a world which yields him no true self-consciousness, but only lets him see himself through the revelation of the other world. It is a peculiar sensation, this double-consciousness, this sense of always looking at one's self through the eyes of others, of measuring one's soul by the tape of a world that looks on in amused contempt and pity. One ever feels his two-ness, – an American, a Negro; two souls, two thoughts, two unreconciled strivings; two warring ideals in one dark body, whose dogged strength alone keeps it from being torn asunder.

The history of the American Negro is the history of this strife, – this longing to attain self-conscious manhood, to merge his double self into a better and truer self. In this merging he wishes neither of the older selves to be lost. He would not Africanize America; for America has too much to teach the world and Africa. He would not bleach his Negro soul in a flood of white Americanism, for he knows that Negro blood has a message for the world.

He simply wishes to make it possible for a man to be both a Negro and an American, without being cursed and spit upon by his fellows, without having the doors of Opportunity closed roughly in his face. ...

...

Away back in the days of bondage they thought to see in one divine event the end of all doubt and disappointment; few men ever worshipped Freedom with half such unquestioning faith as did the American Negro for two centuries. To him, so far as he thought and dreamed, slavery was indeed the sum of all villainies, the cause of all sorrow, the root of all prejudice; Emancipation was the key to a promised land of sweeter beauty than ever stretched before the eyes of wearied Israelites. In song and exhortation swelled one refrain – Liberty; in his tears and curses the God he implored had Freedom in his right hand. At last it came, – suddenly, fearfully, like a dream. With one wild carnival of blood and passion came the message in his own plaintive cadences...

...

Up the new path the advance guard toiled, slowly, heavily, doggedly; only those who have watched and guided the faltering feet, the misty minds, the dull understandings, of the dark pupils of these schools know how faithfully, how piteously, this people strove to learn. It was weary work. The cold statistician wrote down the inches of progress here and there, noted also where here and there a foot had slipped or some one had fallen. To the tired climbers, the horizon was ever dark, the mists were often cold, the Canaan was always dim and far away. If, however, the vistas disclosed as yet no goal, no resting place, little but flattery and criticism, the journey at least gave leisure for reflection and self-examination; it changed the child of Emancipation to the youth with dawning self-consciousness, self-realization, self-respect. In those sombre forests of his striving his own soul rose before him, and he saw himself, – darkly as through a veil; and yet he saw in himself some faint revelation of his power, of his mission. He began to have a dim feeling that, to attain his place in the world, he must be himself, and not another. For the first time he sought to analyze the burden he bore upon his back, that dead-weight of social degradation partially masked behind a half-named Negro problem. He felt his poverty; without a cent, without a home, without land, tools, or savings, he had entered into competition with rich, landed, skilled neighbors. To be a poor man is hard, but to be a poor race in a land of dollars is the very bottom of hardships. He felt the weight of his ignorance, – not simply of letters, but of life, of business, of the humanities; the accumulated sloth and shirking and awkwardness of decades and centuries shackled his hands and feet....

...

A people thus handicapped ought not to be asked to race with the world, but rather allowed to give all its time and thought to its own social problems. But alas! while sociologists gleefully count his bastards and his prostitutes, the very soul of the toiling, sweating black man is darkened by the shadow of a vast despair. Men call the shadow prejudice, and learnedly explain it as the natural defense of culture against barbarism, learning against ignorance, purity against crime, the "higher" against the "lower" races. To which the Negro cries Amen! and swears that to so much of this strange prejudice as is founded on just homage to civilization, culture, righteousness, and progress, he humbly bows and meekly does obeisance. But before that nameless prejudice that leaps beyond all this he stands helpless, dismayed, and well-nigh speechless; before that personal disrespect and mockery, the ridicule and systematic humiliation, the distortion of fact and wanton license of fancy, the cynical ignoring of the better and the boisterous welcoming of the worse, the all-pervading desire to inculcate disdain for everything black, from Toussaint to the devil, – before this there rises a sickening despair that would disarm and discourage any nation save that black host to whom "discouragement" is an unwritten word.

But the facing of so vast a prejudice could not but bring the inevitable self-questioning, self-disparagement, and lowering of ideals which ever accompany repression and breed in an atmosphere of contempt and hate. Whisperings and portents came borne upon the four winds: Lo! we are diseased and dying, cried the dark hosts; we cannot write, our voting is in vain; what need of education, since we must always cook and serve? And the Nation echoed and enforced this self-criticism, saying: Be content to be servants, and nothing more; what need of higher culture for half-men? Away with the black man's ballot, by force or fraud, – and behold the suicide of a race! Nevertheless, out of the evil came something of good, – the more careful adjustment of education to real life, the clearer perception of the Negroes' social responsibilities, and the sobering realization of the meaning of progress.

So dawned the time of ... storm and stress [that] to-day rocks our little boat on the mad waters of the world-sea; there is within and without the sound of conflict, the burning of body and rending of soul; inspiration strives with doubt, and faith with vain questionings. The bright ideals of the past, – physical freedom, political power, the training of brains and the training of hands, – all these in turn have waxed and waned, until even the last grows dim and overcast. Are they all wrong, – all false? No, not that, but each alone was over-simple and incomplete, – the dreams of a credulous race-childhood, or the fond imaginings of the other world which does not know and does not want to know our power. To be really true, all these ideals must be melted and welded into one. The training of the schools we need to-day more than ever, – the training of deft hands, quick eyes and ears, and above all the broader, deeper, higher culture of gifted minds and pure hearts. The power of the ballot we need in sheer self-defense, – else what shall save us from a second slavery? Freedom, too, the long-sought, we still seek, – the freedom of life and limb, the freedom to work and think, the freedom to love and aspire. Work, culture, liberty, – all these we need, not singly but together, not successively but together, each growing and aiding each and all striving toward that vaster ideal that swims before the Negro people, the ideal of human brotherhood, gained through the unifying ideal of Race; the ideal of fostering and developing the traits and talents of the Negro, not in opposition to or contempt for other races, but rather in large conformity to the greater ideals of the American Republic, in order that some day on American soil two world-races may give each to each those characteristics both so sadly lack. We the darker ones come even now not altogether empty-handed: there are to-day no truer exponents of the pure human spirit of the Declaration of Independence than the American Negroes; there is no true American music but the wild sweet melodies of the Negro slave; the American fairy tales and folk-lore are Indian and African; and, all in all, we black men seem the sole oasis of simple faith and reverence in a dusty desert of dollars and smartness. Will America be poorer if she replace her brutal dyspeptic blundering with light-hearted but determined Negro humility? or her coarse and cruel wit with loving jovial good-humor? or her vulgar music with the soul of the Sorrow Songs?

Merely a concrete test of the underlying principles of the great republic is the Negro Problem, and the spiritual striving of the freed-men's sons is the travail of souls whose burden is almost beyond the measure of their strength, but who bear it in the name of an historic race, in the name of this the land of their fathers' fathers, and in the name of human opportunity.

Source: W. E. B. Du Bois, "Of Our Spiritual Strivings," from *The Souls of Black Folk* (Chicago: A. C. McClurg & Co., 1903), pp. 1–12.

7 Black Leaders Disagree with Booker T. Washington: The Niagara Movement, 1905

"this class of American citizens should protest emphatically and continually against the curtailment of their political rights"

In 1905 W. E. B. Du Bois called for a meeting of black leaders frustrated with Booker T. Washington's conciliatory stance on race relations. Coming out of that gathering, the Niagara Movement proffered an assertive agenda focused on black civil rights, but with few resources it could not sustain itself. Still, the organization is important for several reasons: first, Niagara proved that a significant contingent of black Americans disagreed with Washington; second, its manifesto, reprinted here, represents the willingness of black activists to be combative; and finally, Niagara laid the groundwork for the NAACP, founded in 1909. The Movement was unflinching in its belief in the inherent equality of black people; its members identified themselves as Americans regardless of race. Thus, Niagara called upon educated blacks to take responsibility for the racial struggle for civil rights.

The Niagara Movement Statement of Principles

Progress: The members of the conference, known as the Niagara Movement, assembled in annual meeting at Buffalo, July 11th, 12th and 13th, 1905, congratulate the Negro-Americans on certain undoubted evidence of progress in the last decade, particularly the increase of intelligence, the buying of property, the checking of crime, the uplift in home life, the advance in literature and art, and the demonstration of constructive and executive ability in the conduct of great religious, economic and educational institutions.

Suffrage: At the same time, we believe that this class of American citizens should protest emphatically and continually against the curtailment of their political rights. We believe in manhood suffrage; we believe that no man is so good, intelligent or wealthy as to be entrusted wholly with the welfare of his neighbor.

Civil Liberty: We believe also in protest against the curtailment of our civil rights. All American citizens have the right to equal treatment in places of public entertainment according to their behavior and deserts.

Economic Opportunity: We especially complain against the denial of equal opportunities to us in economic life; in the rural districts of the South this amounts to peonage and virtual slavery; all over the South it tends to crush labor and small business enterprises; and everywhere American prejudice, helped often by iniquitous laws, is making it more difficult for Negro-Americans to earn a decent living.

Education: Common school education should be free to all American children and compulsory. High school training should be adequately provided for all, and college training should be the monopoly of no class or race in any section of our common country. We believe that, in defense of our own institutions, the United States should aid common school education, particularly in the South, and we especially recommend concerted agitation to this end. We urge an increase in public high school facilities in the South, where the Negro-Americans are almost wholly without such provisions. We favor well-equipped trade and technical schools for the training of artisans, and the need of adequate and liberal endowment for a few institutions of higher education must be patent to sincere well-wishers of the race.

Courts: We demand upright judges in courts, juries selected without discrimination on account of color and the same measure of punishment and the same efforts at reformation for black as for white offenders. We need orphanages and farm schools for dependent children, juvenile reformatories for delinquents, and the abolition of the dehumanizing convict-lease system.

Public Opinion: We note with alarm the evident retrogression in this land of sound public opinion on the subject of manhood rights, republican government and human brotherhood, and we pray God that this nation will not degenerate into a mob of boasters and oppressors, but rather will return to the faith of the fathers, that all men were created free and equal, with certain unalienable rights.

Health: We plead for health – for an opportunity to live in decent houses and localities, for a chance to rear our children in physical and moral cleanliness.

Employers and Labor Unions: We hold up for public execration the conduct of two opposite classes of men: The practice among employers of importing ignorant Negro-American laborers in emergencies, and then affording them neither protection nor permanent employment; and the practice of labor unions in proscribing and boycotting and oppressing thousands of their fellow-toilers, simply because they are black. These methods have accentuated and will accentuate the war of labor and capital, and they are disgraceful to both sides.

Protest: We refuse to allow the impression to remain that the Negro-American assents to inferiority, is submissive under oppression and apologetic before insults. Through helplessness we may submit, but the voice of protest of ten million Americans must never cease to assail the ears of their fellows, so long as America is unjust.

Color-Line: Any discrimination based simply on race or color is barbarous, we care not how hallowed it be by custom, expediency or prejudice. Differences made on account of ignorance, immorality, or disease are legitimate methods of fighting evil, and against them we have no word of protest; but discriminations based simply and solely on physical peculiarities, place of birth, color of skin, are relics of that unreasoning human savagery of which the world is and ought to be thoroughly ashamed.

"Jim Crow" Cars: We protest against the "Jim Crow" car, since its effect is and must be to make us pay first-class fare for third-class accommodations, render us open to insults and discomfort and to crucify wantonly our man hood, womanhood and self-respect.

Soldiers: We regret that this nation has never seen fit adequately to reward the black soldiers who, in its five wars, have defended their country with their blood, and yet have been systematically denied the promotions which their abilities deserve. And we regard as unjust, the exclusion of black boys from the military and naval training schools.

War Amendments: We urge upon Congress the enactment of appropriate legislation for securing the proper enforcement of those articles of freedom, the thirteenth, fourteenth and fifteenth amendments of the Constitution of the United States.

Oppression: We repudiate the monstrous doctrine that the oppressor should be the sole authority as to the rights of the oppressed. The Negro race in America stolen, ravished and degraded, struggling up through difficulties and oppression, needs sympathy and receives criticism; needs help and is given hindrance, needs protection and is given mob-violence, needs justice and is given charity, needs leadership and is given cowardice and apology, needs bread and is given a stone. This nation will never stand justified before God until these things are changed.

The Church: Especially are we surprised and astonished at the recent attitude of the church of Christ – of an increase of a desire to bow to racial prejudice, to narrow the bounds of human brotherhood, and to segregate black men to some outer sanctuary. This is wrong, unchristian and disgraceful to the twentieth century civilization.

Agitation: Of the above grievances we do not hesitate to complain, and to complain loudly and insistently. To ignore, overlook, or apologize for these wrongs is to prove ourselves unworthy of freedom. Persistent manly agitation is the way to liberty, and toward this goal the Niagara Movement has started and asks the cooperation of all men of all races.

Help: At the same time we want to acknowledge with deep thankfulness the help of our fellowmen from the Abolitionist down to those who today still stand for equal opportunity and who have given and still give of their wealth and of their poverty for our advancement.

Duties: And while we are demanding, and ought to demand, and will continue to demand the rights enumerated above, God forbid that we should ever forget to urge corresponding duties upon our people:

The duty to vote.
The duty to respect the rights of others.
The duty to work.
The duty to obey the laws.
The duty to be clean and orderly.
The duty to send our children to school.
The duty to respect ourselves, even as we respect others.

This statement, complaint and prayer we submit to the American people, and Almighty God.

Source: "The Niagara Declaration of Principles," 1905.

8 Jack Johnson, 1910

In 1908 a black boxer named Jack Johnson (1878–1946) beat white Canadian Tommy Burns to become the heavyweight champion of the world, the first African American to hold the title. His victory directly challenged the primacy of white men, ostensibly demonstrated by the physical prowess of athletics. Johnson's win set off the search for "the Great White Hope," a white boxer who could defeat him. In 1910 James J. Jeffries came out of retirement "to reclaim the heavyweight championship for the white race," but lost to Johnson in what was called the "Battle of the Century." White on black riots ensued in localities across the nation; Texas, Johnson's home state, banned the screening of any films of the fight; and Johnson was harassed continually. To African Americans, however, Jack Johnson represented pride and daring, attitudes portrayed in this 1910 publicity photograph of him.

Figure 2.4   Jack Johnson, *c.* 1910.

Source: Library of Congress, Prints and Photographs Division, George Grantham Bain Collection.

Questions for Consideration

The notion of "the mask" and "double-consciousness" call attention to the shared sense of identity that African Americans shared. How do these documents highlight differences as well as similarities in the experiences of blacks at the end of the nineteenth century? And how did black leaders attempt to mitigate these differences?

Because Jim Crow took many forms, black leaders articulated a variety of tactical and philosophical approaches to progress, from gradualism to outright protest. Which forms of oppression did black leaders consider most egregious and most urgently in need of change, and why? Given the conditions African Americans faced, debate the relative merits of their various proposals and approaches to social change.

How did Ida B. Wells, Booker T. Washington, Mary Church Terrell, and W. E. B. Du Bois assess African Americans' potential to succeed in the South?

How did black women define their roles in the organized movement for black equality? When the Niagara Movement advocated "persistent manly agitation," did this include women? Why or why not? How did racial uplift differ from the struggle for civil rights?

Bibliography

Bay, Mia. *To Tell the Truth Freely: The Life of Ida B. Wells*. Boston: Hill and Wang, 2010.

Brown, Leslie. *Upbuilding Black Durham: Gender, Race, and Black Community Development in the Urban South*. Chapel Hill: University of North Carolina Press, 2008.

Gaines, Kevin K. *Uplifting the Race: Black Leadership, Politics, and Culture in the Twentieth Century*. Chapel Hill: University of North Carolina Press, 1996.

Gidding, Paula. *Sword Among Lions: Ida B. Wells and the Campaign Against Lynching*. New York: Armistad/HarperCollins, 2008.

Gilmore, Glenda Elizabeth. *Gender and Jim Crow: Women and the Politics of White Supremacy in North Carolina, 1896–1920*. Chapel Hill: University of North Carolina Press, 1996.

Hicks, Cheryl D. *Talk With You Like a Woman: African American Women, Justice, and Reform in New York, 1890–1935*. Chapel Hill: University of North Carolina Press, 2010.

Higginbotham, Evelyn. *Righteous Discontent: The Women's Movement in the Black Baptist Church, 1880–1920*. Cambridge, MA: Harvard University Press, 1998.

Lewis, David Levering. *W. E. B. Du Bois: Biography of a Race, 1868–1919*. New York: Henry Holt, 1993.

Litwack, Leon F. *Trouble in Mind: Black Southerners in the Age of Jim Crow*. New York: Vintage Press, 1999.

Murphy, Blair Kelley. *Right to Ride: Streetcar Boycotts and African American Citizenship in the Era of* Plessy v. Ferguson. Chapel Hill: University of North Carolina Press, 2010.

Norrell, Robert J. *Up From History: The Life of Booker T. Washington*. Cambridge, MA: Belknap Press of Harvard University, 2011.

Shaw, Stephanie. *What A Woman Ought to Be and to Do: Black Professional Women Workers During the Jim Crow Era*. Chicago: University of Chicago Press, 1996.

Tolnay, Stewart. *A Festival of Violence: An Analysis of Southern Lynching, 1882–1930*. Urbana: University of Illinois Press, 1995.

Woodward, C. Vann. *The Strange Career of Jim Crow*. Reprint. New York: Oxford University Press, 2001.

Chapter 3   Migration, 1904–1919

What was African American life like for most black people in the early twentieth century? What choices could they make about their lives? What options did they have? Electoral politics and racial segregation aside, work – the doing of it, the search for it, the stresses of the racism attached to it – epitomized most black people's struggle of the early twentieth century. A few managed to make a decent living, but most worked at subservient labor for the sake of survival. In 1900, 90 percent of African Americans lived in the South, and 90 percent of them lived in rural districts, laboring and living as farmers. A few owned land, and some were able to rent, but most worked on shares, that is, they worked for an entire year in exchange for an agreed-upon proportion of the value of harvested crop. Under a fair arrangement, share-cropping proffered a useable agreement for cash- and credit-poor farmers.

But under the control of white landowners, the system was a form of exploitation. The landlord determined the cost of expenses to be deducted from any profits – food, dry goods, fuel, housing, seed, and fertilizer – as well as where those goods could be purchased, the interest accrued, the value of the crop, and, therefore, how much a sharecropping family earned – or owed, usually – at the end of the year. Sharecroppers who defied the landlord by protesting their alleged debt, those who attempted to move or defend themselves, and those in excessive debt were imprisoned. As they assessed their circumstances, black families often decided that women's work outside the home might increase their income. At the end

African American Voices: A Documentary Reader from Emancipation to the Present, First Edition. Edited by Leslie Brown.
© 2014 John Wiley & Sons, Inc. Published 2014 by John Wiley & Sons, Inc.

of the nineteenth century, women dominated the migration streams out of the rural areas to southern and northern cities seeking employment as household laborers. Household labor also echoed slavery, where black women were vulnerable to the sexual predations of white men. Still, more than half of employed African American women worked as domestic servants in 1900, a proportion that increased rather than decreased as the mid-twentieth century approached.

It was the Great Migration, however, the south-to-north shift of African Americans, that changed black demographics significantly. In the 1910s increasing industrial expansion combined with declining European immigration to open employment venues in northern urban centers. As individuals, families, and groups determined whether to stay or go, the Great Migration carried a half-million black folk out of the South, signaling African Americans' willingness to disrupt the status quo. Beyond the official province of southern Jim Crow, wages improved, daily humiliation lessened, and citizenship rights and educational opportunities were broader, but blacks met stubborn barriers. Indeed, black migration revealed that racial animosity was a national inclination, not just a regional anomaly.

1 Voices from *The Independent*, 1904 and 1912

"we lived in a hell on earth"

These two documents appeared as articles in The Independent, *a Progressive-Era magazine whose journalists often published narratives of everyday people's lives based on interviews. It was a dangerous act for African Americans to speak frankly about Jim Crow. Thus, for their protection informants' names and details were withheld in print. Describing the frustrations of living with overt discrimination and hate, these stories tell of the twisted ways that Jim Crow operated to the detriment of blacks and for the benefit of whites. However much or however hard black people worked, whites exploited their labor and often controlled the lot of entire families. And both informants use the term "slavery" to describe this state of affairs.*

"The New Slavery in the South"

I was a man nearly grown before I knew how to count from one to one hundred. I was a man nearly grown before I ever saw a colored school-teacher. I never went to school a day in my life. Today I can't write my own name, tho' I can read a little. I was a man nearly grown before I ever rode on a railroad train, and then I went on an excursion from Elberton to Athens. What was true of me was true of hundreds of other negroes around me – way off there in the country, fifteen or twenty miles from the nearest town.

When I reached twenty-one the Captain [white landowner] told me I was a free man, but he urged me to stay with him. He said he would treat me right, and pay me as much as anybody else would. The Captain's son and I were about the same age, and the Captain said that, as he had owned my mother and uncle during slavery, and as his son didn't want me to leave them (since I had been with them so long), he wanted me to stay with the old family. And I stayed. I signed a contract – that is, I made my mark – for one year. The Captain was to give me $3.50 a week, and furnish me a little house on the plantation – a one-room log cabin similar to those used by his other laborers.

During that year I married Mandy. For several years Mandy had been the house-servant for the Captain, his wife, his son and his three daughters, and they all seemed to think a good deal of her. As an evidence of their regard they gave us a suit of furniture, which cost about $25, and we set up housekeeping in one of the Captain's two-room shanties. I thought I was the biggest man in Georgia. Mandy still kept her place in the "Big House" after our marriage. We did so well for the first year that I renewed my contract for the second year, and for the third, fourth and fifth year I did the same thing. Before the end of the fifth year the Captain had died, and his son, who had married some two or three years before, took charge of the plantation. Also, for two or three years, this son had been serving at Atlanta in some big office to which he had been elected. I think it was in the Legislature or something of that sort – anyhow, all the people called him Senator. At the end of the fifth year the Senator suggested that I sign up a contract for ten years; then, he said, we wouldn't have to fix up papers every year. I asked my wife about it; she consented; and so I made a ten-year contract.

Not long afterward the Senator had a long, low shanty built on his place. A great big chimney, with a wide, open fireplace, was built at one end of it, and on each side of the house, running lengthwise, there was a row of frames or stalls just large enough to hold a single mattress. The places for these mattresses were fixed one above the other, so that there was a double row of these stalls or pens on each side. They looked for all the world like stalls for horses. Since then I have seen cabooses similarly arranged as sleeping quarters for railroad laborers. Nobody seemed to know what the Senator was fixing for. All doubts were put aside one bright day in April when about forty able-bodied negroes, bound in iron chains, and some of them handcuffed were brought out to the Senator's farm in three big wagons. They were quartered in the long, low shanty, and it was afterward called the stockade. This was the beginning of the Senator's convict camp. These men were prisoners who had been leased by the Senator from the State of Georgia at about $200 each per year, the State agreeing to pay for guards and physicians, for necessary inspection, for inquests, all rewards for escaped convicts, the cost of litigation and all other incidental camp expenses. When I saw these men in shackles, and the guards with their guns, I was scared nearly to death. I felt like running away, but I didn't know where to go. And if there had been any place to go to, I would have had to leave my wife and child behind. We free laborers held a meeting. We all wanted to quit. We sent a man to tell the Senator about it. Word came back that we were all under contract for ten years and that the Senator would hold us to the letter of the contract, or put us in chains and lock us up the same as the other prisoners. It was made plain to us by some white people we talked to that in the contracts we had signed we had all agreed to be locked up in a stockade at night or at any other time that our employer saw fit; further, we learned that we could not lawfully break our contract for any reason and go and hire ourselves to somebody else without the consent of our employer, and, more than that, if we got mad and ran away, we could be run down by bloodhounds, arrested without process of law, and be returned to our employer, who, according to the contract, might beat us brutally or administer any other kind of punishment that he thought proper. In other words, we had sold ourselves into slavery – and what could we do about it? The white folks had all the courts, all the guns, all the hounds, all the railroads, all the telegraph wires, all the newspapers, all the money, and nearly all the land – and we had only our ignorance, our poverty and our empty hands. We decided that the best thing to do was to shut our mouths, say nothing, and go back to work. And most of us worked side by side with those convicts during the remainder of the ten years.

But this first batch of convicts was only the beginning. Within six months another stockade was built, and twenty or thirty other convicts were brought to the plantation, among them six or eight women! The Senator had bought an additional thousand acres of land, and to his already large cotton plantation he added two great big saw-mills and went into the lumber business. Within two years the Senator had in all nearly 200 negroes working on his plantation – about half of them free laborers, so-called, and about half of them convicts. The only difference between the free laborers and the others was that the free laborers could come and go as they pleased, at night – that is, they were not locked up at night, and were not, as a general thing, whipped for slight offenses. The troubles of the free laborers began at the close of the ten-year period. To a man, they all wanted to quit when the time was up. To a man, they all refused to sign new contracts – even for one year, not to say anything of ten years. And just when we thought that our bondage was at an end we found that it had really just begun. Two or three years before, or about a year and a half after the Senator had started his camp, he had established a large store, which was called the commissary. All of us free laborers were compelled to buy our supplies – food, clothing, etc. – from that store. We never used any money in our dealings with the commissary, only tickets or orders, and we had a general settlement once each year, in October. In this store we were charged all sorts of high prices for goods, because every year we would come out in debt to our employer. If not that, we seldom had more than $5 or $10 coming to us – and that for a whole year's work. Well, at the close of the tenth year, when we kicked and meant to leave the Senator, he said to some of us with a smile (and I never will forget that smile ... I can see it now):

> "Boys, I'm sorry you're going to leave me. I hope you will do well in your new places – so well that you will be able to pay me the little balances which most of you owe me."

Word was sent out for all of us to meet him at the commissary at 2 o'clock. There he told us that, after we had signed what he called a written acknowledgment of our debts, we might go and look for new places. The storekeeper took us one by one and read to us statements of our accounts. According to the books there was no man of us who owed the Senator less than $100; some of us were put down for as much as $200. I owed $165, according to the bookkeeper. These debts were not accumulated during one year, but ran back for three and four years, so we were told – in spite of the fact that we understood that we had had a full settlement at the end of each year. But no one of us would have dared to dispute a white man's word – oh, no; not in those days. Besides, we fellows didn't care anything about the amounts – we were after getting away; and we had been told that we might go, if we signed the acknowledgments. We would have signed anything, just to get away. So we stepped up, we did, and made our marks. That same night we were rounded up by a constable and ten or twelve white men, who aided him, and we were locked up, every one of us, in one of the Senator's stockades. The next morning it was explained to us by the two guards appointed to watch us that, in the papers we had signed the day before, we had not only made acknowledgment of our indebtedness, but that we had also agreed to work for the Senator until the debts were paid by hard labor. And from that day forward we were treated just like convicts. Really we had made ourselves lifetime slaves, or peons, as the laws called us. But, call it slavery, peonage, or what not, the truth is we lived in a hell on earth what time we spent in the Senator's peon camp.

...

The stockades in which we slept were, I believe, the filthiest places in the world. They were cesspools of nastiness. During the thirteen years that I was there I am willing to swear that a mattress was never moved after it had been brought there, except to turn it over once or twice a month. No sheets were used, only dark-colored blankets. Most of the men slept every night in the clothing that they had worked in all day. Some of the worst characters were made to sleep in chains. The doors were locked and barred each night, and tallow candles were the only lights allowed. Really the stockades were but little more than cow lots, horse stables or hog pens. Strange to say, not a great number of these people died while I was there, tho a great many came away maimed and bruised and, in some cases, disabled for life. As far as I remember only about ten died during the last ten years that I was there, two of these being killed outright by the guards for trivial offenses.

...

When I had served as a peon for nearly three years – and you remember that they claimed that I owed them only $165 – when I had served for nearly three years, one of the bosses came to me and said that my time was up. He happened to be the one who was said to be living with my wife. He gave me a new suit of overalls, which cost about seventy-five cents, took me in a buggy and carried me across the Broad River into South Carolina, set me down and told me to "git." I didn't have a cent of money, and I wasn't feeling well but somehow I managed to get a move on me. I begged my way to Columbia. In two or three days I ran across a man looking for laborers to carry to Birmingham, and I joined his gang. I have been here in the Birmingham district since they released me, and I reckon I'll die either in a coal mine or an iron furnace. It don't make much difference which. Either is better than a Georgia peon camp. And a Georgia peon camp is hell itself!

Source: *The Independent*, 56 (February 25, 1904), pp. 409–414.

More Slavery in the South

I am a negro woman, and I was born and reared in the South. I am now past forty years of age and am the mother of three children. My husband died nearly fifteen years ago, after we had been married about five years. For more than thirty years – or since I was ten years old – I have been a servant in one capacity or another in white families in a thriving Southern city, which has at present a population of more than 50,000. In my early years I was at first what might be called a "house-girl," or, better, a "house-boy." I used to answer the doorbell, sweep the yard, go on errands and do odd jobs. Later on I became a chambermaid and performed the usual duties of such a servant in a home. Still later I was graduated into a cook, in which position I served at different times for nearly eight years in all. During the last ten years I have been a nurse. I have worked for only four different families during all these thirty years. But, belonging to the servant class, which is the majority class among my race at the South, and associating only with servants, I have been able to become intimately acquainted not only with the lives of hundreds of household servants, but also with the lives of their employers. I can, therefore, speak with authority on the so-called servant question; and what I say is said out of an experience which covers many years.

To begin with, then, I should say that more than two-thirds of the negroes of the town where I live are menial servants of one kind or another, and besides that more than two-thirds of the negro women here, whether married or single, are compelled to work for a living, – as nurses, cooks, washer-women, chambermaids, seamstresses, hucksters, janitresses, and the like. I will say, also, that the condition of this vast host of poor colored people is just as bad as, if not worse than, it was during the days of slavery. Tho today we are enjoying a nominal freedom, we are literally slaves. And, not to generalize, I will give you a sketch of the work I have to do – and I'm only one of many.

I frequently work from fourteen to sixteen hours a day. I am compelled to by my contract, which is oral only, to sleep in the house. I am allowed to go home to my own children, the oldest of whom is a girl of 18 years, only once in two weeks, every other Sunday afternoon – even then I'm not permitted to stay all night. I not only have to nurse a little white child, now eleven months old, but I have to act as playmate, or "handy-andy," not to say gov-erness, to three other children in the house, the oldest of whom is only nine years of age. I wash and dress the baby two or three times each day; I give it its meals, mainly from a bottle; I have to put it to bed each night; and, in addition, I have to get up and attend to its every call between midnight and morning. If the baby falls to sleep during the day, as it has been trained to do every day about eleven o'clock, I am not permitted to rest. It's "Mammy, do this," or "Mammy, do that," or "Mammy, do the other," from my mistress, all the time. So it is not strange to see "Mammy" watering the lawn with the garden hose, sweeping the sidewalk, mopping the porch and halls, helping the cook, or darning stockings. Not only so, but I have to put the other three children to bed each night as well as the baby, and I have to wash them and dress them each morning. I don't know what it is to go to church; I don't know what it is to go to a lecture or entertainment of anything of the kind; I live a treadmill life; and I see my own children only when they happen to see me on the streets when I am out with the children, or when my children come to the "yard" to see me, which isn't often, because my white folks don't like to see their servants' children hanging around their premises. You might as well say that I'm on duty all the time – from sunrise to sunrise, every day in the week. I am the slave, body and soul, of this family. And what do I get for this work – this lifetime bondage? The pitiful sum of ten dollars a month! And what am I expected to do with these ten dollars? With this money I'm expected to pay my house rent, which is four dollars per month, for a little house of two rooms, just big enough to turn around in; and I'm expected, also, to feed and clothe myself and three children. For two years my oldest child, it is true, has helped a little toward our support by taking in a little washing at home. She does the washing and ironing of two white families, with a total of five persons; one of these families pays her $1.00 per week, and the other 75 cents per week, and my daughter has to furnish her own soap and starch and wood. For six months my youngest child, a girl about thirteen years old, has been nursing, and she receives $1.50 per week but has no night work. When I think of the low rate of wages we poor colored people receive, and when I hear so much said about our unreliability, our untrustworthiness, and even our vices, I recall the story of the private soldier in a certain army who, once upon a time, being upbraided by the commanding officer because the heels of his shoes were not polished, is said to have replied: "Captain, do you expect all the virtues for $13 per month?"

Of course, nothing is being done to increase our wages, and the way things are going at the present it would seem that nothing could be done to cause an increase of wages. We have no labor unions or organizations of any kind that could demand for us a uniform scale of wages for cooks, washerwomen, nurses, and the like; and, for another thing, if some negroes did here and there refuse to work for seven and eight and ten dollars a month, there would be hundreds of other negroes right on the spot ready to take their places and do the same work, or more, for the low wages that had been refused. So that, the truth is, we have to work for little or nothing, or become vagrants! And that, of course, in this State would mean that we would be arrested, tried, and dispatched to the "State Farm," where we would surely have to work for nothing or be beaten with many stripes!

...

I believe nearly all white men take, and expect to take, undue liberties with their colored female servants – not only the fathers, but in many cases the sons also. Those servants who rebel against such familiarity must either leave or expect a mighty hard time, if they stay. By comparison, those who tamely submit to these improper relations live in clover. They always have a little "spending change," wear better clothes, and are able to get off from work at least once a week – and sometimes oftener. This moral debasement is not at all times unknown to the white women in these homes. I know of more than one colored woman who was openly importuned by white women to become the mistresses of their white husbands, on the ground that they, the white wives, were afraid that, if their husbands did not associate with colored women, they would certainly do so with outside white women, and the white wives, for reasons which ought to be perfectly obvious, preferred to have their husbands do wrong with colored women in order to keep their husbands straight! And again, I know at least fifty places where white men are positively raising two families – a white family in the "Big House" in front, and a colored family in a "Little House" in the backyard.

...

Another thing – it's a small indignity, it may be, but an indignity just the same. No white person, not even the little children just learning to talk, no white person at the South ever thinks of addressing any negro man or woman as Mr., or Mrs., or Miss. The women are called, "Cook," or "Nurse," or "Mammy," or "Mary Jane," or "Lou," or "Dilcey," as the case might be, and the men are called "Bob," or "Boy," or "Old Man," or "Uncle Bill," or "Pate." In many cases our white employers refer to us, and in our presence, too, as their "niggers." No matter what they call us – no matter what we teach our children to call us – we must tamely submit, and answer when we are called; we must enter no protest; if we did object, we should be driven out without the least ceremony, and, in applying for work at other places, we should find it very hard to procure another situation. ...

... Sometimes I have gone on the street cars or the railroad trains with the white children, and, so long as I was in charge of the children, I could sit anywhere I desired, front or back. If a white man happened to ask some other white man, "What is that nigger doing in here?" and was told, "Oh, she's the nurse of those white children in front of her!" immediately there was the hush of peace. Everything was all right, so long as I was in the white man's part of the street car or in the white man's coach as a servant – a slave – but as soon as I did not present myself as a menial, and the relationship of master and servant was abolished by my not having the white children with me, I would be forthwith assigned to the "nigger" seats or the "colored people's coach. ..."

Good cooks in the South receive on an average $8 per month. Porters, butlers, coachmen, janitors, "office boys" and the like receive on an average

$16 per month. Few and far between are the colored men in the South who receive $1 or more per day. Some mechanics do; as, for example, carpenters, brick masons, wheelwrights, blacksmiths, and the like. The vast majority of Negroes in my town are serving in menial capacities in homes, stores and offices. Now taking it for granted, for the sake of illustration, that the husband receives, $16 per month and the wife $8. That would be $24 between the two. The chances are that they will have anywhere from five to thirteen children between them. Now, how far will $24 go toward housing and clothing ten or twelve persons for thirty days? ...

... Perhaps a million of us are introduced daily to the privacy of a million chambers thruout the South, and hold in our arms a million white children, thousands of whom, as infants, are suckled at our breasts – during my life-time I myself have served as "wet nurse" to more than a dozen white chil-dren. On the one hand, we are assailed by white men, and, on the other hand, we are assailed by black men, who should be our natural protectors; and, whether in the cook kitchen, at the washtub, over the sewing machine, behind the baby carriage, or at the ironing board, we are but little more than pack horses, beasts of burden, slaves! In the distant future, it may be, cen-turies and centuries hence, a monument of brass or stone will be erected to the Old Black Mammies of the South, but what we need is present help, present sympathy, better wages, better hours, more protections, and a chance to breathe for once while alive as free women. If none others will help us, it would seem that the Southern white women themselves might do so in their own defense, because we are rearing their children – we feed them, we bathe them, we teach them to speak the English language, and in numberless instances we sleep with them – and it is inevitable that the lives of their chil-dren will in some measure be pure or impure according as they are affected by contact with their colored nurses.

Source: *The Independent*, 72 (January 1912), pp. 196–200.

2 Letters of Negro Migrants, 1916–1917

"I want to get out of this dog hold"

Thousands of southern African Americans wrote letters to race organizations and periodicals seeking information about moving north. In 1919 researcher and journalist Emmet J. Scott published representative correspondence in two issues of the Journal of Negro History, *recognizing "the most significant event in our recent internal history" was underway. Unedited as they appeared in the* Journal, *the letters reprinted below offer a very small sampling, some from southerners wishing to go north, and others from migrants to folks back home.*

TROY, ALA., Oct. 17, 1916.

Dear Sirs I am enclosing a clipping of a lynching again which speaks for itself. I do wish there could be sufficient presure brought about to have federal investigation of such work. I wrote you a few days ago if you could furnish me with the addresses of some firms or co-opporations that needed common labor. So many of our people here are almost starving. The government is feeding quite a number here would go any where to better their conditions. If you can do any thing for us write me as early as posible.

SHERMAN, GA., Nov. 28, 1916.

Dear sir: This letter comes to ask for all infirmations concern emplyoment in your conection in the warmest climate. Now I am in a family of (11) eleven more or less boys and girls (men and women) mixed sizes who want to go north as soon as arrangements can be made and employment given places for shelter an so en (etc) now this are farming people they were raised on the farm and are good farm hands I of course have some experience and qualefication as a coman school teacher and hotel waiter and along few other lines.

I wish you would write me at your first chance and tell me if you can give us employment at what time and about what wages will you pay and what kind of arrangement can be made for our shelter. Tell me when can you best use us now or later.

Will you send us tickets if so on what terms and at what price what is the cost per head and by what route should we come. We are Negroes and try to show ourselves worthy of all we may get from any friendly source we endeavor to be true to all good causes, if you can we thank you to help up to come north as soon as you can.

FAYETTE, GA., January 17, 1917.

Dear Sir: I have learned of the splendid work which you are doing in placing colored men in touch with industrial opportunities. I therefore write you to ask if you have an opening anywhere for me. I am a college graduate and understand Bookkeeping. But I am not above doing hard labor in a foundry or other industrial establishment. Please let me know if you can place me.

MOBILE, ALA., April 25, 1917.

Sir: I was reading in theat paper about the Colored race and while reading it I seen in it where cars would be here for the 15 of May which is one month from to day. Will you be so kind as to let me know where they are coming to and I will be glad to know because I am a poor woman and have a husband and five children living and three dead one single and two twin girls six months old today and my husband can hardly make bread for them in Mobile. This is my native home but it is not fit to live in just as the Chicago Defender say it says the truth and my husband only get $1.50 a day and pays $7.50 a month for house rent and can hardly feed me and his self and children. I am the mother of 8 children 25 years old and I want to get out of this dog hold because I dont know what I am raising them up for in this place and I want to get to Chicago where I know they will be raised and my husband crazy to get there because he know he can get more to raise his children and will you please let me know where the cars is going to stop to so that he can come where he can take care of me and my children. He get there a while and then he can send for me. I heard they wasnt coming here so I sent to find out and he can go and meet them at the place they are going and go from there to Chicago. No more at present. hoping to hear from you soon from your needed and worried friend

ALEXANDRIA, LA., June 6, 1917

Dear Sirs: I am writeing to you all asking a favor of you all. I am a girl of seventeen. School has just closed I have been going to school for nine months and I now feel like I aught to go to work. And I would like very very well for you all to please forward me to a good job. but there isnt a thing here for me to do, the wages here is from a dollar and a half a week. What could I earn Nothing. I have a mother and father my father do all he can for me but it is so hard. A child with any respect about her self or his self wouldnt like to see there mother and father work so hard and earn nothing I feel it my duty to help. I would like for you all to get me a good job and as I havent any money to come on please send me a pass and I would work and pay every cent of it back and get me a good quite place to stay. My father have been getting the defender for three or four months but for the last two weeks we have failed to get it. I dont know why. I am tired of down hear in _____/ I am afraid to say. Father seem to care and then again dont seem to but Mother and I am tired tired of all of this I wrote to you all because I believe you will help I need your help hopeing to here from you all very soon.

DAYTON, OHIO, 7/22/17.

My dear pastor and wife: I reed your letter was Glad to hear from you I am do find hope the same for you I am send you some money for my back salary I will send you some more the 5 of Sept next month Give love to all of the member of church I will be home on a visit in Oct are early so pray for me write to me I would have wrote to you but I did not no just what to say all of the people leaves Go to place up East that I did not no weather are not you care to hear from me are not so I am glad you think of me. Mr. O____ write me was going to take out life insurance with him but he would not send me the paper so I just let it Go as I guess he did not class me with himself I am mak $70 month at this hotel and then not work hard.

PHILADELPHIA, PA., Oct. 7, 1917.

Dear Sir: I take this method of thanking you for yours early responding and the glorious effect of the treatment. Oh. I do feel so fine. Dr. the treatment reach me almost ready to move I am now housekeeping again I like it so much better than rooming. Well Dr. with the aid of God I am making very good I make $75 per month. I am carrying enough insurance to pay me $20 per week if I am not able to be on duty. I don't have to work hard. dont have to mister every little white boy comes along I havent heard a white man call a colored a nigger you no now – since I been in the state of Pa. I can ride in the electric street and steam cars any where I get a seat. I dont care to mix with white what I mean I am not crazy about being with white folks, but if I have to pay the same fare I have learn to want the same acomidation. and if you are first in a place here shoping you dont have to wait until the white folks get thro tradeing yet amid all this I shall ever love the good old South and I am praying that God may give every well wisher a chance to be a man regardless of his color, and if my going to the front would bring about such conditions I am ready any day – well Dr. I dont want to worry you but read between lines; and maybe you can see a little sense in my weak statement the kids are in school every day I have only two and I guess that all. Dr. when you find time I would be delighted to have a word from the good old home state. Wife join me in sending love you and yours.
    I am your friend and patient.

Source: "Letters of Negro Migrants, 1916–18," *Journal of Negro History*, 4 (July 1919): 290–340; and "More Letters of Negro Migrants 1916–1918," *Journal of Negro History*, 4 (October 1919): 412–465.

3 The East St. Louis Riot, 1917

"We can't live South and they don't want us North. Where are we to go?"

Even as they plotted their escape from the South, black southerners also read in the press about the East St. Louis Riot. Over a week's time in July 1917, and with the complicity of law enforcement and the military, whites destroyed some half-million dollars in black property, killed dozens of black people, and left six thousand African Americans homeless. Some among the witnesses were more recent arrivals but many black residents had lived in the city since before the twentieth century. White animosity toward black workers sparked the violence, but the tensions ran deeper than labor issues alone.

W. E. B. Du Bois and Martha Gruening, a white journalist, investigated the riot and published their findings in The Crisis, *the NAACP's journal, in September 1917. Usually,* Crisis *articles were brief, but because authors did not want to understate the events, their report ran more than twenty pages. Concluding that whites launched a deliberate terrorist assault on an enterprising black community, the* Crisis *account included excerpts from the coverage by local white newspapers, quotes from white authorities and observers, and photographs of the damage. The most remarkable parts of the article, excerpted below, are the eyewitness accounts by African Americans caught in the riot.*

"The Massacre of East St. Louis"

...

East St. Louis is a great industrial center, possessing huge packing and manufacturing houses, and is, therefore, one of the biggest markets in the country for common unskilled labor. The war, by the deportation of white foreign workers, caused a scarcity of labor and this brought about the beginning of a noticeable influx of Negroes from the South. Last summer 4,500 white men went on strike in the packing plants of Armour & Co., Morris & Co., and Swift & Co., and Negroes from the South were called into the plants as strike-breakers. When the strike ended the Negroes were still employed and that many white men failed to regain their positions. The leaders of various labor unions realized that the supply of Negroes was practically inexhaustible and that they were receiving the same wages as their white predecessors and so evidently doing the same grade of work. Since it was increasingly possible then to call in as many black strike-breakers as necessary, the effectiveness of any strike was accordingly decreased. It was this realization that caused the small but indicative May riots. Evidently, the leaders of the labor unions thought something must be done, some measure sufficiently drastic must be taken to drive these interlopers away and to restore to these white Americans their privileges. The fact that the Negroes were also Americans meant nothing at such a time as this.

...

The following accounts are published in the somewhat disjointed fashion in which they were necessarily collected by the investigators. No interpolation whatever is added to detract from their simplicity and sincerity.

This is the testimony of Mary Edwards. She is twenty-three years old, directress of a cafeteria at Lincoln School at fifty dollars a month, has lived in East St. Louis for sixteen years:

> Knew at ten o'clock in the morning that white and colored had been fighting, but did not know seriousness of fight until five o'clock in evening when riot started at Broadway and Fourth Street. Heard shooting and yelling, saw mob pull women off street cars and beat them, but did not think rioters would come up to Eighth Street. Fires had started and were as far as Fifth Street and Broadway and swept through Fourth St., to Fifth and on to Eighth. The shooting was so violent that they were afraid to leave home. By this time rioters were on Eighth Street, shooting through homes and setting fire to them. Daughter and father were in house dodging bullets which were coming thick. Building at corner of Eighth and Walnut was occupied by whites. Some of mob yelled, "Save it. Whites live there." Some of the rioters went to Eighth and Broadway and set fire to colored grocery store and colored barber shop. Man in barber shop escaped but the man and wife in store were burned up. By that time Opera House was on fire and flats on side and back of it. East end of Library flats caught and heat was so great that father and daughter tried to escape through alley and up street to Broadway, but encountered mob at Broadway. Soldiers were in line-up on north side of street and offered no assistance. Ran across street to Westbrook's home with bullets flying all around them and rioters shouting, "Kill him, kill him." Here daughter lost track of father. She beat on back door of Westbrook's home but no response, ran across alley to Division Avenue, ran on white lady's porch, but the lady would not let her in. Men were shooting at her for all they were worth, but she succeeded in dodging bullets. Ran across field and got in house and crawled under bed. Mob following right behind her, but lost sight of which house she went in and set fire to each end of flat. Rather than be burned to death she ran out and mob began shooting at her again. Just at that time a man ran out of the house, and mob let girl alone and started at him. She fell in weeds and lay very quiet. Could see them beating man. About one hour afterwards she heard someone say, "Any niggers in here?" She kept very quiet thinking them rioters. One said, "No one does answer. Come on, boys, let's go in after them."

She then raised up not knowing they were soldiers and pleaded for her life. They picked her up and took her over the same ground she had run from the mob; put her in a machine and took her to City Hall. When she came to herself she was in the doctor's office surrounded by friends and her sister, Josephine, who had escaped with the Westbrooks.

...

Nathaniel Cole is twenty-two years old and worked in a steel foundry. He says:

I was on my way from Alton on an Inter-urban car. When our car reached East St. Louis I saw a crowd of whites hollering, "Stop the car and get the nigger." The man pulled out and beaten. In the mean time a white child called "There's another nigger." I was then pulled off the car, beaten and left in the street. After the mob left, I attempted to board a car and was ejected by the conductor. Not knowing anything about East St. Louis or the mob, I ran into a white neighborhood and a woman hollered, "Stop that nigger. Stop that nigger." Two fellows ran out of a gangway, one with a brick and the other with a long club. I ran and was well out of the way when a Ford car came along and about twelve of the rioters got [out] and overtook me after I had entered an alley. They then hemmed me in a yard, where a carpenter was at work and began beating me. The carpenter then asked the rioters not to beat me up there, but to turn me over to the police if I had done anything to deserve it. The rioters replied, "The nigger taken the white man's job." I was beaten in the face with a cane and a rubber hose. I was beaten into insensibility and when I came to they were taking stitches in my head at St. Mary's. Hospital.

...

Rena Cook returned from a day's outing to horror and death. Her statement follows:

While returning from a fishing trip on an Alton St. car, we were met by a mob at Collinsville and Broadway who stopped the car and had the white people get out. The mob came in and dragged my husband and son out, beating them at the same time, threw them off the car and shot both my husband and son, killing them instantly. Two policemen stood by, but did not interfere. The mob came back in the car and ran me out and beat me into insensibility. I knew nothing more until I found myself in St. Mary's Hospital. After staying in the hospital far two days I was taken to City Hall in East St. Louis and from there the police and militia escorted me to St. Louis.

...

Testimony of twenty-year-old Vassie Randall, an employee of the Electric Sack Plant:

The mob had benches stretched across the street facing both directions that no one might escape. A Negro came along and one fellow stepped out and struck him, and then others jumped on him, kicked out his eye and when he tried to get up, they returned and killed him. They then took him to Third and Main and swung him to a telegraph pole ...

...

Testimony of Mary Bell White, age fifty-nine years. She was born in East St. Louis and did laundry-work at $1.25 a day:

Saw two people burn an old man and a very old woman. They were thrown into a burning house. Monday at 4 P. M. I saw three women burned. By that time I was so excited that I ran to Tenth Street, where I met a white-man who offered me and about one hundred others his protection. He had us go into an old building that had been used for a storage house. We stayed there all night. The next day I went to the City Hall and from there to St. Louis. I lost everything.

Testimony of Thomas Crittenden:

Age forty-six years and a resident of East St. Louis for five years. Worked as a laborer at $3.60 a day. Monday night his boss found out about the riot and secreted him and another fellow. The next day he found that the district in which he lived had been burned. His wife was pulled from her house by the women of the mob, who beat her into insensibility and knocked out three teeth ...

...

Testimony of Salena Hubble, age 42 years:

I am a widow. I lived in East St. Louis five years. I came to wait on my sick daughter.

Before the riot the people of both races were friendly and pleasant in manners. On the evening the rioters told me to leave because they were going to burn up the whole block, as they thought I was a white woman, so they warned me to flee. I talked with a neighbor, Mrs. Clemens (a white woman) and asked her if she thought the mob would do any more harm. She said:

"I don't know, but you get ready and leave by the way of the cars over the bridge."

Just as I started over the bridge the mob broke my windows out with rocks. I escaped because the mob didn't know I belonged to the Negro race. Before I got out of East St. Louis I saw the mob with a rope and I heard them say: "There's a nigger. Let us hang the S — of a B — ," and they threw the rope over the telegraph pole, but I didn't know what came of that; I saw the soldiers and they offered no assistance to the colored people. I saw the fire department come before the fire was started, but when the fire was started they did nothing to stop it. I also saw the mob throw a rope around a colored man's neck and shoot him full of holes. The soldiers offered no assistance to the man who was shot, neither did the police. I saw a crowd of soldiers go into a saloon and engage in drinking heavily of beer. The mob burned the houses in the localities where colored lived mostly. The women were as vile as the men in their vile treatment to the Negroes. I saw the soldiers driving a crowd of colored men in the streets. The men were made to hold their hands above their heads as they walked.

Testimony of Beatrice Deshong, age 26 years:

I saw the mob robbing the homes of Negroes and then set fire to them. The soldiers stood with folded arms and looked on as the houses burned. I saw a Negro man killed instantly by a member of the mob, men, small boys, and women and little girls all were trying to do something to injure the Negroes. I saw a colored woman stripped of all of her clothes except her waist. I don't know what became of her. The police and the soldiers were assisting the mob to kill Negroes and to destroy their homes. I saw the mob hang a colored man to a telegraph pole and riddle him with bullets. I saw the mob chasing a colored man who had a baby in his arms. The mob was shooting at him all of the time as long as I saw him. I ran for my life ... The mob stole the jewelry of Negroes and used axes and hatchets to chop up pianos and furniture that belonged to them. The mob was seemingly well arranged to do their desperate work. I recognized some of the wealthy people's sons and some of the bank officials in the mob. They were as vile as they could be.

Testimony of Robert Hersey, age 20 years:

I have lived in East St. Louis since the 25th of March, 1917. I came here because of bad treatment and poor wages. I worked in a tobacco factory in St Louis, Mo., and received two dollars a day.

Before the riot everyone seemed friendly toward me. I never got into the thickest of the men or riot, but they hit me with clubs, bricks, and stamped me on the head. They broke my arm. But for all of that I got away from them.

I shall never return to the South whatever may happen to me here, for in the South it is always killing and burning some of our people. No let up on bad treatment and no wages either. Men must work for eighty cents a day, women for fifty cents a week, and if the whites choose not to pay that, they won't do it. I shall stay in St Louis, Mo.

The damning statements go on and on. Among the Negroes one finds a note sometimes of blank stark despair. John T. Stewart in the *St. Louis Star* draws a pathetic picture:

> One aged Negro woman passed the police station carrying in her arms all that mob spirit and fire had left of her belongings. They consisted of a worn pair of shoes – she was barefooted – an extra calico dress, an old shawl and two puppies. Tears were streaming down her face and she saw neither soldiers nor her enemies as she passed beneath the lights of the City Hall, going she knew not where.

Saddest of all is Miss Gruening's account of the old woman whom she saw poking about in the desolate ruins of what had once been her home. Her family had escaped to St. Louis, but not a fraction of their possessions remained intact. The woman was old – sixty-five – not an easy age at which to begin life anew.

"What are we to do?" she asked Miss Gruening. "We can't live South and they don't want us North. Where are we to go?"

From the statements gathered by the investigators, many of these driven people seem to feel that the example of the South in dealing with Negroes is responsible for the methods of East St. Louis. Many of them express firmly their resolve, in spite of all, never to go back South. They will stay in St. Louis, they say, or push further North.

Source: *The Crisis*, September 1917.

4 Why African Americans Left the South, 1919

"This abnormal movement among the colored people is striking in many ways"

W. T. B. (William Taylor Burwell) Williams (1869–1941), Dean of the College Department at Tuskegee Institute, traveled widely in the North and South as a field agent for several philanthropies that funded black education. In this role he met and talked with black and white leaders. For the US Department of Labor study of the Great Migration, Williams wrote the summary report excerpted below.

The Negro Exodus from the South, 1919
By W. T. B. Williams

For a number of years it has been apparent to even the casual observer that a stream of Negroes has been flowing into the North from the border southern States. Some have been going from the lower South also, but that section has not hitherto been greatly affected. However, recent extraordinary occurrences – the war in Europe, with the consequent shortage of labor in the North, the ravages of the boll weevil and flood conditions in the South – have set on foot a general movement of Negroes northward that is affecting the whole South ...

... The exodus is carrying off in considerable numbers not only the common laborers from the farms and industries of the South but also many of the skilled Negro mechanics from the larger cities, like New Orleans, Montgomery, Birmingham, Savannah, and Charleston; many of the trained workers with less skill; and even Negro business men, ministers, and physicians ...

... This abnormal movement among the colored people is striking in many ways. It seems to be a general response to the call of better economic and social opportunities. The movement is without organization or leadership. The Negroes just quietly move away without taking their recognized leaders into their confidence any more than they do the white people about them. A Negro minister may have all his deacons with him at the mid-week meeting, but by Sunday every church officer is likely to be in the North. They write the minister that they forgot to tell him they were going away. They rarely consult the white people, and never those who may exercise some control over their actions. They will not allow their own leaders to advise them against going North ... They are likely to suspect that such men are in the employ of white people. An influential Negro newspaper in Virginia made an earnest effort at the outset to stem the movement northward. Its supporters brought such influence to bear upon it that, according to the report of its editor, it was forced to change its attitude. In fact, very little positive effort of any kind within the race is made to check the movement. Most Negroes have, of course, no idea of leaving the South themselves. They know that for many reasons the greater part of the race will likely remain better off in the South than in the North. But practically all are convinced that this exodus will result in great good for Negroes generally. It is the universal feeling, in fact, that good has already come out of it.

The exodus has pointedly called attention to the value of Negro labor to the South and to the South's dependence upon it ... The exodus has carried off the surplus labor which has existed in so great abundance that the South has been prodigal and contemptuous of it. The result is less competition among the Negroes for the work the South has to offer and an increased demand among employers for labor. Wages, though still low, are advancing ...

SOME EFFECTS OF THE EXODUS.

Naturally so great a movement of labor from one section would have some harmful effects. The loud and widespread objections to the exodus raised by the farming and industrial interests of the South indicate that the losses and interruptions to business have been considerable and significant ... In a number of industries production has been "slowed down," owing to the necessity of breaking in new men to take the places of experienced men, as in the lumber mills all over the South, in the mines, on the docks, and, as is likely to prove, in the cotton-oil mills ...

Serious costly effects of the exodus are not hard to find in many places. In every State from the Carolinas to Mississippi thousands of acres of land are reported to be lying idle that would have been cultivated had labor been available. And even where good crops have been grown it is a question in many places as to whether sufficient labor for gathering them can be secured ...

... From the cities and towns all over the South a great many colored women and girls have gone North in this movement. This means that many of the best trained domestic servants have been lost to southern homes. That causes more acute suffering of a kind than the loss of the men laborers. New servants from the towns and from the country have taken the places left vacant, but they lack the training of the old servants, and, above all, are not known to nor trusted by their employers, as were the old ones. This means a real hardship for [white] wives and daughters, from whom come the loudest complaints against the migration of the Negroes.

UNDERLYING CAUSES OF THE EXODUS.

... The Negro's success in the North has been far more effective in carrying off labor than agents could possibly have been. Every Negro that makes good in the North, as thousands are doing, and writes back to his friends that "everything is pretty," starts off a new group to the "promised land." It is this quiet, effective work that leads the whites to think that labor agents in large numbers are working secretly still. Then, too, a great deal of money has been sent back into the South by the migrants, and this attracts no end of attention. ...

The treatment accorded the Negro always stood second, when not first, among the reasons given by Negroes for leaving the South. I talked with all classes of colored people from Virginia to Louisiana – farm hands, tenants, farmers, hack drivers, porters, mechanics, barbers, merchants, insurance men, teachers, heads of schools, ministers, druggists, physicians, and lawyers – and in every instance the matter of treatment came to the front voluntarily. This is the all-absorbing, burning question among Negroes ...

The average white man, however, seems to have little knowledge or appreciation of this feeling among Negroes. Few think apparently that anything but money, or the novelty of change, or desire for what they call "social equality" has anything to do with the migration from the South; but they are greatly deceiving themselves ... Indeed, it was rare to find a southern white man who felt, or would at least admit to me, that the South's treatment of the Negro had anything to do with the exodus ...

... Because Negroes have made few public complaints about their condition in the South, the average white man has assumed that they are satisfied; but there is a vast amount of dissatisfaction among them over their lot. There seemed to be no escape and little remedy for it, so there was no point in stirring up trouble for themselves by publicly railing about their plight. The easiest way was the best way. The opportunity to make a living in the North, where hitherto no considerable number of Negroes were wanted, gave them the chance long looked for to move out and to better their condition. Nevertheless these migrants love the South; many of them write back longingly of their homes; still they break their old ties and face a new life in a strange land for the sake of the larger, freer life which they believe awaits them and, particularly, their children. It has taken something more than money to move these masses of people, though money is a necessary condition for the movement and is the immediate occasion of the exodus; but the Negro's list of grievances that have prepared him for this migration is a long one ...

...

... [In addition to wages, a]nother form of injustice that has long been preparing the Negro to escape at his first opportunity is the charging of exorbitant prices by the merchants and planters for the "advances" to the Negroes, and the practice of usury in lending money to them. For example, the tenant contracts for his money advances from the 1st of January. He usually receives no money, however, till the 1st of March and none after the 1st of August. But he must pay interest on the whole amount for a year, and sometimes even for the extra months up to the time of the deferred settlement ...

... Other common practices that keep Negroes stirred up and tend to drive them away are carried on in many places to an extent hardly believable. In a number of the small towns and villages Negroes are roughly handled and severely punished by the whites. The beating of farm hands on the large plantations in the lower South is so common that many colored people look upon every great plantation as a peon camp; and in sawmills and other public works it is not at all unusual for bosses to knock Negroes around with pieces of lumber or anything else that happens to come handy ... On the whole, the plantations or industrial camps that have given any attention worth considering to the housing and general comforts of their employees are rare.

In the cities and towns Negro sections are usually shamefully neglected in the matter of street improvements, sewer facilities, water, and light. Most of the larger southern cities not only exclude Negroes from their fine parks, but make little or no provisions for the recreation of the colored people. Harassing, humiliating "Jim Crow" regulations surround Negroes on every hand and invite unnecessarily severe and annoying treatment from the public and even from public servants. To avoid trouble, interference, and even injury, Negroes must practice eternal vigilance in the streets and on common carriers. The possibilities of trouble are greatly increased if the colored men are accompanied by their wives, daughters, or sweethearts. For then they are more likely to resent violently any rough treatment or abuse and insulting language whether addressed directly to them or to the women. Colored women understand this so well that they frequently take up their own defense rather than expose their male friends to the danger of protecting them.

The abnormal, unwarranted activities of southern police officers are responsible for deep grievances among Negroes. In many cases the police have been the tools of powers higher up. Many colored people believe that employers of convicts urge the police to greater activities among Negroes in order to fill up convict camps; and, as if encouraging arrests, the authorities frequently do not pay the constable and other petty officers salaries for their services but reward them in accordance with the number of arrests made. Naturally, they get all out of it that the business will stand. The Negro suffers and pays the bill ...

... Another source of long slumbering discontent is the matter of Negro schools. Southern white people know so little about the schools for Negroes, or regard their education so lightly, that they do not often look upon the lack of facilities for even elementary education among the colored people as an impelling cause of unrest among them; but in whatever else Negroes may seem to differ they are one in their desire for education for their children. The movement of the Negroes from the country to the cities and towns in the South has been largely an effort in this direction. Naturally, the good schools of the North, together with the opportunity to earn better wages, serve as a strong attraction to the colored people ...

… Another of the more effective causes of the exodus, a cause that appeals to every Negro whether high or low, industrious or idle, respected or contemned, is the Negro's insecurity from mob violence and lynching. He may or may not know of the sporadic cases of lynching in the North, but he does know it is epidemic in the South. … Recent lynchings … have led Negroes generally to feel that character and worth secure no more protection for them than less desirable qualities, and that no Negro is safe …

… The broadening intelligence of the Negroes makes them more restive under these unfavorable conditions than they have been in the past. Even the masses of them feel vaguely something of the great world movement for democracy. They bear unwillingly the treatment usually given them in the South, and they are making use of this first great opportunity to escape from it. To assume that the Negro has been blind and insensible to all his limitations, proscriptions, and persecutions, as so many whites appear to do … There is a good deal in the statement of a leading colored woman of Florida: "Negroes are not so greatly disturbed about wages. They are tired of being treated as children; they want to be men." So they are going where the conditions are more promising in that direction; and the mass of the migrants will in all probability not come back, as the whites generally think they will. Even if they do come back they will be very different people. From a good deal of evidence that is available, it seems that most of the migrants are making good in the North, where they plan to stay …

… During the year I have been repeatedly on practically every great railroad leading out of the South. In every instance I have found groups of Negroes bound for the North. From many southern centers the movement has been large and attended with dramatic incidents. In some instances the public authorities have attempted to use force to check the movement. At Sumter, S. C., a popular Negro minister who went to the station to see some of his members off was arrested as a labor agent. At Albany, Ga., the police tore up the tickets of migrants about to leave for the North, and at Savannah the police arrested and jailed every Negro found in the station on one occasion, without regard as to where he might be going …

… The white South strenuously opposes the Negro movement and loudly objects to the loss of her labor, but she is slow to adopt any constructive measures for retaining it. Indeed many feel that there is nothing to do but to let the movement run its course. The Negroes generally feel that good has already come to them from the exodus. New fields of labor with favorable conditions for larger development have opened to the Negro; his migration has awakened the South to a keener appreciation of the value of Negro labor, admittedly the best labor possible for the South; and selfish interests, at least, should lead the South to make that labor efficient and contented with its pay and treatment. So the Negro feels that there is a better day ahead for him, both north and south.

INITIAL REMEDIES.

How to keep the Negroes in the South and make them satisfied with their lot is the problem now presented to the South. It ought not to be difficult of solution. It is not natural for the Negroes to leave their old homes in this wholesale fashion, and they really do not want to go. Many of the most radical Negroes admit that the colored people will endure objectionable things in the South provided they can be made reasonably safe and comfortable, because it is home. Some planters and industrial establishments are already demonstrating by means of better pay and greater care for their employees what such consideration will do in keeping the Negroes loyally at work in the South ...

... There is no question as to the value of the Negro to the South; but circumstances are bringing other sections to an appreciation of his value also, and the Negro, too, is coming to understand something of his worth to the community. If the South would keep the Negro and have him satisfied she must give more constructive thought than has been her custom to the Negro and his welfare. Negroes must be given better houses to live in and such improved surroundings as will make it possible for them to live decent, sanitary lives. They must also have larger pay for their services in order that they may properly meet the new conditions, and it must be made evident to the Negroes that they are given justice in the courts. It will be necessary also to provide adequate school facilities for colored children, not only for elementary education but for secondary training as well. Practically no provisions for the latter have been made at public expense for colored youth in the South, where Negroes see high schools being placed within reach of every white boy and girl. Some check will have to be put upon the rampant "Jim Crow" legislation and restrictions; the Negro must be made reasonably safe from mob violence and lynching and be given protection against constant irritation, insult, and abuse for no reason other than that he is a black man; and the South must find a way to admit at least the educated, capable colored man to the franchise. The South can no longer afford to do less for the Negro within her gates and upon whom she depends than for any other peoples from anywhere else in the world. Then she should make the same demands of the Negro as of any other citizen. It is too much to expect that Negroes will indefinitely endure their severe limitations in the South when they can escape most of them in a ride of 36 hours ...

Source: W. T. B. Williams, "The Negro Exodus from the South," in George E. Haynes (ed.), *Negro Migration in 1916–17* (Washington, DC: GPO, 1919), pp. 93–113.

Questions for Consideration

Why did the Great Migration cause so much disruption?

How did African Americans make their decisions, and what were the effects of their actions?

Why might black leaders – like Booker T. Washington, who argued in Chapter 2 that African Americans should cast their lot in the South – have disagreed with those who chose to depart?

As a leaderless movement, the Great Migration reflected the profound desire of black southerners to improve their lives. What kinds of initiatives might have offered alternatives?

How did employment for black women and men differ in the North than the South?

Bibliography

Clark-Lewis, Elizabeth. *Living In, Living Out: African American Domestics in Washington, D.C., 1910–1940*. Washington, DC: Smithsonian Books, 1995.

Dodson, Howard, and Sylviana Diouf A. *In Motion: The African American Migration Experience*. Washington, DC: National Geographic, 2005.

Griffin, Farah Jasmine. *"Who Set You Flowin'?": The African-American Migration Narrative*. New York: Oxford University Press, 1996.

Grossman, James R. *Land of Hope: Chicago, Black Southerners, and the Great Migration*. Chicago: University of Chicago Press, 1989.

Phillips, Kimberly L. *Alabama North: African-American Migrants, Community, and Working-Class Activism in Cleveland, 1915–1945*. Urbana: University of Illinois Press, 1999.

Trotter, Joe William, Jr., ed. *The Great Migration in Historical Perspective: New Dimensions of Race, Class, and Gender*. Bloomington: Indiana University Press, 1991.

Wilkerson, Isabel. *The Warmth of Other Suns: The Epic Story of America's Great Migration*. New York: Vintage Press, 2011.

Chapter 4 Determination, 1917–1925

In July 1917, African American organizations – national, local, religious, and secular – held a silent march down Fifth Avenue, a main artery through New York City, protesting the alarming rise in racial violence. On the heels of the East St. Louis Riot, the sound of only marching feet was all the more poignant. "Meetings of protest, with speeches and adopted resolutions, have been so overdone that they now fail to possess any news value," an announcement read. "We ask that you show your courage by taking your place, either as an individual or as a member of some organization, in the line of march." The demonstration suggested that African Americans were hardening their political edge. The ideological framework for World War I, "to make the world safe for democracy," resonated with them, and provided a sturdy rhetoric to challenge the scheme of Jim Crow.

The European war had been waging for three years before President Woodrow Wilson determined in 1917 that Americans would fight for "the rights of those who submit to authority to have a voice in their own government." African Americans did not miss the irony in Wilson's statement. Fighting as citizens, blacks enjoyed neither its privileges not its protections. Expected to sacrifice and labor in support of the war, they also were expected to deal with racism. In all branches of the armed forces, the military segregated black and white servicemen and women. They were denigrated and harassed. Racial attacks against black citizens and soldiers actually increased when African American servicemen and women returned

African American Voices: A Documentary Reader from Emancipation to the Present,
First Edition. Edited by Leslie Brown.
© 2014 John Wiley & Sons, Inc. Published 2014 by John Wiley & Sons, Inc.

Figure 4.1   Silent protest parade in New York City against the East St. Louis riots, 1917.

Source: NAACP Collection, Prints and Photographs Division, Library of Congress (042.00.00), Courtesy of the NAACP. Digital ID # cph-3a34294.

home. So much racial violence occurred during the summer and fall of 1919 that NAACP leader James Weldon Johnson called the season "Red Summer."

Faced with a resurgence of white hostility, black Americans began to fight back. Broadened black perspectives combined with a new assertiveness to generate fresh ideas and approaches to civil and economic rights initiatives. New organizations, some internationalist in scope, emerged and expanded the black political world. Immigration from Africa and the Caribbean to the United States, coupled with black Americans' international travel during the war, engendered a more expansive view of the world and an ideological sense of international connections. Black Americans were fascinated with Marcus Garvey, with the Russian Revolution (1917), and with labor movements like the International Workers of the World (IWW), which articulated race and class analyses that aligned with their experiences. African Americans grasped the inherent conflict between the oppressed (e.g., workers, the proletariat) and their oppressors (the owners of wealth). As a critique of capitalism, communism interested laboring people for its goal of transforming the distribution of resources. Black people also struggled to join the industrial unions, which they viewed as potential protectors of their interests as laborers. All of these ideas fired the black people's political and cultural imagination.

Additionally, as scholars and observers discerned, the Great Migration had loosened a downtrodden folk to seek the opportunities of the city and to affirm themselves. And, too, a generational shift had produced a coterie of educated blacks who enjoined a movement that looked to race as the subject of its pursuits. Centered in New York, and called the "Harlem Renaissance," the movement embraced black artists, musicians, writers, and scholars, a contingent that personified the confident self-assertion of the "New Negro," and accumulated a record of achievements in the arts and letters that remains critical to Africana studies.

Alain LeRoy Locke (1886–1954), referred to as the Dean of the Harlem Renaissance, encouraged young black writers and scholars to take up the issue of racial equality as a political project. In 1925 he edited the renowned collection, *The New Negro: An Interpretation*, an anthology of cultural, artistic, and scholarly works that exemplified the New Negro Movement. "[T]he younger generation is vibrant with a new psychology," Locke wrote in his introduction, and "the new spirit is awake in the masses." Declaring that "the day of 'aunties,' 'uncles' and 'mammies' is equally gone," Locke asked, "Could such a metamorphosis have taken place as suddenly as it has appeared to?" Locke pondered and answered no. "The Negro has been more of a formula than a human being – a something to be argued about, condemned or defended, to be 'kept down,' or 'in his place,' or 'helped up,' to be worried with or worried over, harassed or patronized, a social bogey or a social burden."

Locke continued, "By shedding the old chrysalis of the Negro problem we are achieving something like a spiritual emancipation."

1 W. E. B. Du Bois on African Americans and World War I, 1918 and 1919

"We of the colored race have no ordinary interest in the outcome"

In a 1918 essay in The Crisis, *the journal he edited for the NAACP, W. E. B. Du Bois addressed the meaning of World War I for black Americans. Calling the war "the crisis of the world," he argued that, notwithstanding Jim Crow,*

African Americans should view its goal – democracy – as a larger claim.
Once the war ended and black service people returned in 1919, Du Bois'
racial call to arms rang as strongly as ever in a follow-up essay, "We Return
Fighting."

"Close Ranks," 1918

This is the crisis of the world. For all the long years to come men will point
to the year 1918 as the great Day of Decision, the day when the world decided
whether it would submit to military despotism and an endless armed peace –
if peace it could be called – or whether they could put down the menace of
German militarism and inaugurate the United States of the world ... We of
the colored race have no ordinary interest in the outcome. That which the
German power represents today spells death to the aspirations of Negroes
and all darker races for equality, freedom and democracy. Let us not hesitate.
Let us, while this war lasts, forget our special grievances and close our ranks
shoulder to shoulder with our own white fellow citizens and the allied nations
that are fighting for democracy. We make no ordinary sacrifice, but we make
it gladly and willingly with our eyes lifted to the hills.

Source: W. E. B. Du Bois, "Close Ranks," *The Crisis*, 16 (July 3, 1918), p. 111.

"We Return Fighting," 1919

We are returning from war! *The Crisis* and tens of thousands of black
men were drafted into a great struggle. For bleeding France and what she
means and has meant and will mean to us and humanity and against the
threat of German race arrogance, we fought gladly and to the last drop
of blood; for America and her highest ideals, we fought in far-off hope;
for the dominant southern oligarchy entrenched in Washington, we fought
in bitter resignation. For the America that represents and gloats in lynching, disfranchisement, caste, brutality and devilish insult – for this, in the
hateful upturning and mixing of things, we were forced by vindictive
fate to fight also.

But today we return! We return from the slavery of uniform which the
world's madness demanded us to don to the freedom of civil garb. We stand
again to look America squarely in the face and call a spade a spade. We sing:
This country of ours, despite all its better souls have done and dreamed, is
yet a shameful land.

It lynches.

And lynching is barbarism of a degree of contemptible nastiness unparalleled in human history. Yet for fifty years we have lynched two Negroes a week, and we have kept this up right through the war.

It disfranchises its own citizens.

Disfranchisement is the deliberate theft and robbery of the only protection of poor against rich and black against white. The land that disfranchises its citizens and calls itself a democracy lies and knows it lies.

It encourages ignorance.

It has never really tried to educate the Negro. A dominant minority does not want Negroes educated. It wants servants, dogs, whores and monkeys. And when this land allows a reactionary group by its stolen political power to force as many black folk into these categories as it possibly can, it cries in contemptible hypocrisy: "They threaten us with degeneracy; they cannot be educated."

It steals from us.

It organizes industry to cheat us. It cheats us out of our land; it cheats us out of our labor. It confiscates our savings. It reduces our wages. It raises our rent. It steals our profit. It taxes us without representation. It keeps us consistently and universally poor, and then feeds us on charity and derides our poverty.

It insults us.

It has organized a nation-wide and latterly a world-wide propaganda of deliberate and continuous insult and defamation of black blood wherever found. It decrees that it shall not be possible in travel nor residence, work nor play, education nor instruction for a black man to exist without tacit or open acknowledgment of his inferiority to the dirtiest white dog. And it looks upon any attempt to question or even discuss this dogma as arrogance, unwarranted assumption and treason.

This is the country to which we Soldiers of Democracy return. This is the fatherland for which we fought! But it is our fatherland. It was right for us to fight. The faults of our country are our faults. Under similar circumstances, we would fight again. But by the God of Heaven, we are cowards and jackasses if now that that war is over, we do not marshal every ounce of our brain and brawn to fight a sterner, longer, more unbending battle against the forces of hell in our own land.

We return.

We return from fighting.

We return fighting.

Make way for Democracy! We saved it in France, and by the Great Jehovah, we will save it in the United States of America, or know the reason why.

Source: W. E. B. Du Bois, "We Return Fighting," *The Crisis*, 18 (May 1919), p. 13.

2 Poet Claude McKay Sets a New Tone, 1919

"If We Must Die"

Jamaican-born Claude McKay (1889–1972) expressed his resentment of American racism through his writings. An early voice of the Harlem Renaissance, McKay penned "If We Must Die" during "Red Summer," reflecting a new tenor in black language and letters.

"If We Must Die"

If we must die, let it not be like hogs
Hunted and penned in an inglorious spot,
While round us bark the mad and hungry dogs,
Making their mock at our accursed lot.
If we must die, O let us nobly die
So that our precious blood may not be shed
In vain; then even the monsters we defy
Shall be constrained to honor us though dead!
O kinsmen! We must meet the common foe!
Though far outnumbered let us show us brave,
And for their thousand blows deal one death blow!
What though before us lies the open grave?
Like men we'll face the murderous, cowardly pack,
Pressed to the wall, dying, but fighting back!

Source: Claude McKay, "If We Must Die," in *Harlem Shadows: The Poems of Claude McKay* (New York: Harcourt, Brace and Co., 1922). Courtesy of the Literary Representative for the works of Claude McKay, Schomurg Center for Research in Black Culture, The New York Public Library, Astor, Lenox and Tilden Foundation.

3 Emmett J. Scott Reflects on "What the Negro Got Out of the War," 1919

"a … more sharply defined consciousness"

During World War I Emmett J. Scott (1873–1957) served as the Special Adjutant to the Secretary of the War, facilitating the recruitment, training, and deployment of black troops. The former aide to Booker T. Washington at Tuskegee Institute,

*he traveled the homefront documenting African Americans' experiences. He
found extensive discrimination and violence, but also patriotism and strong
support for black soldiers. In 1919 he published a tome,* Scott's Official History
of the American Negro in the World War, *which remains one of the most
important documents about black Americans' wartime efforts. His last chapter,
excerpted here, assesses "what the Negro got out of the war."*

Chapter XXXI

...

Briefly stated, the Negroes did their full share in the great struggle to make
the world safe for democracy. Four hundred thousand Negro soldiers were
drafted or enlisted and 200,000 served in France under white officers and
1,200 officers of color. Negroes served in all branches of the military establishment – the cavalry, infantry, artillery, signal corps, medical corps, aviation
corps, hospital corps, ammunition trains, stevedore regiments, labor battalions, depot brigades, engineer regiments, as regimental clerks, surveyors and
draftsmen. Negro soldiers acquitted themselves with honor in the battles of
the Argonne Forest, at Chateau Thierry, Belleau Wood, at St. Mihiel, in
Champagne, in the Vosges, and at Metz, and when the Armistice was signed
Negro troops as has been pointed out were nearest the Rhine. Entire regiments of colored troops, including the 369th, 370th, 371st, and 372nd, were
cited for exceptional valor and decorated with the French Croix de Guerre.
Groups of officers and men of the 92nd Division were likewise decorated.
The first battalion of the 367th also received the Croix de Guerre. Many
individuals like Harry Johnson, Needham Roberts, and William Butler were
awarded the Croix de Guerre and scores of officers by devotion to duty
earned, even if they did not receive promotion in their military units.

... [T]he war has brought to the American Negro a keener and more
sharply defined consciousness, not only of his duties as a citizen, but of his
rights and privileges as a citizen of the United States....

A summary of what the Negro wants may be stated: He wants justice in
the courts substituted for lynching, the privilege of serving on juries, the
right to vote, and the right to hold office like other citizens. He wants, moreover, universal suffrage, better educational facilities, the abolition of the
"Jim Crow" car, discontinuance of unjust discriminatory regulations and
segregation in the various departments of the Government, the same military training for Negro Youths as for white, the removal of "dead lines" in
the recognition of fitness for promotion in the army and navy, the destruction of the peonage system, an economic wage scale to be applied to whites

and blacks alike, better housing conditions for Negro employees in industrial centers, better sanitary conditions in the Negro sections of cities, and reforms in the Southern penal institutions. If, after having fulfilled the obligations of citizenship Negroes do not get these things, then indeed, they feel, will the war have been fought in vain.

...

Democracy, they contend, must be made a reality. It must be considered an ideal toward which we struggle and we must not grow impatient and discouraged when we fail to realize it. Democracy must not find it difficult to provide a place for the Negro. He must be treated with justice, his interests must be protected, his life must he held precious, his children must be educated, his health must be preserved, and his rights as an American must be defended ... Since he has made a good soldier, borne wounds, privations and death in the nation's battles to make the world safe for democracy, he deserves to find a place for himself beneath the flag for which he has fought and within the borders of the country for which he was willing to die.

In view of the fact that the Negro faithfully supported the government he expected to get a much larger portion of the benefits of democracy than was given him. The Negro expected above all that as a fundamental concession in the adjustment of affairs necessary, for the reconstruction to herald a new day for the man farthest down, that colored men would at least be given full opportunity to earn a living.

...

The Negroes expected too that the hard and fast rules of labor organizations which have for years barred men of color from the higher pursuits of labor, would be abrogated. It was believed that there would be new avenues for the employment of Negroes and that the so-called friends of Negro labor would be able to effect more than to secure from trade unions mere expressions of interest in behalf of the Negro laborers. It is unfortunate, however, that the Negro still finds himself refused admission to labor unions and then told that he cannot work because he is not a union man. He is denied the chance to care for his family properly and then censured because of his failure to do so. In Northern States where these restrictions have been very rigid it has been difficult to maintain order. Almost any day we hear of reports that some "gang" is hunting Negroes with the intention to do them violence and disturbances and race riots growing out of these conditions are now becoming common.

...

The Negro race and especially the Negro soldier expected that in consideration of what the race as a whole did for the winning of the war, it would receive more consideration in the army when, upon a revelation as to the truth about the slander upon Negro officers the fair-minded people of this country would be convinced as to the worth of the Negroes who led their fellow men at the front and would see to it that hereafter Negro troops be commanded by Negro officers. On the contrary, however, coming out here and there in the army wherever the Negro officer has endeavored permanently to attach himself to the service, have been what appear to be definite efforts to eliminate the Negro officer entirely.

...

Not only has there been an effort to get rid of the Negro officer but in many cases also the Negro private. When, after demobilization of most of the army, it became necessary to call for 50,000 volunteers for special duty it was specifically stated that these volunteers were to be *white*, not Negroes. Here was an opportunity to show one's patriotism and the Negroes nobly volunteered to manifest theirs, but considering the opportunity a much more desirable one than the ordinary enlistment of soldiers, it was reserved to white men. The Negroes then, it would seem, must be patriotic, must make personal sacrifices for the country, and even give their lives to defend it, but they must not expect to get out of it the same returns which will come to white men.

Upon the return to the United States, the Negro soldiers expected that "Jim Crowism" and segregation would receive a check if not eliminated altogether. The Negro soldier returning from the front bore it grievously that on arriving home he had to ride in "Jim Crow" cars, and be excluded from the use of public places. Their contention is that these places are licensed by the Government, established and often wholly maintained by it and, therefore, should be accessible to all. They contended, moreover, that exclusion from these public places often means no such facilities for Negroes or, if at all, decidedly inferior accommodations.

...

The Negro expected, too, a change in the attitude of the white man toward the right of the blacks to exercise the highest functions of citizenship. It has required little argument to convince the Negroes that they are powerless in the hands of the militant whites when the former can neither vote nor hold office. Relying then upon principles long since set forth by the fathers of the Republic that the men who fight for the country ought to share the control of its government, the Negroes have boldly presented their case to the world. This petition has, in most places, fallen upon deaf ears. Instead of a tendency to extend the right of franchise there has been something like a recrudescence, as already stated, of the Ku Klux Klan so as to intimidate the Negroes of the South that they may not seek to reach this end.

Intelligent Negroes, therefore, who got some idea of the real liberty in France although they were not permitted to enjoy it overmuch, are united in demanding better treatment from the American people and to this end have organized a League of Democracy to further their interest. They will not accept excuses, they say; they will not keep silence, they must be heard. They want to enjoy the same rights and privileges vouchsafed to all other citizens regardless of race, creed, or condition. Americans, therefore, they hope, will oppose those enemies to democracy at home that the Junkers were to democracy in Europe. There must come a new day, Negroes feel, for the United States when the country will square itself with its own conscience and with the world in regard to its attitude toward the Negroes in America.

...

With a broad vision, too, the Negroes of this country have looked forward to a better day for the Negro race throughout the world. From the League of Nations the race has expected an amicable adjustment of relations in Africa so as to secure to the natives the opportunities for social, economic and political development. ... Because of the revolting cruelties perpetrated upon the natives in the African dependencies, American Negroes have protested against any contemplation of restoring to Germany her African colonies. Is it too much to say that to restore these helpless black men to their former oppressors would be a terrible betrayal? Has not the hour come when men even in darkest Africa may cry out for the right to elect or ordain their own destinies under an acceptable tutelage, and the guidance of enlightened men rather than under oppressive and cruel masters? If the Senegalese, Algerian and Sudanese troops stayed the Hun and saved civilization to the world, the nations of the world should see to it that these people be removed from the iron heel of malignant oppressors....

Source: Emmett J. Scott, "What the Negro Got Out of the War," in *Scott's Official History of the American Negro in the World War* (1919; reprint, New York: Arno Press, 1969), Chapter XXXI.

4 Program of the NAACP, 1919

"the patience of even colored people can find its limit"

In 1919 writer and organizer James Weldon Johnson became the NAACP's first black director. Confronted with an overwhelming set of priorities, the Association set out to sharpen its focus and to garner the resources necessary to fight the civil rights battles it chose.

Resolutions of the NAACP, 1919

...

[The NAACP] views with gratification the many achievements of the past year along the line of the important work that it has undertaken to perform for the strengthening of the nation's institutions and the eradication of the evils that have permeated it in past years. Public opinion has been enlightened as never before, with regard to the many evils perpetrated against the colored race. The publicity given through the National Office in New York to the special investigations made by competent agents, of lynching occurring in various parts of the country; pleading for the industrial equality of the colored race before the Industrial corporations of the country; scrupulously safeguarding the interest of the colored soldier and obtaining for him better treatment in whole or in part; the organizing of 228 branches in various sections of the country, thereby perfecting more and more the working machinery; the holding of many large anti-lynching meetings in which have appeared leading statesmen of both the North and the South, and many other notable accomplishments which we need not here mention, constitute the program that the Association has carried thru for the year.

While expressing our gratification over these results, we are mindful that much remains to be accomplished which requires sagacity and courage and sacrifice on the part of the members of the Association and on the part of the American public in general who believe in justice and fair play to all Americans. We beg leave to call attention to the following:

All true Americans view with concern the efforts of discontented people to disrupt our government, and we warn the American people that the patience of even colored people can find its limit; that with poor schools, Jim Crow methods of travel, little or no justice in courts or in things economic staring him in the face, while the colored man is called on to bear his part of the burden in taxation, in government, loans, in civic gifts and in fighting the common foes of our government, we are inviting him to grasp the hands which the Bolsheviks, the I.W.W., and other kindred organizations held out to him. It cannot be expected that Negro leaders can forever hold out empty hope to a people deluded in toto.

We are deeply sensible of the campaign of lies that have been subtly and persistently directed against colored officers and men, particularly colored *officers* of the United States army. We have facts to prove that in many instances the least trained among these men were put forward at all; then the Negro's enemies worked zealously to prove that the colored officer was a failure when they ought to "fail" him at the start.

We are aware of the instances in which both officers and men were thrown into prison on the merest pretenses, or on charges which rightfully fell on the shoulders of white officers. We are also cognizant of the fact that the American colored soldiers brigaded with the French did not suffer for recognition through citations, won crosses and even advancement in rank, while the colored soldier's own white countrymen not only stole all possible opportunity for distinctions from him, but actively sought to poison European and American public opinion against their brothers in black.

We demand Congressional investigation of the treatment of colored soldiers at home and abroad. The shameless and cunning manner in which these officers and men have been treated was not only discriminatory, but violative of the spirit of the American people towards men who were offering their lives for a great cause. We make this demand because the facts so evident to us cannot be hidden from all others, and to allow this to go unchallenged is to weaken national and military morale.

We are opposed to race segregation in the army and navy of the United States of America since it cheats our government of that which is best in discipline and spirit; but if that separation is provided by law, then we demand a full division in the new army to be provided for by the present Congress, officered from top to bottom by colored men.

We demand that a larger number of colored men be appointed to West Point and the Naval Academy at Annapolis for training in military and naval service.

We urge an increase in national financial aid to the education of colored people. To keep the colored citizen in the south in ignorance is to chain to this nation a body of death in ignorant colored and white men, from which it can be delivered by no other means than by a square acceptance of the facts and direct application of financial assistance.

Federal aid to a common school training is indispensable and imperative, but wherever separate schools for colored are compulsory all federal appropriations must by law be conditioned on the strict division of the funds between the races according to population and on colored people having representation on the boards that control colored schools.

We regret that much of the advertised improvement of colored public schools of the South finds expression chiefly in promises; that the threadbare illogical argument concerning the proportioning to the education of colored people of taxes paid by colored people is still working overtime. People of other nationalities, even Germans in our American cities, are educated according to the recognized standards and not according to the taxes they pay.

We demand such federal legislation as shall give the government at Washington absolute control of the investigation of and punishment for lynching. This hideous barbarism is murder, and when supposedly civilized democratic states, with laws on their books to prevent or punish murder, openly declare that they are powerless to stop lynching, as declared several southern governors to our Association, they thereby confess that they are to that extent incapable of self-government and subject to this only remedy at hand.

...

We denounce the *Jim Crow* laws of the *South*, as being illegal and unconstitutional, in that such laws interfere with interstate traffic, and deny to a large part of its loyal citizens equal rights guaranteed under the Constitution; and we call upon the *Congress* of the *United States*, to exercise its powers under the *Commerce* clause of the *Constitution* to the end that all such laws be abolished.

We *demand* that the *Congress* take such action as will insure to all citizens, regardless of Race, Color, or Creed *equal* and *unsegregated* service and accommodation on Railroad and Pullman cars.

We demand the enforcement of all constitutional amendments without discrimination. The patience of the colored American is sorely tried by the country's complacent acceptance of these curtailments of his rights. The country has recently called on us to perform unusual duties; we demand that we have the usual rights of American citizens.

We *demand* that the Thirteenth, Fourteenth and Fifteenth Amendments of the Constitution of the United States which guarantee the Citizenship of the Colored American and his enjoyment of all the rights inherent therein and flowing therefrom, be recognized and enforced by the Government, in good faith. To this end we call on all our colored voters in the better civilized parts of the country to see that their representatives in Congress live up to the demands made herein or report the reasons why.

We desire to extend to the members of the Hebrew race our profound sympathy for the cruel and barbarous treatment accorded them in general, and especially in Poland.

Looking to the achievement of the foregoing ends, we declare the platform of the National Association for the Advancement of Colored People to be the following:

1. A vote for every colored man and woman on the same terms as for white men and women.
2. An equal chance to acquire the kind of education that will enable the colored citizen everywhere wisely to use this vote.

3. A fair trial in the courts for all crimes of which he is accused by judges in whose election he has participated without discrimination because of race.
4. A right to sit upon the jury which passes judgment upon him.
5. Defense against lynching and burning at the hands of mobs.
6. Equal service on railroad and other public carriers. This to mean sleeping car service, dining car service, Pullman service, at the same cost and upon the same terms as other passengers.
7. Equal right to the use of public parks, libraries and other community services for which he is taxed.
8. An equal chance for a livelihood in public and private employment.
9. The abolition of color-hyphenation and the substitution of "straight Americanism."

Lynching must be stopped. Many Americans do not believe that such horrible things happen as do happen when Negroes are lynched and burned at the stake. Lynching can be stopped when we can reach the heart and conscience of the American people. Again, money is needed.

Legal work must be done. Defenseless Negroes are every day denied the "equal protection of the laws" because there is not money enough in the Association's treasury to defend them, either as individuals or as a race.

Legislation must be watched. Good laws must be promoted wherever that be possible and bad laws opposed and defeated wherever possible. Once more money is essential.

The public must be kept informed. This means that our regular press service under the supervision of a trained newspaper man must be maintained and strengthened. Every opportunity must be sought out to place before the magazine and periodical reading public, constructive articles on every phase of Negro citizenship ... That colored people are contributing their fair share to the well-being of America must be made known ... That law-abiding colored people are denied the commonest citizenship rights, must be brought home to all Americans who love fair play. Once again, money is needed.

The facts must be gathered and assembled. This requires effort. Facts are not gotten out of one's imagination. Their gathering and interpretation is skilled work. Research workers of a practical experience are needed. Field investigations, in which domain the Association has already made some notable contributions, are essential to good work. More money.

The country must be thoroughly organized. The Association's more than 300 branches are a good beginning. An increased field staff is essential to the upbuilding of this important branch development. A very large percentage of the branch members are colored people. Colored people have less means, and less experience in public organization, than white people. But, they are developing rapidly habits of efficiency in organization. Money, again is needed.

But, not money alone is needed. Men and women are vital to success. Public opinion is the main force upon which the Association relies for a *victory of justice.* Particularly do we seek the active support of all white Americans who realize that a democracy cannot draw the color line in public relations without lasting injury to its best ideals.

Source: National Association for the Advancement of Colored People, "Tenth Annual Report, 1919," reprinted in Herbert Aptheker (ed.), *A Documentary History of the Negro People in the United States,* Vol. 3 (New York: Citadel Press, 1992), pp. 244–273.

5 Marcus Garvey Outlines the Rights of Black Peoples, 1920

"nowhere in the world, with few exceptions, are black men accorded equal treatment with white men"

The Universal Negro Improvement Association (UNIA), founded by Jamaican-born Marcus Garvey (1887–1940), echoed Booker T. Washington's emphasis on self help, but its militancy could not have been more different in tone and intent. Internationalist in scope, Garvey and the UNIA made "Race First," focusing on black peoples subjected to colonialism, imperialism, and exploitation. Garvey believed in "Africa for Africans." Du Bois and other leaders considered Garvey's vision fanciful and unrealistic, and his view of America as a white nation for white people not only outrageous, but also harmful. Yet, millions of ordinary black people embraced Garveyism, attended meetings, and joined divisions. The following document, "Declaration of the Rights of the Negro Peoples of the World," was issued in 1920 at the UNIA meeting at Liberty Hall in Harlem, which was attended by an international contingent of 25,000 people of African descent.

"Declaration of the Rights of the Negro Peoples of the World": The Principles of the Universal Negro Improvement Association

Preamble

Be It Resolved, That the Negro people of the world, through their chosen representatives in convention assembled in Liberty Hall, in the City of

New York and United States of America, from August 1 to August 31, in the year of Our Lord one thousand nine hundred and twenty, protest against the wrongs and injustices they are suffering at the hands of their white brethren, and state what they deem their fair and just rights, as well as the treatment they propose to demand of all men in the future.

We complain:

I. That nowhere in the world, with few exceptions, are black men accorded equal treatment with white men, although in the same situation and circumstances, but, on the contrary, are discriminated against and denied the common rights due to human beings for no other reason than their race and color.

We are not willingly accepted as guests in the public hotels and inns of the world for no other reason than our race and color.

II. In certain parts of the United States of America our race is denied the right of public trial accorded to other races when accused of crime, but are lynched and burned by mobs, and such brutal and inhuman treatment is even practiced upon our women.

III. That European nations have parceled out among them and taken possession of nearly all of the continent of Africa, and the natives are compelled to surrender their lands to aliens and are treated in most instances like slaves.

IV. In the southern portion of the United States of America, although citizens under the Federal Constitution, and in some States almost equal to the whites in population and are qualified land owners and taxpayers, we are, nevertheless, denied all voice in the making and administration of the laws and are taxed without representation by the State governments, and at the same time compelled to do military service in defense of the country.

V. On the public conveyances and common carriers in the southern portion of the United States we are jim-crowed and compelled to accept separate and inferior accommodations and made to pay the same fare charged for first-class accommodations, and our families are often humiliated and insulted by drunken white men who habitually pass through the jim-crow cars going to the smoking car.

VI. The physicians of our race are denied the right to attend their patients while in the public hospitals of the cities and States where they reside in certain parts of the United States.

Our children are forced to attend inferior separate schools for shorter terms than white children, and the public school funds are unequally divided between the white and colored schools.

VII. We are discriminated against and denied an equal chance to earn wages for the support of our families, and in many instances are refused admission into labor unions and nearly everywhere are paid smaller wages than white men.

VIII. In the Civil Service and departmental offices we are everywhere discriminated against and made to feel that to be a black man in Europe, America and the West Indies is equivalent to being an outcast and a leper among the races of men, no matter what the character attainments of the black men may be.

IX. In the British and other West Indian islands and colonies Negroes are secretly and cunningly discriminated against and denied those fuller rights of government to which white citizens are appointed, nominated and elected.

X. That our people in those parts are forced to work for lower wages than the average standard of white men and are kept in conditions repugnant to good civilized tastes and customs.

XI. That the many acts of injustices against members of our race before the courts of law in the respective islands and colonies are of such nature as to create disgust and disrespect for the white man's sense of justice.

XII. Against all such inhuman, unchristian and uncivilized treatment we here and now emphatically protest, and invoke the condemnation of all mankind.

In order to encourage our race all over the world and to stimulate it to overcome the handicaps and difficulties surrounding it, and to push forward to a higher and grander destiny, we demand and insist on the following Declaration of Rights:

1. Be it known to all men that whereas all men are created equal and entitled to the rights of life, liberty and the pursuit of happiness, and because of this we, the duly elected representatives of the Negro peoples of the world, invoking the aid of the just and Almighty God, do declare all men, women and children of our blood throughout the world free denizens, and do claim them as free citizens of Africa, the Motherland of all Negroes.
2. That we believe in the supreme authority of our race in all things racial; that all things are created and given to man as a common possession; that there should be an equitable distribution and apportionment of all such things, and in consideration of the fact that as a race we are now deprived of those things that are morally and legally ours, we believed it right that all such things should be acquired and held by whatsoever means possible.

3. That we believe the Negro, like any other race, should be governed by the ethics of civilization, and therefore should not be deprived of any of those rights or privileges common to other human beings.

4. We declare that Negroes, wheresoever they form a community among themselves should be given the right to elect their own representatives to represent them in Legislatures, courts of law, or such institutions as may exercise control over that particular community.

5. We assert that the Negro is entitled to even-handed justice before all courts of law and equity in whatever country he may be found, and when this is denied him on account of his race or color such denial is an insult to the race as a whole and should be resented by the entire body of Negroes.

6. We declare it unfair and prejudicial to the rights of Negroes in communities where they exist in considerable numbers to be tried by a judge and jury composed entirely of an alien race, but in all such cases members of our race are entitled to representation on the jury.

7. We believe that any law or practice that tends to deprive any African of his land or the privileges of free citizenship within his country is unjust and immoral, and no native should respect any such law or practice.

8. We declare taxation without representation unjust and tyran[n]ous, and there should be no obligation on the part of the Negro to obey the levy of a tax by any law-making body from which he is excluded and denied representation on account of his race and color.

9. We believe that any law especially directed against the Negro to his detriment and singling him out because of his race or color is unfair and immoral, and should not be respected.

10. We believe all men [are] entitled to common human respect and that our race should in no way tolerate any insults that may be interpreted to mean disrespect to our race or color.

11. We deprecate the use of the term "nigger" as applied to Negroes, and demand that the word "Negro" be written with a capital "N."

12. We believe that the Negro should adopt every means to protect himself against barbarous practices inflicted upon him because of color.

13. We believe in the freedom of Africa for the Negro people of the world, and by the principle of Europe for the Europeans and Asia for the Asiatics, we also demand Africa for the Africans at home and abroad.

14. We believe in the inherent right of the Negro to possess himself of Africa and that his possession of same shall not be regarded as an infringement of any claim or purchase made by any race or nation.

15. We strongly condemn the cupidity of those nations of the world who, by open aggression or secret schemes, have seized the territories and

inexhaustible natural wealth of Africa, and we place on record our most solemn determination to reclaim the treasures and possession of the vast continent of our forefathers.

16. We believe all men should live in peace one with the other, but when races and nations provoke the ire of other races and nations by attempting to infringe upon their rights[,] war becomes inevitable, and the attempt in any way to free one's self or protect one's rights or heritage becomes justifiable.

17. Whereas the lynching, by burning, hanging or any other means, of human beings is a barbarous practice and a shame and disgrace to civilization, we therefore declare any country guilty of such atrocities outside the pale of civilization.

18. We protest against the atrocious crime of whipping, flogging and overworking of the native tribes of Africa and Negroes everywhere. These are methods that should be abolished and all means should be taken to prevent a continuance of such brutal practices.

19. We protest against the atrocious practice of shaving the heads of Africans, especially of African women or individuals of Negro blood, when placed in prison as a punishment for crime by an alien race.

20. We protest against segregated districts, separate public conveyances, industrial discrimination, lynchings and limitations of political privileges of any Negro citizen in any part of the world on account of race, color or creed, and will exert our full influence and power against all such.

21. We protest against any punishment inflicted upon a Negro with severity, as against lighter punishment inflicted upon another of an alien race for like offense, as an act of prejudice and injustice, and should be resented by the entire race.

22. We protest against the system of education in any country where Negroes are denied the same privileges and advantages as other races.

23. We declare it inhuman and unfair to boycott Negroes from industries and labor in any part of the world.

24. We believe in the doctrine of the freedom of the press, and we therefore emphatically protest against the suppression of Negro newspapers and periodicals in various parts of the world, and call upon Negroes everywhere to employ all available means to prevent such suppression.

25. We further demand free speech universally for all men.

26. We hereby protest against the publication of scandalous and inflammatory articles by an alien press tending to create racial strife and the exhibition of picture films showing the Negro as a cannibal.

27. We believe in the self-determination of all peoples.

28. We declare for the freedom of religious worship.
29. With the help of Almighty God we declare ourselves the sworn protectors of the honor and virtue of our women and children, and pledge our lives for their protection and defense everywhere and under all circumstances from wrongs and outrages.
30. We demand the right of an unlimited and unprejudiced education for ourselves and our posterity forever[.]
31. We declare that the teaching in any school by alien teachers to our boys and girls, that the alien race is superior to the Negro race, is an insult to the Negro people of the world.
32. Where Negroes form a part of the citizenry of any country, and pass the civil service examination of such country, we declare them entitled to the same consideration as other citizens as to appointments in such civil service.
33. We vigorously protest against the increasingly unfair and unjust treatment accorded Negro travelers on land and sea by the agents and employees of railroad and steamship companies, and insist that for equal fare we receive equal privileges with travelers of other races.
34. We declare it unjust for any country, State or nation to enact laws tending to hinder and obstruct the free immigration of Negroes on account of their race and color.
35. That the right of the Negro to travel unmolested throughout the world be not abridged by any person or persons, and all Negroes are called upon to give aid to a fellow Negro when thus molested.
36. We declare that all Negroes are entitled to the same right to travel over the world as other men.
37. We hereby demand that the governments of the world recognize our leader and his representatives chosen by the race to look after the welfare of our people under such governments.
38. We demand complete control of our social institutions without interference by any alien race or races.
39. That the colors, Red, Black and Green, be the colors of the Negro race.
40. Resolved, That the anthem "Ethiopia, Thou Land of Our Fathers etc.," shall be the anthem of the Negro race....
41. We believe that any limited liberty which deprives one of the complete rights and prerogatives of full citizenship is but a modified form of slavery.
42. We declare it an injustice to our people and a serious Impediment to the health of the race to deny to competent licensed Negro physicians the right to practice in the public hospitals of the communities in which they reside, for no other reason than their race and color.

43. We call upon the various government[s] of the world to accept and acknowledge Negro representatives who shall be sent to the said governments to represent the general welfare of the Negro peoples of the world.

44. We deplore and protest against the practice of confining juvenile prisoners in prisons with adults, and we recommend that such youthful prisoners be taught gainful trades under human[e] supervision.

45. Be it further resolved, That we as a race of people declare the League of Nations null and void as far as the Negro is concerned, in that it seeks to deprive Negroes of their liberty.

46. We demand of all men to do unto us as we would do unto them, in the name of justice; and we cheerfully accord to all men all the rights we claim herein for ourselves.

47. We declare that no Negro shall engage himself in battle for an alien race without first obtaining the consent of the leader of the Negro people of the world, except in a matter of national self-defense.

48. We protest against the practice of drafting Negroes and sending them to war with alien forces without proper training, and demand in all cases that Negro soldiers be given the same training as the aliens.

49. We demand that instructions given Negro children in schools include the subject of "Negro History," to their benefit.

50. We demand a free and unfettered commercial intercourse with all the Negro people of the world.

51. We declare for the absolute freedom of the seas for all peoples.

52. We demand that our duly accredited representatives be given proper recognition in all leagues, conferences, conventions or courts of international arbitration wherever human rights are discussed.

53. We proclaim the 31st day of August of each year to be an international holiday to be observed by all Negroes.

54. We want all men to know that we shall maintain and contend for the freedom and equality of every man, woman and child of our race, with our lives, our fortunes and our sacred honor.

These rights we believe to be justly ours and proper for the protection of the Negro race at large, and because of this belief we, on behalf of the four hundred million Negroes of the world, do pledge herein the sacred blood of the race in defense, and we hereby subscribe our names as a guarantee of the truthfulness and faithfulness hereof, in the presence of Almighty God, on this 13th day of August, in the year of our Lord one thousand nine hundred and twenty.

Sworn before me this 15th day of August, 1920.

[Legal Seal] JOHN G. BAYNE.
Notary Public, New York County.
New York County Clerk's No. 378; New York County Register's No. 12102.
Commission expires March 30, 1922.

Source: Reproduced from Marcus Garvey, "Declaration of the Rights of the Negro Peoples" (1920).

6 Cyril V. Briggs Merges Race Consciousness with Class Consciousness, 1922

> *"12,000,000 Negroes at the heart of an imperialist power could not long be ignored"*

Radicalized by the war and by the Russian Revolution, Caribbean-born Cyril V. Briggs (1888–1966) founded the African Blood Brotherhood (ABB) in 1919. Briggs, a journalist, viewed racism as an extension of capitalism, a means of economic exploitation that not only fixed blacks to the lowest rung of the employment ladder, but also deployed white workers' prejudices against them. Briefly, the ABB was a secret organization, but as it grew, it publicly embraced an evolving range of sentiments, among them anti-colonialist initiatives among nations of color, black self-rule (in the United States and Africa), armed self-defense, industrial unionism, and the critical places of African American workers in the proletarian revolution against capitalism. Briggs and the ABB believed that before barriers could be broken down between white and black labor – in order to achieve a broad unionist front – black workers themselves had to become conscious of their predicament and aware of their own power as a class of workers. The Program of the African Blood Brotherhood, excerpted below, is dated 1919. It is an iteration of Briggs' early ideas.

Program of the African Blood Brotherhood, 1919

The Great Migration of Negro workers from the South continues. Negro workers are pouring North to escape the hellish conditions … in search of higher wages and better living conditions. Shall they be tools for the employers' Open Shop plot against Labor or will Organized Labor move to win these workers to its ranks by (1) opening the doors of the labor unions to them on terms of full equality with white workers, not in theory only but in practice; (2) eliminating all discriminatory practices, non-promotable and "dead-line" clauses, unfair legislative enactments, etc., and (3) acquainting the Negro workers with the benefits of unionism and actively bidding for their membership.

...

The program of the A.B.B. declares:

To gain for Negro Labor a higher rate of compensation and to prevent exploitation because of lack of protective organization we must encourage industrial unionism among our people and at the same time fight to break down the prejudice in the unions which is stimulated and encouraged by the employers. This prejudice is already meeting the attack of the radical and progressive element among white labor union men and must eventually give way before the united onslaught of Colored and White Workers. Wherever it is found impossible to enter the existing labor unions, independent unions should be formed, that Negro Labor be enabled to protect its interests.

The A.B.B. Seeks

To bring about co-operation between colored and white workers on the basis of their identity of interest as workers;

To educate the Negro in the benefits of unionism and to gain admission for him on terms of full equality to the unions;

To bring home to the Negro worker his class interests as a worker and to show him the real source of his exploitation and oppression;

To organize the Negro's labor power into labor and farm organizations;

To foster the principles of consumers' co-operatives as an aid against the high cost of living;

To oppose with counter propaganda the vicious capitalist propaganda against the Negro as a race, which is aimed to keep the workers of both races apart and thus facilitate their exploitation;

To realize a United front of Negro workers and organizations as the first step in an effective fight against oppression and exploitation;

To acquaint the civilized world with the facts about lynchings, peonage, jim-crowism, disfranchisement and other manifestations of race prejudice and mob rule.

Towards These Ends the A.B.B.

Supports a press service – the Crusader Service – for the dissemination to the Negro Press of the facts about conditions and events in the sphere of organized labor; reports of labor's changing and increasingly enlightened attitude towards the colored workers; and sends out news of general race interest, interpreted from the working class point of view. The Service is mailed twice each week and is used regularly by over a hundred Negro papers.

Sends organizers and lecturers into industrial sections to propagate the doctrines of unionism and enlist Negro workers into the ranks of the most militant organization of Negro workers in the country.

Operates forums and classes with the aim of arousing (1) the race consciousness of the Negro workers and (2) their class consciousness. (This is the natural process.)

Guards against the use of the Negro migrants as tools for the Open Shop advocates and other unscrupulous employers who seek to break the power of Organized Labor and to destroy all those gains won for the working class during the last twenty years by those workers who had the good sense to organize for their protection.

Exposes the existence of mob-law, peonage, and other barbarisms in the South and wages relentless war against these evil conditions which force the Southern Negro to flee the South and seek employment in the industrial sections.

The Message to You –

Class-conscious white worker or race-conscious Negro (and the A.B.B. has only one message for both!) – shocked by the conditions under which the Negro is forced to live in the South; the conditions which are driving him northward to create new alignments and strange problems in the industrial sections of the North – you cannot fail to realize the potentialities evoked by this steady stream of unorganized workers from the South. If you are a thinking, rational being you cannot fail to recognize THAT THIS IS YOUR FIGHT and you must help us wage it! The A.B.B. is a workers' organization. It has no source of income other than its membership and the masses. It is upon the workers it must depend. *You* must help us in the work of reaching the Negro masses with the message of unionism, the message of organized power, the message of united action by the workers of both races against the capitalist combinations; against the Wall Streets, the Chambers of Commerce, the Rotarian gang, the Ku Klux Klan, (the American Fascisti) and against all the tools of the interests who would keep the workers apart in order the more effectively to exploit them.

...

A Free Africa: – The A.B.B. stands for the waging of a determined and unceasing fight for the liberation of Africa without, however, making any surrenders or compromises on other fronts. We have no patience, therefore, with those Negroes who would distract the attention of the Negro workers from the fight for better conditions in the United States to an illusory empire or republic on the continent of Africa. We believe that the Negro workers of America can best help their blood-brothers in Africa by first making of their own group a power in America. The position of 12,000,000 Negroes at the heart of an imperialist power could not long be ignored were those Negroes intelligently organized, courageously led, and co-operating with the organized white workers on the basis of identity of interests of the entire working-class of the world.

...

The A.B.B. believes in inter-racial co-operation – not the sham co-operation of the oppressed Negro workers and their oppressors, but the honest co-operation of colored and white workers based upon mutual appreciation of the fact of the identity of their interests as members of the working class. This is the only interracial co-operation the A.B.B. believes in!

Source: Cyril V. Briggs, "Program of the African Blood Brotherhood," reprinted in Herbert Aptheker (ed.), *A Documentary History of the Negro People in the United States*, Vol. 3 (New York: Citadel Press, 1992).

7 Langston Hughes on Being Black in America, 1925

"I am the darker brother"

Writer and poet Langston Hughes epitomized the spirit of the Harlem Renaissance. In a 1926 essay entitled "The Negro Artist and the Racial Mountain," he wrote, "The younger Negro artists who create now intend to express our individual dark-skinned selves without fear or shame." Caring less about who liked their work than about the importance of doing their work, Hughes and his cohort of Harlem Renaissance writers, artists, and scholars set out to make art that relayed a black aesthetic, one that recognized and mediated the perspectives and voices of African Americans and that captured the ways they lived in the world. His poem, "I, Too," was a popular recitation.

"I, Too," 1925

I, too, sing America
I am the darker brother.
They send me to eat in the kitchen
When company comes,
But I laugh,
And eat well,
And grow strong.

Tomorrow,
I'll be at the table
When company comes.
Nobody'll dare
Say to me,
"Eat in the kitchen,"
Then.

Besides,
They'll see how beautiful I am
And be ashamed—

I, too, am America.

Source: Langston Hughes, "I, Too," in Arnold Rampersad (ed.), *The Collected Poems of Langston Hughes* (New York: Vintage Books, 2004), p. 46.

8 Amy Jacques Garvey Calls on Women to Lead, 1925

"Strengthen your shaking knees ... or we will displace you and lead on to victory and to glory"

Editor of and contributor to the UNIA's newspaper The Negro World, *Amy Jacques Garvey (wife of Marcus Garvey) echoed black feminists of her era and before. Whereas nineteenth-century feminists aimed for (eventual) inclusion, the Garvey movement defined its goal as "Race First": autonomy and self-determination for black peoples around the world achieved through building a separate society. In this essay, published in the* World, *Amy Jacques Garvey argues that, as a worldwide liberation struggle, black nation building required the full participation of women.*

The exigencies of this present age require that women take their places beside their men. White women are rallying all their forces and uniting regardless of national boundaries to save their race from destruction, and preserve its ideals for posterity.... White men have begun to realize that as women are the backbone of the home, so can they, by their economic experience and their aptitude for details, participate effectively in guiding the destiny of nation and race.

No line of endeavor remains closed for long to the modern woman. She agitates for equal opportunities and gets them; she makes good on the job and gains the respect of men who heretofore opposed her. She prefers to be a breadwinner than a half-starved wife at home. She is not afraid of hard work, and by being independent she gets more out of the present-day husband than her grandmother did in the good old days.

The women of the East, both yellow and black, are slowly but surely imitating the women of the Western world, and as the white women are bolstering up a decaying white civilization, accordingly women of the darker races are sallying forth to help their men establish a civilization according to their own standards, and to strive for world leadership.

Women of all climes and races have as great a part to play in the development of their particular group as the men. Some readers may not agree with us on this issue, but do they not mould the minds of their children the future men and women? Even before birth a mother can so direct her thoughts and conduct as to bring into the world either a genius or an idiot. Imagine the early years of contact between mother and child, when she directs his form of speech, and is responsible for his conduct and deportment. Many a man has risen from the depths of poverty and obscurity and made his mark in life because of the advices and councils of a good mother whose influence guided his footsteps throughout his life.

Women therefore are extending this holy influence outside the realms of the home, softening the ills of the world by their gracious and kindly contact.

Some men may argue that the home will be broken up and women will become coarse and lose their gentle appeal. We do not think so, because everything can be done with moderation. ... The doll-baby type of woman is a thing of the past, and the wide-awake woman is forging ahead prepared for all emergencies, and ready to answer any call, even if it be to face the cannons on the battlefield.

New York has a woman Secretary of State. Two States have women Governors, and we would not be surprised if within the next ten years a woman graces the White House in Washington, D.C. Women are also filling diplomatic positions, and from time immemorial women have been used as spies to get information for their country.

White women have greater opportunities to display their ability because of the standing of both races, and due to the fact that black men are less appreciative of their women than white men. The former will more readily sing the praises of white women than their own; yet who is more deserving of admiration than the black woman, she who has borne the rigors of slavery, the deprivations consequent on a pauperized race, and the indignities heaped upon a weak and defenseless people? Yet she has suffered all with fortitude, and stands ever ready to help in the onward march to freedom and power.

Be not discouraged black women of the world, but push forward, regardless of the lack of appreciation shown you. A race must be saved, a country must be redeemed, and unless you strengthen the leadership of vacillating Negro men, we will remain marking time until the Yellow race gains leadership of the world, and we be forced to subserviency under them, or extermination.

We are tired of hearing Negro men say, "There is a better day coming," while they do nothing to usher in the day. We are becoming so impatient that we are getting in the front ranks, and serve notice on the world that we will brush aside the halting, cowardly Negro men, and with prayer on our lips and arms prepared for any fray, we will press on and on until victory is over.

Africa must be for Africans, and Negroes everywhere must be independent, God being our guide. Mr. Black man, watch your step! Ethiopia's queens will reign again, and her Amazons protect her shores and people. Strengthen your shaking knees, and move forward, or we will displace you and lead on to victory and to glory.

Source: Amy Jacques Garvey, "Women as Leaders," *The Negro World*, October 25, 1925.

Questions for Consideration

How was the "New Negro" new? What elements of the "New Negro" echoed previous movements?

Why did W. E. B. Du Bois, Emmett J. Scott, and others believe that demonstrations of patriotism and heroism would benefit African Americans and their struggle for equality?

Where do the UNIA and the ABB overlap and where do they diverge? How did their programs differ from that of the NAACP? From black perspectives during this era, which presented the more persuasive or effective course of action? How might African Americans have embraced multiple agendas?

Considering the grievances laid out in Chapter 3 by black southerners and
migrants, how well could the approach of the African Blood Brotherhood
address their economic concerns?

The movement in black arts and letters known as the Harlem Renaissance grew in
tandem with more radical or militant programs presented in this chapter. How
did the poets McKay and Hughes (or other black writers and artists of the era)
express the themes articulated by the political organizations presented here?

Bibliography

Grant, Collin. *Negro with a Hat: The Rise and Fall of Marcus Garvey*. New York:
Oxford University Press, 2010.

Jonas, Gilbert. *Freedom's Sword: The NAACP and the Struggle Against Racism in
America, 1909–1969*. Reprint. New York: Routledge, 2004.

Lentz-Smith, Adriane D. *Freedom Struggles: African Americans and World War I*.
Cambridge, MA: Harvard University Press, 2009.

Lewis, David L. *When Harlem Was in Vogue*. Reprint. Penguin Publishers, 1997.

Rampersad, Arnold. *The Life of Langston Hughes*. 2 volumes. Reprint. New York:
Oxford University Press, 2002.

Sullivan, Patricia. *Lift Every Voice: The NAACP and the Making of the Civil Rights
Movement*. New York: The New Press, 2009.

Taylor, Ula Yvette. *The Veiled Garvey: The Life and Times of Amy Jacques Garvey*.
Chapel Hill: University of North Carolina Press, 2001.

Williams, Chad. *Torchbearers of Democracy: African American Soldiers in the World
War I Era*. Chapel Hill: University of North Carolina Press, 2010.

Wintz, Cary D. *African American Political Thought, 1890–1930: Washington, Du
Bois, Garvey, and Randolph*. Armonk, NY: M. E. Sharpe, 1996.

Chapter 5   Resistance, 1927–1939

> When it rains five days and the skies turn dark as night
> Then trouble's takin' place in the lowlands at night ...
>
> Backwater blues done call me to pack my things and go
> 'Cause my house fell down and I can't live there no more

From "Backwater Blues" (1927) by Bessie Smith

Bessie Smith (1892–1933), the most famous blues performer of her time, wrote "Backwater Blues" about a flood that had occurred in the 1910s. She released it as a record in 1927. Like much of the arts production from the 1920s, the subject proved relevant across time to African Americans. Rains inundated the Mississippi Delta from 1926 to 1927, and when the levees broke, the water subsequently flooded 16 million acres across five states and displaced as many as a million people. Black people comprised 90 percent of those affected, and Smith's song expressed their sorrow, frustration, and anger. In 2005 when the levees broke after Hurricane Katrina and New Orleans flooded, again African Americans suffered most, and "Backwater Blues" became a part of the soundtrack of that disaster.

"Backwater Blues" reflects the instability that marred the decade's economy for rural folk. In 1920, despite the Great Migration, over 70 percent of African Americans still lived and worked as farmers in the rural South. Across the next two decades, migration waned as urban job markets

African American Voices: A Documentary Reader from Emancipation to the Present,
First Edition. Edited by Leslie Brown.
© 2014 John Wiley & Sons, Inc. Published 2014 by John Wiley & Sons, Inc.

declined. Meanwhile discriminatory practices assured that whites displaced black workers, even in positions considered "Negro jobs," pushing black unemployment past white joblessness. With a fragile hold on their place, African Americans felt the economic decline well before the Great Depression.

Black folk were concerned about economic issues, and intended to take their grievances where they could. Loyal traditionally to the Party of Lincoln, and deigning to support the Democratic Party of white supremacy, African Americans reluctantly turned their political attention away from *laissez-faire* Republicans to the Democratic presidency of Franklin Delano Roosevelt. FDR's critique of capitalism run amok resonated with blacks, but they were more interested in his promise to act aggressively on behalf of struggling Americans and his willingness to bring black professionals into his administration in advisory roles. To pass the New Deal, however, Roosevelt needed the political support of the white southerners who controlled Congress. Administered at the state and local level, and accordingly mired in regional – and racial – politics, New Deal programs mostly excluded, segregated, or marginalized blacks.

The New Deal provided limited assistance, and in some ways FDR's softer line on race issues created a new relationship between African Americans and the federal government. Indeed, the migration had created a black urban voting bloc, of interest to the northern Democratic Party. Economic struggles proved as difficult as ever for the black masses everywhere. It should come as no surprise that many found ideas about alternative societal forms including communism attractive.

1 The Scottsboro Boys Write to the Workers of the World, 1932

"We are only workers like you are. Only our skin is black"

Black and white young people, men, women, and children, rode the rails in the 1930s in search of work or whatever better place the trains might take them. In March 1931 nine young black males, some of them children, made such a journey, passing through Scottsboro, Alabama. Two young white women, riders in the same car, were making the same trip. One accused the boys of rape, evidently under pressure by locals furious at the sight of black males and white females in the same space. Neither the boys' statements of innocence nor the facts of the case mattered in terms of southern justice during the 1930s. Eight young black men, the "Scottsboro Boys," as they became known, were found guilty and sentenced to death.

Many civil rights organizations, including the NAACP, took an interest in their case, but it was the Communist Party of the United States of America

(CPUSA), which advocated workers' rights, that provided their defense through its legal arm, International Labor Defense (ILD). The CPUSA set in motion a dynamic campaign that included mass meetings and publications that turned the Scottsboro case into an international cause to expose racial injustice as an American disgrace. The ILD appealed the lower courts' decisions all the way to the Supreme Court, which overturned the Scottsboro convictions, first on the basis of inadequate counsel, and second because the jury pool excluded African Americans.

"Plea of the Scottsboro Boys"

From the death cells in Kilby Prison, where they have been held under conditions of the most ghastly torture ever since the mock trials in the lower court at Scottsboro, Ala., the eight Scottsboro boys send the following appeal to the workers of the whole world to rally to the mass fight to smash the hideous frame-up and lynch murder verdicts:

From the death cell here in Kilby Prison, eight of us Scottsboro boys is writing this to you.

We have been sentenced to die for something we ain't never done. Us poor boys been sentenced to burn up on the electric chair for the reason that we is workers – and the color of our skin is black. We like any one of you workers is none of us older than 20. Two of us is 14 and one is 13 years old.

What we guilty of? Nothing but being out of a job. Nothing but looking for work. Our kinfolk was starving for food. We wanted to help them out. So we hopped a freight – just like any one of you workers might a done – to go down to Mobile to hunt work. We was taken off the train by a mob and framed up on rape charges.

At the trial they give us in Scottsboro we could hear the crowds yelling, "Lynch the Niggers." We could see them toting those big shotguns. Call 'at a fair trial?

And while we lay here in jail, the boss-man make us watch 'em burning up other Negroes on the electric chair. "This is what you'll get," they say to us.

What for? We ain't done nothing to be in here at all. All we done was to look for a job. Anyone of you might have done the same thing – and got framed up on the same charge just like we did.

Only ones helped us down here been the International Labor Defense and the League of Negro Rights. We don't put no faith in the National Association for the Advancement of Colored People. They give some of us boys eats to go against the other boys who talked for the I.L.D. But we wouldn't split. Nohow. We know our friends and our enemies.

Working class boys, we asks you to save us from being burnt on the electric chair. We's only poor working class boys whose skin is black. We shouldn't die for that.

We hear about working people holding meetings for us all over the world. We asks for more big meetings. It'll take a lot of big meetings to help the I.L.D. and the L.S.N.R. to save us from the boss-man down here.

Help us boys. We ain't done nothing wrong. We are only workers like you are. Only our skin is black.

(Signed) Andy Wright, Olen Montgomery, Ozie Powell, Charlie Weems, Clarence Norris, Haywood Patterson, Eugene Williams, Willie Robertson.

Source: "Scottsboro Boys Appeal from Death Cells to the Toilers of the World," *The Negro Worker*, 2 (May 1932), pp. 8–9; reprinted in Manning Marable and Leith Mullings (eds.), *Let Nobody Turn Us Around: Voices of Resistance, Reform, and Renewal: An African American Anthology* (New York: Rowman and Littlefield, 2000), pp. 280–281.

2 Angelo Herndon Joins the Communist Party, 1934

"I had never known that anything could be done about it"

Angelo Herndon (1913–1997) labored in the mines as a boy. His search for work in the 1920s took him southward, where through labor organizations he was introduced to the idea of communism. Stirred by the Party's uncompromising position in support of interracial unity on workers' issues, Herndon agreed to serve as an organizer. In 1932 he was arrested under a nineteenth-century statue for inciting insurrection. His attorneys, supported by the CPUSA and the ILD, argued the unconstitutionality of the case and against the unfairness of a trial by Georgia jury that excluded African Americans. Simultaneously, the CPUSA and the ILD mounted interracial protests outside of the courthouse. Herndon was found guilty, nonetheless, and was sentenced to eighteen to twenty years on a Georgia chain gang. The document below excerpts Herndon's autobiography, a pamphlet published in 1934 and sold by the ILD to fund his defense.

"You Cannot Kill the Working Class"

...

The Jim-Crow system was in full force in the mines of the Tennessee Coal and Iron Company, and all over Birmingham. It had always burnt me up, but I didn't know how to set about fighting it. My parents and grand-parents were hard-boiled Republicans, and told me very often that Lincoln had freed the slaves, and that we'd have to look to the Republican Party for everything good. I began to wonder about that. Here I was, being Jim-Crowed and cheated. Every couple of weeks I read about a lynching some-where in the South. Yet there sat a Republican government up in Washington, and they weren't doing a thing about it.

...

I wish I could remember the exact date when I first attended a meeting of the Unemployment Council, and met up with a couple of members of the Communist Party. That date means a lot more to me than my birthday, or any other day in my life.

The workers in the South, mostly deprived of reading-matter, have devel-oped a wonderful grapevine system for transmitting news. It was over this grapevine that we first heard that there were "reds" in town.

The foremen – when they talked about it – and the newspapers, and the big-shot Negroes in Birmingham, said that the "reds" were foreigners, and Yankees, and believed in killing people, and would get us in a lot of trouble. But out of all the talk I got a few ideas clear about the Reds. They believed in organizing and sticking together. They believed that we didn't have to have bosses on our backs. They believed that Negroes ought to have equal rights with whites. It all sounded O.K. to me. But I didn't meet any of the Reds for a long time.

I Find the Working-Class Movement

One day in June, 1930, walking home from work, I came across some hand-bills put out by the Unemployment Council in Birmingham. They said: "Would you rather fight – or starve?" They called on the workers to come to a mass meeting at 3 o'clock.

Somehow I never thought of missing that meeting. I said to myself over and over: "It's war! It's war! And I might as well get into it right now!" I got to the meeting while a white fellow was speaking. I didn't get everything he said, but this much hit me and stuck with me: that the workers could only get things by fighting for them, and that the Negro and white workers had to stick together to get results. The speaker described the conditions of the Negroes in Birmingham, and I kept saying to myself: "That's it." Then a Negro spoke from the same platform, and somehow I knew that this was what I'd been looking for all my life.

At the end of the meeting I went up and gave my name. From that day to this, every minute of my life has been tied up with the workers' movement.

I joined the Unemployment Council, and some weeks later the Communist Party. I read all the literature of the movement that I could get my hands on, and began to see my way more clearly.
...

All my life I'd been sweated and stepped on and Jim-Crowed. I lay on my belly in the mines for a few dollars a week, and saw my pay stolen and slashed, and my buddies killed. I lived in the worst section of town, and rode behind the "Colored" signs on streetcars, as though there was something disgusting about me. I heard myself called "nigger" and "darky," and I had to say "Yes, sir" to every white man, whether he had my respect or not.

I had always detested it, but I had never known that anything could be done about it. And here, all of a sudden, I had found organizations in which Negroes and whites sat together, and worked together, and knew no difference of race or color. Here were organizations that weren't scared to come out for equality for the Negro people, and for the rights of the workers. The Jim-Crow system, the wage-slave system, weren't everlasting after all! It was like all of a sudden turning a corner on a dirty, old street and finding yourself facing a broad, shining highway.

The bosses, and the Negro misleaders ... told us that these Reds were "foreigners" and "strangers" and that the Communist program wasn't acceptable to the workers in the South. I couldn't see that at all. The leaders of the Communist Party and the Unemployment Council seemed people very much like the ones I'd always been used to. They were workers, and they talked our language ... I felt then, and I know now, that the Communist program is the only program that the Southern workers – whites and Negroes both – can possibly accept in the long run. It's the only program that does justice to the Southern worker's ideas that everybody ought to have an equal chance, and that every man has rights that must be respected.

Work Against Odds

The Communist Party and the Unemployment Council had to work under the most difficult conditions. We tried to have a little headquarters, but it was raided and closed by the police. We collected money for leaflets, penny by penny, and mimeographed them on an old, rickety hand-machine we kept in a private home. We worked very quietly, behind drawn shades, and were always on the look-out for spies and police. We put the leaflets out at night, from door-step to door-step. Some of our members who worked in factories sneaked them in there.

Sometimes we would distribute leaflets in a neighborhood, calling for a meeting in half an hour on a certain corner. We would put up just one speaker, he would give his message in the fewest possible words, we would pass out pamphlets and leaflets, and the meeting would break up before the cops could get on the scene.

The bosses got scared, and the Ku Klux Klan got busy. The Klan would parade up and down the streets, especially in the Negro neighborhoods, in full regalia, warning the Negroes to keep away from the Communists. They passed out leaflets saying: "Communism Must Be Wiped Out. Alabama Is a Good Place for Good Negroes, but a Bad Place for Negroes Who Want Social Equality."

In June, 1930, I was elected a delegate to the National Unemployment Convention in Chicago.

...

A World Movement

In Chicago, I got my first broad view of the revolutionary workers' movement. I met workers from almost every state in the union, and I heard about the work of the same kind of organizations in other countries, and it first dawned on me how strong and powerful the working-class was. There wasn't only me and a few others in Birmingham. There were hundreds, thousands, millions of us!

My family had told me not to come back. What did I care? My real family was the organization. I'd found that I had brothers and sisters in every corner of the world, I knew that we were all fighting for one thing and that they'd stick by me. I never lost that feeling, in all the hard days to come, in Fulton Tower Prison with the threat of the electric chair and the chain-gang looming over me.

I went back to Birmingham and put every ounce of my strength into the work of organization. I built groups among the miners. I read and I studied. I worked in the Young Communist League under the direction of Harry Simms, the young white boy who was later, during the strike of the Kentucky miners, to give his life for the working-class.

I helped organize an Anti-Lynching Conference in Chattanooga. This conference selected delegates to the first convention of the League of Struggle for Negro Rights, held in St. Louis in 1930.

...

Splitting the Workers

[In Atlanta t]he Black Shirts – a fascist organization – held parades quite often, demanding that all jobs be taken away from Negroes and given to whites. They said that all the Negroes should go back to Africa. I smiled the first time I heard this – it amused me to see how exactly the program of Marcus Garvey fitted in with the program of the Klan.

Of course the demand of the Black Shirts to give all the jobs to the whites was an attempt to split the white workers from the Negroes and put an end to joint struggles for relief. As organizer for the Unemployment Council, I had to fight mighty hard against this poison.

From the cradle onward, the Southern white boy and girl are told that they are better than Negroes. Their birth certificates are tagged "white"; they sit in white schools, play in white parks and live on white streets. They pray in white churches, and when they die they are buried in white cemeteries. Everywhere before them are signs: "For White." "For Colored." They are taught that Negroes are thieves, and murderers, and rapists.

I remember especially one white worker, a carpenter, who was one of the first people I talked to in Atlanta. He was very friendly to me. He came to me one day and said that he agreed with the program, but something was holding him back from joining the Unemployment Council.

"What's that, Jim?" I asked. Really, though, I didn't have to ask. I knew the South, and I could guess.

...

The Price of Division

"Well," I said, "I'll tell you why. It's because the bosses have got us all split up down here. We Southern workers are as good fighters as there are anywhere, and yet we haven't been able to get equal wages with the workers in other places, and we haven't got any rights to speak of. That's because we've been divided. When the whites go out on strike, the bosses call in the Negroes to scab. When the Negroes strike, the bosses call in the whites to scab.

"Did you ever figure out why the unions here are so weak? It's because the whites don't want to organize with the Negroes, and the Negroes don't trust the whites.

"We haven't got the simplest human rights down here. We're not allowed to organize and we're not allowed to hold our meetings except in secret. We can't vote – most of us – because the bosses are so anxious to keep the Negroes from voting that they make laws that take this right away from the white workers too.

"We Southern workers are like a house that's divided against itself. We're like an army that goes out to fight the enemy and stops on the way because its men are all fighting each other.

"Take this relief business, now," I said. "The commissioners tell the whites that they can't give them any more relief because they have to feed so many Negroes, and the Negroes ought to be chased back to the farms. Then they turn around and tell the Negroes that white people have to come first on the relief, so there's nothing doing for colored folks. That way they put us off, and get us scrapping with each other.

"Now suppose the white unemployed, and the Negro unemployed, all go to the commissioners together and say: 'We're all starving. We're all in need. We've decided to get together into one strong, powerful organization to make you come across with relief.'

"Don't you think that'll bring results, Jim?" I asked him. "Don't you see how foolish it is to go into the fight with half an army when we could have a whole one? Don't you think that an empty belly is a pretty punk exchange for the honor of being called a 'superior' race? And can't you realize that as long as one foot is chained to the ground the other can't travel very far?"

What Happened to Jim

Jim didn't say anything more that day. I guess he went home and thought it over. He came back about a week later and invited me to his house. It was the first time he'd ever had a Negro in the house as a friend and equal. When I got there I found two other Negro workers that Jim had brought into the Unemployment Council.

About a month later Jim beat up a rent collector who was boarding up the house of an evicted Negro worker. Then he went to work and organized a committee of whites and Negroes to see the mayor about the case. "Today it's the black worker across town; tomorrow it'll be me," Jim told the mayor.

There are a lot of Jims today, all over the South.

...

On the night of July 11, I went to the Post Office to get my mail. I felt myself grabbed from behind and turned to see a police officer.

I was placed in a cell, and was shown a large electric chair, and told to spill everything I knew about the movement. I refused to talk, and was held incommunicado for eleven days. Finally I smuggled out a letter through another prisoner, and the International Labor Defense got on the job.

The Insurrection Law

Assistant Solicitor John Hudson rigged up the charge against me. It was the charge of "inciting to insurrection." It was based on an old statute passed in 1861, when the Negro people were still chattel slaves, and the white masters needed a law to crush slave insurrection and kill those found giving aid to the slaves. The statute read:

"If any person be in any manner instrumental in bringing, introducing or circulating within the state any printed or written paper, pamphlet, or circular for the purpose of exciting insurrection, revolt, conspiracy or resistance on the part of slaves, Negroes or free persons of color in this state he shall be guilty of high misdemeanor which is punishable by death."

Since the days of the Civil War that law had lain, unused and almost forgotten. Now the slaves of the new order – the white and black slaves of capitalism – were organizing. In the eyes of the Georgia masters, it was a crime punishable by death.

The trial was set for January 16, 1933. The state of Georgia displayed the literature that had been taken from my room, and read passages of it to the jury. They questioned me in great detail. Did I believe that the bosses and government ought to pay insurance to unemployed workers? That Negroes should have complete equality with white people? Did I believe in the demand for the self-determination of the Black Belt – that the Negro people should be allowed to rule the Black Belt territory, kicking out the white landlords and government officials? Did I feel that the working-class could run the mills and mines and government? That it wasn't necessary to have bosses at all?

The Unseen Jury

I told them I believed all of that – and more.

The courtroom was packed to suffocation. The I.L.D. attorneys, Benjamin J. Davis, Jr., and John H. Geer, two young Negroes – and I myself – fought every step of the way. We were not really talking to that judge, nor to those prosecutors, whose questions we were answering. Over their heads we talked to the white and Negro workers who sat on the benches, watching, listening, learning. And beyond them we talked to the thousands and millions of workers all over the world to whom this case was a challenge.

We demanded that Negroes be placed on jury rolls. We demanded that the insulting terms, "nigger" and "darky," be dropped in that court. We asserted the right of the workers to organize, to strike, to make their demands, to nominate candidates of their choice. We asserted the right of the Negro people to have complete equality in every field.

The state held that my membership in the Communist Party, my possession of Communist literature, was enough to send me to the electric chair. They said to the jury: "Stamp this damnable thing out now with a conviction that will automatically carry with it a penalty of electrocution."

And the hand-picked lily-white jury responded:

"We, the jury, find the defendant guilty as charged, but recommend that mercy be shown and fix his sentence at from 18 to 20 years."

I had organized starving workers to demand bread, and I was sentenced to live out my years on the chain-gang for it. But I knew that the movement itself would not stop. I spoke to the court and said:

"They can hold this Angelo Herndon and hundreds of others, but it will never stop these demonstrations on the part of Negro and white workers who demand a decent place to live in and proper food for their kids to eat."

I said: "You may do what you will with Angelo Herndon. You may indict him. You may put him in jail. But there will come thousands of Angelo Herndons. If you really want to do anything about the case, you must go out and indict the social system. But this you will not do, for your role is to defend the system under which the toiling masses are robbed and oppressed.

"You may succeed in killing one, two, even a score of working-class organizers. But you cannot kill the working class."

Source: "You Cannot Kill the Working Class," by Angelo Herndon (New York: International Defense Fund, 1934).

3 Ella Baker and Marvel Cooke Report on "The Bronx Slave Market," 1935

"Negro women found themselves being displaced by whites"

The Great Depression worsened conditions for black domestics in several ways. Wages declined; many workers lost steady positions, laid off by white families who chose "day workers" over a permanent employee. As their ranks of unemployed and under-employed swelled, black women gathered on certain urban street corners hoping to be selected for a day's labor. In 1935, two black researchers for the Works Progress Administration (WPA) went to the intersection of 167th St. and Jerome Avenue in The Bronx, New York City, to observe this phenomenon. The following is their report.

The Bronx Slave Market! What is it? Who are its dealers? Who are its victims? What are its causes? How far does its stench spread? What forces are at work to counteract it?

Any corner in the congested sections of New York City's Bronx is fertile soil for mushroom "slave marts." The two where the traffic is heaviest and the bidding is highest are located at 167th Street and Jerome Avenue and at Simpson and Westchester Avenues.

Symbolic of the more humane slave block is the Jerome Avenue "market." There, on benches surrounding a green square, the victims wait, grateful, at least, for some place to sit. In direct contrast is the Simpson Avenue "mart," where they pose wearily against buildings and lampposts, or scuttle about in an attempt to retrieve discarded boxes upon which to rest.

Again, the Simpson Avenue block exudes the stench of the slave market at its worst. Not only is human labor bartered and sold for slave wage, but human love also is a marketable commodity. But whether it is labor, or love that is sold, economic necessity compels the sale. As early as 8 a.m. they come; as late as 1 p.m. they remain.

Rain or shine, cold or hot, you will find them there – Negro women, old and young – sometimes bedraggled, sometimes neatly dressed – but with the invariable paper bundle, waiting expectantly for Bronx housewives to buy their strength and energy for an hour, two hours, or even for a day at the munificent rate of fifteen, twenty, twenty-five, or, if luck be with them, thirty cents an hour. If not the wives themselves, maybe their husbands, their sons, or their brothers, under the subterfuge of work, offer worldly-wise girls higher bids for their time.

Who are these women? What brings them here? Why do they stay? In the boom days before the onslaught of the depression in 1929, many of these women who are now forced to bargain for day's work on street corners, were employed in grand homes in the rich Eighties, or in wealthier homes in Long Island and Westchester, at more than adequate wages. Some are former marginal industrial workers, forced by the slack in industry to seek other means of sustenance. In many instances there had been no necessity for work at all. But whatever their standing prior to the depression, none sought employment where they now seek it. They come to the Bronx, not because of what it promises, but largely in desperation.

Paradoxically, the crash of 1929 brought to the domestic labor market a new employer class. The lower middle-class housewife, who, having dreamed of the luxury of a maid, found opportunity staring her in the face in the form of Negro women pressed to the wall by poverty, starvation and discrimination.

Where once color was the "gilt edged" security for obtaining domestic and personal service jobs, here, even, Negro women found themselves being displaced by whites. Hours of futile waiting in employment agencies, the fee that must be paid despite the lack of income, fraudulent agencies that sprung up during the depression, all forced the day worker to fend for herself or try the dubious and circuitous road to public relief.

As inadequate as emergency relief has been, it has proved somewhat of a boon to many of these women, for with its advent, actual starvation is no longer their ever-present slave driver and they have been able to demand twenty-five and even thirty cents an hour as against the old fifteen and twenty cent rate. In an effort to supplement the inadequate relief received, many seek this open market.

And what a market! She who is fortunate (?) enough to please Mrs. Simon Legree's scrutinizing eye is led away to perform hours of multifarious household drudgeries. Under a rigid watch, she is permitted to scrub floors on her bended knees, to hang precariously from window sills, cleaning window after window, or to strain and sweat over steaming tubs of heavy blankets, spreads and furniture covers.

Fortunate, indeed, is she who gets the full hourly rate promised. Often, her day is rewarded with a single dollar bill or whatever her unscrupulous employer pleases to pay. More often, the clock is set back for an hour or more. Too often she is sent away without any pay at all.

Source: "The Bronx Slave Market," by Ella Baker and Marvel Cooke, *The Crisis*, 42 (November 1935). We wish to thank the Crisis Publishing Co., Inc., the publisher of the magazine of the National Association for the Advancement of Colored People, for the use of the material first published in the November 1935 issue of *The Crisis*.

4 Richard Wright Observes a Black Response to Joe Louis' Victory, 1935

"Something ... popped loose"

In separate racial clusters around radios throughout the nation, Americans listened to the 1935 boxing match between Joe Louis and Max Baer. The fight posed an epic battle between the races that recalled Jack Johnson's days. A win by Baer meant the triumph of white supremacy; his defeat by Louis, its denial. In this essay that appeared in The New Masses, *writer Richard Wright details blacks' response on Chicago's South Side.*

"Joe Louis Uncovers Dynamite"

"Wun-tuh-threee-fooo-fiive-seex-seven-eight-niine-thuun!"

Then:

"JOE LOUIS – THE WINNAH!"

On Chicago's South Side five minutes after these words were yelled and Joe Louis' hand was hoisted as victor in his four-round go with Max Baer, Negroes poured out of beer taverns, pool rooms, barber shops, rooming houses and dingy flats and flooded the streets.

"LOUIS! LOUIS! LOUIS!" they yelled and threw their hats away. They snatched newspapers from the stands of astonished Greeks and tore them up, flinging the bits into the air. They wagged their heads. Lawd, they'd never seen or heard the like of it before. They shook the hands of strangers. They clapped one another on the back. It was like a revival. Really there was a religious feeling in the air. Well, it wasn't exactly a religious feeling, but it was something, and you could feel it. It was a feeling of unity, of oneness.

Two hours after the fight the area between South Parkway and Prairie Avenue on 47th Street was jammed with no less than twenty-five thousand Negroes, joy-mad and moving to they didn't know where. Clasping hands, they formed long writhing snake-lines and wove in and out of traffic. They seeped out of doorways, oozed from alleys, trickled out of tenements, and flowed down the street; a fluid mass of joy. White storekeepers hastily closed their doors against the tidal wave and stood peeping through plate glass with blanched faces.

Something had happened, all right. And it had happened so confoundingly sudden that the whites in the neighborhood were dumb with fear. They felt – you could see it in their faces – that something had ripped loose, exploded. Something which they had long feared and thought was dead. Or if not dead, at least so safely buried under the pretence of good-will that they no longer had need to fear it. Where in the world did it come from? And what was worst of all, how far would it go? Say, what's got into these Negroes?

And the whites and the blacks began to feel themselves. The blacks began to remember all the little slights, and discriminations and insults they had suffered; and their hunger too and their misery. And the whites began to search their souls to see if they had been guilty of something, some time, somewhere against which this wave of feeling was rising.

As the celebration wore on, the younger Negroes began to grow bold. They jumped on the running boards of automobiles going east or west on 47th Street and demanded of the occupants:

"Who yuh fer – Baer or Louis?"

In the stress of the moment it seemed that the answer to the question marked out friend and foe.

A hesitating reply brought waves of scornful laughter. Baer, huh? That was funny. Now, hadn't Joe Louis just whipped Max Baer? Didn't think we had it in us, did you? Thought Joe Louis was scared, didn't you? Scared because Max talked loud and made boasts. We ain't scared either. We'll fight too when the time comes. We'll win, too.

A taxicab driver had his cab wrecked when he tried to put up a show of bravado.

Then they began stopping street cars. Like a cyclone sweeping through a forest, they went through them, shouting, stamping. Conductors gave up and backed away like children. Everybody had to join in this celebration. Some of the people ran out of the cars and stood, pale and trembling, in the crowd. They felt it, too.

In the crush a pocketbook snapped open and money spilled on the street for eager black fingers.

"They stole it from us, anyhow," they said as they picked it up.

When an elderly Negro admonished them, a fist was shaken in his face. Uncle Tomming, huh?

"What in hell yuh gotta do wid it?" they wanted to know.

Something had popped loose, all right. And it had come from deep down. And nobody could have said just what it was, and nobody wanted to say. Blacks and whites were afraid. But it was a sweet fear, at least for the blacks. It was a mingling of fear and fulfillment. Something dreaded and yet wanted. A something had popped out of a dark hole, something with a hydra-like head, and it was darting forth its tongue.

You stand on the borderline, wondering what's beyond. Then you take one step and you feel a strange, sweet tingling. You take two steps and the feeling becomes keener. You want to feel some more. You break into a run. You know it's dangerous, but you're impelled in spite of yourself.

Four centuries of oppression, of frustrated hopes, of black bitterness, felt even in the bones of the bewildered young, were rising to the surface. Yes, unconsciously they had imputed to the brawny image of Joe Louis all the balked dreams of revenge, all the secretly visualized moments of retaliation, and he had won! Good Gawd Almighty! Yes, by Jesus, it could be done! Didn't Joe do it? You see, Joe was the consciously-felt symbol. Joe was the concentrated essence of black triumph over white. And it comes so seldom, so seldom. And what could be sweeter than long nourished hate vicariously gratified? From the symbol of one's strength they took strength, and in that moment all fear, all obstacles were wiped out, drowned. They stepped out of the mire of hesitation and irresolution and were free! Invincible! A merciless victor over a fallen foe! Yes, they had felt all that – for a moment. ...

And then the cops came.

Not the carefully picked white cops who were used to batter the skulls of white workers and intellectuals who came to the South Side to march with the black workers to show their solidarity in the struggle against Mussolini's impending invasion of Ethiopia; no, no, black cops, but trusted black cops and plenty tough. Cops who knew their business, how to handle delicate situations. They piled out of patrols, swinging clubs.

"Git back! Gawdammit, git back!"

But they were very careful, very careful. They didn't hit anybody. They, too, sensed something. And they didn't want to trifle with it. And there's no doubt but that they had been instructed not to. Better go easy here. No telling what might happen. They swung clubs, but pushed the crowd back with their hands.

Finally, the street cars moved again. The taxis and automobiles could go through. The whites breathed easier. The blood came back to their cheeks.

The Negroes stood on the sidewalks, talking, wondering, looking, breathing hard. They had felt something, and it had been sweet – that feeling. They wanted some more of it, but they were afraid now. The spell was broken.

And about midnight down the street that feeling ebbed, seeping home – flowing back to the beer tavern, the pool room, the café, the barber shop, the dingy flat. Like a sullen river it ran back to its muddy channel, carrying a confused and sentimental memory on its surface, like a water-soaked driftwood.

Say, Comrade, here's the wild river that's got to be harnessed and directed. Here's that something, that pent-up folk consciousness. Here's a fleeting glimpse of the heart of the Negro, the heart that beats and suffers and hopes – for freedom. Here's the fluid something that's like iron. Here's the real dynamite that Joe Louis uncovered!

Source: "Joe Louis Uncovers Dynamite," by Richard Wright, *New Masses*, 17 (October 8, 1935), pp. 18–19.

5 The Southern Negro Youth Congress on Freedom, Equality, and Opportunity, 1937

"America cannot be America to us until we share its benefits as we have gladly shared its burdens"

Inspired by the 1936 meeting of the National Negro Council (NNC), an umbrella organization that sought to link black economic and civil rights, the Southern Negro Youth Congress (SNYC) differentiated itself generationally and regionally from other organizations. Dedicated to voting rights and union organizing among southern blacks, the SNYC issued the statement below after its first conference in Richmond, Virginia.

Proclamation of Southern Negro Youth: For Freedom, Equality, and Opportunity

We are the Negro youth of the South. We are proud of every inch of Southern soil. We, and our fathers before us, have given our toil and the sweat of our brow that the land of our birth might prosper. We are proud of the generations of the Negro people of the South. We are proud of the traditions of Frederick Douglass, Sojourner Truth, Nat Turner, Harriet Tubman, and other Negro sons and daughters of the South who gave their lives that all men might be free and equal. And we are no less proud of the heritage given to all Americans alike by such fighters for liberty and democracy as Thomas Jefferson and Patrick Henry.

We Negro youth of the South know that ours is the duty to keep alive the traditions of freedom and democracy. We know that ours must be the ceaseless task to win the status of citizenship for the Negro people. From Douglass and Lincoln our hands received the torch of freedom and we shall hold it high.

We realize that the majority of white Southerners are not responsible for the conditions under which we live. These conditions are caused, not by the many – but by the few, those who profit by pitting white labor against black labor to the harm of both. To all white youth of the South we extend our hand in warmest brotherhood. For we know, and we would make them know, that as one rises all must rise, and as one falls all must fall. The right to live as citizens, the right to education, the right to all the benefits of life in a democratic land cannot be fully theirs unless these things are fully ours. We would be friends with them, friends in the deepest sense of the word, working together for our common good.

We have a right to a school that is free and equal; to a home around which the spectre of poverty, sickness, and want does not hover; to playgrounds and swimming pools and all those recreations which build young bodies and make them strong. We have a right to jobs at equal pay for equal work, to jobs which end in no blind alley.

Our generation cannot and must not grow into manhood a voteless generation. We have the right to vote, to serve on juries, to share in the government of this land of ours. We cannot prosper and the South cannot prosper as long as lynching and mob violence shadow our path of progress and stain with the blood of innocent victims the Constitution of our land. Lynching must end. The Jim-Crow system must end. For these are shackles which bind Negro and white youth alike.

We who are the sharecroppers and tenant farmers must be freed from the relics of slavery. Peonage must be abolished. We, who till the soil, must be given the opportunity to own land. Negro girls of the South, who toil as domestics, as laundresses, and on the farms must be free from the degradation to which low-paid toil and unequal opportunity now condemn them.

We, who work in mine, mill and factory, must win improved conditions of work and a higher standard of living. We must win the right to organize, with white workers, into large and powerful trade unions – for the union makes us strong.

Our bodies and our souls are destined for higher things than cannon fodder in banker-made wars. For this reason we take our stand with those who fight for peace, with those who fight against war and fascism. The tragic lessons of Ethiopia and Spain teach us that it is the growing menace of fascism which breeds war. We have seen tendencies towards fascism in our own country: the Ku Klux Klan. Realizing that fascism presents a world-wide danger, particularly to minority groups, we must unite with all those forces throughout the world which strike out boldly for the preservation of peace and democracy.

These things must be ours because we know them to be right and just. In our churches and schools we have been taught to love and respect the ideals of the brotherhood of man and the equality of all Americans. We dedicate ourselves to the attainment of these things because we know that America cannot be America to us until we share its benefits as we have gladly shared its burdens.

But we are under no illusions. We know that to win these rights there must be endless work. We know that Negro youth of the South, from church and school, from the plantations, from mine and mill and factory must be united. And for that unity we pledge our lives. Unity for us is no mere phrase. It is the practical device through which we will win our freedom. We will build this unity to win free schools, decent American homes and the right to play. We shall join our hands together to build trade unions in the South free from prejudice. We shall unite in the struggle for the right to work.

We have no higher duty than to bend our backs and lend our joint energies in a struggle to end the Jim-Crow system, to wipe out lynching and mob violence. We will not stop until Angelo Herndon and the nine Scottsboro boys are completely free.

United with youth of every land and every nation we will fight for peace and democracy.

United we will struggle to improve the status of Negro girls – the future Negro womanhood of the South.

Hands locked together and with heads erect we march into the future, fearless and unafraid. We are Americans! We are the hope of our people! We have the right to live!

Source: "Proclamation of Southern Negro Youth: For Freedom, Equality, and Opportunity," reproduced with permission from Herbert Aptheker (ed.), *A Documentary History of the Negro People in the United States*, Vol. 4 (reprint, New York: Carroll Publishing, 1992), pp. 258–261. Courtesy of B. Aptheker.

6 The Coordinating Committee for Employment, New York, 1938

"serious business in Harlem"

Since the nineteenth century African Americans had used direct action protests to express their dissatisfaction. In the 1930s major cities witnessed a wave of boycotts against business that refused to hire blacks. In New York

City, the Coordinating Committee for Employment organized protests against not only stores, but also utility and other companies. These documents were written by Adam Clayton Powell, Jr., a young minister from Harlem, for his column "Soap Box," published in the black newspaper, the Amsterdam News. *A Democrat, Powell went on to represent the district in the House of Representatives from 1945 to 1971.*

"The Fight For Jobs"

The Coordinating Committee for Employment is beginning a serious business in Harlem. It is beginning a fight for jobs. It has asked for work. It has pleaded for work. It has held work conferences. It has utilized every means at its disposal to get the employers of New York City to stop starving the Negroes of New York. These means have failed.

The Committee is now inaugurating a mass boycott and picketing of every enterprise in Greater New York that refuses to employ Negroes. The Gas and Electric Company has seen the light, the telephone company must also. The big department stores must follow suit. If Negroes can work at Ovington's, Wanamaker's, Macy's and Bloomingdale's, then an appreciable percentage must work at Gimbel's, Klein's, Hearn's, Saks and other stores.

The milk companies are next. No more subterfuges, no more passing the buck, but black faces must appear on Harlem milk wagons immediately or the milk concerns shall be boycotted.

Three hundred and fifty thousand consumers are not anything to be sneezed at and if anyone dares try to sneeze, we are killing him with the worst cold he ever had. The same thing goes for the Metropolitan Life. As long as we have Negro insurance companies there is no reason why Negroes should pay one cent to any other insurance company that refuses to employ Negroes.

Platform for Jobs Campaign

1. AIMS: To provide a greater measure of employment for Negro workers in the institutions and establishments which are sustained by the purchasing power of the Negro.
2. All jobs obtained must provide for a standard living wage equal to that prevailing at the time of employment.
3. Wherever Negroes obtain jobs and union conditions prevail, the Negro workers must be, or must become members of the established union.
4. Workers are to be hired on the qualifying standards set by the employer.
5. Applicants for employment shall not be confined to any organization, or individual.

6. Employment of Negroes outside of the Harlem area must not be sacrificed for any possible local increases.
7. Any increase in employment of Negroes in Harlem must be accomplished without the victimization of white for black workers.
8. The Harlem Job Committee shall charge no fee or in any way exact profit of any kind from any employer or employee.
9. In pursuance of the above objectives the Committee will secure and utilize the cooperation and support of all responsible institutions and organizations in Harlem.
10. The Harlem Job Committee will cooperate with those employers recognizing the justice of the Committee's objectives. The Committee will, however, utilize every legal and recognized means to obtain its aims, in cases where employers either fail or are unwilling to cooperate.

Source: Reproduced with permission from Adam Clayton Powell, Jr., "Soap Box: The Fight For Jobs," New York *Amsterdam News*, May 7 and 14, 1938.

7 Marian Anderson at the Lincoln Memorial, 1939

Marian Anderson was, perhaps, the world's most notable voice in 1939. Nonetheless, the Daughters of the American Revolution used its "whites only" policy to deny the renowned contralto use of Constitution Hall for a concert in Washington, DC. With the support of Eleanor and Franklin Roosevelt and Harold Ickes at the Department of the Interior, Anderson gave a concert on Easter Sunday at the Lincoln Memorial, before an audience of 75,000 on the national Mall. Millions around the world heard the NBC broadcast. The concert included her usual program, ranging from opera to spirituals. That day she performed a particularly memorable rendition of the national hymn, "My country 'tis of thee / Sweet land of liberty / Of thee we sing."

Questions for Consideration

How and why did the identity of African Americans as workers emerge in the 1930s? What did this new collective identity mean for black political organizations and for the movement for civil rights?

How did the Great Depression and the New Deal change employment and relief options for black Americans?

What did the cases of Angelo Herndon and the Scottsboro Boys reveal about the vulnerabilities of ordinary black southerners? What did the response to their cases reveal about the priorities and resources of black political organizations?

Figure 5.1   75,000 people gather to hear singer Marian Anderson in Potomac Park, April 9, 1939.

Source: Courtesy National Archives, Still Pictures Records Section, photo Double Delta Industries Inc.

Why did African Americans find communism and the Communist Party so compelling?
Compare the strategies and rhetoric used by activists in the 1930s to those of the New Negro Era. How did they overlap and how did they differ in their understanding of and abilities to address the needs of the masses of black Americans?
How – and how effectively – would the Platform for Jobs Campaign, put out in 1938 by the Coordinating Committee for Employment, address the conditions that created the Bronx Slave Market described by Ella Baker and Marvel Cooke?

Bibliography

Bates, Beth Tompkins. *Pullman Porters and the Rise of Protest Politics in Black America, 1925–1945*. Chapel Hill: University of North Carolina Press, 2001.
Bynum, Cornelius L. *A. Philip Randolph and the Struggle for Civil Rights*. Urbana: University of Illinois Press, 2010.

Chafe, William H., et al., eds. *Remembering Jim Crow: African Americans Tell About Life in the Segregated South*. Reprint. New York: New Press, 2008.

Kelley, Robin D. G. *Hammer and Hoe: Alabama Communists During the Great Depression*. Chapel Hill: University of North Carolina Press, 1990.

McDuffie, Erik S. *Sojourning for Freedom: Black Women, American Communism, and the Making of Black Left Feminism*. Durham, NC: Duke University Press, 2011.

Naison, Mark. *The Cry Was Unity: Communists and African Americans, 1917–1936*. Jackson: University Press of Mississippi, 1998.

Sullivan, Patricia. *Days of Hope: Race and Democracy in the New Deal Era*. Chapel Hill: University of North Carolina Press, 1996.

Wolcott, Victoria W. *Remaking Respectability: African American Women in Interwar Detroit*. Chapel Hill: University of North Carolina Press, 2000.

Valk, Anne M., and Leslie Brown, eds. *Living with Jim Crow: African American Women and Memories of the Segregated South*. New York: Palgrave Macmillan, 2010.

Chapter 6   Resolve, 1941–1952

Doris "Dorie" Miller (1919–1944) joined the Navy in 1939. He was serving as a mess attendant on the USS *West Virginia* at Pearl Harbor on December 7, 1941. Miller carried injured sailors and his commanding officer to safety, then manned an anti-aircraft gun. For his heroism Miller received a medal, the Navy Cross. He continued to serve, still in a support position, but was lost in 1944 when the *Liscombe Bay* was sunk in the South Pacific. His image, used for this recruiting poster entitled "Above and Beyond the Call of Duty," survived. Created by the Office of War Information, the poster was one among many in the campaign to garner Americans' support and compliance for the war effort, and proudly African Americans hung it in barbershops, beauty parlors, churches, libraries, and classrooms.

The Miller poster targeted a black audience, but the story behind it also belies the usual patterns of Jim Crow. It was African Americans who demanded to know the details of Miller's acts and who carried his story in the press. Then, when produced, the poster was distributed only in black communities, and only by black Boy Scout troops, who in reality were neither sanctioned nor affiliated with the segregationist Boy Scouts of America. Under the pressure of evident irony, all Scout troops eventually were allowed to distribute Miller's image, that his story might persuade whites of blacks' capacity for courage and that the gesture might project to the world an inclusive depiction of America.

African American Voices: A Documentary Reader from Emancipation to the Present, First Edition. Edited by Leslie Brown.
© 2014 John Wiley & Sons, Inc. Published 2014 by John Wiley & Sons, Inc.

Figure 6.1   David Stone Martin, "Above and Beyond the Call of Duty": Dorie Miller Received the Navy Cross at Pearl Harbor, May 27, 1942.

Source: Library of Congress, Prints and Photographs Division.

As the Miller story reveals, however, the hypocrisies of black life in the United States were as evident during World War II as they had been in World War I. Called upon to support the war, again black people shared the nation's sacrifices disproportionately and confronted its racial brutalities. Whites assaulted black men in uniform, black workers, and black communities. In the armed forces, African Americans were segregated. Working mostly in menial positions, they lived in appalling conditions and suffered humiliation perpetuated by military policy. Black servicemen and women were refused service in places that served German prisoners of war. The War Department set up training programs at Tuskegee Institute where the Tuskegee Airmen (and the lesser known Tuskegee Signal Corps) prepared, but they were excluded from battle, until protests and war demands forced the military to change its position. The Tuskegee contingent excelled, and for their valor, eighty-eight Tuskegee pilots earned the Distinguished Flying Cross.

African Americans seized on Roosevelt's Four Freedoms – of speech and of religion, from want and from fear – as they had Wilson's World War I rhetoric about making the world safe for democracy, but it remained dangerous to protest, especially in the South. Ideological objections to black demands masked whites' resentment. Strong anti-communist sentiments treated black people's arguments for rights and equality as anti-America rhetoric and traitorous disloyalty. Still, black organizations employed a progressively stronger language of protest. At the same time boycotts of transportation, stores, and schools, and protest rallies and marches posed direct challenges to Jim Crow. And individuals like Jackie Robinson, who in 1947 cracked the color line in baseball, continued to publicly refute theories of white supremacy.

It was duplicitous, black Americans believed, for the United States to have waged war against fascism and racism abroad, and yet sanction the same at home or elsewhere in the world. Jim Crow was a form of apartheid, state-sanctioned racism that excluded, segregated, and discriminated – and killed – a particular class of citizens on the basis of race. As colonized nations of color sought independence, they challenged global realignments and old patterns of white domination. While the United States vied with Russia for international influence in the post-war era, President Harry S. Truman gave serious consideration to the civil rights issue, forming an interracial commission to study race in America.

The resulting report, "To Secure these Rights," reiterated much of what black organizations like the NAACP had stated before, and it made many of the same recommendations: to desegregate the military, to provide equal opportunities in education, employment, and housing, and to enforce the right to vote, among other objectives. Although it offered little new, the report was important as a presidential statement that directly broached the pattern of inequality. Southern congressional obstinance foiled legislative attempts at change, but by executive order, Truman desegregated the military. The process took years, and white resistance was immense. But if the military and baseball reflected the society that created them, then in the post-war era, Truman's order and Robinson's feats could have enormous ramifications.

1 The March on Washington Movement, 1941

"The Negroes' greatest opportunity to rise"

In the run-up to World War II, a Second Great Migration drew African Americans out of the South. Poised along with black northern residents to enter industry, they found racial limitations to their employment options. In

*the summer of 1941, labor leader A. Philip Randolph organized the March
on Washington Movement (MOWM) that threatened to draw 10,000 blacks
to the nation's capital to protest. Under this pressure, President Franklin D.
Roosevelt issued Executive Order 8802, prohibiting discrimination in
defense industries. In return Randolph agreed to call off the march, but not
the movement. In cities throughout the United States, blacks and their allies
rallied for jobs and fair wages, for enforcement of the Constitution, and for
an end to lynching and racial violence. This document urged African
Americans to keep up the protest.*

CALL TO THE MARCH

We call upon you to fight for jobs in National Defense.

We call upon you to struggle for the integration of Negroes in the armed forces such as the Air Corps, Navy, and Marine Corps of the Nation.

We call upon you to demonstrate for the abolition of Jim-Crowism in all Government departments and defense employment.

This is an hour of crisis. It is a crisis of democracy. It is a crisis of minority groups. It is a crisis of Negro Americans.

What is this crisis?

To American Negroes, it is the denial of jobs in Government defense projects. It is racial discrimination in Government departments. It is widespread Jim-Crowism in the armed forces of the Nation.

While billions of the taxpayers' money are being spent for war weapons, Negro workers are being turned away from the gates of factories, mines and mills – being flatly told, "NOTHING DOING." Some employers refuse to give Negroes jobs when they are without "union cards," and some unions refuse Negro workers union cards when they are "without jobs."

What shall we do?

What a dilemma!

What a runaround!

What a disgrace!

What a blow below the belt!

Though dark, doubtful and discouraging, all is not lost, all is not hopeless.

Though battered and bruised, we are not beaten, broken or bewildered.

Verily, the Negroes' deepest disappointments and direst defeats, their tragic trials and outrageous oppressions in these dreadful days of destruction and disaster to democracy and freedom, and the rights of minority peoples, and the dignity and independence of the human spirit, is the Negroes' greatest opportunity to rise to highest heights of struggle for freedom and justice in Government, in industry, in labor unions, education, social service, religion and culture.

With faith and confidence of the Negro people in their own power for self-liberation, Negroes can break down the barriers of discrimination against employment in National Defense. Negroes can kill the deadly serpent of race hatred in the Army, Navy, Air and Marine Corps, and smash through and blast the Government, business and labor-union red tape to win the right to equal opportunity in vocational training and re-training in defense employment.

Most important and vital to all, Negroes, by the mobilization and coordination of their mass power, can cause PRESIDENT ROOSEVELT TO ISSUE AN EXECUTIVE ORDER ABOLISHING DISCRIMINATIONS IN ALL GOVERNMENT DEPARTMENTS, ARMY, NAVY, AIR CORPS AND NATIONAL DEFENSE JOBS.

Of course, the task is not easy. In very truth, it is big, tremendous and difficult.

It will cost money.

It will require sacrifice.

It will tax the Negroes' courage, determination and will to struggle. But we can, must and will triumph.

The Negroes' stake in national defense is big. It consists of jobs, thousands of jobs. It may represent millions, yes, hundreds of millions of dollars in wages. It consists of new industrial opportunities and hope. This is worth fighting for.

But to win our stakes, it will require an "all out," bold and total effort and demonstration of colossal proportions.

Negroes can build a mammoth machine of mass action with a terrific and tremendous driving and striking power that can shatter and crush the evil fortress of race prejudice and hate, if they will only resolve to do so and never stop, until victory comes.

Dear fellow Negro Americans, be not dismayed in these terrible times. You possess power, great power. Our problem is to harness and hitch it up for action on the broadest, daring and most gigantic scale.

In this period of power politics, nothing counts but pressure, more pressure, and still more pressure, through the tactic and strategy of broad, organized, aggressive mass action behind the vital and important issues of the Negro.

To this end, we propose that ten thousand Negroes MARCH ON WASHINGTON FOR JOBS IN NATIONAL DEFENSE AND EQUAL INTEGRATION IN THE FIGHTING FORCES OF THE UNITED STATES.

An "all-out" thundering march on Washington, ending in a monster and huge demonstration at Lincoln's Monument will shake up white America.

It will shake up official Washington.

It will give encouragement to our white friends to fight all the harder by our side, with us, for our righteous cause.

It will gain respect for the Negro people.

It will create a new sense of self-respect among Negroes.

But what of national unity?

We believe in national unity which recognizes equal opportunity of black and white citizens to jobs in national defense and the armed forces, and in all other institutions and endeavors in America. We condemn all dictatorships, Fascist, Nazi and Communist. We are loyal, patriotic Americans, all.

But, if American democracy will not defend its defenders; if American democracy will not protect its protectors; if American democracy will not give jobs to its toilers because of race or color; if American democracy will not insure equality of opportunity, freedom and justice to its citizens, black and white, it is a hollow mockery and belies the principles for which it is supposed to stand.

To the hard, difficult and trying problem of securing equal participation in national defense, we summon all Negro Americans to march on Washington. We summon Negro Americans to form committees in various cities to recruit and register marchers and raise funds through the sale of buttons and other legitimate means for the expenses of marchers to Washington by buses, train, private automobiles, trucks, and on foot.

We summon Negro Americans to stage marches on their City Halls and Councils in their respective cities and urge them to memorialize the President to issue an executive order to abolish discrimination in the Government and national defense.

However, we sternly counsel against violence as ill-considered and intemperate as the abuse of power. Mass power, like physical power, when misdirected is more harmful than helpful.

We summon you to mass action that is orderly and lawful, but aggressive and militant, for justice, equality and freedom.

Crispus Attucks marched and died as a martyr for American independence. Nat Turner, Denmark Vasey, Gabriel Prosser, Harriet Tubman and Frederick

Douglass fought, bled and died for emancipation of Negro slaves and the preservation of American democracy.

Today, we call upon President Roosevelt, a great humanitarian and idealist, to follow in the footsteps of his noble and illustrious predecessor and take the second decisive step in this world and national emergency and free American Negro citizens of the stigma, humiliation and insult of discrimination and Jim-Crowism in Government departments and national defense.

The Federal Government cannot with clear conscience call upon private industry and labor unions to abolish discrimination based upon race and color as long as it practices discrimination itself against Negro Americans.

Source: Reprinted with permission of the A. Philip Randolph Institute.

2 The "Double V" Campaign, 1942

"against the enemies of democracy"

In a 1942 letter to the Pittsburgh Courier, *a prominent black newspaper, a reader suggested that African Americans fought for a double victory: against enemies abroad and enemies at home. The* Courier *produced an image, the "Double V" symbol, writing, "In continuing the policy of* The Courier *to fight for the rights of the Negro race, the paper recently started the 'Double V' drive for victory at home against prejudice and discrimination as well as victory abroad against the enemies of democracy. ..."*

3 A Black Army Chaplain Protests the Treatment of Black Soldiers, 1944

"My job, it seemed, was to build *morale, not to* have *it"*

Grant Reynolds (1908–2004) served as an Army chaplain during World War II. In each camp where black soldiers trained – North, South, or West – Reynolds observed shamelessly racist practices that humiliated African American servicemen. His protests marked him as a troublemaker. Reynolds quit the military and took his protests public. In a series of articles, excerpted

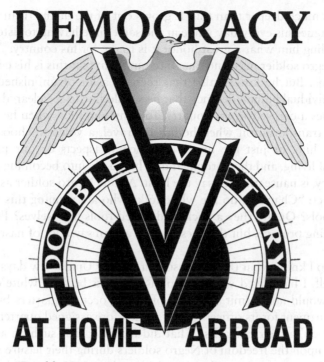

Figure 6.2 "Double V" image.

Source: "Nation Lauds *Courier's* and 'Double V' Campaign: Race Unites for Drive to Secure Real Democracy," Pittsburgh *Courier*, March 7, 1942. Proquest.

> *below, he described the black military experience in unflinching terms. Published in* The Crisis, *the articles reveal what African Americans thought – but rarely spoke directly – about the war and their world.*

I

   … Negro soldiers are damned tired of the treatment they are getting. This dislike cannot be attributed to the natural antipathy of the majority of soldiers, white and black, developed out of their efforts to adjust themselves to the rigors and uncertainties of war. Now the Negro soldier is as easily adaptable as any other American soldier. I'd even go as far as to say that he is more adaptable. His lifetime of adjusting himself to the whims and inconsistencies of the American white man substantiates this claim. His resentment then goes much deeper than this. It grows out of the unamerican treatment which plagues his every day while at the same time having to listen to loud voices telling him what a great honor it is to die for his country.

The Negro soldier needs no one to remind him that this is his country. He knows this. But he knows also that there is a lot of unfinished business about individual human decency that he would like to see cleared up before he becomes a corpse for *any* country. To deny him food when he is hungry, dignified transportation when he has to travel, a voice in choosing those who rule him, or just the most fundamental aspects or our proclaimed method of living, and then propagandize him daily into becoming a hero for democracy, is nauseating, to say the least. As one Negro soldier asked me in this respect: "Chaplain, do the white folks who are running this war think we are fools? Or, are they a pack of damned fools themselves? Excuse me, sir, for being profane, but this mess makes a man say a lot of nasty things."

...

How do I know what the Negro soldier thinks? Until a few days ago I was one myself. I have lived with him in his barracks because white officers in Virginia would not permit a colored officer to occupy quarters built by the War Department for its officers ... I was therefore assigned quarters with the enlisted men in their barracks. What did it matter that such an assignment infringed upon the freedom of Negro soldiers during their leisure moments? What did it matter how this personal embarrassment and humiliation impaired my morale? My job, it seemed, was to *build* morale, not to *have* it.

...

[Secretary of War Henry L.] Stimson must have been told that the Negro soldier is demoralized, that he does not want to fight – unless a second front is opened in Mississippi, Texas, Georgia, South Carolina, Louisiana, or just *anywhere* below the Mason and Dixon Line – that his heart is not in this war. Such a soldier cannot be depended upon to offer up his life against German or Japanese soldiers who know why they are fighting and demonstrate each day their willingness to die for their beliefs. Where are the American soldiers, of any color, who would destroy their own lives rather than fall into the hands of a hated enemy?

...

Who among our military authorities would admit that the nation's indecent treatment of the Negro soldier had rendered him unfit for combat with a foreign enemy? So following the traditional point of view, since this point of view led to the creation of the dilemma in the first place, the Negro soldier was promptly discredited. Not because he could not master the technique of modern weapons of war – this was the Secretary of War's claim – but because this is the logical stand that the traditional race haters were bound to use in defense of their hypocritical and infamous conduct. Talk about impeding the war effort! What *is* treason anyway?

...

But [Stimson's] blanket statement about the Negro soldier's inability in this respect not only insults the thousands of intelligent Negro youth in our armed forces from all sections of the country, but by indirection it classifies them as morons incapable of attaining the intelligence level of the most ignorant southern cracker. What does the Negro soldier think about this? He considers it a vicious attack upon his manhood. And what is more he thinks that the Administration continues to insult him as long as such men are allowed to control his destiny in this war. The Negro soldier will not give his life for the perpetuation of this outright lynching of his ability, nor for the right of domestic nazis to make of him a military scapegoat.

Every factual pronouncement which falls from the lips of Anglo-Saxon war leaders in this conflict lays a foundation for the Negro soldier's conviction that this is a war to maintain the white man's right to keep the colored man in social and economic bondage. The Negro soldier is not so dumb as far too many people in authority lead themselves to believe. He is asking a lot of questions. Does the Atlantic Charter apply to colored people now enslaved by the British, Dutch, Portuguese, and other imperialistic powers? ... Why does our foreign policy fail to make clear America's stand in regard to spilling the blood of its sons to dictate the destiny of people who admittedly have a right to self-determination? But most important of all, the Negro soldier is asking how he can be expected to give his last full measure of devotion for his country when each day, while he wears the uniform of his country, he is insulted, humiliated, and even murdered for attempting to be an American?

My experience with Negro soldiers has led me to oppose the idea that the majority of them consider this a "race war." One must confess, however, that at times they are given strong evidence to the contrary. To say that all Negro soldiers share this or any one point of view is to engage in deliberate falsehood. Many of them think that this is a white man's war, "lock, stock, and barrel." This conclusion is reached in spite of Hitler's treatment of the people in the occupied countries and what the Chinese have suffered at the hands of the Japanese ...

...

In spite of his frustration the Negro soldier sees a New World A-Coming. But he hasn't read about it in anybody's book. He sees its light beginning to break across the dark and distant horizon of time, and events. It won't dawn tomorrow, nor on any tomorrow for a long time to come. This knowledge makes him sad. But that light has begun to shine, dimly 'tis true, and the darkness of man's inhumanity will not prevail against it because it is the light of determined millions of men and women marching toward freedom [in Russia, China, and India].

...

II

The War Department has sold the Negro soldier a rotten bill of goods. ... In the first instance he observes his daily treatment which is both lamentable on the one hand and unsupported by decency on the other. Having a record of loyalty and devotion to the nation that is unequaled as well as unquestioned, he sees the War Department destroy his love for his country by making him a military "untouchable." All other American citizens, irrespective of racial origin, serve in American units – all except the Negro. He serves in a jim crow unit, separated from other Americans, giving stark evidence each day of the War Department's unqualified disrespect for his status as an American citizen.

...

The Constitution and its accompanying Bill of Rights have been literally torn up and the bits insultingly thrown into the Negro soldier's face. Yet these sons of American mothers are expected to die and are dying in the face of such indignity. It is a widely known fact that Nazi prisoners of war receive better treatment in this country than do hundreds of thousands of Negro soldiers.... As it prepares him for death on the foreign battlefields of the world, and actually sends him to his death, it winks at conditions which torture him physically and which mob and lynch his spirit. Under these conditions the War Department sends the sons of American mothers into battle ill-prepared indeed. It is small wonder that among many Negro soldiers, there is the feeling that the War Department itself is helping to destroy their lives.

...

Historians of the future when writing the history of this war will undoubtedly include the great sociological changes which took place. ... This has resulted in the development of new skills for thousands of men which points to an incalculable influence on post-war employment. Vast population changes will have resulted not only from the deployment of soldiers into many sections of the nation hitherto unfamiliar to them, but from the creation of the incentive whereby thousands of women and children have followed these men. Scores of such families will never return to their native communities and will thus influence by virtue of their regional culture whatever area they settle.

... The provincialism of untold millions will have been changed because of the vast geographical nature of the military undertaking. And also the very nature of war itself induces within men a restlessness and dissatisfaction which leads to serious changes in their modes of behavior and which in themselves make serious inroads into previously existing community patterns.

Thus when War Department spokesmen plead their inability to change contemporary practices in such instances as the creation of a mixed division, the very facts themselves deny the validity of their claims. When they state that the War Department is not "running a sociological laboratory" the Negro takes such an excuse for the continuation of military segregation as so much poppycock. And if War Department officials are stupid enough to make such an excuse for their un-American behavior, the Negro soldier is not stupid enough to believe them.

...

Let us assume that you are a colored service man and that you were faced with any of the aforementioned insults. If after your white commanding officer had in a lecture declared that he was going to see to it that Negro soldiers suffered their full share of casualties in this war, what would be your attitude? If after you had been abused and insulted and then expected to demonstrate a high degree of *esprit de corps* and you found that you were incapable of being a super man, what would be your state of mind?

Source: Grant Reynolds, "What the Negro Soldier Thinks About This War," *The Crisis*, 51 (September, October, and November 1944). We wish to thank the Crisis Publishing Co., Inc., the publisher of the magazine of the National Association for the Advancement of Colored People, for the use of the material first published in the September, October, and November 1944 issue of *The Crisis*.

4 Pauli Murray on Student Protests in Washington, DC, 1944

"The revolt against jim crow started with a mutter and a rumble"

Black Washingtonians had boycotted and picketed business that refused to hire them in the 1930s. During World War II, Howard University students launched a new form of protest, "the stool-sitting technique." Howard University Law School student Pauli Murray (1910–1985) published the piece excerpted below in The Crisis in 1944, describing a movement that started in 1942. Murray downplays her role as an organizer here, but at the time she was involved with the Fellowship of Reconciliation and later its successor the Congress of Racial Equality, which used such protests in other cities. The concept had resilience.

"A Blueprint for First Class Citizenship"

Howard University traditionally has been called the "Capstone of Negro Education." When 2,000 young Americans, fresh from 45 states and students from 24 foreign countries arrived there two years ago, their futures uncertain, their draft numbers coming up every day, and their campus surrounded by the dankest kind of degradation they were tempted to call their alma mater the "keptstone" of education. More than half of these students had come from northern or border states or western and middle-western communities. Many of them had never tasted the bitter fruits of jim crow. They were of a generation who tended to think for themselves as Americans without a hyphen.

Thrown rudely into the nation's capital where jim crow rides the American Eagle, if indeed he does not put the poor symbol to flight, these students were psychologically and emotionally unprepared for the insults and indignities visited upon them when they left the campus and went downtown to see the first-run shows, or stopped in a cafe to get a hotdog and a "coke." The will to be free is strong in the young, and their sensitive souls recoiled with a violence that reverberated throughout the war time campus.

The revolt against jim crow started with a mutter and a rumble. It was loudest in the Law School where men students, unprotected by any kind of deferment, were being yanked out of their classes and into a G.I. uniform. "I don't want to fight in a jim crow army." "I'd rather die first!" "I'll go to jail first," were some of the remarks daily. During the first tense days of war time conscription, classes were almost entirely disrupted by the feeling of futility and frustration that settled over these young men.

And then the spirit of revolt took shape. It started in the fall of 1942 with the refusal of Lewis Jones, Morehouse graduate, to be inducted into a jim crow army ...

In January 1943, three women students were arrested in downtown Washington for the simple act of refusing to pay an overcharge for three hot chocolates in a United Cigar store on Pennsylvania Avenue. The young women sat down at the counter and ordered hot chocolate. The waitress refused to serve them at first and they asked for the manager. They were told the manager was out, and they replied they would wait, keeping their seats at the counter. After hurried legal consultation the "management" ordered the waitress to serve them, but upon looking at their checks they were charged twenty-five cents each instead of the standard dime charged for a packaged hot drink. The young women laid thirty-five cents on the counter and started for the door where they were met by a half dozen policemen, hauled off to a street corner, held until the arrival of a Black Maria, and landed in prison in a cell with prostitutes and other criminal suspects. It was not until they were searched and scared almost out of their wits that the dean of women at Howard University was notified and they were dismissed in her care without any charges lodged against them.

The flood of resentment against the whole system of segregation broke loose. Conservative administration members frowned upon this "incident" and advised the three young women they should not stage individual demonstrations against jim crow. It was suggested they should work through an organization concerned with such matters.

These young women of Howard were determined. Others joined them. They took the matter to the student chapter of the N.A.A.C.P. In the meantime from the Law School issued a new trend of thought. The men had spent hours in their "bull sessions" discussing attack and counter-attack upon jim crow. One second-year student, a North Carolinian and former leader in N.A.A.C.P., William Raines, had agitated for months for what he called "the stool-sitting technique." "If the white people want to deny us service, let them pay for it," Raines said. "Let's go downtown some lunch hour when they're crowded. They're open to the public. We'll take a seat on a lunch stool, and if they don't serve us, we'll just sit there and read our books. They lose trade while that seat is out of circulation. If enough people occupy seats, they'll lose so much trade, they'll start thinking."

...

The Civil Rights Committee [formed in March with strong student support] undertook a campaign to bring equal accommodations to the District of Columbia. They set up five subcommittees, publicity and speakers' bureau, program and legislative, committee on correspondence, finance, and direct action. They lobbied in groups with the representatives and senators from their states. They made ingenious little collection cans out of hot chocolate cups and collected pennies from their classmates to pay for paper and postage. They held pep rallies around campus and broadcast their campaign from the tower of Founders Library. They sponsored a Town Hall Meeting at Douglass Hall and brought in community speakers to lead a discussion on "Civil Rights" and the techniques by which they were to be attained.

...

The direct action sub-committee spent a week studying the disorderly conduct and picketing laws of D.C. They spent hours threshing out the pros and cons of public conduct, anticipating and preparing for the reactions of the white public, the Negro public, white customers and the management. They pledged themselves to exemplary behavior, no matter what the provocation. And one rainy Saturday afternoon in April, they started out. In groups of four, with one student acting as an "observer" on the outside, they approached the café. Three went inside and requested service. Upon refusal they took their seats and pulled out magazines, books of poetry, or pencils and pads. They sat quietly. Neither the manager's panicky efforts to dismiss them nor the presence of a half dozen policemen outside could dislodge them. Five minutes later another group of three would enter. This pilgrimage continued until the Little Cafeteria was more than half-filled with staring students on the inside, and a staring public grouped in the street. In forty-five minutes the management had closed the cafeteria. The students took up their vigil outside the restaurant with attractive and provocative picket signs, "There's No Segregation Law in D.C. – What's Your Story Little Palace?" "We die together – Why Can't We Eat Together?" and so on. The picketing continued on Monday morning when the restaurant reopened its doors. The students had arranged a picketing schedule and gave their free hours to the picket line. In two days the management capitulated and changed its policy.

In the spring of 1944, the Civil Rights Committee decided to carry the fight downtown into the heart of Washington. They selected a Thompson's cafeteria at 14th and Pennsylvania in the shadow of the White House. They took off a Saturday afternoon, dressed in their best, and strolled into Thompson's in two's and three's at intervals of ten minutes. They threw up a small picket line outside. Three white sympathizers polled the customers inside and found that only 3 out of 10 expressed objection to their being served. They scrupulously observed the picketing laws, and neither the jeers of undisciplined white members of the Armed Forces, nor cheers of W.A.C.s, W.A.V.E.s and other sympathetic members of the public brought any outward response. When 55 of them, including 6 Negro members of the Armed Forces, had taken seats at the tables, and the Thompson's trade had dropped 50 percent in four hours, the management, after frantic calls to its main office in Chicago, was ordered to serve them.

Before the Civil Rights Committee was able to negotiate with the local management of Thompson's with reference to a changed policy, the Howard University Administration, through the voice of Dr. Mordecai W. Johnson, requested them to suspend their activities until there was a clarification of Administration policy. A hurried meeting of the Deans and Administrators was called and a directive issued requesting the students to cease all activities "designed to accomplish social reform affecting institutions other than Howard University itself."

The students were quick to take up this challenge. They then directed their efforts at "social reform" toward the Administration itself. They had already requested a discussion with representatives of the faculty and administration. They indicated their unwillingness to give up their direct action program, and appealed the ruling of the Administration to the Board of Directors which meets in October, 1944.

...

The question remains to be settled during the coming months whether Howard students shall participate in social action directed against the second-class citizenship to which they have been victimized. There are those who believe the energy and the dynamics of social change must originate in democratic institutions which form test-tubes of democracy and that there must be a realistic relation of one's activities in the community to one's studies in the classroom. There are others who believe that education is a static affair and must not be related to the community at large. Between these two points of view Howard University must make a choice.

But whatever the final outcome, Howard may be proud of those students who have led the way toward new, and perhaps successful techniques to achieve first class citizenship in one area of life in these United States.

Source: Pauli Murray, "A Blueprint for First Class Citizenship," *The Crisis*, 51 (November 1944), pp. 359–359. We wish to thank the Crisis Publishing Co., Inc., the publisher of the magazine of the National Association for the Advancement of Colored People, for the use of the material first published in the November 1944 issue of *The Crisis*.

5 The Civil Rights Congress Charges the US with Genocide, 1951

"We Charge Genocide"

The United Nations, founded in 1945, provided a place where nations might negotiate their disagreements, and the world's oppressed people could bring their grievances. From the late 1940s through the present, various African American organizations have petitioned the UN to investigate racial conditions in the United States, each accompanied by hundreds of pages of evidence. "We Charge Genocide," submitted by the Civil Rights Congress, one of several petitions black organizations submitted right after the war, used particularly strong language to present a "record of mass slayings on the basis of race, of lives deliberately warped and distorted by the willful creation of conditions making for premature death, poverty and disease." As evidence it cited hundreds of incidents of racial violence that had occurred in the US since 1945. The introduction is excerpted below.

"We Charge Genocide: The Historic Petition to the United Nations for Relief From a Crime of The United States Government Against the Negro People"

Introduction:

Out of the inhuman black ghettos of American cities, out of the cotton plantations of the South, comes this record of mass slayings on the basis of race, of lives deliberately warped and distorted by the willful creation of conditions making for premature death, poverty and disease. It is a record that calls aloud for condemnation, for an end to these terrible injustices that constitute a daily and ever-increasing violation of the United Nations Convention on the Prevention and Punishment of the Crime of Genocide.

It is sometimes incorrectly thought that genocide means the complete and definitive destruction of a race or people. The Genocide Convention, however, adopted by the General Assembly of the United Nations on December 9, 1948, defines genocide as … any intent to destroy, in whole or in part, a national, racial, ethnic or religious group is genocide, according to the Convention. "[C]ausing serious bodily or mental harm to members of the group," is genocide as well as "killing members of the group."

We maintain, therefore, that the oppressed Negro citizens of the United States, segregated, discriminated against and long the target of violence, suffer from genocide as the result of the consistent, conscious, unified policies of every branch of government.

…

To the General Assembly of the United Nations:

The responsibility of being the first in history to charge the government of the United States of America with the crime of genocide is not one your petitioners take lightly. The responsibility is particularly grave when citizens must charge their own government with mass murder of its own nationals, with institutionalized oppression and persistent slaughter of the Negro people in the United States on a basis of "race," a crime abhorred by mankind and prohibited by the conscience of the world as expressed in the Convention on the Prevention and Punishment of the Crime of Genocide adopted by the General Assembly of the United Nations on December 9, 1948.

Genocide Leads to Fascism and to War

If our duty is unpleasant it is historically necessary both for the welfare of the American people and for the peace of the world. We petition as American patriots, sufficiently anxious to save our countrymen and all mankind from the horrors of war to shoulder a task as painful as it is important. We cannot forget Hitler's demonstration that genocide at home can become wider massacre abroad, that domestic genocide develops into the larger genocide that is predatory war. The wrongs of which we complain are so much the expression of predatory American reaction and its government that civilization cannot ignore them nor risk their continuance without courting its own destruction. We agree with those members of the General Assembly who declared that genocide is a matter of world concern because its practice imperils world safety.

But if the responsibility of your petitioners is great, it is dwarfed by the responsibility of those guilty of the crime we charge. Seldom in human annals has so iniquitous a conspiracy been so gilded with the trappings of respectability. Seldom has mass murder on the score of "race" been so sanctified by law, so justified by those who demand free elections abroad even as they kill their fellow citizens who demand free elections at home. Never have so many individuals been so ruthlessly destroyed amid many tributes to the sacredness of the individual. The distinctive trait of this genocide is a cant that mouths aphorisms of Anglo-Saxon jurisprudence even as it kills.

The genocide of which we complain is as much a fact as gravity. The whole world knows of it. The proof is in every day's newspapers, in every one's sight and hearing in these United States. In one form or another it has been practiced for more than three hundred years although never with such sinister implications for the welfare and peace of the world as at present. Its very familiarity disguises its horror. It is a crime so embedded in law, so explained away by specious rationale, so hidden by talk of liberty, that even the conscience of the tender minded is sometimes dulled. Yet the conscience of mankind cannot be beguiled from its duty by the pious phrases and the deadly legal euphemisms with which its perpetrators seek to transform their guilt into high moral purpose.

Killing Members of the Group

...

We shall submit evidence proving "killing members of the group," in violation of Article II of the Convention. We cite killings by police, killings by incited gangs, killings at night by masked men, killings always on the basis of "race," killings by the Ku Klux Klan, that organization which is charted by the several states as a semi-official arm of government and even granted the tax exemptions of a benevolent society.

Our evidence concerns the thousands of Negroes who over the years have been beaten to death on chain gangs and in the back rooms of sheriff's offices, in the cells of county jails, in precinct police stations and on city streets, who have been framed and murdered by sham legal forms and by a legal bureaucracy. It concerns those Negroes who have been killed, allegedly for failure to say "sir" or tip their hats or move aside quickly enough, or, more often, on trumped up charges of "rape," but in reality for trying to vote or otherwise demanding the legal and inalienable rights and privileges of United States citizenship formally guaranteed them by the Constitution of the United States, rights denied them on the basis of "race," in violation of the Constitution of the United States, the United Nations Charter, and the Genocide Convention.

Economic Genocide

We shall offer proof of economic genocide, or in the words of the Convention, proof of "deliberately inflicting on the group conditions of life calculated to bring about its destruction in whole or in part." We shall prove that such conditions so swell the infant and maternal death rate and the death rate from disease, that the American Negro is deprived, when compared with the remainder of the population of the United States, of eight years of life on the average.

Further we shall show a deliberate national oppression of these 15,000,000 Negro Americans on the basis of "race" to perpetuate these "conditions of life." Negroes are the last hired and the first fired. They are forced into city ghettos or their rural equivalents. They are segregated legally or through sanctioned violence into filthy, disease-bearing housing, and deprived by law of adequate medical care and education. From birth to death, Negro Americans are humiliated and persecuted, in violation of the Charter and Convention. They are forced by threat of violence and imprisonment into inferior, segregated accommodations, into jim crow busses, jim crow trains, jim crow hospitals, jim crow schools, jim crow theaters, jim crow restaurants, jim crow housing, and finally into jim crow cemeteries.

We shall prove that the object of this genocide, as of all genocide, is the perpetuation of economic and political power by the few through the destruction of political protest by the many. Its method is to demoralize and divide an entire nation; its end is to increase the profits and unchallenged control by a reactionary clique. We shall show that those responsible for this crime are not the humble but the so-called great, not the American people but their misleaders, not the convict but the robed judge, not the criminal but the police, not the spontaneous mob but organized terrorists licensed and approved by the state to incite to a Roman holiday.

We shall offer evidence that this genocide is not plotted in the dark but incited over the radio into the ears of millions, urged in the glare of public forums by Senators and Governors. It is offered as an article of faith by powerful political organizations, such as the Dixiecrats, and defended by influential newspapers, all in violation of the United Nations charter and the Convention forbidding genocide.

This proof does not come from the enemies of the white supremacists but from their own mouths, their own writings, their political resolutions, their racist laws, and from photographs of their handiwork ...

Through this and other evidence we shall prove this crime of genocide is the result of a massive conspiracy, more deadly in that it is sometimes "understood" rather than expressed, a part of the mores of the ruling class often concealed by euphemisms, but always directed to oppressing the Negro people. Its members are so well-drilled, so rehearsed over the generations, that they can carry out their parts automatically and with a minimum of spoken direction. They have inherited their plot and their business is but to implement it daily so that it works daily. This implementation is sufficiently expressed in decision and statute, in depressed wages, in robbing millions of the vote and millions more of the land, and in countless other political and economic facts, as to reveal definitively the existence of a conspiracy backed by reactionary interests in which are meshed all the organs of the Executive, Legislative and Judicial branches of government. It is manifest that a people cannot be consistently killed over the years on the basis of "race" – and more than 10,000 Negroes have so suffered death – cannot be uniformly segregated, despoiled, impoverished, and denied equal protection before the law, unless it is the result of the deliberate, all-pervasive policy of government and those who control it.

Emasculation of Democracy

We shall show, more particularly, how terror, how "killing members of the group," in violation of Article II of the Genocide Convention, has been used to prevent the Negro people from voting in huge and decisive areas of the United States in which they are the preponderant population, thus dividing the whole American people, emasculating mass movements for democracy and securing the grip of predatory reaction on the federal, state, county and city governments. We shall prove that the crimes of genocide offered for your action and the world's attention have in fact been incited, a punishable crime under Article III of the Convention, often by such officials as Governors, Senators, Judges and peace officers whose phrases about white supremacy and the necessity of maintaining inviolate a white electorate resulted in bloodshed as surely as more direct incitement.

We shall submit evidence showing the existence of a mass of American law, written[,] as was Hitler's law[,] solely on the basis of "race," providing for segregation and otherwise penalizing the Negro people, in violation not only of Articles II and III of the Convention but also in violation of the

Charter of the United Nations. Finally we shall offer proof that a conspiracy exists in which the Government of the United States, its Supreme Court, its Congress, its Executive branch, as well as the various state, county and municipal governments, consciously effectuate policies which result is the crime of genocide being consistently and constantly practiced against the Negro people of the United States.

The Negro Petitioners

Many of your petitioners are Negro citizens to whom the charges herein described are not mere words. They are facts felt on our bodies, crimes inflicted on our dignity. We struggle for deliverance, not without pride in our valor, but we warn mankind that our fate is theirs …

We, Negro petitioners whose communities have been laid waste, whose homes have been burned and looted, whose children have been killed, whose women have been raped, have noted with peculiar horror that the genocidal doctrines and actions of the American white supremacists have already been exported to the colored peoples of Asia. We solemnly warn that a nation which practices genocide against its own nationals may not be long deterred, if it has the power, from genocide elsewhere. White supremacy at home makes for colored massacres abroad. Both reveal contempt for human life in a colored skin. Jellied gasoline in Korea and the lynchers' faggot at home are connected in more ways than that both result in death by fire. The lyncher and the atom bomber are related. The first cannot murder unpunished and unrebuked without so encouraging the latter that the peace of the world and the lives of millions are endangered. Nor is this metaphysics. The tie binding both is economic profit and political control. It was not without significance that it was President Truman who spoke of the possibility of using the atom bomb on the colored peoples of Asia, that it is American statesmen who prate constantly of "Asiatic hordes."

"Our Humanity Denied and Mocked"

We Negro petitioners protest this genocide as Negroes and we protest it as Americans, as patriots. We know that no American can be truly free while 15,000,000 other Americans are persecuted on the grounds of "race," that few Americans can be prosperous while 15,000,000 are deliberately pauperized. Our country can never know true democracy while millions of its citizens are denied the vote on the basis of their color.

But above all we protest this genocide as human beings whose very humanity is denied and mocked. We cannot forget that after Congressman Henderson Lovelace Lanham, of Rome, Georgia, speaking in the halls of

Congress, called William L. Paterson, one of the leaders of the Negro people, "a God-damned black son-of-bitch," he added, "We gotta keep the black apes down." We cannot forget it because this is the animating sentiment of the white supremacists, of a powerful segment of American life. We cannot forget that in many American states it is a crime for a white person to marry a Negro on the racist theory that Negroes are "inherently inferior as an immutable fact of Nature." The whole institution of segregation, which is training for killing, education for genocide, is based on the Hitler-like theory of the "inherent inferiority of the Negro." The tragic fact of segregation is the basis for the statement, too often heard after murder, particularly in the South, "Why I think no more of killing a n----r, than of killing a dog."

We petition in the first instance because we are compelled to speak by the unending slaughter of Negroes. The fact of our ethnic origin, of which we are proud – our ancestors were building the world's first civilizations 3,000 years before our oppressors emerged from barbarism in the forests of western Europe – is daily made the signal for segregation and murder. There is infinite variety in the cruelty we will catalogue, but each case has the common denominator of racism. This opening statement is not the place to present our evidence in detail. Still, in this summary of what is to be proved, we believe it necessary to show something of the crux of our case, something of the pattern of genocidal murder, the technique of incitement to genocide, and the methods of mass terror.

Our evidence begins with 1945 and continues to the present. It gains in deadliness and in number of cases almost in direct ratio to the surge towards war. We are compelled to hold to this six years span if this document is to be brought into manageable proportions.

Causes Celèbres

We Negro petitioners are anxious that the General Assembly know of our tragic *causes celèbres*, ignored by the American white press but known nevertheless the world over, but we also wish to inform it of the virtually unknown killed almost casually, as an almost incidental aspect of institutionalized murder.

We want the General Assembly to know of Willie McGee, framed on perjured testimony and murdered in Mississippi because the Supreme Court of the United States refused even to examine vital new evidence proving his innocence. But we also want it to know of the two Negro children, James Lewis, Jr., fourteen years old, and Charles Trudell, fifteen, of Natchez, Mississippi who were electrocuted in 1947, after the Supreme Court of the United States refused to intervene.

We want the General Assembly to know of the martyred Martinsville Seven, who died in Virginia's electric chair for a rape they never committed, in a state that has never executed a white man for that offense. But we want it to know, too, of the eight Negro prisoners who were shot down and murdered on July 11, 1947 at Brunswick, Georgia, because they refused to work in a snake-infested swamp without boots.

We shall inform the Assembly of the Trenton Six, of Paul Washington, the Daniels cousins, Jerry Newsom, Wesley Robert Wells, of Rosalee Ingram, of John Derrick, of Lieutenant Gilbert, of the Columbia, Tennessee destruction, the Freeport slaughter, the Monroe killings – all important cases in which Negroes have been framed on capital charges or have actually been killed. But we want it also to know of the typical and less known – of William Brown, Louisiana farmer, shot in the back and killed when he was out hunting on July 19, 1947 by a white game warden who casually announced his unprovoked crime by saying, "I just shot a n---r. Let his folks know." The game warden, one Charles Ventrill, was not even charged with the crime.

Source: Civil Rights Congress, *We Charge Genocide: The Historic Petition to the United Nations for Relief From a Crime of The United States Government Against the Negro People* (New York: Civil Rights Congress, 1951), pp. xi–xiii, 3–10. Reproduced with permission from Civil Rights Congress, 1951. © 1970 International Publishers. Also see BlackPast.org, an online reference guide to African American history.

6 African Americans Petition the President and the American Delegation to the United Nations, 1952

"we share the world-wide concern for finding the way to peace"

The similarities between white supremacy exercised in the United States and colonial power exerted by European nations over their territories linked the interests of African Americans with people of color around the world. After World War II, as Western and Eastern powers carved the globe into spheres of influence, colonized peoples from Africa, Asia, and Latin America brought to the United Nations their claims for self-determination and independence. There, despite public declarations about freedom, the United States – in collaboration with Western allies – maneuvered to deny such demands, consequently revealing clear hypocrisies in American foreign policy. Against the wishes of nations, Western powers expanded military footprints in South Asia, North Africa, and the Middle East, and allowed – if not endorsed – the white minority government of South Africa to impose apartheid on that nation's black majority. In the following document, a group of black leaders – among them W. E. B. Du Bois, Mary Church Terrell, Sidney Poitier, and Paul

*Robeson – petitioned President Dwight D. Eisenhower and the American
delegation to the United Nations, naming specific examples of actions taken by
the United States which, the petitioners believed, contradicted Western
articulations of democratic principles and threatened world peace.*

As human beings we share the world-wide concern for finding the way to
peace. As Americans we share the common concern of our fellow citizens as
to our country's foreign policy and where it is leading us. As Negroes we
have deep bonds of sympathy, growing out of a common experience of
suffering and struggle, with the two-thirds of the world that is called colored
and which has been or still remains under the domination of the United
States, Great Britain, France and other countries in what is called the Western
World.

We address this petition to you, Mr. President, and to this government's
Delegation to the United Nations, because we believe that the policy our
government is pursuing with respect to these hundred of millions of subject
people in Africa, Asia, the Pacific, and the Caribbean – a policy reflected in
the status of this country's own Negro citizens – will decisively determine
the issue of world war or world peace.

This petition is motivated by what in our view is the indefensible position
on several important questions taken by the United States Delegation to the
United Nations General Assembly meeting in Paris, and also by certain
recent Presidential pronouncements.

First, we deplore the fact that the United States Delegation has again, as
in previous sessions of the U.N. General Assembly, refused to support the
forthright condemnation of the vicious system of racial discrimination
practiced by the government of the Union of South Africa. While the
majority of the U.N. members assailed South Africa's "apartheid" policy,
exemplified by the Group Areas Act, and urged suspension of that law
pending settlement of the South African-Indian dispute, the United States
Delegation abstained.

...

Does the United States Delegation's stand on these matters perhaps arise
from fear of U.N. exposure and criticism of discriminatory practices in the
United States? Or is it because of the close financial ties between this
country and South Africa? Dr. Malan's government, a fascist government,
has lately been the beneficiary of substantial United States loans from New
York banks and through the International Bank for Reconstruction and
Development. And were it not for the gold which the United States takes

from South Africa – not to mention manganese, uranium ore, copper and other minerals and raw materials – and were it not for the large investments of American corporations in that country, it is generally agreed that South Africa's slave-labor economy would quickly collapse.

Secondly, we deplore the major role played by the United States Delegation to the Paris U.N. General Assembly meeting in forcing through the decision of that body not to take up consideration of the Moroccan charges brought against France. According to the *N.Y. Times* (Dec. 4, 1951), Sir Mohammed Zafrullah Khan, Pakistani Prime Minister, told the U.N. delegates that the United States representative would have to bear responsibility for the further shedding of Moroccan blood.

The Western powers, he observed, always supported the general principle of freedom for colonial peoples but almost invariably voted against specific implementation of the principle; whereas the Eastern European countries has won the gratitude of Asian countries by always supporting such implementation.

Did not this American support of the French on the Moroccan question result from the fact that it was with the French government, and without consultation or the consent of the Moroccan people, that the United States government negotiated for the construction of a network of U.S. air bases in Morocco estimated to cost a half billion dollars ...

As in Morocco[,] so in other areas United States political policy has been dictated by United States military objectives – to the detriment of the interest of the inhabitants ... The U.N. grant of "independence" to Libya was in effect bought with agreements for the long-term maintenance by the United States of its Wheelus Air Base in Tripoli and for continued occupation of the territory by U.S.-British-French military forces.

Third, we are deeply disturbed, Mr. President, by the communiqué of January 9, 1952, on your talks with Mr. Churchill, with reference to "a complete identity of aims between us" with regard to the Middle East, and to your agreement to "continue to work out together agreed policies to give effect to this aim." We ask whether this can mean anything except the continued application of pressure by every possible means, including the use of military force in Egypt, in order to maintain Anglo-American influence and economic and military dominance in Iran, Egypt, and other Middle Eastern countries now striving for independence.

"Some United States Middle Eastern experts," says *Business Week* (Oct. 27, 1951), "feel that the only policy that would have a chance of success now would be a barefaced return to old-fashioned gunboat imperialism – sugar coated with a lot of economic assistance." Is this the agreed-upon Anglo-American policy, Mr. President?

A leading Negro newspaper, the *Afro-American* (Nov. 3, 1951), commenting editorially on our government's support of Britain in Iran and Egypt, states: "It appears that neither England nor the United States seems to be interested in the fundamental right of these darker nations to be supreme in their own territories and compel all foreigners to leave, if that is their desire."

…

Fourth, we object to the continued alliance of the United States with Britain, France, and other colonial powers in the Trusteeship Committee at the Paris U.N. Assembly meeting in opposition, as at previous sessions, to various proposals for the advancement of the interests of colonial peoples. *The N.Y. Times* (Jan. 16, 1952) reports that a "unique" development of the Paris meetings was the fact that "the small nations took the initiative and carried a series of resolutions on dependencies that at best are unwelcome to the Western Powers."

Among the colonial resolutions opposed or not supported by the United States Delegation was one asking the nations administering the U.N. trust territories to set deadlines for the independence of those areas. This has been repeatedly demanded ever since the establishment of the trusteeship system, and repeatedly opposed and defeated by the colony-holding powers. Here is one instance of what Sir Zafrullah referred to as the readiness of the Western Powers to endorse the general principle of colonial liberation while consistently opposing action on specific issues toward that end.

Fifth, we regard it as a deplorable backward step that the United States at the Paris U.N. meeting won its fight by the narrow margin of 30 to 24 votes, to exclude economic and social rights from the proposed U.N. Covenant on Human Rights, to be left for inclusion in a separate and later covenant. The United States Delegation argued that to include economic, social and cultural rights in the same covenant with political rights would prevent some countries from ratifying the instrument because state-guaranteed economic rights tended in the direction of the welfare state.

This seems to us to be an evident effort to appease the Dixiecrat and other reactionary elements in our government who have for so long blocked enactment of effective Fair Employment Practices legislation. We believe with the opponents of the United States position that political freedom is impaired if not negated unless it is accompanied by effective guarantees of economic and social freedom. The Negro people in the United States certainly know this.

Another instance of apparent appeasement of the anti-democratic forces in the United States is the insistence of the American Delegation upon inserting a qualifying provision in the Covenant of Human Rights virtually relieving federal governments, such as the United States, of responsibility for violations of the Covenant in the component units of the federal government – for example the state of Florida or Mississippi.

...

The Negro people of the United States are deeply concerned with the achievement of effective international safe-guards for human rights – for themselves and for darker peoples throughout the world who are the victims of racist doctrines of white supremacy. From this racism stems the failure of our government to protect the lives and rights of its Negro citizens – in Cicero, Illinois; in Groveland and Mims, Florida; and from it stems also the inhuman repression of non-white persons in Asia and Africa by the Western Powers. Those non-white peoples most assuredly want none of the "American way of life" experienced by 15 million Negro Americans. Nor can the continued rule of racism in the United States be ended as long as the enslavement of darker peoples throughout the world continues.

In your recent State of the Union Message, Mr. President, you declared, "The peoples of Asia want to be free to follow their own way of life." We agree whole-heartedly, and we would add that the peoples of Africa, the Caribbean, Latin America and other lands want the same. However, the quoted sentence in its context actually meant that the peoples of Asia must be "free" to remain within the Western sphere of influence. It seems to us truly extraordinary that in both your state of the Union and Budget Messages to Congress you could deal with the subject of hunger and need of the Asian and other peoples without once even mentioning the root of their miserable condition – namely, their long-suffering subjection to Western economic and colonial overlords.

In the above-mentioned Messages to Congress you placed great emphasis, Mr. President, upon the aid programs which the United States can provide for economically backward peoples. But, as is well known, these same peoples have a deep suspicion of this aid; ... [they have] a popular saying that their overlords were willing to do most anything for them except get off their backs. These peoples realize that in order to use economic or other assistance for its *own* benefit, a nation must first of all be free to determine its *own* economic and social goals. As an African leader has recently said, "Self-government and independence must be the initial capital to be invested in the non-self-governing territories."

We submit, Sir, that though it may be possible for the Western Powers to find and bribe puppet-spokesmen among oppressed nations, it is impossible to either bribe or coerce whole peoples whose national consciousness and will to freedom have become articulate. This is the inescapable meaning of national revolts today sweeping Asia, the Middle East, and Africa.

If America's name is not to be hated throughout the world wherever people struggle for liberty, our government must completely revise its foreign policy and give concrete evidence, through its conduct in the United Nations and in all areas of international economic, political, and military relations, of its genuine and unequivocal support of the principle of national self-determination.

The policy now pursued, the policy of bribery and coercion to make the American or Western way of life prevail, can lead only to national and international disaster. This policy if continued, we believe, will surely lead only to more Koreas. Peace cannot be won with either guns or dollars. The only conceivable world of lasting peace is a world of free peoples living together in mutual cooperation, equality and respect.

WE PETITION YOU to work to build such a world. We urge:

1. that our government go on record condemning, as a flagrant violation of human rights and serious threat to world peace, the racist program of the government of the Union of South Africa exemplified in the Group Areas Act, and that it use its full influence to press for the South African government's adherence to the recommendation of the United Nations respecting South West Africa and the grievances of the Indians in South Africa.
2. that our government seek the fullest and speediest implementation of the Charter provisions and recommendations of the United Nations relating to the advancement of the welfare and freedom of colonial peoples;
3. that our government strive for the creation and adoption of the U.N. Covenant of Human Rights which will provide truly effective protection of the economic, social, civil and political rights of all peoples in all countries;
4. that our government lend its full support to the fulfillment of the demands for national self-determination voiced by subject peoples in Africa and all other areas of the world, and that it withhold assistance of any kind from any government engaged in suppressing such demands;
5. that our government and all other governments withdraw their military forces and installations from all foreign territories where their presence is not authorized by agreement of all the major powers;
6. that our government, together with other major powers, undertake sincere and serious efforts toward reaching general agreement so that the world of lasting peace which we seek may become a glorious reality.

Source: "A Petition to the President of the United States and the U.S. Delegation to the United Nations," reproduced with permission from Herbert Aptheker (ed.), *A Documentary History of the Negro People in the United States*, Volume 6 (reprint, New York: Citadel Press, 1993), pp. 98–105. Courtesy of B. Aptheker.

Questions for Consideration

How did African Americans weigh the importance of patriotism and unity at a
  time of national emergency against the demands of their own group interests?
Why did FDR respond to the March on Washington Movement's pressure?
As the United States took on a more muscular international role during and after
  World War II, how did the strategies and approaches of African American
  political organizations shift?
Why did African Americans petition the United Nations? Why did they use the
  charge "genocide"? What did they hope to achieve?
In the 1952 petition to Eisenhower and the US delegation to the UN, African
  Americans argued that true political freedom was impossible to achieve without
  social and economic freedom. In what ways do the experiences of black
  Americans support or contradict this assertion?

Bibliography

Anderson, Carol. *Eyes off the Prize: The United Nations and the African American
  Struggle for Human Rights, 1944–1955.* New York: Cambridge University Press,
  2003.
Biondi, Martha. *To Stand and Fight: The Struggle for Civil Rights in Post-War
  New York City.* Cambridge, MA: Harvard University Press, 2006.
Buchanan, A. Russell. *Black Americans in World War II.* Santa Barbara, CA: Clio
  Books, 1983.
Gore, Dayo F. *Radicalism at the Crossroads: African American Women Activists in
  the Cold War.* New York: New York University Press, 2011.
Katznelson, Ira. *When Affirmative Action Was White: An Untold History of Racial
  Inequality in Twentieth Century America.* New York: W. W. Norton, 2005.
Korstad, Robert Rodgers. *Civil Rights Unionism: Tobacco Workers and the Struggle
  for Democracy in the Mid-Twentieth Century South.* Chapel Hill: University of
  North Carolina Press, 2007.
McGuire, Phillip, ed. *Taps of a Jim Crow Army: Letters from Black Soldiers in World
  War II.* Lexington: University Press of Kentucky, 1993.
Moye, J. Todd, ed. *Freedom Flyers: The Tuskegee Airmen of World War II: An Oral
  History.* New York: Oxford University Press, 2010.
Plummer, Brenda Gayle. *Rising Wind: Black Americans and U.S. Foreign Affairs,
  1935–1960.* Chapel Hill: University of North Carolina Press, 1996.
Savage, Barbara. *Broadcasting Freedom: Radio, War, and the Politics of Race, 1938–48.*
  Chapel Hill: University of North Carolina Press, 1999.
von Eshen, Penny. *Race Against Empire: Black Americans and Anti-Colonialism,
  1937–1957.* Ithaca: Cornell University Press, 1999.

Chapter 7   Discontent, 1953–1959

In *Smith v. Allwright* (1944), argued by the NAACP, the Supreme Court struck down southern Democrats' practice of racial exclusion in state primaries. But when a group of black vets including Medgar Evers (1925–1963), head of the Mississippi NAACP, attempted to register to vote, he and his colleagues met a mob of armed whites determined to bar them from the polls. Against Harry S. Truman's support for expanded civil rights, South Carolina Senator Strom Thurmond mounted an alternative candidacy in 1948 on a segregationist platform. In the face of white defiance and inaction African Americans expanded the black freedom struggle, launching concurrent challenges through court cases, voting campaigns, and targeted demonstrations.

From site to site, local people responded to the circumstances of particular places. For example, *Brown v. Board of Education* (1954) was composed of five local cases. *Davis v. County School Board of Prince Edward County* came out of Virginia where high school student Barbara Johns called a student strike to protest inadequate facilities for blacks. In the case from Washington, DC, *Bolling v. Sharpe*, parents had tried to transfer their students from an overcrowded black school to an underutilized white school, and were denied. Two cases, *Bulah v. Gebhart* (Delaware) and *Briggs v. Elliot* (South Carolina), began when local school boards denied black parents' requests for bus transportation. In Topeka, Kansas, Linda Brown, barred from the white school seven blocks from home, had to walk a mile to the nearest black school.

African American Voices: A Documentary Reader from Emancipation to the Present, First Edition. Edited by Leslie Brown.
© 2014 John Wiley & Sons, Inc. Published 2014 by John Wiley & Sons, Inc.

Brown v. Board of Education was a momentous victory in black Americans' drive for equal education. But desegregation only ran one way; select black students could attend some white schools. African Americans cheered, but also sustained their doubts about the process. Anthropologist and writer Zora Neale Hurston (1891–1960) – who had exemplified the inclinations of Harlem Renaissance artists by turning to ordinary African Americans for the substance of her work – questioned the decision. Writing to the *Orlando Sentinel*, Hurston asserted, "The whole matter revolves around the self-respect of my people. How much satisfaction can I get from a court order for somebody to associate with me who does not wish me near them?"

In the meantime, in Montgomery, Alabama, the Women's Political Council organized a boycott of public transportation. Once it was launched, in December 1955, it lasted a year and most of the protesters were black women domestics. Out of Montgomery, Martin Luther King, Jr., emerged as a prominent leader, with a message that linked the social gospel of Christianity to the morality of righteous action against unjust laws and then to Constitutional principles. In 1957 King founded an organization of black ministers, the Southern Christian Leadership Conference (SCLC), to assist with local demonstration and to encourage African Americans' efforts to achieve citizenship rights. SCLC's signature, however, was its commitment to mass demonstrations utilizing non-violence.

Philosophically, King argued, non-violence extended to a personal commitment to the redemptive power of love. The language alone, as yet unheard in American racial rhetoric, proved inspirational. Tactically, non-violence operated as non-cooperation with unjust laws. Psychologically, passive resistance disconcerted the perpetrator in tense situations. Still, non-violence did not stop the battering rams of white resistance. In Monroe, North Carolina, where the public swimming pool banned African Americans, Robert F. Williams, a veteran and president of the Monroe NAACP, led a series of protests in 1957, asking initially not for integration but for a day set aside when black people could use the facility. Whites responded with direct assaults on peaceful demonstrators whom police refused to protect. Nor would law enforcement stop the Ku Klux Klan from terrorizing Monroe's black neighborhoods. Drawing on his military experience, Williams organized local blacks to arm themselves in defense. Faced with black resistance, white violence in Monroe subsided.

Whatever infrastructural changes were underway in terms of race in American institutions during the 1950s, white opposition persisted. As the 1950s closed, the distinctions between the non-violent philosophy articulated by King and armed self-defense maintained by Williams revealed the breadth of perspectives present within the black freedom movement. African Americans continued to incorporate new methods of confrontation in their struggle, even as they realized that bloodshed might follow.

1 Thurgood Marshall Reargues *Brown v. Board of Education*, 1953

"the Fourteenth Amendment prevents states from according differential treatment to American children on the basis of their color or race"

Brown v. Board of Education *was the culmination of several strategies grounded in an historic struggle for civil rights: first, on the part of Howard University Law School's program to train lawyers as social engineers, dedicated to creating Constitutional changes through legal challenges; second, on the part of the NAACP and its Legal Defense Fund's work to set precedents that dismantled segregation in graduate and professional schools in the 1930s and 1940s; third, on the part of social sciences researchers who brought new analyses to bear on racial issues; and finally, and most importantly, on the part of individual students, families, and communities willing to challenge white authorities on the local level.*

Howard Law graduate Thurgood Marshall (1908–1993) of the NAACP Legal Defense Fund argued the landmark case. The brief excerpted below, written for a second round in 1953, reiterates the central point of the case, notes that the fact of – and rationale for – inequality had been established in earlier cases (for example, Sweatt and McLaurin, as noted here), and answers a central question posed to the plaintiffs by the Court: In proposing the Fourteenth Amendment, did Congress at the time understand that the Amendment would prohibit racial segregation in public schools? The NAACP legal team's historical research answered convincingly. Finally, the brief argues that there was no reason for the Court to delay implementation of an affirmative decision. Brown carried far-reaching and immediate consequences not only for public education as a core institution of American society, but also with regard to public accommodations.

Oliver Brown, et al. v. Board of Education, et al., 347 U.S. 483

...

The substantive question common to all is whether a state can, consistently with the Constitution, exclude children, solely on the ground that they are Negroes, from public schools which otherwise they would be qualified to attend. It is the thesis of this brief, submitted on behalf of the excluded children, that the answer to the question is in the negative: the Fourteenth Amendment prevents states from according differential treatment to American children on the basis of their color or race ...

Denying this thesis, the school authorities, relying in part on language originating in this Court's opinion in *Plessy v. Ferguson*, 163 U.S. 537, urge that exclusion of Negroes, qua Negroes, from designated public schools is permissible when the excluded children are afforded admittance to other schools especially reserved for Negroes, qua Negroes, if such schools are equal.

...

The importance to our American democracy of the substantive question can hardly be overstated. The question is whether a nation founded on the proposition that "all men are created equal" is honoring its commitments to grant "due process of law" and "the equal protection of the laws" to all within its borders when it, or one of its constituent states, confers or denies benefits on the basis of color or race.

1. Distinctions drawn by state authorities on the basis of color or race violate the Fourteenth Amendment, *Shelley v. Kraemer*, 334 U.S. 1; *Buchanan v. Warley*, 245 U.S. 60. This has been held to be true even as to the conduct of public educational institutions. *Sweatt v. Painter*, 339 U.S. 629; *McLaurin v. Oklahoma State Regents*, 339 U.S. 637. Whatever other purposes the Fourteenth Amendment may have had, it is indisputable that its primary purpose was to complete the emancipation provided by the Thirteenth Amendment by ensuring to the Negro equality before the law. The Slaughter House Cases, 16 Wall. 36; *Strauder v. West Virginia*, 100 U.S. 303.

2. Even if the Fourteenth Amendment did not per se invalidate racial distinctions as a matter of law, the racial segregation challenged in the instant cases would run afoul of the conventional test established for application of the equal protection clause because the racial classifications here have no reasonable relation to any valid legislative purpose ...

3. Appraisal of the facts requires rejection of the contention of the school authorities. The educational detriment involved in racially constricting a student's associations has already been recognized by this Court. *Sweatt v. Painter*, 339 U.S. 629; *McLaurin v. Oklahoma State Regents*, 339 U.S. 637.

4. The argument that the requirements of the Fourteenth Amendment are met by providing alternative schools rests, finally, on reiteration of the separate but equal doctrine enunciated in *Plessy v. Ferguson*.

    Were these ordinary cases, it might be enough to say that the *Plessy* case can be distinguished – that it involved only segregation in transportation. But these are not ordinary cases, and in deference to their importance it seems more fitting to meet the Plessy doctrine head-on and to declare that doctrine erroneous.

Candor requires recognition that the plain purpose and effect of seg-regated education is to perpetuate an inferior status for Negroes which is America's sorry heritage from slavery. But the primary purpose of the Fourteenth Amendment was to deprive the states of all power to perpet-uate such a caste system.

5. The first and second of the five questions propounded by this Court requested enlightenment as to whether the Congress which submitted, and the state legislatures and conventions which ratified, the Fourteenth Amendment contemplated or understood that it would prohibit segre-gation in public schools, either of its own force or through subsequent legislative or judicial action. The evidence, both in Congress and in the legislatures of the ratifying states, reflects the substantial intent of the Amendment's proponents and the substantial understanding of its opponents that the Fourteenth Amendment would, of its own force, proscribe all forms of state-imposed racial distinctions, thus necessarily including all racial segregation in public education.

The Fourteenth Amendment was actually the culmination of the determined efforts of the Radical Republican majority in Congress to incorporate into our fundamental law the well-defined equalitarian principle of complete equality for all without regard to race or color. The debates in the 39th Congress and succeeding Congresses clearly reveal the intention that the Fourteenth Amendment would work a rev-olutionary change in our state-federal relationship by denying to the states the power to distinguish on the basis of race.

The Civil Rights Bill of 1866, as originally proposed, possessed scope sufficiently broad in the opinion of many Congressmen to entirely destroy all state legislation based on race. A great majority of the Republican Radicals – who later formulated the Fourteenth Amendment – understood and intended that the Bill would prohibit segregated schools. Opponents of the measure shared this understanding. The scope of this legislation was narrowed because it was known that the Fourteenth Amendment was in process of preparation and would itself have scope exceeding that of the original draft of the Civil Rights Bill.

6. The evidence makes clear that it was the intent of the proponents of the Fourteenth Amendment, and the substantial understanding of its oppo-nents, that it would, of its own force, prohibit all state action predicated upon race or color. The intention of the framers with respect to any specific example of caste state action – in the instant cases, segregated

education – cannot be determined solely on the basis of a tabulation of contemporaneous statements mentioning the specific practice. The framers were formulating a constitutional provision setting broad standards for determination of the relationship of the state to the individual. In the nature of things they could not list all the specific categories of existing and prospective state activity which were to come within the constitutional prohibitions. The broad general purpose of the Amendment – obliteration of race and color distinctions – is clearly established by the evidence. So far as there was consideration existing, both proponents and opponents of the Amendment understood that it would proscribe all racial segregation in public education.

7. While the Amendment conferred upon Congress the power to enforce its prohibitions, members of the 39th Congress and those of subsequent Congresses made it clear that the framers understood and intended that the Fourteenth Amendment was self-executing and particularly pointed out that the federal judiciary had authority to enforce its prohibitions without Congressional implementation.

8. The evidence as to the understanding of the states is equally convincing. Each of the eleven states that had seceded from the Union ratified the Amendment, and concurrently eliminated racial distinctions from its laws, and adopted a constitution free of requirement or specific authorization of segregated schools. Many rejected proposals for segregated schools, and none enacted a school segregation law until after readmission. The significance of these facts is manifest from the consideration that ten of these states, which were required, as a condition of readmission, to ratify the Amendment and to modify their constitutions and laws in conformity therewith, considered that the Amendment required them to remove all racial distinctions from their existing and prospective laws, including those pertaining to public education.

Twenty-two of the twenty-six Union states also ratified the Amendment. Although unfettered by Congressional surveillance, the overwhelming majority of the Union states acted with an understanding that it prohibited racially segregated schools and necessitated conformity of their school laws to secure consistency with that understanding.

9. In short, the historical evidence fully sustains this Court's conclusion in the Slaughter House Cases, 16 Wall. 36, 81, that the Fourteenth Amendment was designed to take from the states all power to enforce caste or class distinctions.

10. The Court … assumes that segregation is declared unconstitutional and inquires as to whether relief should be granted immediately or gradually. Appellants, recognizing the possibility of delay of a purely

administrative character, do not ask for the impossible. No cogent reasons justifying further exercise of equitable discretion, however, have as yet been produced.

It has been indirectly suggested in the briefs and oral argument of appellees that some such reasons exist. Two plans were suggested by the United States in its Brief as Amicus Curiae. We have analyzed each of these plans as well as appellees' briefs and oral argument and find nothing there of sufficient merit on which this Court, in the exercise of its equity power, could predicate a decree permitting an effective gradual adjustment from segregated to non-segregated school systems. Nor have we been able to find any other reasons or plans sufficient to warrant the exercise of such equitable discretion in these cases. Therefore, in the present posture of these cases, appellants are unable to suggest any compelling reasons for this Court to postpone relief.

Source: Appellant Brief in *Brown v. Board of Education*, reargued December 8, 1953, from *Brown v. Board of Education*, in Gerhard Casper and Kathleen Sullivan (eds.), *Landmark Briefs and Arguments of the Supreme Court of the United States: Constitutional Law* (UPA Collections, Lexis-Nexis). Reprinted by permission of ProQuest LLC. Further reproduction prohibited. www.proquest.com.

2 The Montgomery Bus Boycott, 1955

"Another Negro woman has been arrested and thrown into jail"

The Women's Political Council, a black women's organization in Montgomery, Alabama, already had outlined plans for a bus boycott when Rosa Parks (1913–2005) was arrested in December 1955 for refusing to give up her seat so a white man could sit. The three documents below illustrate how the event unfolded.

A Letter from the Women's Political Council to the Mayor of Montgomery, 1954

Dear Sir:

The Women's Political Council is very grateful to you and the City Commissioners for the hearing you allowed our representatives during the month of March, 1954, when the "city-busfare-increase case" was being reviewed. There were several things the Council asked for:

1. A city law that would make it possible for Negroes to sit from back toward front, and whites from front toward back until all the seats are taken;
2. That Negroes not be asked or forced to pay fare at front and go to the rear of the bus to enter;
3. That busses stop at every corner in residential sections occupied by Negroes as they do in communities where whites reside.

We are happy to report that busses have been stopping at more corners now in some sections where Negroes live than previously. However, the same practices in seating and boarding the bus continue.

Mayor [W. A.] Gayle, three-fourths of the riders of these public conveyances are Negroes. If Negroes did not patronize them, they could not possibly operate. More and more of our people are already arranging with neighbors and friends to ride to keep from being insulted and humiliated by bus drivers.

There has been talk from twenty-five or more local organizations of planning a city-wide boycott of busses. We, sir, do not feel that forceful measures are necessary in bargaining for a convenience which is right for all bus passengers. We, the Council, believe that when this matter has been put before you and the Commissioners, that agreeable terms can be met in a quiet and sensible manner to the satisfaction of all concerned.

Many of our Southern cities in neighboring states have practiced the policies we seek without incident whatsoever. Atlanta, Macon and Savannah in Georgia have done this for years. Even Mobile, in our own state, does this and all the passengers are satisfied.

Please consider this plea, and if possible, act favorably upon it, for even now plans are being made to ride less, or not at all, on our busses. We do not want this.

Respectfully yours,

The Women's Political Council
Jo Ann Robinson, President

Leaflet Announcing the Boycott

This is for Monday, December 5, 1955

Another Negro woman has been arrested and thrown into jail because she refused to get up out of her seat on the bus for a white person to sit down.

It is the second time since the Claudette Colbert case that a Negro woman has been arrested for the same thing. This has to be stopped.

Negroes have rights, too, for if Negroes did not ride the buses, they could not operate. Three-fourths of the riders are Negroes, yet we are arrested, or have to stand over empty seats. If we do not do something to stop these arrests, they will continue. The next time it may be you, or your daughter, or mother.

This woman's case will come up on Monday. We are, therefore, asking every Negro to stay off the buses Monday in protest of the arrest and trial. Don't ride the buses to work, to town, to school, or anywhere on Monday.

You can afford to stay out of school for one day if you have no other way to go except by bus.

You can also afford to stay out of town for one day. If you work, take a cab, or walk. But please, children and grown-ups, don't ride the bus at all on Monday. Please stay off all buses.

Memo to the City Council, 1956

NEGROES' MOST URGENT NEEDS

FOLLOWING ARE A FEW OF THE MOST URGENT NEEDS OF OUR PEOPLE. IMMEDIATE ATTENTION SHOULD BE GIVEN EACH OF THESE. WHAT IS YOUR STAND TOWARD THEM?

1. The present bus situation. Negroes have to stand over empty seats of city buses, because the first ten seats are reserved for whites who sometimes never ride. We wish to fill the bus from the back toward the front until <u>all</u> the seats are taken. This is done in Atlanta, Georgia, Mobile, Alabama, and in most of our larger southern cities.
2. Negro Representation on the Parks and Recreation Board. Our parks are in a deplorable condition. We have protested, yet nothing has been done toward improving them. Juvenile delinquency continues to increase. In many instances these children are not responsible. The city is. Nobody knows better than Negroes what their needs are.
3. Sub-division for housing. Just recently a project for a sub-division for Negroes was presented before the City commission for approval. Protests from whites and other objections prevented the development. There is no section wherein Negroes can expand to build decent homes. What of Lincoln Heights?
4. Jobs for qualified Negroes. Certain civil service jobs are not open to Negroes, yet many are qualified. Negroes need jobs commensurate with their training. Everybody can not teach.

5. Negro representation on all boards affecting Negroes. Negroes are tax-payers; they are property owners or renters. They constitute about fifty percent of the city's population. Many boards determine their destinies without any kind of representation whatsoever. Only Negroes are qualified to represent themselves adequately and properly.
6. Congested areas, with inadequate or no fireplugs. Fire hazards are inviting.
7. Lack of sewage disposals make it necessary to resort to out-door privies, which is a health hazard.
8. Narrow streets, lack of curbing, unpaved streets in some sections. Immediate action should be taken on this traffic hazard.

Gentlemen, what is your stand on these issues? What will you do to improve these undemocratic practices? Your stand on these issues will enable us to better decide on whom we shall cast our ballot in the March election.

Very truly yours,

Montgomery Negroes

Source: Reproduced from Jo Ann Gibson Robinson with David Garrow, *The Montgomery Bus Boycott and the Women Who Started It: The Memoir of Jo Ann Gibson Robinson* (Knoxville: University of Tennessee Press, 1987).

3 Rev. Dr. Martin Luther King, Jr., Writes on Non-Violence, 1957

"Violence solves no social problems"

A range of activist personalities influenced Martin Luther King, Jr., including Bayard Rustin, a noted black pacifist who possessed a deep history of non-violent direct action. Encouraged to embrace non-violence not just as a strategy, but as a philosophy and a force, King, a scholar as well as a minister, published the document below in the Christian Century.

"Nonviolence and Racial Justice"

It is commonly observed that the crisis in race relations dominates the arena of American life. This crisis has been precipitated by two factors: the determined resistance of reactionary elements in the south to the Supreme Court's momentous decision outlawing segregation in the public schools, and the radical change in the Negro's evaluation of himself. While southern legislative halls ring with open defiance through "interposition" and "nullification," while a modern version of the Ku Klux Klan has arisen in the form of "respectable" white citizens' councils, a revolutionary change has taken place in the Negro's conception of his own nature and destiny. Once he thought of himself as an inferior and patiently accepted injustice and exploitation. Those days are gone.

This new self-respect and sense of dignity on the part of the Negro undermined the south's negative peace, since the white man refused to accept the change. The tension we are witnessing in race relations today can be explained in part by this revolutionary change in the Negro's evaluation of himself and his determination to struggle and sacrifice until the walls of segregation have been finally crushed by the battering rams of justice.

The determination of Negro Americans to win freedom from every form of oppression springs from the same profound longing for freedom that motivates oppressed peoples all over the world. The rhythmic beat of deep discontent in Africa and Asia is at the bottom a quest for freedom and human dignity on the part of people who have long been victims of colonialism. The struggle for freedom on the part of oppressed people in general and of the American Negro in particular has developed slowly and is not going to end suddenly. Privileged groups rarely give up their privileges without strong resistance. But when oppressed people rise up against oppression there is no stopping point short of full freedom. Realism compels us to admit that the struggle will continue until freedom is a reality for all the oppressed peoples of the world.

Hence the basic question which confronts the world's oppressed is: How is the struggle against the forces of injustice to be waged? There are two possible answers. One is resort to the all too prevalent method of physical violence and corroding hatred. The danger of this method is its futility. Violence solves no social problems; it merely creates new and more complicated ones.... The shores of history are white with the bleached bones of nations and communities that failed to follow this command. If the American Negro and other victims of oppression succumb to the temptation of using violence in the struggle for justice, unborn generations will live in a desolate night of bitterness, and their chief legacy will be an endless reign of chaos.

The alternative to violence is nonviolent resistance. This method was made famous in our generation by Mohandas K. Gandhi, who used it to free India from the domination of the British empire. Five points can be made concerning nonviolence as a method in bringing about better racial conditions.

First, this is not a method for cowards; it *does* resist. The nonviolent resister is just as strongly opposed to the evil against which he protests as is the person who uses violence. His method is passive or nonaggressive in the sense that he is not physically aggressive toward his opponent. But his mind and emotions are always active, constantly seeking to persuade the opponent that he is mistaken. This method is passive physically but strongly active spiritually; it is nonaggressive physically but dynamically aggressive spiritually.

A second point is that nonviolent resistance does not seek to defeat or humiliate the opponent, but to win his friendship and understanding. The nonviolent resister must often express his protest through noncooperation or boycotts, but he realizes that noncooperation and boycotts are not ends themselves; they are merely means to awaken a sense of moral shame in the opponent. The end is redemption and reconciliation. The aftermath of nonviolence is the creation of the beloved community, while the aftermath of violence is tragic bitterness.

A third characteristic of this method is that the attack is directed against forces of evil rather than against persons who are caught in those forces. It is evil we are seeking to defeat, not the persons victimized by evil. Those of us who struggle against racial injustice must come to see that the basic tension is not between races. As I like to say to the people in Montgomery, Alabama: "The tension in this city is not between white people and Negro people. The tension is at bottom between justice and injustice, between the forces of light and the forces of darkness. And if there is a victory it will be a victory not merely for 50,000 Negroes, but a victory for justice and the forces of light. We are out to defeat injustice and not white persons who may happen to be unjust."

A fourth point that must be brought out concerning nonviolent resistance is that it avoids not only external physical violence but also internal violence of spirit. At the center of nonviolence stands the principle of love. In struggling for human dignity the oppressed people of the world must not allow themselves to become bitter or indulge in hate campaigns. To retaliate with hate and bitterness would do nothing but intensify the hate in the world. Along the way of life, someone must have sense enough and morality enough to cut off the chain of hate. This can be done only by projecting the ethics of love to the center of our lives.

In speaking of love at this point, we are not referring to some sentimental emotion. It would be nonsense to urge men to love their oppressors in an affectionate sense. "Love" in this connection means understanding good will ... When we speak of loving those who oppose us ...; we speak of a love which is expressed in the Greek word *agape*. *Agape* means nothing sentimental or basically affectionate; it means understanding, redeeming good will for all men, an overflowing love which seeks nothing in return. It is the love of God working in the lives of men. When we love on the *agape* level we love men not because we like them, not because their attitudes and ways appeal to us, but because God loves them. Here we rise to the position of loving the person who does the evil deed while hating the deed he does.

Finally, the method of nonviolence is based on the conviction that the universe is on the side of justice. It is this deep faith in the future that causes the nonviolent resister to accept suffering without retaliation. He knows that in his struggle for justice he has cosmic companionship. This belief that God is on the side of truth and justice comes down to us from the long tradition of our Christian faith. There is something at the very center of our faith which reminds us that Good Friday may reign for a day, but ultimately it must give way to the triumphant beat of the Easter drums. Evil may so shape events that Caesar will occupy a palace and Christ a cross, but one day that same Christ will rise up and split history into A.D. and B.C., so that even the life of Caesar must be dated by his name. So in Montgomery we can walk and never get weary, because we know that there will be a great camp meeting in the promised land of freedom and justice.

This, in brief, is the method of nonviolent resistance. It is a method that challenges all people struggling for justice and freedom. God grant that we wage the struggle with dignity and discipline. May all who suffer oppression in this world reject the self-defeating method of retaliatory violence and choose the method that seeks to redeem. Through using this method wisely and courageously we will emerge from the bleak and desolate midnight of man's inhumanity to man into the bright daybreak of freedom and justice.

Source: Rev. Dr. Martin Luther King, Jr., "Nonviolence and Racial Justice," *Christian Century*, 74 (February 6, 1957), pp. 165–167. Reprinted by arrangement with The Heirs to the Estate of Martin Luther King, Jr., c/o Writers House as agent for the proprietor New York, NY. Copyright 1957 Dr. Martin Luther King, Jr.; copyright renewed 1995 Coretta Scott King.

4 Robert F. Williams Advocates Armed Self-Defense, 1959

"meeting violence with violence"

Robert F. Williams (1925–1996), a military veteran and leader of the NAACP in Monroe, North Carolina, embraced the use of non-violent direct action as a tactic. But he urged African Americans to arm themselves – a constitutional right – against the violent retaliation by whites, a position he espoused in the 1959 article excerpted below. His statement garnered enthusiastic support, but also brought him into conflict with the NAACP, which removed him from his post. In a debate published in 1959, Martin Luther King, Jr., responded to Williams, arguing, "There is more power in socially organized masses on the march than there is in guns in the hands of a few desperate men." Williams held his ground.

"Can Negroes Afford to Be Pacifists?"

...

Since my release from the Marine Corps I could cite many cases of unprovoked violence that have been visited upon my people. Some, like the Emmett Till case, the Asbury Howard case and the Mack Parker incident, have been widely publicized. There are more, many many more, occurring daily in the South that never come to the light of the press because of a news blackout sponsored by local racist officials.

Laws serve to deter crime and to protect the weak from the strong in civilized society. When there is a breakdown of law and the right of equal protection by constituted authority, where is the force of deterrent? It is the nature of people to respect law when it is just and strong. Only highly civilized and moral individuals respect the rights of others. The low-mentality bigots of the South have shown a wanton disregard for the wellbeing and rights of their fellowmen of color, but there is one thing that even the most savage beast respects, and that is force. Soft, polished words whispered into the ears of a brute make him all the more confused and rebellious against a society that is more than he can understand or feel secure in. The Southern brute respects only force. Non-violence is a very potent weapon when the opponent is civilized, but non-violence is no match or repellent for a sadist. I have great respect for the pacifist, that is, for the pure pacifist. I think a pure pacifist is one who resents violence against nations as well as individuals and is courageous enough to speak out against jingoistic governments (including his own) without an air of self-righteousness and pious moral individuality. I am not a pacifist and I am sure that I may safely say that most of my people are not. Passive resistance is a powerful weapon in gaining concessions from oppressors, but I venture to say that if Mack Parker had had an automatic shotgun at his disposal, he could have served as a great deterrent against lynching.

Rev. Martin Luther King is a great and successful leader of our race. The Montgomery bus boycott was a great victory for American democracy. However, most people have confused the issues facing the race. In Montgomery the issue was a matter of struggle for human dignity. Non-violence is made to order for that type of conflict. While praising the actions of those courageous Negroes who participated in the Montgomery affair, we must not allow the complete aspects of the Negro struggle throughout the South to be taken out of their proper perspective. In a great many localities in the South Negroes are faced with the necessity of combating savage violence. The struggle is for mere existence. The Negro is in a position of begging for life. There is no lawful deterrent against those who would do him violence. An open declaration of non-violence, or turn-the-other-cheekism is an invitation that the white racist brutes will certainly honor by brutal attack on cringing, submissive Negroes. It is time for the Negro in the South to reappraise his method of dealing with his ruthless oppressor.

In 1957 the Klan moved into Monroe and Union County. In the beginning we did not notice them much. Their numbers steadily increased to the point where in the local press reported as many as seventy-five hundred racists massed at one rally. They became so brazen that mile-long motorcades started invading the Negro community. These hooded thugs fired pistols from car windows, screamed, and incessantly blew their automobile horns. On one occasion they caught a Negro woman on the street and tried to force her to dance for them at gun-point. She escaped into the night, screaming and hysterical. They forced a Negro merchant to close down his business on direct orders from the Klan. Drivers of cars tried to run Negroes down when seen walking on the streets at night. Negro women were struck with missiles thrown from passing vehicles. Lawlessness was rampant. A Negro doctor was framed to jail on a charge of performing an abortion on a white woman. This doctor, who was vice-president of the National Association for the Advancement of Colored People, was placed in a lonely cell in the basement of a jail, although men prisoners are usually confined upstairs. A crowd of white men started congregating around the jail. It is common knowledge that a lynching was averted. We have had the usual threats of the Klan here, but instead of cowering, we organized an armed guard and set up a defense force around the doctor's house. On one occasion, we had to exchange gunfire with the Klan. Each time the Klan came on a raid they were led by police cars. We appealed to the President of the United States to have the Justice Department investigate the police. We appealed to Governor Luther Hodges. All our appeals to constituted law were in vain. Governor Hodges, in an underhanded way, defended the Klan. He publicly made a statement, to the press, that I had exaggerated Klan activity in Union County – despite the fact that they were operating openly and had gone so far as to build a Klan club-house and advertise meetings in the local press and on the radio.

A group of non-violent ministers met the city Board of Aldermen and pleaded with them to restrict the Klan from the colored community. The city fathers advised these cringing, begging Negro ministers that the Klan had constitutional rights to meet and organize in the same way as the N.A.A.C.P. Not having been infected by turn-the-other-cheekism, a group of Negroes who showed a willingness to fight, caused the city officials to deprive the Klan of its constitutional rights after local papers told of dangerous incidents between Klansmen and armed Negroes. Klan motorcades have been legally banned from the City of Monroe.

The possibility of tragedy's striking both sides of the tracks has caused a mutual desire to have a peaceful coexistence. The fact that any racial brutality may cause white blood to flow as well as Negro is lessening racial tension. The white bigots are sparing Negroes from brutal attack, not because of a new sense of morality, but because Negroes have adopted a policy of meeting violence with violence.

I think there is enough latitude in the struggle for Negro liberation for the acceptance of diverse tactics and philosophies. There is need for pacifists and non-pacifists. I think each freedom fighter must unselfishly contribute what he has to offer. I have been a soldier and a Marine. I have been trained in the way of violence. I have been trained to defend myself. Self-defense to a Marine is a reflex action. People like Rev. Martin Luther King have been trained for the pulpit. I think they would be as out of place in a conflict that demanded real violent action as I would in a pulpit praying for an indifferent God to come down from Heaven and rescue a screaming Mack Parker or Emmett Till from an ungodly howling mob. I believe if we are going to pray, we ought to pass the ammunition while we pray. If we are too pious to kill in our own self-defense, how can we have the heart to ask a Holy God to come down to this violent fray and smite down our enemies?

Three Centuries of Prayer

As a race, we have been praying for three hundred years. The N.A.A.C.P. boasts that it has fought against lynching for fifty years. A fifty-year fight without victory is not impressive to me. An unwritten anti-lynch law was initiated overnight in Monroe. It is strange that so-called Negro leaders have never stopped to think why a simple thing like an anti-lynch law in a supposedly democratic nation is next to impossible to get passed. Surely every citizen in a republic is entitled not to be lynched. To seek an anti-lynch law in the present situation is to seek charity. Individuals and governments are more inclined to do things that promote the general welfare and wellbeing of the populace. A prejudiced government and a prejudiced people are not going to throw a shield of protection around the very people in the South on whom they vent pent-up hatreds as scapegoats. When white people in the South start needing such a law, we will not even have to wait fifty days to get it.

On May 5, 1959, while president of the Union County branch of the National Association for the Advancement of Colored People, I made a statement to the United Press International after a trial wherein a white man was supposed to have been tried for kicking a Negro maid down a flight of stairs in a local white hotel. In spite of the fact that there was an eyewitness, the defendant failed to show up for his trial, [he] was completely exonerated. Another case in the same court involved a white man who had come to a pregnant Negro mother's home and attempted to rape her. In recorder's court the only defense offered for the defendant was that "he's not guilty. He was just drunk and having a little fun." Despite the fact that this pregnant Negro mother was brutally beaten and driven from her home because she refused to submit, and a white woman neighbor testified that the woman had come to her house excited, her clothes torn, her feet bare, and begging her for assistance, the court was unmoved. The defendant's wife was allowed to sit with him throughout the trial, and his attorney asked the jury if they thought this white man would leave "this beautiful white woman, the flower of life for this Negro woman." Some of the jurymen laughed and the defendant went free. This great miscarriage of justice left me sick inside, and I said then what I say now. I believe that Negroes must be willing to defend themselves, their women, their children and their homes. They must be willing to die and to kill in repelling their assailants. There is no Fourteenth Amendment, no equal protection under the law. Negroes *must* protect themselves. It is obvious that the federal government will not put an end to lynching; therefore it becomes necessary for us to stop lynching with violence. We must defend ourselves. Even though I made it known that I spoke as an individual American citizen, I was suspended by the N.A.A.C.P. for advocating violence …

It is obvious that the Negro leadership is caught in a terrible dilemma. It is trying to appease both white liberals who want to see Negro liberation given to us in eye-dropper doses; and the Negro masses, who are growing impatient and restive under brutal oppression. There is a new Negro coming into manhood on the American scene and an indifferent government must take cognizance of this fact. The Negro is becoming more militant, and pacifism will never be accepted wholeheartedly by the masses of Negroes so long as violence is rampant in Dixie. Even Negroes like King who profess to be pacifists are not pure pacifists and at times speak proudly of the Negro's role of violence in this violent nation's wars. In a speech at the N.A.A.C.P. convention, he said, "In spite of all of our oppression, we have never turned to a foreign ideology to solve our problems. Communism has never invaded our ranks. And now we are simply saying we want our freedom, we have stood with you in every crisis. For you, America, our sons died in the trenches of France, in the foxholes of Germany, on the beachheads of Italy and on the islands of Japan. And now, America, we are simply asking you to guarantee our freedom." King may not be willing to partake in expeditions of violence, but he has no compunction about cashing in on the spoils of war. There are too many Negro leaders who are afraid to talk violence against the violent racist, and are too weak-kneed to protest the warmongering of the atom-crazed politicians of Washington.

Some Negro leaders have cautioned me that if Negroes fight back, the racist will have cause to exterminate the race. How asinine can one get? This government is in no position to allow mass violence to erupt, let alone allow twenty million Negroes to be exterminated. I am not half so worried about being exterminated as I am about my children's growing up under oppression and being mentally twisted out of human proportions.

We live in perilous times in America, and especially in the South. Segregation is an expensive commodity, but liberty and democracy too, have their price. So often the purchase check of democracy must be signed in blood. Someone must be willing to pay the price, despite the scoffs from the Uncle Toms. I am told that patience is commendable and that we must never tire of waiting, yet it is instilled at an early age that men who violently and swiftly rise to oppose tyranny are virtuous examples to emulate. I have been taught by my government to fight, and if I find it necessary I shall do just that. All Negroes must learn to fight back, for nowhere in the annals of history does the record show a people delivered from bondage by patience alone.

Source: Reproduced with permission from Robert F. Williams, "Can Negroes Afford to Be Pacifists?" *Liberation*, 4 (September 1959), pp. 4–7.

Questions for Consideration

How did the variety of approaches – law suits, boycotts, voter registration drives, direct action protests, armed resistance – work together to advance the black freedom movement?

Thinking back to the Emancipation era and to World Wars I and II, connect the frustrations and expectations of black servicemen and women across time. How do the activities of black veterans like Medgar Evers and Robert F. Williams link to those concerns?

What is non-violence? What is armed self-defense? Given the realities of Jim Crow and massive white resistance to change (including the use of aggressive violence), debate the merits and drawbacks of each.

What roles are young people – teenagers and children – asked to play in 1950s freedom struggles?

In what ways was the freedom movement of the 1950s NOT a campaign against racial segregation?

Bibliography

Branch, Taylor. *Parting the Waters: America in the King Years, 1954–63*. New York: Simon and Schuster, 1988.

Dudziak, Mary L. *Cold War Civil Rights: Race and the Image of American Democracy*. Princeton: Princeton University Press, 2000.

Kluger, Richard. *Simple Justice: The History of Brown v. Board of Education and Black America's Struggle for Equality*. New York: Alfred A. Knopf, 1976.

Lewis, David Levering. *W. E. B. Du Bois, 1919–1963: The Fight for Equality and the American Century*. New York: Henry Holt, 2001.

McGuire, Danielle L. *At the Dark End of the Street: Black Women, Rape, and Resistance – A New History of the Civil Rights Movement from Rosa Parks to the Rise of Black Power*. New York: Vintage, 2011.

Patterson, James T. *Brown v. Board of Education: A Civil Rights Milestone and Its Troubled Legacy*. New York: Oxford University Press, 2001.

Robinson, JoAnn Gibson (with David J. Garrow). *The Montgomery Bus Boycott and the Women Who Started It: The Memoir of JoAnn Gibson Robinson*. Knoxville: University of Tennessee Press, 1987.

Savage, Barbara Dianne. *Your Spirits Walk Beside Us: The Politics of Black Religion*. Cambridge, MA: Belknap Press of Harvard University, 2008.

Tyson, Timothy B. *Radio Free Dixie: Robert F. Williams and the Roots of Black Power*. Chapel Hill: University of North Carolina Press, 1999.

Chapter 8   Revolt, 1960–1963

The sit-ins at the Woolworth's in Greensboro, North Carolina, on February 1, 1960, set off a mass movement that had been simmering. The approach had been utilized spottily before, for example, by Howard University students in 1942. This time the tactic exploded. Within weeks of the Greensboro action young blacks and some white allies repeated it across the South. Scornful whites escalated from rebuff to violence, and mass arrests ensued. But one wave of protesters removed was followed by another to take its place. Unmet demands for desegregation led to boycotts and marches. Media savvy as a generation, the students' demeanor projected seriousness of purpose and righteous intent. And the more brutal the white response, the more intensely they held their position.

The scale and rapidity of these protests surprised older civil rights activists and introduced a new phase. The students called it "the Movement." A new generation of impatient participants, insistent on change, drew on legacies of the past, but also generated new organizations, articulated new ideas, and deployed new strategies. The Student Nonviolent Coordinating Committee (SNCC), formed out of the wave of sit-ins, became the vanguard of this new freedom movement. Unable initially to decide between direct action against segregation in public accommodation or for voter registration campaigns, SNCC elected to do both, and more. Setting up field offices in cities and rural counties across the South, SNCC focused on issues relevant to those communities, joining local activists already at work while

African American Voices: A Documentary Reader from Emancipation to the Present,
First Edition. Edited by Leslie Brown.
© 2014 John Wiley & Sons, Inc. Published 2014 by John Wiley & Sons, Inc.

recruiting new participants. In Albany, Georgia, for instance, SNCC workers connected with members of the NAACP youth chapter. In Nashville, Tennessee, students organized as a group examining the principles of non-violence and passive resistance.

Along with SNCC, other groups coordinated local campaigns and regional efforts to push local and federal authorities to enforce civil rights. The Congress on Racial Equality (CORE) organized the Freedom Rides in 1961, a follow-up to a similar effort in the 1940s. The rides brought interracial groups of travelers onto interstate buses to test court decisions that prohibited segregated interstate transportation and facilities. The rides provoked horrendous violence that demanded federal intervention. In Birmingham, Alabama, the sit-in movement stalled, but a local organization called the Alabama Christian Movement for Human Rights (ACMHR) called on SCLC and Martin Luther King, Jr., to regenerate the efforts. Project C, the Children's Crusade, generated a series of children's marches. City police with dogs and firemen with hoses attacked the children, and the images splashed across international news. Declaring that the nation faced a moral crisis on the issue of black freedom, President John F. Kennedy proclaimed in 1963 that the movement was underway:

It cannot be met by repressive police action. It cannot be left to increased demonstrations in the streets. It cannot be quieted by token moves or talk. It is a time to act in the Congress, in your State and local legislative body and, above all, in all of our daily lives. It is not enough to pin the blame on others, to say this is a problem of one section of the country or another, or deplore the facts that we face. A great change is at hand, and our task, our obligation, is to make that revolution, that change, peaceful and constructive for all. Those who do nothing are inviting shame, as well as violence. Those who act boldly are recognizing right, as well as reality.

These "whirlwinds of revolt," as King described them in the "I Have a Dream" speech in 1963, forced the federal government to take action. Relentless white violence obliged the Justice Department to promise (if not provide) protection for protesters. But it was the courageous activists who worked on the ground who built a movement of collective action that demanded and compelled the federal government to pass new legislation. In 1964, President Lyndon B. Johnson signed a Civil Rights Act, legislation initially proposed by President John F. Kennedy, requiring desegregation in public accommodations. But southern authorities mostly ignored the law, and Jim Crow sustained its regime. What black people lacked in America was power. In the years that followed, that goal rose to the top of the black agenda.

1 Young Activists Form the Student Nonviolent Coordinating Committee (SNCC), 1960

"a genuine spirit of love and good-will"

SNCC began as a small, diverse group – 126 southern students from fifty-six sit-in centers, twelve states, and delegates from nineteen northern colleges – who in 1960 attended a meeting at Shaw University in Raleigh, North Carolina, organized by Ella Baker who worked with SCLC. SNCC transformed from a loose association of individuals and groups into a forceful "organization of organizers" that challenged the status quo. Its founding statement, printed below, foregrounds the organization's moral underpinnings, its members' sense of personal responsibility to each other as a part of the freedom struggle, and its embrace of non-violence. It seems modest against the organization's future accomplishments, including an aggressive voter registration project that changed electoral politics in the South and the nation.

Student Nonviolent Coordinating Committee Founding Statement, 1960

We affirm the philosophical or religious ideal of nonviolence as the foundation of our purpose, the presupposition of our belief, and the manner of our action.

Nonviolence, as it grows from the Judeo-Christian tradition, seeks a social order of justice permeated by love. Integration of human endeavor represents the crucial first step towards such a society.

Through nonviolence, courage displaces fear. Love transcends hate. Acceptance dissipates prejudice; hope ends despair. Faith reconciles doubt. Peace dominates war. Mutual regards cancel enmity. Justice for all overthrows injustice. The redemptive community supersedes immoral social systems.

By appealing to conscience and standing on the moral nature of human existence, nonviolence nurtures the atmosphere in which reconciliation and justice become actual possibilities.

Although each local group in this movement must diligently work out the clear meaning of this statement of purpose, each act or phase of our corporate effort must reflect a genuine spirit of love and good-will.

Source: "SNCC Founding Statement".

2 Ella Baker Reports on the Founding of SNCC, 1960

"they have a destined date with freedom"

Ella Baker (1903–1986) possessed profound ideas about the importance of politics and meaning of freedom. Her philosophy of "participatory democracy" influenced SNCC's strategies for community organizing: valuing the contributions, participation, and expertise of ordinary people; downplaying hierarchy; and directly addressing apprehension. In the document below, written for The Southern Patriot, *a liberal-leaning publication for readers interested in race relations, Baker offers her initial assessment of the students who founded SNCC.*

"Bigger Than a Hamburger"

Raleigh, NC – The Student Leadership Conference made it crystal clear that current sit-ins and other demonstrations are concerned with something much bigger than a hamburger or even a giant-sized Coke.

Whatever may be the difference in approach to their goal, the Negro and white students, North and South, are seeking to rid America of the scourge of racial segregation and discrimination – not only at lunch counters, but in every aspect of life.

In reports, casual conversations, discussion groups, and speeches, the sense and the spirit of the following statement that appeared in the initial newsletter of the students at Barber-Scotia College, Concord, N.C., were re-echoed time and again:

> "We want the world to know that we no longer accept the inferior position of second-class citizenship. We are willing to go to jail, be ridiculed, spat upon and even suffer physical violence to obtain First Class Citizenship."

By and large, this feeling that they have a destined date with freedom, was not limited to a drive for personal freedom, or even freedom for the Negro in the South. Repeatedly it was emphasized that the movement was concerned with the moral implications of racial discrimination for the "whole world" and the "Human Race."

This universality of approach was linked with a perceptive recognition that "it is important to keep the movement democratic and to avoid struggles for personal leadership."

It was further evident that desire for supportive cooperation from adult leaders and the adult community was also tempered by apprehension that adults might try to "capture" the student movement. The students showed willingness to be met on the basis of equality, but were intolerant of anything that smacked of manipulation or domination.

This inclination toward group-centered leadership, rather than toward a leader-centered group pattern of organization, was refreshing indeed to those of the older group who bear the scars of the battle, the frustrations and the disillusionment that come when the prophetic leader turns out to have heavy feet of clay.

However hopeful might be the signs in the direction of group-centeredness, the fact that many schools and communities, especially in the South, have not provided adequate experience for young Negroes to assume initiative and think and act independently accentuated the need for guarding the student movement against well-meaning, but nevertheless unhealthy, over-protectiveness.

Here is an opportunity for adult and youth to work together and provide genuine leadership – the development of the individual to his highest potential for the benefit of the group.

Many adults and youth characterized the Raleigh meeting as the greatest or most significant conference of our period.

Whether it lives up to this high evaluation or not will, in a large measure, be determined by the extent to which there is more effective training in and understanding of non-violent principles and practices, in group dynamics, and in the re-direction into creative channels of the normal frustrations and hostilities that result from second-class citizenship.

Source: Reproduced from "Bigger Than a Hamburger" by Ella Baker, *The Southern Patriot*, May 1960.

3 Robert Moses Writes from Jail in Magnolia, Mississippi, 1961

"the middle of the iceberg"

Robert Parris Moses (b. 1935) was among the most influential of SNCC activists. Fearless and personally committed to non-violence, Moses attracted people through his fierce dedication to the struggle for civil rights and human dignity. Jailed in Magnolia, Mississippi, in 1961, with a cohort of fellow activists, he wrote the letter below to Tom Hayden, then leader of Students for a Democratic Society (SDS).

We are smuggling this note from the drunk tank of the county jail in Magnolia, Mississippi. Twelve of us are here, sprawled out along the concrete bunker; Curtis Hayes, Hollis Watkins, Ike Lewis, and Robert Talbert, four veterans of the bunker, are sitting up talking – mostly about girls; Charles McDew ("Tell the story") is curled into the concrete and the wall; Harold Robinson, Stephen Ashley, James Wells, Lee Chester Vick, Leotus Eubanks, and Ivory Diggs lay cramped on the cold bunker; I'm sitting with smuggled pen and paper, thinking a little, writing a little; Myrtis Bennett and Janie Campbell are across the way wedded to a different icy cubicle.

Later on Hollis will lead out with a clear tenor into a freedom song; Talbert and Lewis will supply jokes; and McDew will discourse on the history of the black man and the Jew. McDew – a black by birth, a Jew by choice, and a revolutionary by necessity – has taken on the deep hates and deep loves which America, and the world, reserves for those who dare to stand in a strong sun and cast a sharp shadow.

In the words of Judge Brumfield, who sentenced us, we are "cold calculators" who design to disrupt the racial harmony (harmonious since 1619) of McComb into racial strife and rioting; we, he said, are the leaders who are causing young children to be led like sheep to the pen to be slaughtered (in a legal manner). "Robert," he was addressing me, "haven't some of the people from your school been able to go down and register without violence here in Pike county?" I thought to myself that southerners are most exposed when they boast.

It's mealtime now: we have rice and gravy in a flat pan, dry bread and a "big town cake"; we lack eating and drinking utensils. Water comes from a faucet and goes into a hole.

This is Mississippi, the middle of the iceberg. Hollis is leading off with his tenor, "Michael, row the boat ashore, Alleluia; Christian brothers don't be slow, Alleluia; Mississippi's next to go, Alleluia." This is a tremor in the middle of the iceberg – from a stone that the builders rejected.

Source: Reproduced from Robert Moses, Letter from Magnolia County Jail to Tom Hayden (1961). Courtesy of R. Moses.

4 The Freedom Rides, 1961

"Jail, no bail"

The Supreme Court's decision in Boynton v. Virginia *(1960) outlawed segregated facilities on interstate routes. In 1961 CORE organized the "Freedom Rides" to test the decision. An interracial contingent left on two buses from Washington, DC, bound for Jackson, Mississippi. In Anniston, Alabama, one bus was bombed. In Birmingham, a mob of whites brutally*

*beat exiting riders including John Lewis of SNCC and white participant
James Peck. CORE considered calling off the rides, but, unwilling to accept
defeat, SNCC picked up the protest. Along the routes local white officials
arrested riders, but many elected to go to jail rather than accept bail. "Jail, no
bail" became the goal of the demonstration, to rebuke the criminal justice
system, to reveal the immorality of punishing individuals for exercising their
rights, and to undermine the force of a tactic that white authorities used not
only to stymie movement activists but also to repress blacks. Joined by
students from across the nation, Freedom Rides continued throughout the
year. The document below indicates multiple routes of the Rides.*

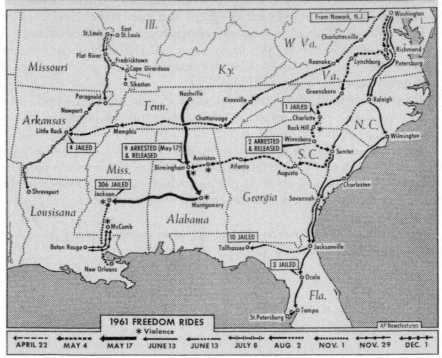

Figure 8.1   Background map, Freedom Rides, 1961.

Source: New York, Associated Press Newsfeature, 1962, p. 3. Used with permission
from the Associated Press. Copyright © 2013. All rights reserved. Photo Library of
Congress, Geography and Map Division.

5 Diane Nash Recalls the Early Student Movement, 1960–1961

"We felt we were right"

When the Greensboro sit-ins began in 1960, Diane Nash was a student at Fisk University, an historically black college in Nashville, Tennessee, where a coalition of student groups had been planning a similar action. She also was among the contingent of Nashville students who attended the April 1960 meeting called by Ella Baker at which the Student Nonviolent Coordinating Committee (SNCC) was founded. In 1961 Nash coordinated SNCC's participation in the Freedom Rides. In the interview below – conducted in 1985 for the film series Eyes on the Prize *– Nash remembers the impetus, approach, and sentiments of the Nashville student movement. For pedagogical purposes, the original transcript of the interview has been slightly edited and modified so that it flows more smoothly as a narrative, but it retains the integrity, perspectives, and words that Nash used to describe events of the early 1960s.*

As a teenager, I think I really started emerging into being a real person, and I was very much aware of [civil rights issues], and I was looking forward in college to really expanding myself, and growing … When I got to Nashville, I keenly resented segregation, and not being allowed to do basic kinds of things like eating at restaurants, in the ten-cent stores even. I really felt stifled. I heard about the Little Rock story, on the radio. I remember the Emmett Till situation really keenly. In fact, even now I can, I have a good image of that picture that appeared in Jet magazine, of him. However, I had never traveled to the south at that time. And I didn't have an emotional relationship to segregation. When I actually went south, and actually saw signs that said "white" and "colored" and I actually could not drink out of that water fountain, or go to that ladies' room, I had a real emotional reaction. I remember the first time it happened, was at the Tennessee State Fair. And I had a date with this, this young man. And I started to go the ladies' room. And it said, "white and colored" and I really resented that. I was outraged. So, it, it had a really emotional effect.

… I recall talking to a number of people in the dormitories at school and on campus, and asking them if they knew any people who were trying to – to bring about some type of change. And I remember being, getting almost depressed, because I encountered what I thought was so much apathy. At first, I couldn't find anyone, and many of the students were saying, why are you concerned about that? You know, they were not interested in trying to effect some kind of change, I thought, they certainly didn't seem to be. And then, I did talk to Paul Lefred, who told me about the non-violent workshops, that Jim Lawson was conducting. They were taking place a couple of blocks off campus. And the reason that I said earlier that I thought the other students were apathetic was that after the movement got started, and there was something that they could do, i.e., sit at a lunch counter, march, take part, many of those same students, who were right there, going to jail, taking part in marches, and sit-ins, and what have you, it was that they didn't have a concept of what they really could do, so when they got one, they were on fire. They wanted a change.

Jim Lawson was a very interesting person. He had been to India, and he had studied the movement, Mohandas Gandhi, in India. He also had been a conscientious objector, and had refused to fight in the Korean War. And he really is the person that brought Gandhi's philosophy and strategies of non-violence to this country. And he conducted weekly workshops, where students in Nashville, as well as some of the people who lived in the Nashville community, were really trained and educated in these philosophies, and strategies. I remember we used to role-play, and we would do things like actually sit-in, pretending we were sitting at lunch counters, in order to prepare ourselves to do that. And we would practice things such as how to protect your head from a beating, how to protect each other, if one person was taking a severe beating, we would practice other people putting their bodies in between that person and the violence. So that the violence could be more distributed and hopefully no one would get seriously injured. We would practice not striking back, if someone struck us. There were many things that I learned in those workshops, that I not only was able to put into practice at the time that we were demonstrating and so forth, but that I have used for the rest of my life. That have been invaluable, in, in shaping the kind of person I've become.

I discovered that practical and real power of truth and love. When you're really honest with yourself, and honest with other people, you give yourself and them the opportunity to solve problems, using reality, instead of lack of reality. That makes problem-solving much more efficient. I could give you an example. We felt we were right. We felt we were right, and rational. When we took a position that segregation was, was wrong, and we really tried to be open and honest and loving with our opposition. A person who is being truthful and honest, actually is, is standing in a much more powerful position than a person who's lying, or trying to maintain his preference, even though on some level he knows he's wrong. I think, on some level, most people really deep-down know that segregation was wrong, just based on race, and disregarding everything else about the person.

You know, during the workshops, we had begun what we called testing the lunch counters. We had actually sent teams of people into department store restaurants, to attempt to be served, and we had anticipated that we'd be refused, and we were. And we established the fact that we were not able to be served, and we asked to speak to the manager, and engaged him in a conversation about why not, the fact that it really was immoral to discriminate against people because of their skin color. And then Christmas break had happened. And we had intended to start the demonstrations afterwards, and we hadn't really started up again. So when the students in Greensboro sat-in on February 1, we simply made plans to join their effort by sitting-in at the same chains that they sat-in at. After we had started sitting-in, we were surprised and delighted to hear reports of other cities joining in the sit-ins. And I think we started feeling the power of the idea whose time had come. Before we did the things that we did, we had no inkling that the movement would become as widespread as it, as it was.

It was a total surprise, when other cities joined in the same chains that we were sitting-in. And I can remember being in the dorm any number of times and hearing the newscasts, that Orangeburg had demonstrations, or Knoxville or, you know, other, other towns. And we were really excited. I can remember, we'd applaud, and say yea. When you are that age, you don't feel powerful. I remember realizing that with what we were doing, trying to abolish segregation, we were coming up against governors of seven states, judges, politicians, businessmen, and I remember thinking, I'm only 22 years old, what do I know, what am I doing? And I felt very vulnerable. So when we heard these newscasts, that other cities had demonstrations, it really helped. Because there were more of us.

I can remember sitting in class, many times, before demonstrations, and I knew, like, we were going to have a demonstration that afternoon. And the palms of my hands would be so sweaty, and I would be so tense and tight inside. I was really afraid. The movement had a way of reaching inside me and bringing out things that I never knew were there. Like courage, and love for people who would put their bodies between you and danger.

...

The movement had a way of reaching inside you and bringing out things that even you didn't know were there. Such as courage. When it – when it was time to go jail, I was much too busy to be afraid. The sit-ins were really highly charged, emotionally. I'm – I'm thinking of one in particular where, in our non-violent workshops, we had decided to be respectful to the opposition, and try to keep issues geared towards desegregation, not get sidetracked. And the first sit-in we had was really funny, because the waitresses were nervous. And they must have dropped $2,000 worth of dishes that day [laughter]. I mean, literally, it was almost a cartoon ... [S]he was so nervous, she picked up dishes and she dropped one and, and she'd pick up another one, and she'd drop it and another. It was really funny, and we were sitting there trying not to laugh, because we thought that, that laughing would be insulting and you know, we didn't want to create that kind of atmosphere. At the same time, we were scared to death.

...

The day that the police first arrested us was interesting too, because their attitude, they had made a decision they were going to arrest us if we sat-in that day, and so, they announced to us "O.K., all you nigras, get up from the lunch counter or we're going to arrest you." And their attitude was like, well, we warned you. So they repeated it a couple of times, and nobody moved. And of course, we were prepared for this. So they said, "Well, we warned you, you won't move, O.K. Everybody's under arrest." So we all get up and marched to the wagon. And the police turned and they looked around the lunch counter again, and the second wave of students had all taken seats. And they were confounded, kind of looked at each other like, "now what do we do," you know? They said well, O.K., we'll arrest those too, and they did it. Then the third wave. No matter what they did and how many they arrested, there was still a lunch counter full of students, there. It was interesting to watch their response. They didn't quite know how to act, and pretty soon it just got to be a problem for them.

[After whites bombed the home of black civil rights attorney Z. Alexander Loobey] we decided to have the mass march, consisting of students from all of the schools, who were participating.... The students met on Tennessee A&T's campus, and we marched, I think, three abreast. We were very organized. One of the things that we made it a point to do was that whenever there was a demonstration, we were to be overly dressed. The men generally wore suits and ties, and the women – we looked like we were dressing up for Sunday. And anyway, we marched quietly – we were met later by students at Fisk. We passed Fisk campus. And other students, other schools had points where they joined in to the march. There were many thousands of people that marched that day. We marched silently, really. And the – the long line of students must have continued for many, many blocks. Miles, maybe.

We had sent telegrams ahead of time, telling him that as a result of the bombing, turning the Loobeys' home into a state of violence, tension, violence in the city of Nashville, we felt like we needed to talk to the mayor. So we met him on the steps of City Hall. And confronted him with what his feelings as a man, were. As a person, I was particularly interested in that, as opposed to just his being a mayor. And I have a lot of respect for the way he responded. He didn't have to respond the way he did. He said, that he felt like it was wrong, for citizens of Nashville to be discriminated against at the lunch counters, solely on the basis of the color of their skin. And, I think that was the turning point. The Nashville newspaper reported that, in the headlines, the next day, and it was one more step towards desegregating the lunch counters. And I think that day was very important. One of the things that we were able to do in the movement, which was one of the things that we were also, that we learned, also, from Gandhi's movement, was to turn the energy of violence, that was perpetrated against us, into advantage. And so if Attorney Loobey's house was burned, that was used as a catalyst to draw many thousands of people to express their opposition to segregation.

...

I remember receiving the invitation to attend the conference that would bring together student leadership from many campuses where there were sit-ins, sit-ins going on. And, of course, we had been really excited by the fact that there was a national movement in many cities involved. We felt a real kinship with the students who were working in other cities, to bring about the same things that we were. And it, it felt like a good idea. We were interested in meeting the people that – meeting as individuals the people that we had heard about. And we decided to send a large delegation to Raleigh, North Carolina.

The impetus, we understood later, for that meeting had come from Ella Baker. She was a person who I think was very central to setting the direction that the student movement ... Ella Baker was very important to giving direction to the student movement, and not giving direction in a way of her making decisions as to what the students ought to do, but to recognize that the students should set the goals and directions, and maintain control of the student movement.

... [And] she was constantly aware of the fact that the differences that the students had were probably not as important as the similarities that we had, in terms of what we were trying to do. So, very often, she was the person who was able to make us see, and work together. I think her participation as a person some years older than we, could really serve as a model of how older people can give energy and help to younger people, at the same time, not take over and tell them what to do, really strengthen them as individuals and also strengthen – she strengthened our organization.

...

We heard about the Freedom Rides in Nashville, when they were starting, and we all agreed with their purposes and agreed that it was really an important thing for CORE to do. We also were very aware of the fact that taking the route that they were taking, which was down the eastern seacoast, into the deep south, through Georgia, Florida, Alabama and Mississippi, we knew that that was awfully dangerous, and that they would probably meet with violence a number of times. So in Nashville we decided that we would watch them, as they, as the Freedom Ride, progressed. And if there were ways that we could help, we'd stand by, and be available. And true enough, they were beaten and attacked, many, many times. When the buses were burned in

Anniston, on Mother's Day, the Nashville group met. Since there was such a close kinship, between us and the Freedom Riders, we understood exactly what they were doing, and it was our fight, every bit as much as theirs. It was as though we had been attacked. And a contingency of students left Nashville to go and pick up the Freedom Ride where it had stopped, been stopped. Now, that was really one of the times where I saw people face death. Because nobody went and joined the Freedom Ride without – it would have been really unwise to have gone without realizing that they might not come back. Some of the students that left gave me sealed letters to be mailed, in case they were killed. That's how prepared they were, for death.

You know, if the Freedom Ride had been stopped as a result of violence, I strongly felt that the future of the movement was going to be cut short. Because the impression would have been given that whenever a movement starts, all that has to be done is attack it, [use] massive violence and blacks would stop. And I thought that was a very dangerous thing to happen. So, under those circumstances, it was really important that the Ride continue. And again, part of the non-violent strategy understands that when that type of negative image is directed at you, one of the important things to do is find ways to convert it to, to positive energy, which we were able to do as a result of continuing.

Of course, our whole way of operating was that we took ultimate responsibility for what we were going to do, so we made our decisions, and then we told the federal government what that would be. It was felt that they should be advised, in Washington, of what our plans were and what we were going to do, and we certainly made sure that they did know what we were going to do, [although] Jim Lawson cautioned against relying on hoping for federal protection.

The students from Nashville who were going to pick up the Freedom Ride elected me coordinator. And as coordinator, part of my responsibility was to stay in touch with the Justice Department. I was to keep the press informed, the Justice Department, keep the communities that were participating informed, such as Birmingham, Montgomery, Jackson, Nashville, etc. To coordinate the training and recruitment of more people to take up the Freedom Ride, etc. etc., so I advised the Justice Department regularly as to what our plans were, and what kinds of things were happening ... Everything was so uncertain. We never knew what the situation would be like ten minutes from the time that it was. During the Freedom Ride, in my job as coordinator, I was very well aware of the fact that when I went to sleep at night, some of [the people I loved] might not be alive the next night. And during that particular time I think I, I cried just every night, profusely. And I needed to, as an energy release. It was so much tension. It was like being at war. And we were very upset when they were attacked and injured, and I remember visiting them in the hospital, and there was so much concern over which of these injuries would be permanent. People really stood to be permanently injured for the rest of their lives.

I think it's really important that young people today understand that the movement of the sixties was really a people's movement. The media and history seems to record it as Martin Luther King's movement, but if young people realized that it was people just like them, their age, that formulated goals and strategies, and actually developed the movement, that when they look around now, and see things that need to be changed, that they, instead of saying, I wish we had a leader like Martin Luther King today, they would say, what can I do, what can my roommate and I do to effect that change. And that's not to take anything away from Martin. I personally think he made a tremendous contribution. And I liked him a great deal, as an individual, thought he was a really nice guy. And I, still feel the pain of his not being with us, but I think that it's really important to realize that each individual shoulders a great deal of responsibility, and, and, and that's the way the movement in the sixties was accomplished.

Source: Reproduced with permission from interview with Diane Nash, November 12, 1985, Chicago, Illinois, for Blackside, Inc., *Eyes on the Prize: America's Civil Rights Years (1954–1965)*, edited transcript. Henry Hampton Collection, Film & Media Archive, Washington University Libraries.

6 Rev. Dr. Martin Luther King, Jr., Writes a Letter from Birmingham Jail, 1963

"freedom is never voluntarily given by the oppressor; it must be demanded by the oppressed"

Rev. Dr. Martin Luther King, Jr. (1929–1968) was arguably the most prominent civil rights personality of the mid-twentieth century, if not always for his leadership, then for his rhetoric. King was a highly controversial figure, without the cache his legacy carries in history. Yet, his writings, in particular, transformed the racial attitudes of uninformed audiences. "Letter from Birmingham Jail" not only quelled his critics among southern white clergy, but also garnered ecumenical admirers and allies, black and white. Published widely, for instance in the New York Post *and the* Atlantic Monthly, *"Letter from Birmingham Jail" is considered one of the most important documents of American history.*

Birmingham City Jail, April 16, 1963

My dear Fellow Clergymen,

While confined here in the Birmingham City Jail, I came across your recent statement calling our present activities "unwise and untimely." Seldom, if ever, do I pause to answer criticism of my work and ideas. ... But since I feel that you are men of genuine goodwill and your criticisms are sincerely set forth, I would like to answer your statement in what I hope will be patient and reasonable terms.

I think I should give the reason for my being in Birmingham, since you have been influenced by the argument of "outsiders coming in." I have the honor of serving as president of the Southern Christian Leadership Conference, an organization operating in every Southern state with head-quarters in Atlanta, Georgia. We have some eighty-five affiliate organizations all across the South – one being the Alabama Christian Movement for Human Rights. Whenever necessary and possible we share staff, educational, and financial resources with our affiliates. Several months ago our local affiliate here in Birmingham invited us to be on call to engage in a nonviolent direct action program if such were deemed necessary. We readily consented and when the hour came we lived up to our promises. So I am here, along with several members of my staff, because we were invited here. I am here because I have basic organizational ties here. Beyond this, I am in Birmingham because injustice is here ...

Moreover, I am cognizant of the interrelatedness of all communities and states. I cannot sit idly by in Atlanta and not be concerned about what happens in Birmingham. Injustice anywhere is a threat to justice everywhere. We are caught in an inescapable network of mutuality tied in a single garment of destiny. Whatever affects one directly affects all indirectly. Never again can we afford to live with the narrow, provincial "outside agitator" idea. Anyone who lives inside the United States can never be considered an outsider anywhere in this country.

You deplore the demonstrations that are presently taking place in Birmingham. But I am sorry that your statement did not express a similar concern for the conditions that brought the demonstrations into being. I am sure that each of you would want to go beyond the superficial social analyst who looks merely at effects, and does not grapple with underlying causes. I would not hesitate to say that it is unfortunate that so-called demonstrations are taking place in Birmingham at this time, but I would say in more emphatic terms that it is even more unfortunate that the white power structure of this city left the Negro community with no other alternative.

In any nonviolent campaign there are four basic steps: (1) Collection of the facts to determine whether injustices are alive; (2) Negotiation; (3) Self-purification; and (4) Direct action. We have gone through all of these steps in Birmingham. There can be no gainsaying of the fact that racial injustice engulfs this community. Birmingham is probably the most thoroughly segregated city in the United States. Its ugly record of police brutality is known in every section of this country. Its unjust treatment of Negroes in the courts is a notorious reality. There have been more unsolved bombings of Negro homes and churches in Birmingham than any city in this nation. These are the hard, brutal, and unbelievable facts. On the basis of these conditions Negro leaders sought to negotiate with the city fathers. But the political leaders consistently refused to engage in good faith negotiation.

Then came the opportunity last September to talk with some of the leaders of the economic community. In these negotiating sessions certain promises were made by the merchants – such as the promise to remove the humiliating racial signs from the stores. On the basis of these promises Rev. Shuttlesworth and the leaders of the Alabama Christian Movement for Human Rights agreed to call a moratorium on any type of demonstrations. As the weeks and months unfolded we realized that we were the victims of a broken promise. The signs remained. As in so many experiences of the past we were confronted with blasted hopes, and the dark shadow of a deep disappointment settled upon us. So we had no alternative except that of preparing for direct action, whereby we would present our very bodies as a means of laying our case before the conscience of the local and national community ...

... You may well ask, "Why direct action? Why sit-ins, marches, etc.? Isn't negotiation a better path?" You are exactly right in your call for negotiation. Indeed, this is the purpose of direct action. Nonviolent direct action seeks to create such a crisis and establish such creative tension that a community that has constantly refused to negotiate is forced to confront the issue. It seeks so to dramatize the issue that it can no longer be ignored. I just referred to the creation of tension as a part of the work of the nonviolent resister. This may sound rather shocking. But I must confess that I am not afraid of the word tension. I have earnestly worked and preached against violent tension, but there is a type of constructive nonviolent tension that is necessary for growth ...

[T]he purpose of the direct action is to create a situation so crisis-packed that it will inevitably open the door to negotiation. We, therefore, concur with you in your call for negotiation. Too long has our beloved Southland been bogged down in the tragic attempt to live in monologue rather than dialogue.

One of the basic points in your statement is that our acts are untimely....
My friends, I must say to you that we have not made a single gain in civil
rights without determined legal and nonviolent pressure. History is the long
and tragic story of the fact that privileged groups seldom give up their privileges voluntarily. Individuals may see the moral light and voluntarily give
up their unjust posture; but as Reinhold Niebuhr has reminded us, groups
are more immoral than individuals.

We know through painful experience that freedom is never voluntarily
given by the oppressor; it must be demanded by the oppressed. Frankly I
have never yet engaged in a direct action movement that was "well timed,"
according to the timetable of those who have not suffered unduly from the
disease of segregation. For years now I have heard the word "Wait!" It rings
in the ear of every Negro with a piercing familiarity. This "wait" has almost
always meant "never." It has been a tranquilizing thalidomide, relieving the
emotional stress for a moment, only to give birth to an ill-formed infant of
frustration. We must come to see with the distinguished jurist of yesterday
that "justice too long delayed is justice denied."

We have waited for more than three hundred and forty years for our constitutional and God-given rights. The nations of Asia and Africa are moving with
jet-like speed toward the goal of political independence, and we still creep at
horse and buggy pace toward the gaining of a cup of coffee at a lunch counter....

Perhaps it is easy for those who have never felt the stinging darts of segregation to say wait. But when you have seen vicious mobs lynch your mothers
and fathers at will and drown your sisters and brothers at whim; when you
have seen hate filled policemen curse, kick, brutalize, and even kill your black
brothers and sisters with impunity; when you see the vast majority of your
twenty million Negro brothers smothering in an air-tight cage of poverty in
the midst of an affluent society; when you suddenly find your tongue twisted
and your speech stammering as you seek to explain to your six-year-old
daughter why she can't go to the public amusement park that has just been
advertised on television, and see tears welling up in her little eyes when she is
told that Funtown is closed to colored children, and see the depressing clouds
of inferiority begin to form in her little mental sky, and see her begin to dis-
tort her little personality by unconsciously developing a bitterness toward
white people; when you have to concoct an answer for a five-year-old son
asking in agonizing pathos: "Daddy, why do white people treat colored people so mean?"; when you take a cross-country drive and find it necessary to
sleep night after night in the uncomfortable corners of your automobile
because no motel will accept you; when you are humiliated day in and day
out by nagging signs reading "white" men and "colored"; when your first
name becomes "nigger" and your middle name becomes "boy" (however old

you are) and your last name becomes "John," and when your wife and mother are never given the respected title "Mrs."; when you are harried by day and haunted by night by the fact that you are a Negro, living constantly at tip-toe stance never quite knowing what to expect next, and plagued with inner fears and outer resentments; when you are forever fighting a degenerating sense of "nobodiness" – then you will understand why we find it difficult to wait. There comes a time when the cup of endurance runs over, and men are no longer willing to be plunged into an abyss of injustice where they experience the bleakness of corroding despair. I hope, sirs, you can understand our legitimate and unavoidable impatience.

You express a great deal of anxiety over our willingness to break laws. This is certainly a legitimate concern. Since we so diligently urge people to obey the Supreme Court's decision of 1954 outlawing segregation in the public schools, it is rather strange and paradoxical to find us consciously breaking laws. One may well ask: "How can you advocate breaking some laws and obeying others?" The answer is found in the fact that there are two types of laws: There are just laws and there are unjust laws. I would be the first to advocate obeying just laws. One has not only a legal but moral responsibility to obey just laws. Conversely, one has a moral responsibility to disobey unjust laws. I would agree with Saint Augustine that "An unjust law is no law at all."

Now what is the difference between the two? How does one determine when a law is just or unjust? A just law is a man-made code that squares with the moral law or the law of God. An unjust law is a code that is out of harmony with the moral law. To put it in the terms of Saint Thomas Aquinas, an unjust law is a human law that is not rooted in eternal and natural law. Any law that uplifts human personality is just. Any law that degrades human personality is unjust. All segregation statutes are unjust because segregation distorts the soul and damages the personality.

...

Let me give another explanation. An unjust law is a code inflicted upon a minority which that minority had no part in enacting or creating because they did not have the unhampered right to vote. Who can say that the legislature of Alabama which set up the segregation laws was democratically elected? Throughout the state of Alabama all types of conniving methods are used to prevent Negroes from becoming registered voters and there are some counties without a single Negro registered to vote despite the fact that the Negro constitutes a majority of the population. Can any law set up in such a state be considered democratically structured?

I hope you can see the distinction I am trying to point out. In no sense do I advocate evading or defying the law as the rabid segregationist would do.

This would lead to anarchy. One who breaks an unjust law must do it openly, lovingly (not hatefully as the white mothers did in New Orleans when they were seen on television screaming "nigger, nigger, nigger") and with a willingness to accept the penalty. I submit that an individual who breaks a law that conscience tells him is unjust, and willingly accepts the penalty by staying in jail to arouse the conscience of the community over its injustice, is in reality expressing the very highest respect for law.

...

We can never forget that everything Hitler did in Germany was "legal" and everything the Hungarian freedom fighters did in Hungary was "illegal." It was "illegal" to aid and comfort a Jew in Hitler's Germany ...

I must make two honest confessions to you, my Christian and Jewish brothers. First, I must confess that over the last few years I have been gravely disappointed with the white moderate. I have almost reached the regrettable conclusion that the Negroes' great stumbling block in the stride toward freedom is not the White Citizen's "Counciler" or the Ku Klux Klanner, but the white moderate who is more devoted to "order" than to justice; who prefers a negative peace which is the absence of tension to a positive peace which is the presence of justice; who constantly says "I agree with you in the goal you seek, but I can't agree with your methods of direct action"; who paternalistically feels that he can set the timetable for another man's freedom; who lives by the myth of time and who constantly advises the Negro to wait until a "more convenient season." Shallow understanding from people of good will is more frustrating than absolute misunderstanding from people of ill will. Lukewarm acceptance is much more bewildering than outright rejection.

I had hoped that the white moderate would understand that law and order exist for the purpose of establishing justice, and that when they fail to do this they become dangerously structured dams that block the flow of social progress. I had hoped that the white moderate would understand that the present tension in the South is merely a necessary phase of the transition from an obnoxious negative peace, where the Negro passively accepted his unjust plight, to a substance-filled positive peace, where all men will respect the dignity and worth of human personality. Actually, we who engage in nonviolent direct action are not the creators of tension. We merely bring to the surface the hidden tension that is already alive. We bring it out in the open where it can be seen and dealt with ...

...

... We must come to see, as federal courts have consistently affirmed, that it is immoral to urge an individual to withdraw his efforts to gain his basic constitutional rights because the quest precipitates violence. Society must protect the robbed and punish the robber.

I had also hoped that the white moderate would reject the myth concerning time in relation to the struggle for freedom.... It is the strangely irrational notion that there is something in the very flow of time that will inevitably cure all ills. Actually time is neutral. It can be used either destructively or constructively. I am coming to feel that the people of ill will have used time much more effectively than the people of good will.

Human progress never rolls in on wheels of inevitability ... We must use time creatively, and forever realize that the time is always ripe to do right. Now is the time to make real the promise of democracy, and transform our pending national elegy into a creative psalm of brotherhood. Now is the time to lift our national policy from the quicksand of racial injustice to the solid rock of human dignity.

...

Oppressed people cannot remain oppressed forever. The urge for freedom will eventually come. This is what has happened to the American Negro. Something within has reminded him of his birthright of freedom; something without has reminded him that he can gain it. Consciously and unconsciously, he has been swept in by what the Germans call the Zeitgeist, and with his black brothers of Africa, and his brown and yellow brothers of Asia, South America, and the Caribbean, he is moving with a sense of cosmic urgency toward the promised land of racial justice. Recognizing this vital urge that has engulfed the Negro community, one should readily understand public demonstrations. The Negro has many pent-up resentments and latent frustrations. He has to get them out. So let him march sometime; let him have his prayer pilgrimages to the city hall; understand why he must have sit-ins and freedom rides. If his repressed emotions do not come out in these nonviolent ways, they will come out in ominous expressions of violence. This is not a threat; it is a fact of history. So I have not said to my people, "Get rid of your discontent." But I have tried to say that this normal and healthy discontent can be channeled through the creative outlet of nonviolent direct action. Now this approach is being dismissed as extremist. I must admit that I was initially disappointed in being so categorized.

But as I continued to think about the matter I gradually gained a bit of satisfaction from being considered an extremist. Was not Jesus an extremist in love? "Love your enemies, bless them that curse you, pray for them that despitefully use you." ... Was not Abraham Lincoln an extremist – "This nation cannot survive half slave and half free." Was not Thomas Jefferson an extremist – "We hold these truths to be self-evident, that all men are created equal." So the question is not whether we will be extremist but what kind of extremist will we be. Will we be extremists for hate or will we be extremists for love? Will we be extremists for the preservation of injustice – or will we be extremists for the cause of justice? ... So, after all, maybe the South, the nation, and the world are in dire need of creative extremists.

I had hoped that the white moderate would see this. Maybe I was too optimistic. Maybe I expected too much. I guess I should have realized that few members of a race that has oppressed another race can understand or appreciate the deep groans and passionate yearnings of those that have been oppressed, and still fewer have the vision to see that injustice must be rooted out by strong, persistent, and determined action. I am thankful, however, that some of our white brothers have grasped the meaning of this social revolution and committed themselves to it. They are still all too small in quantity, but they are big in quality. Some like Ralph McGill, Lillian Smith, Harry Golden, and James Dabbs have written about our struggle in eloquent, prophetic, and understanding terms. Others have marched with us down nameless streets of the South. They have languished in filthy, roach-infested jails, suffering the abuse and brutality of angry policemen who see them as "dirty nigger lovers." They, unlike so many of their moderate brothers and sisters, have recognized the urgency of the moment and sensed the need for powerful "action" antidotes to combat the disease of segregation.

Let me rush on to mention my other disappointment. I have been so greatly disappointed with the white Church and its leadership. ...

I have heard numerous religious leaders of the South call upon their worshippers to comply with a desegregation decision because it is the law, but I have longed to hear white ministers say follow this decree because integration is morally right and the Negro is your brother. In the midst of blatant injustices inflicted upon the Negro, I have watched white churches stand on the sideline and merely mouth pious irrelevancies and sanctimonious trivialities. In the midst of a mighty struggle to rid our nation of racial and economic injustice, I have heard so many ministers say, "Those are social issues with which the gospel has no real concern," and I have watched so many churches commit themselves to a completely other-worldly religion which made a strange distinction between body and soul, the sacred and the secular.

So here we are moving toward the exit of the twentieth century with a religious community largely adjusted to the status quo, standing as a tail-light behind other community agencies rather than a headlight leading men to higher levels of justice.

...

I must close now. But before closing I am impelled to mention one other point in your statement that troubled me profoundly. You warmly commend the Birmingham police force for keeping "order" and "preventing violence." I don't believe you would have so warmly commended the police force if you had seen its angry violent dogs literally biting six unarmed, nonviolent Negroes. I don't believe you would so quickly commend the policemen if you would observe their ugly and inhuman treatment of Negroes here in the city jail; if you would watch them push and curse old Negro women and young Negro girls; if you would see them slap and kick old Negro men and young Negro boys; if you will observe them, as they did on two occasions, refuse to give us food because we wanted to sing our grace together. I'm sorry that I can't join you in your praise for the police department.

...

I wish you had commended the Negro sit-inners and demonstrators of Birmingham for their sublime courage, their willingness to suffer, and their amazing discipline in the midst of the most inhuman provocation. One day the South will recognize its real heroes. They will be the James Merediths, courageously and with a majestic sense of purpose, facing jeering and hostile mobs and the agonizing loneliness that characterizes the life of the pioneer. They will be old, oppressed, battered Negro women, symbolized in a seventy-two year old woman of Montgomery, Alabama, who rose up with a sense of dignity and with her people decided not to ride the segregated buses, and responded to one who inquired about her tiredness with ungrammatical profundity: "My feets is tired, but my soul is rested." They will be the young high school and college students, young ministers of the gospel and a host of their elders courageously and nonviolently sitting-in at lunch counters and willingly going to jail for conscience sake. One day the South will know that when these disinherited children of God sat down at lunch counters they were in reality standing up for the best in the American dream and the most sacred values in our Judaeo-Christian heritage, and thus carrying our whole nation back to great wells of democracy which were dug deep by the founding fathers in the formulation of the Constitution and the Declaration of Independence.

...

Yours for the cause of

Peace and Brotherhood,

Martin Luther King, Jr.

7 The March on Washington for Jobs and Freedom, 1963

"We are now involved in a serious revolution"

*Racial segregation merely symbolized the larger issues African Americans
wanted to change. Access to better jobs, adequate housing, equal educational
opportunities, and civil rights comprised a broad agenda of freedom
movement demands. Echoing the claims presented in 1941, Bayard Rustin
and A. Philip Randolph planned another March on Washington for Jobs and
Freedom. This 1963 March similarly hoped to force the passage of significant
legislative and policy changes. As Franklin D. Roosevelt had done in 1941,
President John F. Kennedy asked civil rights leaders to call off the march.
This time they refused. An interracial alliance of prominent figures from
religious, labor, and civil rights groups supported the event. Among the
speakers, John Lewis (b. 1940), then Chair of SNCC, wanted to express
activists' frustration, and planned to tell the Kennedy administration that the
civil rights bill he proposed was "too little too late." To hold the coalition
together, however, Lewis had to tone down his critique. And in the end,
King's "I Have a Dream" speech is remembered, ironically, for lines that
were not his point. Below is the speech John Lewis planned to give.*

Original Draft of SNCC Chairman John Lewis' Speech to the March

We march today for jobs and freedom, but we have nothing to be proud of,
for hundreds and thousands of our brothers are not here. They have no
money for their transportation, for they are receiving starvation wages, or
no wages at all.

In good conscience, we cannot support wholeheartedly the administration's civil rights bill, for it is too little and too late. There's not one thing in
the bill that will protect our people from police brutality.

This bill will not protect young children and old women from police dogs
and fire hoses, for engaging in peaceful demonstrations: This bill will not
protect the citizens in Danville, Virginia, who must live in constant fear in a
police state. This bill will not protect the hundreds of people who have been
arrested on trumped up charges. What about the three young men in
Americus, Georgia, who face the death penalty for engaging in peaceful
protest?

The voting section of this bill will not help thousands of black citizens
who want to vote. It will not help the citizens of Mississippi, of Alabama
and Georgia, who are qualified to vote but lack a sixth-grade education.
"ONE MAN, ONE VOTE" is the African cry. It is ours, too. It must be ours.

People have been forced to leave their homes because they dared to exercise their right to register to vote. What is there in this bill to ensure the equality of a maid who earns $5 a week in the home of a family whose income is $100,000 a year?

For the first time in one hundred years this nation is being awakened to the fact that segregation is evil and that it must be destroyed in all forms. Your presence today proves that you have been aroused to the point of action.

We are now involved in a serious revolution. This nation is still a place of cheap political leaders who build their careers on immoral compromises and ally themselves with open forms of political, economic and social exploitation. What political leader here can stand up and say, "My party is the party of principles?" The party of Kennedy is also the party of Eastland. The party of Javits is also the party of Goldwater. Where is *our* party?

In some parts of the South we work in the fields from sunup to sundown for $12 a week. In Albany, Georgia, nine of our leaders have been indicted not by Dixiecrats but by the federal government for peaceful protest. But what did the federal government do when Albany's deputy sheriff beat attorney C. B. King and left him half dead? What did the federal government do when local police officials kicked and assaulted the pregnant wife of Slater King, and she lost her baby?

It seems to me that the Albany indictment is part of a conspiracy on the part of the federal government and local politicians in the interest of expediency.

I want to know, which side is the federal government on?

The revolution is at hand, and we must free ourselves of the chains of political and economic slavery. The nonviolent revolution is saying, "We will not wait for the courts to act, for we have been waiting for hundreds of years. We will not wait for the President, the Justice Department, nor Congress, but we will take matters into our own hands and create a source of power, outside of any national structure, that could and would assure us a victory."

To those who have said, "Be patient and wait," we must say that "patience" is a dirty and nasty word. We cannot be patient, we do not want to be free gradually. We want our freedom, and we want it *now*. We cannot depend on any political party, for both the Democrats and the Republicans have betrayed the basic principles of the Declaration of Independence.

We all recognize the fact that if any radical social, political and economic changes are to take place in our society, the people, the masses, must bring them about. In the struggle, we must seek more than civil rights; we must work for the community of love, peace and true brotherhood. Our minds, souls and hearts cannot rest until freedom and justice exist for *all people*.

The revolution is a serious one. Mr. Kennedy is trying to take the revolution out of the streets and put it into the courts. Listen, Mr. Kennedy. Listen, Mr. Congressman. Listen, fellow citizens. The black masses are on the march for jobs and freedom, and we must say to the politicians that there won't be a "cooling-off" period.

All of us must get in the revolution. Get in and stay in the streets of every city, every village and every hamlet of this nation until true freedom comes, until the revolution is complete. In the Delta of Mississippi, in southwest Georgia, in Alabama, Harlem, Chicago, Detroit, Philadelphia and all over this nation, the black masses are on the march!

We won't stop now. All of the forces of [Senator James] Eastland [Mississippi], [Governor Ross] Barnett [Arkansas], [Governor George] Wallace [Alabama] and [Senator Strom] Thurmond won't stop this revolution. The time will come when we will not confine our marching to Washington. We will march through the South, through the heart of Dixie, the way Sherman did. We shall pursue our own "scorched earth" policy and burn Jim Crow to the ground – nonviolently. We shall fragment the South into a thousand pieces and put them back together in the image of democracy. We will make the action of the past few months look petty. And I say to you, WAKE UP AMERICA!

We will not stop. If we do not get meaningful legislation out of this Congress, the time will come when we will not confine our marching to Washington. We will march through the South, through the streets of Jackson, through the streets of Danville, through the streets of Cambridge, through the streets of Birmingham. But we will march with the spirit of love and with the spirit of dignity that we have shown here today.

By the force of our demands, our determination and our numbers, we shall splinter the desegregated South into a thousand pieces and put them back together in the image of God and democracy.

We must say, "Wake up, America. *Wake up!!!* For we cannot stop, and we *will* not be patient."

Questions for Consideration

The 1960s brought a generational shift in the work of black freedom where young people moved to the forefront of activism. What motivated them to forge a new movement? How did their age influence the tactics they deployed?

How did the resistance of white segregationists affect the movement?
Explain non-violence. How did it work? Why did King, SNCC, and others believe
it was the right approach to take in the South?
How did activists balance their critical view of the federal government with their
convictions about its role in attaining freedom, equality, and democracy?

Bibliography

Arsenault, Raymond. *Freedom Riders 1961 and the Struggle for Racial Justice*. New
York: Oxford University Press, 2006.
Carson, Clayborne. *In Struggle: SNCC and the Black Awakening of the 1960s*.
Cambridge, MA: Harvard University Press, 1981.
Chafe, William H. *Civilities and Civil Rights: Greensboro North Carolina and the
Black Struggle for Freedom*. New York: Oxford University Press, 1981.
Dittmer, John. *Local People: The Struggle for Civil Rights in Mississippi*. Urbana:
University of Illinois Press, 1994.
Garrow, David. *Bearing the Cross: Martin Luther King, Jr., and the Southern
Christian Leadership Conference*. New York: William Morrow, 1986.
Hogan, Wesley C. *Many Minds, One Heart: SNCC's Dream for a New America*.
Chapel Hill: University of North Carolina Press, 2007.
Holsaert, Faith S., et al., eds. *Hands on the Freedom Plow: Personal Accounts by
Women in SNCC*. Urbana: University of Illinois Press, 2012.
Lee, Chana Kai. *For Freedom's Sake: The Life of Fannie Lou Hamer*. Urbana:
University of Illinois Press, 1999.
Lewis, John. *Walking with the Wind: A Memoir of the Movement*. New York:
Mariner Books, 1999.
Ransby, Barbara. *Ella Baker and the Black Freedom Movement: A Radical
Democratic Vision*. Chapel Hill: University of North Carolina Press, 2005.

Chapter 9   Power, 1964–1966

Although African Americans persisted in using direct action campaigns for desegregation, the larger goal of the civil rights movement was to secure for African Americans the ability to effect significant changes in their lives, in short, power. If not about the methods – or the rhetoric – employed to attain it, black activists mostly agreed on the goal. By the mid-1960s, movement forces had coalesced around the vote, theorizing that black ballots would reshape southern governance and law, and, by extension, the American political system. White resistance mounted, however, such that the frequency of violence demanded an innovative response.

With SNCC on the frontline, a coalition of civil rights groups, the Council of Federated Organizations (COFO), organized massive voter registration campaigns. Robert Moses developed a new plan to expand the number of organizers on the ground, bring national attention to the conditions faced by blacks in the South, and challenge white power directly. For "Freedom Summer" in 1964, hundreds of black and white students and young professionals from the North went South to work together, setting up freedom schools and health clinics, providing legal assistance, collecting and distributing resources, and doing voter education and registration. Followed by the media, SNCC understood, whites' presence would garner national attention, especially when – not if – violence ensued. Almost immediately, a contingent of law enforcement officers and Klansmen in Philadelphia, Mississippi, executed two white and one black civil rights workers.

African American Voices: A Documentary Reader from Emancipation to the Present, First Edition. Edited by Leslie Brown.
© 2014 John Wiley & Sons, Inc. Published 2014 by John Wiley & Sons, Inc.

The second phase of Freedom Summer took on the Dixiecrats with alternative political organizations through which African Americans could enter the electoral process. At the 1964 Democratic National Convention elected representatives of the Mississippi Freedom Democratic Party (MFDP) argued that the regular delegation, which was all white by design, had no right to represent the state. MFDP made a strong case, and refused to accept a compromise that offered them two seats at large. Returning home disappointed, MFDP still managed to sustain an effective grassroots program that grew the black vote and thus black political influence.

Meanwhile, President Lyndon Johnson won re-election with a large enough margin to push through a second civil rights bill, the Voting Rights Act of 1965. White southern Democrats began defecting to the Republican Party, which welcomed them. To address the larger issues raised by activists, Johnson initiated his "Great Society" programs, declaring war on poverty (black and white). But national resources drained away to the war in Southeast Asia. Dismantling the obvious manifestations of Jim Crow, moreover, raised new questions. Exactly how could or should African Americans use the vote to their advantage? How effective were coalitions, given the misapprehensions of white liberals? Could black ballots attain the right to make a living or to access a quality education? Could they stop police brutality or end the war?

1 Malcolm X Reflects on the Approaches African Americans Must Use, 1964

"either the ballot or the bullet"

Malcolm X (El-Hajj Malik El-Shabazz) (1929–1965), minister in the Nation of Islam (NOI), held fast to many principles that African Americans and black organizations articulated historically: race consciousness and pride, a strong sense of morality and respectability, self-help and autonomy. In 1964, after making the hajj to Mecca, Malcolm rejected the NOI philosophy that embraced black supremacy, and, disappointed in the Nation's leader, the Honorable Elijah Muhammad, he left the group to found his own. Although he continued to question non-violence – not as a tactic but as a philosophy – he engaged the goals of the black freedom movement. The document below excerpts a speech he gave at a public meeting in Cleveland in 1964. In it he makes a black nationalist case for the use of the ballot.

"The Ballot or the Bullet" (1964)

... The question tonight, as I understand it, is "The Negro Revolt, and Where Do We Go From Here?" or "What Next?" In my little humble way of understanding it, it points toward either the ballot or the bullet.

...

1964 threatens to be the most explosive year America has ever witnessed. The most explosive year. Why? It's also a political year. It's the year when all of the white politicians will be back in the so-called Negro community jiving you and me for some votes. The year when all of the white political crooks will be right back in your and my community with their false promises, building up our hopes for a letdown, with their trickery and their treachery, with their false promises which they don't intend to keep. As they nourish these dissatisfactions, it can only lead to one thing, an explosion ...

...

I'm not a politician, not even a student of politics; in fact, I'm not a student of much of anything. I'm not a Democrat. I'm not a Republican, and I don't even consider myself an American. If you and I were Americans, there'd be no problem ...

...

No, I'm not an American. I'm one of the 22 million black people who are the victims of Americanism. One of the 22 million black people who are the victims of democracy, nothing but disguised hypocrisy. ...

... These 22 million victims are waking up. Their eyes are coming open. They're beginning to see what they used to only look at. They're becoming politically mature. They are realizing that there are new political trends from coast to coast ... [B]lack people have a bloc of votes of their own, it is left up to them to determine who's going to sit in the White House and who's going to be in the dog house.

...

The Dixiecrats in Washington, D.C., control the key committees that run the government. The only reason the Dixiecrats control these committees is because they have seniority. The only reason they have seniority is because they come from states where Negroes can't vote. This is not even a government that's based on democracy. It is not a government that is made up of representatives of the people. Half of the people in the South can't even vote ...

...

If the black man in these Southern states had his full voting rights, the key Dixiecrats in Washington, D. C., which means the key Democrats in Washington, D.C., would lose their seats. The Democratic Party itself would lose its power. It would cease to be powerful as a party. When you see the amount of power that would be lost by the Democratic Party if it were to lose the Dixiecrat wing, or branch, or element, you can see where it's against the interests of the Democrats to give voting rights to Negroes in states where the Democrats have been in complete power and authority ever since the Civil War. You just can't belong to that Party without analyzing it.

I say again, I'm not anti-Democrat, I'm not anti-Republican, I'm not anti-anything. I'm just questioning their sincerity, and some of the strategy that they've been using on our people by promising them promises that they don't intend to keep ... That's why, in 1964, it's time now for you and me to become more politically mature and realize what the ballot is for; what we're supposed to get when we cast a ballot; and that if we don't cast a ballot, it's going to end up in a situation where we're going to have to cast a bullet. It's either a ballot or a bullet.

...

So, what I'm trying to impress upon you, in essence, is this: You and I in America are faced not with a segregationist conspiracy, we're faced with a government conspiracy. Everyone who's filibustering is a senator – that's the government. Everyone who's finagling in Washington, D.C., is a congressman – that's the government. You don't have anybody putting blocks in your path but people who are a part of the government. The same government that you go abroad to fight for and die for is the government that is in a conspiracy to deprive you of your voting rights, deprive you of your economic opportunities, deprive you of decent housing, deprive you of decent education. You don't need to go to the employer alone, it is the government itself, the government of America, that is responsible for the oppression and exploitation and degradation of black people in this country. And you should drop it in their lap. This government has failed the Negro. This so-called democracy has failed the Negro. And all these white liberals have definitely failed the Negro.

So, where do we go from here? First, we need some friends. We need some new allies. The entire civil-rights struggle needs a new interpretation, a broader interpretation. We need to look at this civil-rights thing from another angle – from the inside as well as from the outside. To those of us whose philosophy is black nationalism, the only way you can get involved in the civil-rights struggle is give it a new interpretation.

...

The black nationalists, those whose philosophy is black nationalism, in bringing about this new interpretation of the entire meaning of civil rights, look upon it as meaning ... equality of opportunity. Well, we're justified in seeking civil rights, if it means equality of opportunity, because all we're doing there is trying to collect for our investment. Our mothers and fathers invested sweat and blood. Three hundred and ten years we worked in this country without a dime in return – I mean without a dime in return …

…

Not only did we give of our free labor, we gave of our blood. Every time we had a call to arms, we were the first ones in uniform. We died on every battlefield the white man had. We have made a greater sacrifice than anybody who's standing up in America today. We have made a greater contribution and have collected less. Civil rights, for those of us whose philosophy is black nationalism, means: "Give it to us now. Don't wait for next year. Give it to us yesterday, and that's not fast enough."

I might stop right here to point out one thing. Whenever you're going after something that belongs to you, anyone who's depriving you of the right to have it is a criminal. Understand that. Whenever you are going after something that is yours, you are within your legal rights to lay claim to it. And anyone who puts forth any effort to deprive you of that which is yours, is breaking the law, is a criminal. And this was pointed out by the Supreme Court decision. It outlawed segregation.

Which means segregation is against the law. Which means a segregationist is breaking the law. A segregationist is a criminal. You can't label him as anything other than that. And when you demonstrate against segregation, the law is on your side. The Supreme Court is on your side.

Now, who is it that opposes you in carrying out the law? The police department itself. With police dogs and clubs. Whenever you demonstrate against segregation, whether it is segregated education, segregated housing, or anything else, the law is on your side, and anyone who stands in the way is not the law any longer. They are breaking the law; they are not representatives of the law …

If you don't take this kind of stand, your little children will grow up and look at you and think "shame." … Any time you know you're within the law, within your legal rights, within your moral rights, in accord with justice, then die for what you believe in. But don't die alone. Let your dying be reciprocal. This is what is meant by equality. What's good for the goose is good for the gander.

When we begin to get in this area, we need new friends, we need new allies. We need to expand the civil-rights struggle to a higher level – to the level of human rights. Whenever you are in a civil-rights struggle, whether you know it or not, you are confining yourself to the jurisdiction of Uncle Sam. No one from the outside world can speak out in your behalf as long as your struggle is a civil-rights struggle. Civil rights comes within the domestic affairs of this country. All of our African brothers and our Asian brothers and our Latin-American brothers cannot open their mouths and interfere in the domestic affairs of the United States. And as long as it's civil rights, this comes under the jurisdiction of Uncle Sam.

...

When you expand the civil-rights struggle to the level of human rights, you can then take the case of the black man in this country before the nations in the UN. You can take it before the General Assembly. You can take Uncle Sam before a world court. But the only level you can do it on is the level of human rights. Civil rights keeps you under his restrictions, under his jurisdiction. Civil rights keeps you in his pocket. Civil rights means you're asking Uncle Sam to treat you right. Human rights are something you were born with. Human rights are your God-given rights. Human rights are the rights that are recognized by all nations of this earth. And any time any one violates your human rights, you can take them to the world court.

... Expand the civil-rights struggle to the level of human rights. Take it into the United Nations, where our African brothers can throw their weight on our side, where our Asian brothers can throw their weight on our side, where our Latin-American brothers can throw their weight on our side, and where 800 million Chinamen are sitting there waiting to throw their weight on our side.

Let the world know how bloody [Uncle Sam's] hands are. Let the world know the hypocrisy that's practiced over here. Let it be the ballot or the bullet. Let him know that it must be the ballot or the bullet.

...

The political philosophy of black nationalism means that the black man should control the politics and the politicians in his own community; no more. The black man in the black community has to be re-educated into the science of politics so he will know what politics is supposed to bring him in return. Don't be throwing out any ballots. A ballot is like a bullet. You don't throw your ballots until you see a target, and if that target is not within your reach, keep your ballot in your pocket.

The political philosophy of black nationalism is being taught in the Christian church. It's being taught in the NAACP. It's being taught in CORE meetings. It's being taught in SNCC Student Nonviolent Coordinating Committee meetings. It's being taught in Muslim meetings. It's being taught where nothing but atheists and agnostics come together. It's being taught everywhere. Black people are fed up with the dillydallying, pussyfooting, compromising approach that we've been using toward getting our freedom. We want freedom now, but we're not going to get it saying "We Shall Overcome." We've got to fight until we overcome.

The economic philosophy of black nationalism is pure and simple. It only means that we should control the economy of our community. Why should white people be running all the stores in our community? Why should white people be running the banks of our community? Why should the economy of our community be in the hands of the white man? Why? If a black man can't move his store into a white community, you tell me why a white man should move his store into a black community. The philosophy of black nationalism involves a re-education program in the black community in regards to economics. Our people have to be made to see that any time you take your dollar out of your community and spend it in a community where you don't live, the community where you live will get poorer and poorer, and the community where you spend your money will get richer and richer.

...

So the economic philosophy of black nationalism means in every church, in every civic organization, in every fraternal order, it's time now for our people to become conscious of the importance of controlling the economy of our community. If we own the stores, if we operate the businesses, if we try and establish some industry in our own community, then we're developing to the position where we are creating employment for our own kind. Once you gain control of the economy of your own community, then you don't have to picket and boycott and beg some cracker downtown for a job in his business.

The social philosophy of black nationalism only means that we have to get together and remove the evils, the vices, alcoholism, drug addiction, and other evils that are destroying the moral fiber of our community. We our selves have to lift the level of our community, the standard of our community to a higher level, make our own society beautiful so that we will be satisfied in our own social circles and won't be running around here trying to knock our way into a social circle where we're not wanted. So I say, in spreading a gospel such as black nationalism, it is not designed to make the black man re-evaluate the white man – you know him already – but to make the black man re-evaluate himself. Don't change the white man's mind – you can't change his mind, and that whole thing about appealing to the moral conscience of America – America's conscience is bankrupt. She lost all conscience a long time ago. Uncle Sam has no conscience.

...

[The black Muslim] gospel is black nationalism. We're not trying to threaten the existence of any organization, but we're spreading the gospel of black nationalism. Anywhere there's a church that is also preaching and practicing the gospel of black nationalism, join that church. If the NAACP is preaching and practicing the gospel of black nationalism, join the NAACP. If CORE is spreading and practicing the gospel of black

nationalism, join CORE. Join any organization that has a gospel that's for the uplift of the black man. And when you get into it and see them pussy-footing or compromising, pull out of it because that's not black nationalism. We'll find another one.
...

We will work with anybody, anywhere, at any time, who is genuinely interested in tackling the problem head-on, nonviolently as long as the enemy is nonviolent, but violent when the enemy gets violent. We'll work with you on the voter-registration drive, we'll work with you on rent strikes, we'll work with you on school boycotts; I don't believe in any kind of integration; I'm not even worried about it, because I know you're not going to get it anyway ... But we will still work with you on the school boycotts because we're against a segregated school system. A segregated school system produces children who, when they graduate, graduate with crippled minds. But this does not mean that a school is segregated because it's all black. A segregated school means a school that is controlled by people who have no real interest in it whatsoever.

Let me explain what I mean. A segregated district or community is a community in which people live, but outsiders control the politics and the economy of that community. They never refer to the white section as a segregated community. It's the all-Negro section that's a segregated community. Why? The white man controls his own school, his own bank, his own economy, his own politics, his own everything, his own community; but he also controls yours. When you're under someone else's control, you're segregated. They'll always give you the lowest or the worst that there is to offer, but it doesn't mean you're segregated just because you have your own. You've got to control your own. Just like the white man has control of his, you need to control yours.

You know the best way to get rid of segregation? The white man is more afraid of separation than he is of integration. Segregation means that he puts you away from him, but not far enough for you to be out of his jurisdiction; separation means you're gone. And the white man will integrate faster than he'll let you separate. So we will work with you against the segregated school system because it's criminal, because it is absolutely destructive, in every way imaginable, to the minds of the children who have to be exposed to that type of crippling education.

Last but not least, I must say this concerning the great controversy over rifles and shotguns. The only thing that I've ever said is that in areas where the government has proven itself either unwilling or unable to defend the lives and the property of Negroes, it's time for Negroes to defend themselves. Article number two of the constitutional amendments provides you and me the right to own a rifle or a shotgun. It is constitutionally legal to own a shotgun or a rifle. This doesn't mean you're going to get a rifle and form battalions and go out looking for white folks, although you'd be within your rights – I mean, you'd be justified; but that would be illegal and we don't do anything illegal. If the white man doesn't want the black man buying rifles and shotguns, then let the government do its job.

...

The black nationalists aren't going to wait. Lyndon B. Johnson is the head of the Democratic Party. If he's for civil rights, let him go into the Senate next week and declare himself. Let him go in there right now and declare himself. Let him go in there and denounce the Southern branch of his party. Let him go in there right now and take a moral stand – right now, not later. Tell him don't wait until election time. If he waits too long, brothers and sisters, he will be responsible for letting a condition develop in this country which will create a climate that will bring seeds up out of the ground with vegetation on the end of them looking like something these people never dreamed of. In 1964, it's the ballot or the bullet.

Source: Reproduced from "The Ballot or the Bullet," in George Breitman (ed.), *Malcolm X Speaks: Selected Speeches and Statements* (Grove Weidenfeld, 1969). Copyright © 1965, 1989 by Betty Shabazz and Pathfinder Press. Reprinted by permission.

2 Fannie Lou Hamer Testifies on Behalf of the Mississippi Freedom Democratic Party, 1964

"All of this is on account of us wanting to register"

The Mississippi Freedom Democratic Party (MFDP) was created as a mechanism through which African Americans could register to vote in the state. Mounting a direct challenge to the Democratic Party's practice of white supremacy, MFDP put up delegates to send to the Democratic National Convention in Atlantic City the summer of 1964. Claiming that its representatives were the true Democrats from Mississippi, MFDP attempted to replace the state's all-white regular delegation. Fannie Lou Hamer (1917–1977), a native Mississippian and a sharecropper, fired and harassed for attempting to register, had joined SNCC as an organizer, and emerged as a formidable leader. While activists and allies demonstrated outside and lobbied other delegations at the Convention, Hamer gave the testimony below to the Credentials Committee.

July 22, 1964

Mr. Chairman, and the Credentials Committee, my name is Mrs. Fannie Lou Hamer, and I live at 626 East Lafayette Street, Ruleville, Mississippi, Sunflower County, the home of Senator James O. Eastland and Senator Stennis.

It was the 31st of August in 1962 that 18 of us traveled 26 miles to the country courthouse in Indianola to try to register to try to become first-class citizens.

We was met in Indianola by Mississippi men, Highway Patrolmens and they only allowed two of us in to take the literacy test at the time. After we had taken this test and started back to Ruleville, we was held up by the City Police and the State Highway Patrolmen and carried back to Indianola where the bus driver was charged that day with driving a bus the wrong color.

After we paid the fine among us, we continued on to Ruleville, and Reverend Jeff Sunny carried me four miles in the rural area where I had worked as a timekeeper and sharecropper for 18 years. I was met there by my children, who told me that the plantation owner was angry because I had gone down to try to register.

After they told me, my husband came, and said that the plantation owner was raising cain because I had tried to register, and before he quit talking the plantation owner came, and said, "Fannie Lou, do you know – did Pap tell you what I said?"

And I said, "yes, sir."

He said, "I mean that," he said, "If you don't go down and withdraw your registration, you will have to leave," said, "Then if you go down and with-draw," he said, "You will – you might have to go because we are not ready for that in Mississippi."

And I addressed him and told him and said, "I didn't try to register for you. I tried to register for myself."

I had to leave that same night.

On the 10th of September 1962, 16 bullets was fired into the home of Mr. and Mrs. Robert Tucker for me. That same night two girls were shot in Ruleville, Mississippi. Also Mr. Joe McDonald's house was shot in.

And in June the 9th, 1963, I had attended a voter registration workshop, was returning back to Mississippi. Ten of us was traveling by the Continental Trailway bus. When we got to Winona, Mississippi, which is in Montgomery County, four of the people got off … to use the restaurant, two of the people wanted to use the washroom.

The four people that had gone in to use the restaurant was ordered out. During this time I was on the bus. But when I looked through the window and saw they had rushed out[,] I got off of the bus to see what had happened, and one of the ladies said, "It was a State Highway Patrolman and a Chief of Police ordered us out."

I got back on the bus and one of the persons had used the washroom got back on the bus, too.

As soon as I was seated on the bus, I saw when they began to get the four people in a highway patrolman's car, I stepped off of the bus to see what was happening and somebody screamed from the car that the four workers was in and said, "Get that one there," and ... when the man told me I was under arrest, he kicked me.

I was carried to the county jail, and put in the booking room. They left some of the people in the booking room and began to place us in cells. I was placed in a cell with a young woman called Miss Ivesta Simpson. After I was placed in the cell I began to hear the sound of kicks and horrible screams, and I could hear somebody say, "Can you say, yes, sir, nigger? Can you say yes, sir?"

And they would say other horrible names.

She would say, "Yes, I can say yes, sir."

"So say it."

She says, "I don't know you well enough."

They beat her, I don't know how long, and after a while she began to pray, and asked God to have mercy on those people.

And it wasn't too long before three white men came to my cell. One of these men was a State Highway Patrolman and he asked me where I was from and I told him Ruleville, he said, "We are going to check this."

And they left my cell and it wasn't too long before they came back. He said, "You are from Ruleville all right," and he used a curse word, and he said, "We are going to make you wish you was dead."

I was carried out of that cell into another cell where they had two Negro prisoners. The State Highway Patrolmen ordered the first Negro to take the blackjack.

The first Negro prisoner ordered me, by orders from the State Highway Patrolman for me, to lay down on a bunk bed on my face, and I laid on my face.

The first Negro began to beat, and I was beat by the first Negro until he was exhausted, and I was holding my hands behind me at that time on my left side because I suffered from polio when I was six years old.

After the first Negro had beat until he was exhausted the State Highway Patrolman ordered the second Negro to take the blackjack.

The second Negro began to beat and I began to work my feet, and the State Highway Patrolman ordered the first Negro who had beat me to sit upon my feet to keep me from working my feet. I began to scream and one white man got up and began to beat me in my head and told me to hush.

One white man – since my dress had worked up high, walked over and pulled my dress down and he pulled my dress back, back up.

I was in jail when Medgar Evers was murdered.

All of this is on account of us wanting to register, to become first-class citizens, and if the Freedom Democratic Party is not seated now, I question America, is this America, the land of the free and the home of the brave where we have to sleep with our telephones off of the hooks because our lives be threatened daily because we want to live as decent human beings, in America?

Thank you.

Source: Fannie Lou Hamer, "I'm Sick and Tired of Being Sick and Tired," Speech to the Credentials Committee, Democratic National Convention, 1964.

3 Bayard Rustin Considers the Future of the Movement, 1965

"the Negro today finds himself stymied by obstacles of far greater magnitude than the legal barriers he was attacking before"

Since the 1930s, Bayard Rustin (1912–1987) had been active in civil rights, labor, and pacifist movements. Openly gay, he remained in the background, but as a masterful tactician, he was central to organizing the Freedom Rides and the Marches on Washington. To Rustin the Civil Rights Act (1964) and the Voting Rights Act (1965), passed after long and bitter battles, were significant victories, but the movement needed to shift, he believed, from protest to politics. To do so, he argued, African Americans needed to strengthen their historical coalitions. The excerpts below are from an influential article Rustin wrote in 1965.

"From Protest to Politics"

I

The decade spanned by the 1954 Supreme Court decision on school desegregation and the Civil Rights Act of 1964 will undoubtedly be recorded as the period in which the legal foundations of racism in America were destroyed. To be sure, pockets of resistance remain; but it would be hard to quarrel with the assertion that the elaborate legal structure of segregation and discrimination, particularly in relation to public accommodations, has virtually collapsed. On the other hand, without making light of the human sacrifices involved in the direct-action tactics (sit-ins, freedom rides, and the rest) that were so instrumental to this achievement, we must recognize that in desegregating public accommodations, we affected institutions which are relatively peripheral both to the American socio-economic order and to the fundamental conditions of life of the Negro people. In a highly industrialized, 20th-century civilization, we hit Jim Crow precisely where it was most anachronistic, dispensable, and vulnerable – in hotels, lunch counters, terminals, libraries, swimming pools, and the like. For in these forms, Jim Crow does impede the flow of commerce in the broadest sense: it is a nuisance in a society on the move (and on the make). Not surprisingly, therefore, it was the most mobility-conscious and relatively liberated groups in the Negro community – lower-middle-class college students – who launched the attack that brought down this imposing but hollow structure.

...

[But] what is the value of winning access to public accommodations for those who lack money to use them? The minute the movement faced this question, it was compelled to expand its vision beyond race relations to economic relations, including the role of education in modern society. And what also became clear is that all these interrelated problems, by their very nature, are not soluble by private, voluntary efforts but require government action – or politics. Already Southern demonstrators had recognized that the most effective way to strike at the police brutality they suffered from was by getting rid of the local sheriff – and that meant political action, which in turn meant, and still means, political action within the Democratic party where the only meaningful primary contests in the South are fought.

And so, in Mississippi, thanks largely to the leadership of Bob Moses, a turn toward political action has been taken. More than voter registration is involved here. A conscious bid for *political power* is being made, and in the course of that effort a tactical shift is being effected: direct-action techniques are being subordinated to a strategy calling for the building of community institutions or power bases. Clearly, the implications of this shift reach far beyond Mississippi. What began as a protest movement is being challenged to translate itself into a political movement. Is this the right course? And if it is, can the transformation be accomplished?

II
The very decade which has witnessed the decline of legal Jim Crow has also seen the rise of *de facto* segregation in our most fundamental socio-economic institutions. More Negroes are unemployed today than in 1954, and the

unemployment gap between the races is wider. The median income of Negroes has dropped from 57 per cent to 54 per cent of that of whites. A higher percentage of Negro workers is now concentrated in jobs vulnerable to automation than was the case ten years ago. More Negroes attend *de facto* segregated schools today than when the Supreme Court handed down its famous decision; while school integration proceeds at a snail's pace in the South, the number of Northern schools with an excessive proportion of minority youth proliferates. And behind this is the continuing growth of racial slums, spreading over our central cities and trapping Negro youth in a milieu which, whatever its legal definition, sows an unimaginable demoralization. Again, legal niceties aside, a resident of a racial ghetto lives in segregated housing, and more Negroes fall into this category than ever before.

[T]he task of the movement is vastly complicated by the failure of many whites of good will to understand the nature of our problem. There is a widespread assumption that the removal of artificial racial barriers should result in the automatic integration of the Negro into all aspects of American life. This myth is fostered by facile analogies with the experience of various ethnic immigrant groups, particularly the Jews. But the analogies with the Jews do not hold for three simple but profound reasons. First, Jews have a long history as a literate people, a resource which has afforded them opportunities to advance in the academic and professional worlds, to achieve intellectual status even in the midst of economic hardship, and to evolve sustaining value systems in the context of ghetto life. Negroes, for the greater part of their presence in this country, were forbidden by law to read or write. Second, Jews have a long history of family stability, the importance of which in terms of aspiration and self-image is obvious. The Negro family structure was totally destroyed by slavery and with it the possibility of cultural transmission (the right of Negroes to marry and rear children is barely a century old). Third, Jews are white and have the *option* of relinquishing their cultural-religious identity, intermarrying, passing, etc. Negroes, or at least the overwhelming majority of them, do not have this option. There is also a fourth, vulgar reason. If the Jewish and Negro communities are not comparable in terms of education, family structure, and color, it is also true that their respective economic roles bear little resemblance.

This matter of economic role brings us to the greater problem – the fact that we are moving into an era in which the natural functioning of the market does not by itself ensure every man with will and ambition a place in the productive process. The immigrant who came to this country during the late 19th and early 20th centuries entered a society which was expanding territorially and/or economically. It was then possible to start at the bottom, as an unskilled or semi-skilled worker, and move up the ladder, acquiring new skills along the way. Especially was this true when industrial unionism was burgeoning, giving new dignity and higher wages to organized workers. Today the situation has changed. We are not expanding territorially, the western frontier is settled, labor organizing has leveled off, our rate of economic growth has been stagnant for a decade. And we are in the midst of a technological revolution which is altering the fundamental structure of the labor force, destroying unskilled and semi-skilled jobs – jobs in which Negroes are disproportionately concentrated.

Whatever the pace of this technological revolution may be, the *direction* is clear: the lower rungs of the economic ladder are being lopped off. This means that an individual will no longer be able to start at the bottom and work his way up; he will have to start in the middle or on top, and hold on tight. It will not even be enough to have certain specific skills, for many skilled jobs are also vulnerable to automation. A broad educational background, permitting vocational adaptability and flexibility, seems more imperative than ever …

…

III

Let me sum up what I have thus far been trying to say: the civil rights movement is evolving from a protest movement into a full-fledged *social movement* – an evolution calling its very name into question. It is now concerned not merely with removing the barriers to full *opportunity* but with achieving the fact of *equality*. From sit-ins and freedom rides we have gone into rent strikes, boycotts, community organization, and political action. As a consequence of this natural evolution, the Negro today finds himself stymied by obstacles of far greater magnitude than the legal barriers he was attacking before: automation, urban decay, *de facto* school segregation. These are problems which, while conditioned by Jim Crow, do not vanish upon its demise. They are more deeply rooted in our socio-economic order; they are the result of the total society's failure to meet not only the Negro's needs, but human needs generally.

…

The revolutionary character of the Negro's struggle is manifest in the fact that this struggle may have done more to democratize life for whites than for Negroes. Clearly, it was the sit-in movement of young Southern Negroes which, as it galvanized white students, banished the ugliest features of McCarthyism from the American campus and resurrected political debate. It was not until Negroes assaulted *de facto* school segregation in the urban centers that the issue of quality education for *all* children stirred into motion. Finally, it seems reasonably clear that the civil rights movement, directly and through the resurgence of social conscience it kindled, did more to initiate the war on poverty than any other single force.

... But the term revolutionary, as I am using it, does not connote violence; it refers to the qualitative transformation of fundamental institutions, more or less rapidly, to the point where the social and economic structure which they comprised can no longer be said to be the same. The Negro struggle has hardly run its course; and it will not stop moving until it has been utterly defeated or won substantial equality. But I fail to see how the movement can be victorious in the absence of radical programs for full employment, abolition of slums, the reconstruction of our educational system, new definitions of work and leisure. Adding up the cost of such programs, we can only conclude that we are talking about a refashioning of our political economy. ...

... It is clear that Negro needs cannot be satisfied unless we go beyond what has so far been placed on the agenda. How are these radical objectives to be achieved? The answer is simple, deceptively so: *through political power.*

...

Neither [the] movement nor the country's twenty million black people can win political power alone. We need allies. The future of the Negro struggle depends on whether the contradictions of this society can be resolved by a coalition of progressive forces which becomes the *effective* political majority in the United States. I speak of the coalition which staged the March on Washington, passed the Civil Rights Act, and laid the basis for the Johnson landslide – Negroes, trade unionists, liberals, and religious groups.

[T]he issue is which coalition to join and how to make it responsive to your program. Necessarily there will be compromise. But the difference between expediency and morality in politics is the difference between selling out a principle and making smaller concessions to win larger ones. The leader who shrinks from this task reveals not his purity but his lack of political sense.

The task of molding a political movement out of the March on Washington coalition is not simple, but no alternatives have been advanced. We need to choose our allies on the basis of common political objectives. It has become fashionable in some no-win Negro circles to decry the white liberal as the main enemy (his hypocrisy is what sustains racism); by virtue of this reverse recitation of the reactionary's litany (liberalism leads to socialism, which leads to Communism) the Negro is left in majestic isolation, except for a tiny band of fervent white initiates. But the objective fact is that *Eastland and Goldwater* are the main enemies – they and the opponents of civil rights, of the war on poverty, of medicare, of social security, of federal aid to education, of unions, and so forth. The labor movement, despite its obvious faults, has been the largest single organized force in this country pushing for progressive social legislation. And where the Negro-labor-liberal axis is weak, as in the farm belt, it was the religious groups that were most influential in rallying support for the Civil Rights Bill.

The 1964 elections marked a turning point in American politics. The Democratic landslide was not merely the result of a negative reaction to Goldwaterism; it was also the expression of a majority liberal consensus. ... Beyond adding to Johnson's total national margin, [Negro support] was specifically responsible for his victories in Virginia, Florida, Tennessee, and Arkansas. ... [T]he 1.6 million Southern Negroes who voted have had a shattering impact on the Southern political party structure. ... It may be premature to predict a Southern Democratic party of Negroes and white moderates and a Republican Party of refugee racists and economic conservatives, but there certainly is a strong tendency toward such a realignment. ...Even the *tendency* toward disintegration of the Democratic party's racist wing defines a new context for Presidential and liberal strategy in the congressional battles ahead ...

    ...

Here is where the cutting edge of the civil rights movement can be applied. We must see to it that the reorganization of the "consensus party" proceeds along lines which will make [the Democratic Party] an effective vehicle for social reconstruction, a role it cannot play so long as it furnishes Southern racism with its national political power. (One of Barry Goldwater's few attractive ideas was that the Dixiecrats belong with him in the same party.) And nowhere has the civil rights movement's political cutting edge been more magnificently demonstrated than at Atlantic City, where the Mississippi Freedom Democratic Party not only secured recognition as a bona fide component of the national party, but in the process routed the representatives of the most rabid racists – the white Mississippi and Alabama delegations. While I still believe that the FDP made a tactical error in spurning the compromise, there is no question that they launched a political revolution whose logic is the displacement of Dixiecrat power. They launched that revolution within a major political institution and as part of a coalitional effort.

The role of the civil rights movement in the reorganization of American political life is programmatic as well as strategic. We are challenged now to broaden our social vision, to develop functional programs with concrete objectives. We need to propose alternatives to technological unemployment, urban decay, and the rest. We need to be calling for public works and training, for national economic planning, for federal aid to education, for attractive public housing – all this on a sufficiently massive scale to make a difference. We need to protest the notion that our integration into American life, so long delayed, must now proceed in an atmosphere of competitive scarcity instead of in the security of abundance which technology makes possible. We cannot claim to have answers to all the complex problems of modern society. That is too much to ask of a movement still battling barbarism in Mississippi. But we can agitate the right questions by probing at the contradictions which still stand in the way of the "Great Society." The questions having been asked, motion must begin in the larger society, for there is a limit to what Negroes can do alone.

Source: Bayard Rustin, "From Protest to Politics: The Future of the Civil Rights Movement," *Commentary Magazine*, February 1965. Reprinted with permission of Commentary Magazine.

4 Stokely Carmichael Explains Black Power, 1966

"Black people must do things for themselves"

Many SNCC activists became impatient with the snail's pace of change, the futility of non-violence in the face of violence, the resistance of white opponents, and the reticence of white liberals. At a 1966 march, Stokely Carmichael (who changed his name to Kwame Ture) (1941–1998) deployed a new rhetorical tool, a call for "black power." The slogan was wildly popular with the crowd, but disconcerting to leaders like King, who reproved the phrase. "Black power" suggested a militancy that some African American activists wished to eschew, lest it produce anxieties among whites. "If we had said 'Negro Power,'" Carmichael commented at a speech at Berkeley in 1966, "nobody would have minded." Yet, the ultimate struggle against racism was the pursuit of power, and on this activists agreed.

"Black power" proffered a new rhetoric, but not a new idea; it stipulated that African Americans act in their own interests. That is, black freedom should translate into autonomy and self-determination, and by extension the economic and electoral strength to end poverty and effect political change. The article excerpted below appeared in the New York Review of Books. *In it Carmichael responds to the critical howls that the term "black power" evoked.*

"What We Want" (1966)

...

An organization which claims to speak for the needs of a community – as does the Student Nonviolent Coordinating Committee – must speak in the tone of that community, not as somebody else's buffer zone. This is the significance of black power as a slogan. For once, black people are going to use the words they want to use – not just the words whites want to hear. And they will do this no matter how often the press tries to stop the use of the slogan by equating it with racism or separatism. An organization which claims to be working for the needs of a community – as SNCC does – must work to provide that community with a position of strength from which to make its voice heard. This is the significance of black power beyond the slogan.

...

Almost from its beginning, SNCC sought to address itself to both conditions with a program aimed at winning political power for impoverished Southern blacks. We had to begin with politics because black Americans are a propertyless people in a country where property is valued above all. We had to work for power, because this country does not function by morality, love, and nonviolence, but by power. Thus we determined to win political power, with the idea of moving on from there into activity that would have economic effects. With power, the masses could make or participate in making the decisions which govern their destinies, and thus create basic change in their day-to-day lives.

But if political power seemed to be the key to self-determination, it was also obvious that the key had been thrown down a deep well many years earlier. Disenfranchisement, maintained by racist terror, makes it impossible to talk about organizing for political power in 1960. The right to vote had to be won, and SNCC workers devoted their energies to this from 1961 to 1965. They set up voter registration drives in the Deep South. They created pressure for the vote by holding mock elections in Mississippi in 1963 and by helping to establish the Mississippi Freedom Democratic Party (MFDP) in 1964. That struggle was eased, though not won, with the passage of the 1965 Voting Rights Act. SNCC workers could then address themselves to the question: "Who can we vote for, to have our needs met – how do we make our vote meaningful?"

...

But the concept of "black power" is not a recent or isolated phenomenon: It has grown out of the ferment of agitation and activity by different people and organizations in many black communities over the years. Our last year of work in Alabama added a new concrete possibility. In Lowndes County, for example, black power will mean that if a Negro is elected sheriff, he can end police brutality. If a black man is elected tax assessor, he can collect and channel funds for the building of better roads and schools serving black people thus advancing the move from political power into the economic arena. In such areas as Lowndes, where black men have a majority, they will attempt to use it to exercise control. This is what they seek: control.

Where Negroes lack a majority, black power means proper representation and sharing of control. It means the creation of power bases from which black people can work to change statewide or nationwide patterns of oppression through pressure from strength – instead of weakness. Politically, black power means what it has always meant to SNCC: the coming-together of black people to elect representatives and to force those representatives to speak to their needs. It does not mean merely putting black faces into office. A man or woman who is black and from the slums cannot be automatically expected to speak to the needs of black people. Most of the black politicians we see around the country today are not what SNCC means by black power. The power must be that of a community, and emanate from there.

SNCC today is working in both North and South on programs of voter registration and independent political organizing. ... We have no infallible master plan and we make no claim to exclusive knowledge of how to end racism; different groups will work in their own different ways. SNCC cannot spell out the full logistics of self-determination but it can address itself to the problem by helping black communities define their needs, realize their strength, and go into action along a variety of lines which they must choose for themselves. Without knowing all the answers, it can address itself to the basic problem of poverty; to the fact that in Lowndes County, [Alabama] eighty-six white families own 90 percent of the land. What are black people in that county going to do for jobs, where are they going to get money? There must be reallocation of land, of money.

Ultimately, the economic foundations of this country must be shaken if black people are to control their lives. The colonies of the United States – and this includes the black ghettoes within its borders, North and South – must be liberated. For a century, this nation has been like an octopus of exploitation, its tentacles stretching from Mississippi and Harlem to South America, the Middle East, southern Africa, and Vietnam; the form of exploitation varies from area to area but the essential result has been the same – a powerful few have been maintained and enriched at the expense of the poor and voiceless colored masses. This pattern must be broken. As its grip loosens here and there around the world, the hopes of black Americans become more realistic. For racism to die, a totally different America must be born.

This is what the white society does not wish to face; this is why that society prefers to talk about integration. But integration speaks not at all to the problem of poverty, only to the problem of blackness. Integration today means the man who "makes it," leaving his black brothers behind in the ghetto as fast as his new sports car will take him ...

Integration, moreover, speaks to the problem of blackness in a despicable way. As a goal, it has been based on complete acceptance of the fact that in order to have a decent house or education, blacks must move into a white neighborhood or send their children to a white school. This reinforces, among both black and white, the idea that "white" is automatically better and "black" is by definition inferior. This is why integration is a subterfuge for the maintenance of white supremacy. It allows the nation to focus on a handful of Southern children who get into white schools, at great price, and to ignore the 94 percent who are left behind in unimproved all-black schools.

Such situations will not change until black people have power – to control their own school boards, in this case. Then Negroes become equal in a way that means something, and integration ceases to be a one-way street. Then integration doesn't mean draining skills and energies from the ghetto into white neighborhoods ...

To most whites, black power seems to mean that the Mau Mau are coming to the suburbs at night. The Mau Mau are coming, and whites must stop them. Articles appear about plots to "get Whitey," creating an atmosphere in which "law and order must be maintained." Once again, responsibility is shifted from the oppressor to the oppressed. Other whites chide, "Don't forget – you're only 10 percent of the population; if you get too smart, we'll wipe you out." If they are liberals, they complain, "What about me? – don't you want my help any more?" These are people supposedly concerned about black Americans, but today they think first of themselves, of their feelings of rejection. Or they admonish, "You can't get anywhere without coalitions," when there is in fact no group at present with whom to form a coalition in which blacks will not be absorbed and betrayed. Or they accuse us of "polarizing the races" by our calls for black unity, when the true responsibility for polarization lies with whites who will not accept their responsibility as the majority power for making the democratic process work.

White America will not face the problem of color, the reality of it. The well-intended say: "We're all human, everybody is really decent, we must forget color." But color cannot be "forgotten" until its weight is recognized and dealt with. White America will not acknowledge that the ways in which this country sees itself are contradicted by being black – and always have been. Whereas most of the people who settled this country came here for freedom or for economic opportunity, blacks were brought here to be slaves.

When the Lowndes County Freedom Organization chose the black panther as its symbol, it was christened by the press "the Black Panther Party" – but the Alabama Democratic Party, whose symbol is a rooster, has never been called the White Cock Party. No one ever talked about "white power" because power in this country is white. All this adds up to more than merely identifying a group phenomenon by some catchy name or adjective. The furor over that black panther reveals the problems that white America has with color and sex; the furor over "black power" reveals how deep racism runs and the great fear which is attached to it.

...

From birth, black people are told a set of lies about themselves. We are told that we are lazy – yet I drive through the Delta area of Mississippi and watch black people picking cotton in the hot sun for fourteen hours. We are told, "If you work hard, you'll succeed" – but if that were true, black people would own this country. We are oppressed because we are black – not because we are ignorant, not because we are lazy, not because we're stupid (and got good rhythm), but because we're black ... It takes time to reject the most important lie: That black people inherently can't do the same things white people can do, unless white people help them.

... Only black people can convey the revolutionary idea that black people are able to do things themselves. Only they can help create in the community an aroused and continuing black consciousness that will provide the basis for political strength. In the past, white allies have furthered white supremacy without the whites involved realizing it – or wanting it, I think. Black people must do things for themselves; they must get poverty money they will control and spend themselves; they must conduct tutorial programs themselves so that black children can identify with black people. This is one reason Africa has such importance: The reality of black men ruling their own natives gives blacks elsewhere a sense of possibility, of power, which they do not now have.

This does not mean we don't welcome help or friends. But we want the right to decide whether anyone is, in fact, our friend. In the past, black Americans have been almost the only people whom everybody and his momma could jump up and call their friends. We have been tokens, symbols, objects – as I was in high school to many young whites, who liked having "a Negro friend." We want to decide who is our friend, and we will not accept someone who comes to us and says: "If you do X, Y, and Z, then I'll help you." We will not be told whom we should choose as allies. We will not be isolated from any group or nation except by our own choice. We cannot have the oppressors telling the oppressed how to rid themselves of the oppressor.

I have said that most liberal whites react to "black power" with the question, What about me?, rather than saying: Tell me what you want me to do and I'll see if I can do it. There are answers to the right question. One of the most disturbing things about almost all white supporters of the movement has been that they are afraid to go into their own communities – which is where the racism exists – and work to get rid of it. They want to run from Berkeley to tell us what to do in Mississippi; let them look instead at Berkeley. They admonish blacks to be nonviolent; let them preach nonviolence in the white community. They come to teach me Negro history; let them go to the suburbs and open up freedom schools for whites. Let them work to stop America's racist foreign policy; let them press this government to cease supporting the economy of South Africa.

...

As for white America, perhaps it can stop crying out against "black supremacy," "black nationalism," "racism in reverse," and begin facing reality. The reality is that this nation, from top to bottom, is racist; that racism is not primarily a problem of "human relations" but of an exploitation maintained – either actively or through silence – by the society as a whole. Camus and Sartre have asked, can a man condemn himself? Can whites, particularly liberal whites, condemn themselves? Can they stop blaming us, and blame their own system? Are they capable of the shame which might become a revolutionary emotion?

...

Source: Stokely Carmichael, "What We Want," New York Review of Books, Vol. 7 (September 22, 1966), pp. 5–6, 8.

Questions for Consideration

How did Malcolm X's approach to civil rights compare to that expressed by
   Martin Luther King, Jr.'s "Letter from a Birmingham Jail?" Where do they agree?
   And where do they differ?
What common themes emerge among these documents? What differences do they
   reflect?
Why did black activists view the vote as critical to their goals?
All of the documents in this chapter relate to "black power." On what historical
   themes of black freedom does "black power" draw? What made the theme of
   "power" so important at this moment?
How effective was the goal of integration as a strategy for black freedom?
How did activists in the mid-1960s understand the relationship between power and
   equality? Is racial equality possible without black power?
How did the views of Bayard Rustin and Stokely Carmichael differ on the matter
   of allies? Why might they have disagreed?

Bibliography

Branch, Taylor. Pillar of Fire: America in the King Years, 1963–1965. New York:
   Simon and Schuster, 1998.
Countryman, Matthew J. Up South: Civil Rights and Black Power in Philadelphia.
   Philadelphia: University of Pennsylvania Press, 2007.

D'Emilio, John. *Lost Prophet: The Life and Times of Bayard Rustin*. Chicago: Chicago University Press, 2004.

Jeffries, Hasan Kwame. *Bloody Lowndes: Civil Rights and Black Power in Alabama's Black Belt*. New York: New York University Press, 2010.

Joseph, Peniel E. *Waiting for the Midnight Hour: A Narrative History of Black Power in America*. New York: Henry Holt, 2005.

Lawson, Steven F. *Running for Freedom: Civil Rights and Black Politics in America Since 1941*. 3rd ed. Oxford: Blackwell Publishing, 2009.

Lewis, Andrew B. *The Shadows of Youth: The Remarkable Journey of the Civil Rights Generation*. New York: Hill and Wang, 2010.

Marable, Manning. *Malcolm X: A Life of Reinvention*. New York: Penguin, 2011.

Nagin, Tomiko-Brown. *Courage to Dissent: Atlanta and the Long History of the Civil Rights Movement*. New York: Oxford University Press, 2011.

Payne, Charles. *I've Got the Light of Freedom: The Organizing Tradition and the Mississippi Freedom Struggle*. Reprint. Berkeley: University of California Press, 2007.

Self, Robert O. *American Babylon: Race and the Struggle for Post-War Oakland*. Princeton: Princeton University Press, 2003.

Ture, Kwame [Stokely Carmichael]. *Ready for Revolution: The Life and Struggles of Stokely Carmichael*. New York: Scribner, 2005.

Ture, Kwame [Stokely Carmichael], and Charles V. Hamilton. *Black Power: The Politics of Liberation in America*. Reprint. New York: Vintage Books, 1992.

Chapter 10   Revolution, 1966–1977

The Rustin–Carmichael discourse of 1965–1966 reiterated an old debate in a new context. Should black people turn inward? Or, as Du Bois had believed, could they bring "the Negro Genius" to bear on making a better world? African Americans historically had made alliances with labor, gays, communists, religionists, feminists, pacifists, reformers, radicals, and Leftists, as well as with Democrats, Republicans, liberals, and conservatives. At the same time, they always had possessed their own institutions and organizations that reflected black self-interests, upbuilding, uplift, civil rights, and power. Whatever their affiliations or tactics – armed self-defense, direct action protest, racial separatism, moral suasion, coalition building, or intellectual analyses – African Americans possessed both a shared disillusionment with American society and a common desire to effect positive change.

In the late 1960s and early 1970s, black nationalist voices multiplied, building consciousness and pride as part of a reclamation project. Seeking ideas and allies, extant organizations expanded, contracted, disappeared, and reformed, and new ones emerged. Across different venues, activists deployed varying interpretations of "black power," defined as African Americans' ability to effect consequential transformations that applied not only to themselves. But the goals also extended to oppressed people generally. In short, the black freedom movement was fluid. It had demolished the underpinnings of constitutional inequality, opening important American institutions – political, cultural, and economic – for whole groups of

African American Voices: A Documentary Reader from Emancipation to the Present,
First Edition. Edited by Leslie Brown.
© 2014 John Wiley & Sons, Inc. Published 2014 by John Wiley & Sons, Inc.

Americans, among them whites and women, who historically had been excluded. Common use of the term "revolution" in this era recognized the significance of the societal changes activists proposed and pursued. The question of the moment asked: Could the freedom movement – the revolution – coalesce into a larger human struggle?

1 The Black Panther Party Articulates a Platform, 1966

"black people will not be free until we are able to determine our destiny"

The Black Panther Party for Self-Defense (BPP) was founded in 1966 in Oakland, California, by college students Huey Newton and Bobby Seale. As a community organization it focused on problems that plagued black neighborhoods, including education, housing, employment, health care, hunger, safety, and police brutality. A political party, the BPP articulated a black nationalist perspective grounded in a sense of shared responsibility that called upon the black community to protect and provide for itself. Its talk of liberation translated into actively "politicizing" residents through "observation and participation," that is, encouraging people to learn about the system by engaging the system.

Its assertiveness, coupled with its willingness to establish working relationships and to forge political coalitions, made the BPP influential on the political landscape of the late 1960s and early 1970s. Considered the vanguard of "the revolution" – the societal upheaval unfolding – the Party attracted a range of supporters among liberal and Leftist groups, even as it distressed moderates and antagonized authorities. Its platform, the Ten Point Program, was a statement of goals as well as a list of demands. It was widely distributed in Panther publications.

The Black Panther Party Ten Point Program, October 1966

1. We want freedom. We want power to determine the destiny of our Black Community.

    We believe that black people will not be free until we are able to determine our destiny.

2. We want full employment for our people.

    We believe that the federal government is responsible and obligated to give every man employment or a guaranteed income. We believe that if the white American businessmen will not give full employment, then the means of production should be taken from the businessmen and placed in the community so that the people of the community can organize and employ all of its people and give a high standard of living.

3. We want an end to the robbery by the white man of our Black Community.

We believe that this racist government has robbed us and now we are demanding the overdue debt of forty acres and two mules. Forty acres and two mules was promised 100 years ago as restitution for slave labor and mass murder of black people. We will accept the payment as currency which will be distributed to our many communities. The Germans are now aiding the Jews in Israel for the genocide of the Jewish people. The Germans murdered six million Jews. The American racist has taken part in the slaughter of over twenty million black people; therefore, we feel that this is a modest demand that we make.

4. We want decent housing, fit for shelter of human beings.

We believe that if the white landlords will not give decent housing to our black community, then the housing and the land should be made into cooperatives so that our community, with government aid, can build and make decent housing for its people.

5. We want education for our people that exposes the true nature of this decadent American society. We want education that teaches us our true history and our role in the present-day society.

We believe in an educational system that will give to our people a knowledge of self. If a man does not have knowledge of himself and his position in society and the world, then he has little chance to relate to anything else.

6. We want all black men to be exempt from military service.

We believe that Black people should not be forced to fight in the military service to defend a racist government that does not protect us. We will not fight and kill other people of color in the world who, like black people, are being victimized by the white racist government of America. We will protect ourselves from the force and violence of the racist police and the racist military, by whatever means necessary.

7. We want an immediate end to police brutality and murder of black people.

We believe we can end police brutality in our black community by organizing black self-defense groups that are dedicated to defending our black community from racist police oppression and brutality. The Second Amendment to the Constitution of the United States gives us a right to bear arms. We therefore believe that all black people should arm themselves for self-defense.

8. We want freedom for all black men held in federal, state, county and city prisons and jails.

We believe that all black people should be released from the many jails and prisons because they have not received a fair and impartial trial.

9. We want all black people when brought to trial to be tried in court by a jury of their peer group or people from their black communities, as defined by the Constitution of the United States.

We believe that the courts should follow the United States Constitution so that black people will receive fair trials. The 14th Amendment of the U.S. Constitution gives a man a right to be tried by his peer group. A peer is a person from a similar economic, social, religious, geographical, environmental, historical and racial background. To do this the court will be forced to select a jury from the black community from which the black defendant came. We have been, and are being tried by all-white juries that have no understanding of the "average reasoning man" of the black community.

10. We want land, bread, housing, education, clothing, justice and peace. And as our major political objective, a United Nations-supervised plebiscite to be held throughout the black colony in which only black colonial subjects will be allowed to participate for the purpose of determining the will of black people as to their national destiny.

When in the course of human events, it becomes necessary for one people to dissolve the political bands which have connected them with another, and to assume, among the powers of the earth, the separate and equal station to which the laws of nature and nature's God entitle them, a decent respect to the opinions of mankind requires that they should declare the causes which impel them to the separation.

We hold these truths to be self evident, that all men are created equal; that they are endowed by their Creator with certain unalienable rights; that among these are life, liberty, and the pursuit of happiness. That, to secure these rights, governments are instituted among men, deriving their just powers from the consent of the governed; that, whenever any form of government becomes destructive of these ends, it is the right of the people to alter or to abolish it, and to institute a new government, laying its foundation on such principles, and organizing its powers in such form, as to them shall seem most likely to effect their safety and happiness. Prudence, indeed, will dictate that governments long established should not be changed for light and transient causes; and accordingly, all experience hath shown, that mankind are more disposed to suffer, while evils are sufferable, than to right themselves by abolishing the forms to which they are accustomed. But, when a long train of abuses and usurpations, pursuing invariably the same object,

evinces a design to reduce them under absolute despotism, it is their right, it
is their duty, to throw off such government, and to provide new guards for
their future security.

Source: Reproduced from *War Against the Panthers* by Huey P. Newton, by Writers &
Readers Publishing, Inc. (now For Beginners LLC), 1996. Reprinted with permission.

2 Rev. Dr. Martin Luther King, Jr., Opposes the War in Vietnam, 1967

*"A true revolution of values will lay hand on the world order and say
of war, 'This way of settling differences is not just'"*

*Rev. Dr. Martin Luther King, Jr., was honored in 1964 with a Nobel Prize
for Peace, which cited him as "the first person in the Western world to have
shown us that a struggle can be waged without violence." In the mid-1960s,
he began to speak out against the war in Vietnam; he was roundly criticized,
even by allies. King delivered this speech to an ecumenical group, Clergymen
and Laymen Concerned About Vietnam, at the prestigious Riverside Church
in New York City.*

"Time to Break the Silence"

...

Over the past two years, as I have moved to break the betrayal of my
own silences and to speak from the burnings of my own heart, as I have
called for radical departures from the destruction of Vietnam, many persons have questioned me about the wisdom of my path. At the heart of
their concerns, this query has often loomed large and loud: "Why are you
speaking about the war, Dr. King? Why are you joining the voices of dissent?" "Peace and civil rights don't mix," they say. "Aren't you hurting the
cause of your people?" they ask. And when I hear them, though I often
understand the source of their concern, I am nevertheless greatly saddened,
for such questions mean that the inquirers have not really known me, my
commitment, or my calling. Indeed, their questions suggest that they do not
know the world in which they live. In the light of such tragic misunderstanding, I deem it of signal importance to state clearly, and I trust con-
cisely, why I believe that the path from Dexter Avenue Baptist Church – the
church in Montgomery, Alabama, where I began my pastorate – leads
clearly to this sanctuary tonight.

I come to this platform tonight to make a passionate plea to my beloved nation. This speech is not addressed to Hanoi or to the National Liberation Front. It is not addressed to China or to Russia. Nor is it an attempt to overlook the ambiguity of the total situation and the need for a collective solution to the tragedy of Vietnam. Neither is it an attempt to make North Vietnam or the National Liberation Front paragons of virtue, nor to overlook the role they must play in the successful resolution of the problem. While they both may have justifiable reasons to be suspicious of the good faith of the United States, life and history give eloquent testimony to the fact that conflicts are never resolved without trustful give and take on both sides. Tonight, however, I wish not to speak with Hanoi and the National Liberation Front, but rather to my fellow Americans.

Since I am a preacher by calling, I suppose it is not surprising that I have several major reasons for bringing Vietnam into the field of my moral vision. There is at the outset a very obvious and almost facile connection between the war in Vietnam and the struggle I and others have been waging in America. A few years ago there was a shining moment in that struggle. It seemed as if there was a real promise of hope for the poor, both black and white, through the poverty program. There were experiments, hopes, new beginnings. Then came the buildup in Vietnam, and I watched this program broken and eviscerated as if it were some idle political plaything on a society gone mad on war. And I knew that America would never invest the necessary funds or energies in rehabilitation of its poor so long as adventures like Vietnam continued to draw men and skills and money like some demonic, destructive suction tube. So I was increasingly compelled to see the war as an enemy of the poor and to attack it as such.

Perhaps a more tragic recognition of reality took place when it became clear to me that the war was doing far more than devastating the hopes of the poor at home. It was sending their sons and their brothers and their husbands to fight and to die in extraordinarily high proportions relative to the rest of the population. We were taking the black young men who had been crippled by our society and sending them eight thousand miles away to guarantee liberties in Southeast Asia which they had not found in southwest Georgia and East Harlem. So we have been repeatedly faced with the cruel irony of watching Negro and white boys on TV screens as they kill and die together for a nation that has been unable to seat them together in the same schools. So we watch them in brutal solidarity burning the huts of a poor village, but we realize that they would hardly live on the same block in Chicago. I could not be silent in the face of such cruel manipulation of the poor.

My third reason moves to an even deeper level of awareness, for it grows out of my experience in the ghettos of the North over the last three years, especially the last three summers. As I have walked among the desperate, rejected, and angry young men, I have told them that Molotov cocktails and rifles would not solve their problems. I have tried to offer them my deepest compassion while maintaining my conviction that social change comes most meaningfully through nonviolent action. But they asked, and rightly so, "What about Vietnam?" They asked if our own nation wasn't using massive doses of violence to solve its problems, to bring about the changes it wanted. Their questions hit home, and I knew that I could never again raise my voice against the violence of the oppressed in the ghettos without having first spoken clearly to the greatest purveyor of violence in the world today: my own government. For the sake of those boys, for the sake of this government, for the sake of the hundreds of thousands trembling under our violence, I cannot be silent.

For those who ask the question, "Aren't you a civil rights leader?" and thereby mean to exclude me from the movement for peace, I have this further answer. In 1957, when a group of us formed the Southern Christian Leadership Conference, we chose as our motto: "To save the soul of America." We were convinced that we could not limit our vision to certain rights for black people, but instead affirmed the conviction that America would never be free or saved from itself until the descendants of its slaves were loosed completely from the shackles they still wear.

...

Finally, as I try to explain for you and for myself the road that leads from Montgomery to this place, I would have offered all that was most valid if I simply said that I must be true to my conviction that I share with all men the calling to be a son of the living God. Beyond the calling of race or nation or creed is this vocation of sonship and brotherhood. Because I believe that the Father is deeply concerned, especially for His suffering and helpless and outcast children, I come tonight to speak for them. This I believe to be the privilege and the burden of all of us who deem ourselves bound by allegiances and loyalties which are broader and deeper than nationalism and which go beyond our nation's self-defined goals and positions. We are called to speak for the weak, for the voiceless, for the victims of our nation, for those it calls "enemy," for no document from human hands can make these humans any less our brothers.

And as I ponder the madness of Vietnam and search within myself for ways to understand and respond in compassion, my mind goes constantly to the people of that peninsula. I speak now not of the soldiers of each side, not of the ideologies of the Liberation Front, not of the junta in Saigon, but simply of the people who have been living under the curse of war for almost three continuous decades now. I think of them, too, because it is clear to me that there will be no meaningful solution there until some attempt is made to know them and hear their broken cries.

They must see Americans as strange liberators. ... So they go, primarily women and children and the aged. They watch as we poison their water, as we kill a million acres of their crops. They must weep as the bulldozers roar through their areas preparing to destroy the precious trees. They wander into the hospitals with at least twenty casualties from American firepower for one Vietcong-inflicted injury. So far we may have killed a million of them, mostly children. They wander into the towns and see thousands of the children, homeless, without clothes, running in packs on the streets like animals. They see the children degraded by our soldiers as they beg for food. They see the children selling their sisters to our soldiers, soliciting for their mothers.

What do the peasants think as we ally ourselves with the landlords and as we refuse to put any action into our many words concerning land reform? What do they think as we test out our latest weapons on them, just as the Germans tested out new medicine and new tortures in the concentration camps of Europe? Where are the roots of the independent Vietnam we claim to be building? Is it among these voiceless ones?

...

... I am as deeply concerned about our own troops there as anything else. For it occurs to me that what we are submitting them to in Vietnam is not simply the brutalizing process that goes on in any war where armies face each other and seek to destroy. We are adding cynicism to the process of death, for they must know after a short period there that none of the things we claim to be fighting for are really involved. Before long they must know that their government has sent them into a struggle among Vietnamese, and the more sophisticated surely realize that we are on the side of the wealthy, and the secure, while we create a hell for the poor.

Surely this madness must cease. We must stop now. I speak as a child of God and brother to the suffering poor of Vietnam. I speak for those whose land is being laid waste, whose homes are being destroyed, whose culture is being subverted. I speak for the poor in America who are paying the double price of smashed hopes at home, and dealt death and corruption in Vietnam. I speak as a citizen of the world, for the world as it stands aghast at the path we have taken. I speak as one who loves America, to the leaders of our own nation: The great initiative in this war is ours; the initiative to stop it must be ours.

...

Now there is something seductively tempting about stopping there and sending us all off on what in some circles has become a popular crusade against the war in Vietnam. I say we must enter that struggle, but I wish to go on now to say something even more disturbing.

The war in Vietnam is but a symptom of a far deeper malady within the American spirit, and if we ignore this sobering reality [applause] ..., we will find ourselves organizing "clergy and laymen concerned" committees for the next generation. They will be concerned about Guatemala and Peru. They will be concerned about Thailand and Cambodia. They will be concerned about Mozambique and South Africa. We will be marching for these and a dozen other names and attending rallies without end unless there is a significant and profound change in American life and policy. [sustained applause] So such thoughts take us beyond Vietnam, but not beyond our calling as sons of the living God.

...

[T]he words of the late John F. Kennedy come back to haunt us. Five years ago he said, "Those who make peaceful revolution impossible will make violent revolution inevitable." [applause] Increasingly, by choice or by accident, this is the role our nation has taken, the role of those who make peaceful revolution impossible by refusing to give up the privileges and the pleasures that come from the immense profits of overseas investments. I am convinced that if we are to get on to the right side of the world revolution, we as a nation must undergo a radical revolution of values. We must rapidly begin [applause], we must rapidly begin the shift from a thing-oriented society to a person-oriented society. When machines and computers, profit motives and property rights, are considered more important than people, the giant triplets of racism, extreme materialism, and militarism are incapable of being conquered.

A true revolution of values will soon look uneasily on the glaring contrast of poverty and wealth. With righteous indignation, it will look across the seas and see individual capitalists of the West investing huge sums of money in Asia, Africa, and South America, only to take the profits out with no concern for the social betterment of the countries, and say, "This is not just." It will look at our alliance with the landed gentry of South America and say, "This is not just." The Western arrogance of feeling that it has everything to teach others and nothing to learn from them is not just.

A true revolution of values will lay hand on the world order and say of war, "This way of settling differences is not just." This business of burning human beings with napalm, of filling our nation's homes with orphans and widows, of injecting poisonous drugs of hate into the veins of peoples normally humane, of sending men home from dark and bloody battlefields physically handicapped and psychologically deranged, cannot be reconciled with wisdom, justice, and love. A nation that continues year after year to spend more money on military defense than on programs of social uplift is approaching spiritual death. [sustained applause]

America, the richest and most powerful nation in the world, can well lead the way in this revolution of values. There is nothing except a tragic death wish to prevent us from reordering our priorities so that the pursuit of peace will take precedence over the pursuit of war. There is nothing to keep us from molding a recalcitrant status quo with bruised hands until we have fashioned it into a brotherhood.

...

A genuine revolution of values means in the final analysis that our loyalties must become ecumenical rather than sectional. Every nation must now develop an overriding loyalty to mankind as a whole in order to preserve the best in their individual societies.

We can no longer afford to worship the god of hate or bow before the altar of retaliation. The oceans of history are made turbulent by the ever-rising tides of hate. History is cluttered with the wreckage of nations and individuals that pursued this self-defeating path of hate.

...

We are now faced with the fact, my friends, that tomorrow is today. We are confronted with the fierce urgency of now. In this unfolding conundrum of life and history, there is such a thing as being too late. Procrastination is still the thief of time. Life often leaves us standing bare, naked, and dejected with a lost opportunity. The tide in the affairs of men does not remain at flood – it ebbs. We may cry out desperately for time to pause in her passage, but time is adamant to every plea and rushes on. Over the bleached bones and jumbled residues of numerous civilizations are written the pathetic words, "Too late." There is an invisible book of life that faithfully records our vigilance or our neglect. Omar Khayyam is right: "The moving finger writes, and having writ moves on."

We still have a choice today: nonviolent coexistence or violent coannihilation. We must move past indecision to action. We must find new ways to speak for peace in Vietnam and justice throughout the developing world, a world that borders on our doors. If we do not act, we shall surely be dragged down the long, dark, and shameful corridors of time reserved for those who possess power without compassion, might without morality, and strength without sight.

...

Source: Rev. Dr. Martin Luther King, Jr., "Beyond Vietnam – A Time to Break Silence." Reprinted by arrangement with The Heirs to the Estate of Martin Luther King, Jr., c/o Writers House as agent for the proprietor New York, NY. Copyright 1957 Dr. Martin Luther King, Jr.; copyright renewed 1995 Coretta Scott King.

3 The Poor People's Campaign, 1968

Evolving with the black freedom movement, SCLC pledged to use "any means of legitimate nonviolent protest necessary to move our nation and our

government on a new course of social, economic, and political reform." The
Poor People's Campaign was a masterful stroke of direct action genius,
seeking to make poverty visible with a multiracial, multi-ethnic march on
Washington, DC, that started from different points across the United States
and a mass encampment on the national Mall.

   Martin Luther King, Jr., was gunned down in the midst of planning the
Poor People's March. The Campaign continued, however, with one group
setting off from Grenada, Mississippi, in early May 1968. The first
photograph below depicts the procession arriving in Washington, DC, where
thousands marched, led by Coretta Scott King, on Mother's Day. Over
50,000 people participated in Solidarity Day in June. The second photograph
is of a Poor People's Rally at Lafayette Park, across from the White House.
The momentum proved hard to sustain, even though the number of
participants exceeded expectations. Moreover, they were met with apathy
by federal officials in DC, and the encampment, Resurrection City, was undone
by a combination of relentless rain and organizational problems inherent
to such a large enterprise.

Figure 10.1   Poor People's Campaign Procession into Washington, DC.

Source: *From Eyes on the Prize II*, in the Henry Hampton Collection, Film and
Media Archives, Washington University. © Bettmann/Corbis.

Figure 10.2   Poor People's Campaign Rally in Lafayette Park across from the White House.

Source: Photograph by Warren K. Leffler. Library of Congress, Prints and Photographs Division, LC-DIG-ppmsca-04302.

4 The Black Panther Party Convenes a Revolutionary People's Constitutional Convention, 1970

"We call upon the American people to rise up, repudiate, and restrain the forces of fascism"

With chapters across the nation, including in the South, the Black Panther Party had garnered a broad constituency by 1970 through its grassroots projects including health clinics, free breakfast programs, food and clothing drives, and legal assistance. Its political education programs encouraged community residents to get involved in municipal affairs. In the spring of 1970, the Black Panther Party issued a call for a Revolutionary People's Constitutional Convention. Articles about the event appeared in both Leftist and national publications including The New York Times *and* Life *magazine. It was a fanciful idea, but interracial groups of thousands of activists from among the Panthers' vast networks of affiliations attended.*

MESSAGE TO AMERICA
Delivered on the 107th Anniversary of the Emancipation Proclamation at
Washington, D.C.
Capitol of Babylon, World Racism, and Imperialism June 19, 1970
BY THE BLACK PANTHER PARTY

As oppressed people held captive within the confines of the Fascist-
Imperialist United States of America, we Black Americans take a dim view
of the position that we, as a people, find ourselves in at the beginning of the
7th decade of the Twentieth Century.

...

Black people within the domestic confines of the U.S.A. have reached
another cross road. This is a time for the most serious decisions that we, as
a people, have ever been called upon to make. The decisions that we make
in our time, the actions that we take or fail to take, will determine whether
we, as a people, will survive or fall victims to genocidal extermination at the
hands of the FASCIST MAJORITY which the Nixon clique are rapidly
mobilizing into a beastly vigilante weapon to be unleashed against us.

THE U.S.A. MONSTER

The United States of America is a barbaric organization controlled and
operated by avaricious, sadistic, bloodthirsty thieves. The United States of
America is the Number One exploiter and oppressor of the peoples of the
whole world. The inhuman capitalistic system which defines the core of
reality of the U.S.A., is the root of the evil that has polluted the very fabric
of existence within the U.S.A. Exploitation of man by man; the rule of man
over man instead of the rule of the laws of Human Rights and Justice; savage
wars of aggression, mass murder, genocide, and shameless slaughter of the
people of the world; impudent, arrogant White Racism; and a naked, brazen
attempt to perpetuate White Supremacy on a world scale—these are a few of
the unsavory characteristics of the U.S.A. Monster with which we have to deal.

We did not ask for this situation. We did not create it. And we do not
prefer it but we must deal with it.

THE EMANCIPATION PROCLAMATION

Today, June 19th, is the anniversary of the issuance by President Abraham
Lincoln of THE EMANCIPATION PROCLAMATION during the Civil
War, officially dated January 1, 1863. The end result of the EMANCIPATION
PROCLAMATION was supposed to be the freedom and liberation of Black
people from the cruel shackles of chattel slavery. And yet, 100 and 7 years
later, today, Black people still are not free. Where is that freedom supposedly

granted to our people by THE EMANCIPATION PROCLAMATION and guaranteed to us by the Constitution of the United States?

Is it in the many "Civil Rights Bills" that have been passed to try to hide the irrelevance of the Constitution for Black People?

Is it in the blood-shed and lives lost by Black People when America brings "Law and Order" to the ghetto in the same fashion and by those same forces that export "Freedom and Democracy" to Korea, to Vietnam, to Africa, Asia, and Latin America?

Is it the right to "political activity" when the U.S.A. attempts to legally murder Bobby Seale, Chairman of the Black Panther Party, for his political beliefs?

Where was that right when brother Malcolm was murdered, when Martin Luther King was gunned down?

Where is Freedom when a peoples right to "Freedom of Speech" is denied to the point of murder? When attempts at "Freedom of the Press" brings bombings and lynchings?

Where is Freedom when the right to "peacefully assemble" brings on massacres? Where is our right to "keep and bear arms" when Black People are attacked by the Racist Gestapo of America? Where is "religious freedom" when places of worship become the scene of shoot-ins and bomb-ins? Where is the right to vote "regardless of race or color" when murder takes place at the voting polls? Are we free when we are not even secure from being savagely murdered in our sleep by policemen who stand blatantly before the world but yet go unpunished? Is that "…equal protection of the laws"? The empty promise of the Constitution to "establish Justice" lies exposed to the world by the reality of Black Peoples' existence. For 400 years now, Black people have suffered an unbroken chain of abuse at the hands of White America. For 400 years we have been treated as America's footstool. This fact is so clear that it requires no argumentation.

THE CONSTITUTION

The Constitution of the U.S.A. does not and never has protected our people or guaranteed to us those lofty ideals enshrined within it. When the Constitution was first adopted we were held as slaves. We were held in slavery under the Constitution. We have suffered every form of indignity and imposition under the Constitution, from economic exploitation, political subjugation, to physical extermination.

We need no further evidence that there is something wrong with the Constitution of the United States of America. We have had our Human

Rights denied and violated perpetually under this Constitution—for hundreds of years. As a people, we have received neither the Equal Protection of the Laws nor Due Process of Law. Where Human Rights are being daily violated there is denial of Due Process of Law and there is no Equal Protection of the Law. The Constitution of the United States does not guarantee and protect our Economic Rights, or our Political Rights, nor our Social Rights. It does not even guarantee and protect our most basic Human Right, the right to LIVE!

IMPLEMENTING POINT NO. 10 OF THE BLACK PANTHER PARTY PLATFORM AND PROGRAM

Point No. 10 of the Black Panther Party's Platform and Program addresses itself to the question of the National Destiny of Black people. We feel that, in practical terms, it is time for Black people as a whole to address their attention to the question of our National Destiny.

Black People can no longer either respect the U.S. Constitution, look to it with hope, or live under it. The Constitution is the social contract that binds the American people together into a sovereign nation and defines authority and the distribution of power, rights, and privileges. By shoving the Constitution aside, rendering it null and void, in order to carry out fascist oppression and repression of Black People, the fascists have, by that very fact, destroyed even the false foundations of authority in this society. We live in a lawless society where racist pigs have usurped the Legislative, Judicial, and Executive branches of government and perverted them towards the prosperity of their private interests. We repudiate, most emphatically, all documents, Laws, Conventions, and Practices that allow this sorry state of affairs to exist—including the Constitution of the United States.

For us, the case is absolutely clear: Black people have no future within the present structure of power and authority in the United States under the present Constitution. For us, also, the alternatives are absolutely clear: the present structure of power and authority in the United States must be radically changed or we, as a people, must extricate ourselves from entanglement with the United States.

If we are to remain a part of the United States, then we must have a new Constitution that will strictly guarantee our Human Rights to Life, Liberty, and the Pursuit of Happiness, which is promised but not delivered by the present Constitution. We shall not accept one iota less than this, our full, unblemished Human Rights. If this is not to be, if we cannot make a new arrangement within the United States, then we have no alternative but to declare ourselves free and independent of the United States. If it is our national destiny to follow the latter course, then we must declare ourselves into self-governing machinery, and seek the recognition of the freedom loving nations of the world.

The Black Panther Party fully realizes that the two roads open to us as set forth above involve monumental undertakings. But we are trapped in a monstrous situation that requires a monumental solution. And no task, however great, is too much to deal with when the very welfare, survival, and national destiny of our people are at stake. Having already struggled up from the dismal depths of chattel slavery, no obstacles can be too high for us to surmount in order to liberate our people and take back the freedom and security that was taken away from us and denied us for so long.

CALL FOR A REVOLUTIONARY PEOPLE'S CONSTITUTIONAL CONVENTION

The hour is late and the situation is desperate. As a nation, America is now in the middle of the greatest crisis in its history. The Black Panther Party believes that the American people are capable of rising to the task which history has [been] laid before the nation. We believe that the American people are capable of rejecting the fascist solution to the national crisis which the fascist Nixon clique, the George Wallaces, Lester Maddoxes, Ronald Reagans, Spiro Agnews, etc. hold out to the people.

WE THEREFORE, CALL FOR A REVOLUTIONARY PEOPLE'S CONSTI TUTIONAL CONVENTION, TO BE CONVENED BY THE AMERICAN PEOPLE, TO WRITE A NEW CONSTITUTION THAT WILL GUARANTEE AND DELIVER TO EVERY AMERICAN CITIZEN THE INVIOLABLE HUMAN RIGHT TO LIFE, LIBERTY, AND THE PURSUIT OF HAPPINESS!

We call upon the American people to rise up, repudiate, and restrain the forces of fascism that are now rampant in the land and which are the only real obstacles standing between us and a rational resolution of the national crisis.

We believe that Black people are not the only group within America that stands in need of a new Constitution. Other oppressed ethnic groups, the youth of America, Women, young men who are slaughtered as cannon fodder in mad, avaricious wars of aggression, our neglected elderly people all have an interest in a new Constitution that will guarantee us a society in which Human Rights are supreme and Justice is assured to every man, woman, and child within its jurisdiction. For it is only through this means that America, as a nation, can live together in peace with our brothers and sisters the world over. Only through this means can the present character of America, the purveyor of exploitation, misery, death, and wanton destruction all over the planet earth, be changed.

WARNING TO AMERICA

We are from 25 to 30 million strong, and we are armed. And we are conscious of our situation. And we are determined to change it. And we are unafraid. Because we have our guarantee …

It had best be understood, now, that the power we rely upon ultimately, as our only guarantee against Genocide at the hands of the Fascist Majority, is our strategic ability to lay this country in ruins, from the bottom to the top. If forced to resort to this guarantee, we will not hesitate to do so.

FOR THE SALVATION, LIBERATION, AND FREEDOM OF OUR PEOPLE, WE WILL NOT HESITATE TO EITHER KILL OR DIE!

ALL POWER TO THE PEOPLE

Source: "Call for a Revolutionary People's Constitutional Convention," *Black Panther*, June 1970.

5 Gil Scott-Heron Warns: "The Revolution Will Not Be Televised," 1971

*"There will be no pictures of pigs shooting
down brothers in the instant replay"*

The Black Arts Movement emerged in the 1970s with the specific objective of doing the cultural work of black freedom: to encourage purveyors and audiences to see the arts as an arena of political engagement and to use African Americans' experiences as inspiration in their productions. Like the Harlem Renaissance of the 1920s, the Black Arts Movement produced novels, plays, poetry, music, and art. Similarly it influenced more than one generation. In 1971 Gil Scott-Heron (1949–2011) recorded "The Revolution Will Not Be Televised," a forerunner of what would later be called rap music. Its rhythm and rhyme employed pop culture references from both popular media and American politics of the era to speak of black frustrations. The song, a call to consciousness, urges black people to prepare for the street-level rebellion at hand.

The Revolution Will Not Be Televised

You will not be able to stay home, brother.
You will not be able to plug in, turn on and cop out.

You will not be able to lose yourself on skag and skip,
Skip out for beer during commercials,
Because the revolution will not be televised.

The revolution will not be televised.
The revolution will not be brought to you by Xerox
In 4 parts without commercial interruptions.
The revolution will not show you pictures of Nixon
blowing a bugle and leading a charge by John
Mitchell, General Abrams and Spiro Agnew to eat
hog maws confiscated from a Harlem sanctuary.

The revolution will not be televised.
The revolution will not be brought to you by the
Schaefer Award Theatre and will not star Natalie
Woods and Steve McQueen or Bullwinkle and Julia.
The revolution will not give your mouth sex appeal.
The revolution will not get rid of the nubs.
The revolution will not make you look five pounds
thinner, because the revolution will not be televised, Brother.

There will be no pictures of you and Willie Mays
pushing that shopping cart down the block on a dead run,
or trying to slide that color television into a stolen ambulance.
NBC will not be able to predict the winner at 8:32
or report from 29 districts.

The revolution will not be televised.
There will be no pictures of pigs shooting down
brothers in the instant replay.
There will be no pictures of Whitney Young being
run out of Harlem on a rail with a brand new process.
There will be no slow motion or still life of Roy
Wilkins strolling through Watts in a Red, Black and
Green liberation jumpsuit that he had been saving
For just the proper occasion.

Green Acres, The Beverly Hillbillies, and Hooterville
Junction will no longer be so damned relevant, and
women will not care if Dick finally gets down with
Jane on Search for Tomorrow because Black people
will be in the street looking for a brighter day.

The revolution will not be televised.
There will be no highlights on the eleven o'clock
news and no pictures of hairy armed women
liberationists and Jackie Onassis blowing her nose.
The theme song will not be written by Jim Webb,
Francis Scott Key, nor sung by Glen Campbell, Tom
Jones, Johnny Cash, Englebert Humperdink, or Rare Earth.

The revolution will not be televised.
The revolution will not be right back after a message
about a white tornado, white lightning, or white people.
You will not have to worry about a dove in your
bedroom, a tiger in your tank, or the giant in your toilet bowl.
The revolution will not go better with Coke
The revolution will not fight the germs that may cause bad breath.
The revolution will put you in the driver's seat.

The revolution will not be televised,
will not be televised,
will not be televised,
will not be televised.

The revolution will be no re-run brothers;
The revolution will be live.

Source: Gil Scott-Heron, "The Revolution Will Not Be Televised" (New York: RCA Records, 1971). Courtesy of the estate of Gil Scott-Heron.

6 The Combahee River Collective Statement Explains Black Feminism, 1977

"The synthesis of these oppressions creates the conditions of our lives"

The National Black Feminist Organization (NBFO) was founded in 1973 to address the relationship between African American women and the feminist movement. Its members – among them writer Michelle Wallace and artist Faith Ringgold – also participated in civil rights, women's movement, anti-war, and anti-poverty activism. Precisely because feminism had come under attack by black nationalists, NBFO sought to reclaim and articulate a feminism that reflected black women's experiences, traditions, and conventions, one born of their lives. Emerging from NBFO, the Combahee River Collective (CRC) also veterans of black freedom, women's and

*feminist, anti-war and anti-poverty movements, turned to writing as a
political act.*

*Taking its name from the route Harriet Tubman used to lead escaping
slaves out of South Carolina, the CRC framed its work as an act of black
women's liberation. Drawing theory from participants' experiences as black
women, lesbians, feminists, nationalists, and activists, the Collective's
statement describes how the group came to its analysis: that the major
systems of oppression are interlocking. The work of the CRC was significant
in several ways. First, members came out as black lesbian feminists and
staked a claim for their own liberation. Second, the CRC framed an enduring
intellectual theory, grounded in black feminism, that offers an important
critique of American cultural politics expressed in academia and the media.
Finally, the Collective founded Kitchen Table Press. Part of a renaissance in
independent publishing, KTP provided a venue where women of color found
an outlet and an audience for their work. The Collective's statement
continues to influence the work of scholars and activists.*

The Combahee River Collective Statement

We are a collective of Black feminists who have been meeting together since
1974. During that time we have been involved in the process of defining and
clarifying our politics, while at the same time doing political work within
our own group and in coalition with other progressive organizations and
movements. The most general statement of our politics at the present time
would be that we are actively committed to struggling against racial, sexual,
heterosexual, and class oppression, and see as our particular task the
development of integrated analysis and practice based upon the fact that the
major systems of oppression are interlocking. The synthesis of these oppressions creates the conditions of our lives. As Black women we see Black feminism as the logical political movement to combat the manifold and
simultaneous oppressions that all women of color face.

We will discuss four major topics in the paper that follows: (1) the genesis
of contemporary Black feminism; (2) what we believe, i.e., the specific province of our politics; (3) the problems in organizing Black feminists, including
a brief herstory of our collective; and (4) Black feminist issues and practice.

1. The Genesis of Contemporary Black Feminism

Before looking at the recent development of Black feminism we would like
to affirm that we find our origins in the historical reality of Afro-American
women's continuous life-and-death struggle for survival and liberation.
Black women's extremely negative relationship to the American political

system (a system of white male rule) has always been determined by our membership in two oppressed racial and sexual castes ... There have always been Black women activists – some known, like Sojourner Truth, Harriet Tubman, Frances E. W. Harper, Ida B. Wells Barnett, and Mary Church Terrell, and thousands upon thousands unknown – who have had a shared awareness of how their sexual identity combined with their racial identity to make their whole life situation and the focus of their political struggles unique. Contemporary Black feminism is the outgrowth of countless generations of personal sacrifice, militancy, and work by our mothers and sisters.

A Black feminist presence has evolved most obviously in connection with the second wave of the American women's movement beginning in the late 1960s. Black, other Third World, and working women have been involved in the feminist movement from its start, but both outside reactionary forces and racism and elitism within the movement itself have served to obscure our participation. In 1973, Black feminists, primarily located in New York, felt the necessity of forming a separate Black feminist group. This became the National Black Feminist Organization (NBFO).

Black feminist politics also have an obvious connection to movements for Black liberation, particularly those of the 1960s and 1970s. Many of us were active in those movements (Civil Rights, Black nationalism, the Black Panthers), and all of our lives were greatly affected and changed by their ideologies, their goals, and the tactics used to achieve their goals. It was our experience and disillusionment within these liberation movements, as well as experience on the periphery of the white male left, that led to the need to develop a politics that was anti-racist, unlike those of white women, and anti-sexist, unlike those of Black and white men.

There is also undeniably a personal genesis for Black Feminism, that is, the political realization that comes from the seemingly personal experiences of individual Black women's lives. Black feminists and many more Black women who do not define themselves as feminists have all experienced sexual oppression as a constant factor in our day-to-day existence. As children we realized that we were different from boys and that we were treated differently. For example, we were told in the same breath to be quiet both for the sake of being "ladylike" and to make us less objectionable in the eyes of white people. As we grew older we became aware of the threat of physical and sexual abuse by men. However, we had no way of conceptualizing what was so apparent to us, what we knew was really happening.

Black feminists often talk about their feelings of craziness before becoming conscious of the concepts of sexual politics, patriarchal rule, and most importantly, feminism, the political analysis and practice that we women use to struggle against our oppression. The fact that racial politics and indeed racism are pervasive factors in our lives did not allow us, and still does not allow most Black women, to look more deeply into our own experiences and, from that sharing and growing consciousness, to build a politics that will change our lives and inevitably end our oppression. Our development must also be tied to the contemporary economic and political position of Black people. The post World War II generation of Black youth was the first to be able to minimally partake of certain educational and employment options, previously closed completely to Black people. Although our economic position is still at the very bottom of the American capitalistic economy, a handful of us have been able to gain certain tools as a result of tokenism in education and employment which potentially enable us to more effectively fight our oppression.

A combined anti-racist and anti-sexist position drew us together initially, and as we developed politically we addressed ourselves to heterosexism and economic oppression under capitalism.

2. *What We Believe*

Above all else, our politics initially sprang from the shared belief that Black women are inherently valuable, that our liberation is a necessity not as an adjunct to somebody else's [but] because of our need as human persons for autonomy. This may seem so obvious as to sound simplistic, but it is apparent that no other ostensibly progressive movement has ever considered our specific oppression as a priority or worked seriously for the ending of that oppression. Merely naming the pejorative stereotypes attributed to Black women (e.g. mammy, matriarch, Sapphire, whore, bulldagger), let alone cat-aloguing the cruel, often murderous, treatment we receive, indicates how little value has been placed upon our lives during four centuries of bondage in the Western hemisphere. We realize that the only people who care enough about us to work consistently for our liberation are us. Our politics evolve from a healthy love for ourselves, our sisters and our community which allows us to continue our struggle and work.

This focusing upon our own oppression is embodied in the concept of identity politics. We believe that the most profound and potentially most radical politics come directly out of our own identity, as opposed to working to end somebody else's oppression. In the case of Black women this is a particularly repugnant, dangerous, threatening, and therefore revolutionary concept because it is obvious from looking at all the political movements that have preceded us that anyone is more worthy of liberation than ourselves. We reject pedestals, queenhood, and walking ten paces behind. To be recognized as human, levelly human, is enough.

We believe that sexual politics under patriarchy is as pervasive in Black women's lives as are the politics of class and race. We also often find it difficult to separate race from class from sex oppression because in our lives they are most often experienced simultaneously. We know that there is such a thing as racial-sexual oppression which is neither solely racial nor solely sexual, e.g., the history of rape of Black women by white men as a weapon of political repression.

Although we are feminists and Lesbians, we feel solidarity with progressive Black men and do not advocate the fractionalization that white women who are separatists demand. Our situation as Black people necessitates that we have solidarity around the fact of race, which white women of course do not need to have with white men, unless it is their negative solidarity as racial oppressors. We struggle together with Black men against racism, while we also struggle with Black men about sexism.

We realize that the liberation of all oppressed peoples necessitates the destruction of the political-economic systems of capitalism and imperialism as well as patriarchy. We are socialists because we believe that work must be organized for the collective benefit of those who do the work and create the products, and not for the profit of the bosses. Material resources must be equally distributed among those who create these resources. We are not convinced, however, that a socialist revolution that is not also a feminist and anti-racist revolution will guarantee our liberation ... We need to articulate the real class situation of persons who are not merely raceless, sexless workers, but for whom racial and sexual oppression are significant determinants in their working/economic lives. Although we are in essential agreement with Marx's theory as it applied to the very specific economic relationships he analyzed, we know that his analysis must be extended further in order for us to understand our specific economic situation as Black women.

A political contribution which we feel we have already made is the expansion of the feminist principle that the personal is political ... We have spent a great deal of energy delving into the cultural and experiential nature of our oppression out of necessity because none of these matters has ever been looked at before. No one before has ever examined the multilayered texture of Black women's lives. An example of this kind of revelation/conceptualization occurred at a meeting as we discussed the ways in which our early intellectual interests had been attacked by our peers, particularly Black males. We discovered that all of us, because we were "smart" had also been considered "ugly," i.e., "smart-ugly." "Smart-ugly" crystallized the way in which most of us had been forced to develop our intellects at great cost to our "social" lives. The sanctions in the Black and white communities against

Black women thinkers [are] comparatively much higher than for white women, particularly ones from the educated middle and upper classes.

As we have already stated, we reject the stance of Lesbian separatism because it is not a viable political analysis or strategy for us. It leaves out far too much and far too many people, particularly Black men, women, and children. We have a great deal of criticism and loathing for what men have been socialized to be in this society: what they support, how they act, and how they oppress. But we do not have the misguided notion that it is their maleness, per se – i.e., their biological maleness – that makes them what they are. As Black women we find any type of biological determinism a particularly dangerous and reactionary basis upon which to build a politic. We must also question whether Lesbian separatism is an adequate and progressive political analysis and strategy, even for those who practice it, since it so completely denies any but the sexual sources of women's oppression, negating the facts of class and race.

3. Problems in Organizing Black Feminists

During our years together as a Black feminist collective we have experienced success and defeat, joy and pain, victory and failure ... The major source of difficulty in our political work is that we are not just trying to fight oppression on one front or even two, but instead to address a whole range of oppressions. We do not have racial, sexual, heterosexual, or class privilege to rely upon, nor do we have even the minimal access to resources and power that groups who possess any one of these types of privilege have.

The psychological toll of being a Black woman and the difficulties this presents in reaching political consciousness and doing political work can never be underestimated. There is a very low value placed upon Black women's psyches in this society, which is both racist and sexist. As an early group member once said, "We are all damaged people merely by virtue of being Black women." We are dispossessed psychologically and on every other level, and yet we feel the necessity to struggle to change the condition of all Black women ...

...

The reaction of Black men to feminism has been notoriously negative. They are, of course, even more threatened than Black women by the possibility that Black feminists might organize around our own needs. They realize that they might not only lose valuable and hardworking allies in their struggles but that they might also be forced to change their habitually sexist ways of interacting with and oppressing Black women. Accusations that Black feminism divides the Black struggle are powerful deterrents to the growth of an autonomous Black women's movement.

Still, hundreds of women have been active at different times during the three-year existence of our group. And every Black woman who came, came out of a strongly-felt need for some level of possibility that did not previously exist in her life.

Currently we are planning to gather together a collection of Black feminist writing. We feel that it is absolutely essential to demonstrate the reality of our politics to other Black women and believe that we can do this through writing and distributing our work. The fact that individual Black feminists are living in isolation all over the country, that our own numbers are small, and that we have some skills in writing, printing, and publishing makes us want to carry out these kinds of projects as a means of organizing Black feminists as we continue to do political work in coalition with other groups.

4. Black Feminist Issues and Projects

During our time together we have identified and worked on many issues of particular relevance to Black women. The inclusiveness of our politics makes us concerned with any situation that impinges upon the lives of women, Third World and working people. We are of course particularly committed to working on those struggles in which race, sex, and class are simultaneous factors in oppression. We might, for example, become involved in workplace organizing at a factory that employs Third World women or picket a hospital that is cutting back on already inadequate health care to a Third World community, or set up a rape crisis center in a Black neighborhood. Organizing around welfare and daycare concerns might also be a focus. The work to be done and the countless issues that this work represents merely reflect the pervasiveness of our oppression.

Issues and projects that collective members have actually worked on are sterilization abuse, abortion rights, battered women, rape and health care. We have also done many workshops and educationals on Black feminism on college campuses, at women's conferences, and most recently for high school women.

One issue that is of major concern to us and that we have begun to publicly address is racism in the white women's movement. As Black feminists we are made constantly and painfully aware of how little effort white women have made to understand and combat their racism, which requires among other things that they have a more than superficial comprehension of race, color, and Black history and culture. Eliminating racism in the white women's movement is by definition work for white women to do, but we will continue to speak to and demand accountability on this issue.

In the practice of our politics we do not believe that the end always justifies the means. Many reactionary and destructive acts have been done in the name of achieving "correct" political goals. As feminists we do not want to mess over people in the name of politics.

As Black feminists and Lesbians we know that we have a very definite revolutionary task to perform and we are ready for the lifetime of work and struggle before us.

Source: Combahee River Collective, *The Combahee River Collective Statement: Black Feminist Organizing in the Seventies and Eighties* (Albany, NY: Kitchen Table Press, 1986).

Questions for Consideration

The notion of revolution informed the approaches of all of the activists in this chapter. What kind of transformation did they imagine and why did they see them as revolutionary? What analyses did they share? And where did they differ? How do each of them put "power" to work in their agendas?

Compare the approaches to the fight against poverty used by Martin Luther King, Jr., and the Black Panther Party.

Martin Luther King's speech on Vietnam and the call for the Revolutionary People's Constitutional Convention both place the situations of African Americans in the United States in international contexts. How did they define or describe that relationship? How did their understandings of black Americans' place in the world differ from activists of earlier eras?

What is the impact of the Black Panther Party's use of the Declaration of Independence and the Constitution in their statements?

What is black feminism? How is it relevant to black freedom and the black freedom movement?

How did the Combahee River Collective and the Black Panther Party understand the relationship between their organizations and white activists? Who did they see as allies?

Bibliography

Branch, Taylor. *At Canaan's Edge: America in the King Years, 1965–68*. New York: Simon and Schuster, 2007.

Brown, Elaine. *A Taste of Power: A Black Woman's Story*. Reprint. New York: Pantheon Books, 1992.

Dyson, Michael Eric. *I May Not Get There With You: The True Martin Luther King, Jr*. New York: Free Press, 2000.

Jackson, Thomas F. *From Civil Rights to Human Rights: Martin Luther King, Jr., and the Struggle for Economic Justice*. Philadelphia: University of Pennsylvania Press, 2007.

Joseph, Peniel E. *The Black Power Movement: Rethinking the Civil Rights-Black Power Era*. New York: Routledge, 2006.

Murch, Donna. *Living for the City: Migration, Education, and the Rise of the Black Panther Party in Oakland, California*. Chapel Hill: University of North Carolina Press, 2011.

Seale, Bobby. *Seize the Time: The Story of the Black Panther Party and Huey Newton*. Reprint. Baltimore: Black Classic Press, 1991.

Springer, Kimberly. *Living for the Revolution: Black Feminist Organizations, 1968–1980*. Durham, NC: Duke University Press, 2005.

Valk, Anne M. *Radical Sisters: Second Wave Feminism and Black Liberation in Washington, DC*. Urbana: University of Illinois Press, 2008.

Van de Burg, William L. *New Day in Babylon: The Black Power Movement and American Culture, 1965–1975*. Chicago: University of Chicago Press, 1992.

Chapter 11   Crosscurrents, 1982–2001

> Don't push me 'cuz I'm close to the edge
> I'm tryin' not to lose my head
>
> It's like a jungle sometimes
> It makes me wonder how I keep from going under

"The Message" (1982), Grand Master Flash and the Furious Five

The rhetoric of revolution and black nationalism had fallen out of fashion by 1982 when Grandmaster Flash and the Furious Five recorded "The Message." The first to grow up without legal discrimination, the hip-hop generation reconstructed the black spoken word tradition to offer a new refrain. The legal moorings of Jim Crow had loosened but the struggle for survival against its forces – "to keep from going under" – remained. Examining the lives of the disempowered, the movement critiqued the persistence of poverty in the age of conspicuous wealth, and asked: what can – and can't – under-resourced people do about their situation?

Certainly the moral force of civil rights had made overt racism unacceptable. By the 1980s, African Americans had made critical inroads to major American institutions, business, education, media, sports, and politics. But these were mostly singular accomplishments, achieved against great odds. In truth, the first wave of African Americans to pass the color barrier held a tenuous grip on any benefits to desegregation. Legal or policy

African American Voices: A Documentary Reader from Emancipation to the Present, First Edition. Edited by Leslie Brown.
© 2014 John Wiley & Sons, Inc. Published 2014 by John Wiley & Sons, Inc.

interventions intended to redress structural inequities – open housing and open employment initiatives, affirmative action, empowerment zones – had yielded only briefly to the freedom movement's momentum. As Bayard Rustin had predicted, the "technological revolution" altered "the fundamental structure of the labor force, destroying unskilled and semi-skilled jobs" where blacks were unduly concentrated. At the same time, withering local tax bases combined with state and federal budget cuts and a conservative political turn under the presidency of Ronald Reagan to leave black communities with limited services or protections. Mostly segregated, under-resourced, and crumbling schools proved unable to prepare students for a quickly shifting economy. Black youth faced extensive joblessness, while draconian laws and circuitous enforcement policies ensnared many blacks, especially young men, in the criminal justice system.

The civil rights movement and freedom struggles had effected expansive efforts for social justice not only for African Americans, but also for women and other minorities, immigrants, gays, the poor, and the elderly. However, the conservative uprising of the end of the twentieth century determined to sap activists' energies and to roll back gains. In a cultural milieu that celebrated individuality and questioned the value of diversity, moreover, it was difficult to generate the kind of racial consciousness that had invigorated movements of the past. Yet, African Americans organized – among themselves and in coalitions – around an array of local, regional, national, and international issues. At the same time, black people renewed their discourse of self-reflection, calling upon themselves to reappraise the sense of hopelessness especially among youth, and to revive the process of upbuilding their communities.

1 Activists Call for Americans to Break Ties with South Africa, 1980

"Under apartheid the beneficiaries of South Africa's wealth are the whites"

Historically, African Americans have expressed solidarity with struggles for self-determination among people of color internationally, especially condemning the system of apartheid imposed by the South African white minority on that nation's black majority. In 1980, when President Ronald Reagan signaled support for the white South African regime – even as its human rights violations mounted – anti-apartheid activism swept the nation. Linked nationally and internationally, African Americans and allies – through organizations, churches, localities, colleges, and unions – launched informational campaigns, direct action protests, and product boycotts to buttress demands that institutions divest from American corporations and banks that conducted business in South Africa, arguing that such investments benefited from apartheid's abuses.

A CALL FOR LEGISLATIVE ACTION TO BREAK THE TIES WITH APARTHEID

NEBRASKA: The Legislature of the State of Nebraska declares that investment of Nebraska state funds in institutions which support the apartheid system of South Africa is contrary to Nebraska's principles of human rights and social equality and calls on the Nebraska Investment Council to remove from the approved list for investment of Nebraska trust funds corporations and banks which invest in South Africa

BERKELEY, CALIFORNIA: The people of Berkeley, California declare that public monies should be removed from banks and other financial institutions doing business in or with South Africa and reinvested according to a policy that takes ethical, social, and economic considerations into full account.

Nebraska and Berkeley are not alone in their rejection of economic ties to South Africa, and the impact of their actions will grow as other state and local governments, universities, churches, black organizations, and unions take similar steps.

WHY THE FOCUS ON SOUTH AFRICA?

South Africa is a rich and beautiful land. It produces most of the Western World's gold and diamonds, and supplies platinum and manganese vital for advanced industrial economies. Its mills and factories pour out a growing stream of wealth, attracting an ever increasing number of U.S. and other foreign investors. But the whole country is dominated by a racist system which decrees that all power and prosperity shall be "for whites only."

Under apartheid the beneficiaries of South Africa's wealth are the whites who number about 4.5 million out of a total population of almost 24 million. Lopsided statistics are the norm in South Africa. Eighty-seven percent of the land, including all the major cities and industrial installations, is in the hands of the whites; thirteen percent of the land is reserved for Africans. The average monthly wage for a white South African miner is $772; for a black miner it is $103. One half of the children born in the black reservations die before reaching the age of five, a death rate 25 times higher than that of white children.

Prosperity for white South Africans and for their financial backers is paid for by the exploitation of the black majority which has been reduced to serving as a source of cheap labor, without economic or political rights. The white government considers Africans transient migrant labor units who are only allowed in the "white areas" to perform designated tasks. The system of apartheid that governs the country deprives blacks of freedom of movement, land ownership, organizing rights, education, and citizenship in the land of their birth. It is enforced by a vast network of repressive laws and a powerfully equipped military and police force.

The South African Government, architect of apartheid, searches for and cultivates foreign investors. There has been a parallel growth over the last 20 years of ever increasing control of the black population – more laws, more restrictions, more destruction of black leaders and their organizations – and an ever increasing investment in apartheid by foreign corporations. Since 1960, U.S. corporate investment in South Africa has grown from $286 million to more than $2 billion in 1980, making the U.S. the second largest foreign investor after Britain. More than 300 U.S. companies operate there, and U.S. banks have bolstered the economy with more than $2.2 billion in recent loans. This U.S. corporate and financial involvement has helped provide the capital and technology for the nuclear, military, police and prison systems needed to maintain control of the black majority.

Of growing concern in the U.S. is the investment of public trust funds, education funds and pension funds in South Africa rather than in the cities and states where the money has been earned and where it is badly needed. Many corporations and banks are unsympathetic to this concern. David Packard, chairman of Hewlett-Packard, has been very straightforward about his company's priorities. Speaking in South Africa he said, "Some states back home say they intend to boycott U.S. companies which trade with South Africa. Well that doesn't worry us at all, we're going to continue to trade. I'd much rather lose business with Nebraska than with South Africa."

CALL FOR ACTION

Already this year, more than thirty people have been killed by the South African police as they demonstrated for better education and an end to apartheid. Protest is escalating, involving black South Africans in strikes, demonstrations and sabotage. The Government has responded with the harshest ban on public meetings issued in twenty years, outlawing all gatherings "of a political nature" involving more than 10 people. It is time to act here in the United States. In South Africa opponents of the apartheid regime have called for foreign corporations and banks to withdraw; that call deserves support.

What has been done: More than twenty universities and colleges have already taken steps to break ties with South Africa. Among these,

Michigan State University voted for full divestment involving $7.5 million in December, 1978, and Yale University divested $1.6 million from Morgan Guaranty Trust because of its policy of lending to South Africa. The AFL-CIO, at its 1979 convention, passed a resolution urging "total cessation of U.S. Government support for economic transactions with South Africa."

In early 1980, the National Council of Churches withdrew from Citibank a payroll account through which $4.7 million flowed annually, and the United Methodist Board of Global Ministries severed all relations with Citibank, including 28 separate accounts with annual cash flows of over $57 million. Citibank is America's largest lender to South Africa and the only U.S. bank with branches in the Republic.

What you can do: Join the following states and cities where action for divestment has been begun and, in some cases, completed:

Connecticut
Gary, Indiana
Illinois
Davis, California
Massachusetts
Cotati, California
Michigan
Berkeley, California
Minnesota
Madison, Wisconsin
Nebraska
Cambridge, Massachusetts

Pass this Model Bill:

After the date of enactment of this Act, no public pension, state educational, or public trust funds shall be invested in any bank or financial institution which makes loans to South Africa or to a national corporation of South Africa, or to a subsidiary or affiliate of a United States company operating in South Africa, and no assets shall remain invested in the stocks, securities or other obligations of any company doing business in or with South Africa.

A network of organizations has formed to facilitate the passage of appropriate legislation. For more information contact:

The American Committee on Africa
American Friends Service Committee

Washington Office on Africa
Interfaith Center on Corporate Responsibility
TransAfrica
Clergy and Laity Concerned

Source: African Activist Archive.

2 Toxic Wastes and Race in the United States, 1987

"Race proved to be the most significant among variables"

Led by Rev. Ben Chavis (b. 1948), whose roots ran deep in black freedom movements, the Commission of Racial Justice of the United Church of Christ underwrote a research project that identified an unmistakable connection between the placement of toxic waste facilities and the racial or ethnic composition of the communities where those facilities were placed, an intentional act of racism which the report defined as follows:

Racism is racial prejudice plus power. Racism is the intentional or unintentional use of power to isolate, separate and exploit others. This use of power is based on a belief in superior racial origin, identity or supposed racial characteristics. Racism confers certain privileges on and defends the dominant group, which in turn sustains and perpetuates racism. Both consciously and unconsciously, racism is enforced and maintained by the legal, cultural, religious, educational, economic, political, environmental and military institutions of societies. Racism is more than just a personal attitude; it is the institutionalized form of that attitude.

The study, excerpted below, sparked a campaign against environmental racism and forged new coalitions among African Americans and other minority communities and the environmentalist movement.

EXECUTIVE SUMMARY

Recently, there has been unprecedented national concern over the problem of hazardous wastes. This concern has been focused upon the adverse environmental and health effects of toxic chemicals and other hazardous substances emanating from operating hazardous waste treatment, storage and disposal facilities as well as thousands of abandoned waste sites. Efforts to address this issue, however, have largely ignored the specific concerns of

African Americans, Hispanic Americans, Asian Americans, Pacific Islanders and Native Americans. Unfortunately, racial and ethnic Americans are far more likely to be unknowing victims of exposure to such substances.

Public policies ushered in by the Reagan Administration signaled a reduction of domestic programs to monitor the environment and protect public health. Reduction of efforts to protect public health is especially disturbing in light of the many citizens who unknowingly may be exposed to substances emanating from hazardous waste sites. According to a December 1986 U.S. General Accounting Office (GAO) report, the U.S. Environmental Protection Agency (EPA) "does not know if it has identified 90 percent of the potentially hazardous wastes or only 10 percent."

Issues surrounding the siting of hazardous waste facilities in racial and ethnic communities gained national prominence in 1982. The Commission for Racial Justice joined ranks with residents of predominantly Black and poor Warren County, North Carolina, in opposing the establishment of a polychlorinated biphenyl (PCB) disposal landfill. This opposition culminated in a nonviolent civil disobedience campaign and more than 500 arrests. As a result of the protests in Warren County, the GAO studied the racial and socio-economic status of communities surrounding four landfills in southeastern United States. It found that Blacks comprised the majority of the population in three of the four communities studied.

Previous to the Warren County demonstrations, racial and ethnic communities had been marginally involved with issues of hazardous wastes. One reason for this can be traced to the nature of the environmental movement which has historically been white middle- and upper-class in its orientation. This does not mean, however, that racial and ethnic communities do not care about the quality of their environment and its effect on their lives. Throughout the course of the Commission for Racial Justice's involvement with issues of hazardous wastes and environmental pollution, we have found numerous grassroots racial and ethnic groups actively seeking to deal with this problem in their communities.

Racial and ethnic communities have been and continue to be beset by poverty, unemployment and problems related to poor housing, education and health. These communities cannot afford the luxury of being primarily concerned about the quality of their environment when confronted by a plethora of pressing problems related to their day-to-day survival. Within this context, racial and ethnic communities become particularly vulnerable to those who advocate the siting of a hazardous waste facility as an avenue for employment and economic development. Thus, proposals that economic incentives be offered to mitigate local opposition to the establishment of new hazardous waste facilities raise disturbing social policy questions.

...

"Hazardous wastes" is the term used by the EPA to define by-products of industrial production which present particularly troublesome health and environmental problems. Newly generated hazardous wastes must be managed in an approved "facility" which is defined by the EPA as any land and structures thereon which are used for treating, storing or disposing of hazardous wastes (TSD facility). Such facilities may include landfills, surface impoundments or incinerators. A "commercial" facility is defined as any facility (public or private) which accepts hazardous wastes from a third party for a fee or other remuneration.

"Uncontrolled toxic waste sites" refer to closed and abandoned sites on the EPA's list of sites which pose a potential threat to human health and the environment. The problem of human exposure to uncontrolled hazardous wastes is national in its scope. By 1985, the EPA had inventoried approximately 20,000 uncontrolled sites containing hazardous wastes across the nation. The potential health problems associated with the existence of these sites is highlighted by the fact that approximately 75 percent of U.S. cities derive their water supplies, in total or in part, from groundwater.

MAJOR FINDINGS

...

Demographic Characteristics of Communities with Commercial Hazardous Waste Facilities:

- Race proved to be the most significant among variables tested in association with the location of commercial hazardous waste facilities. This represented a consistent national pattern.
- Communities with the greatest number of commercial hazardous waste facilities had the highest composition of racial and ethnic residents. In communities with two or more facilities or one of the nation's five largest landfills the average minority percentage of the population [In this report, "minority percentage of the population" was used as a measure of "race"] was more than three times that of communities without facilities (38 percent vs. 12 percent).
- In communities with one commercial hazardous waste facility, the average minority percentage of the population was twice the average minority percentage of the population in communities without such facilities (24 percent vs. 12 percent).
- Although socio-economic status appeared to play an important role in the location of commercial hazardous waste facilities, race still proved to be more significant. This remained true after the study

controlled for urbanization and regional differences. Incomes and home values were substantially lower when communities with commercial facilities were compared to communities in the surrounding counties without facilities.

– Three out of the five largest commercial hazardous waste landfills in the United States were located in predominantly Black or Hispanic communities. These three landfills accounted for 40 percent of the total estimated commercial landfill capacity in the nation.

Demographic Characteristics of Communities with Uncontrolled Toxic Waste Sites

– Three out of every five Black and Hispanic Americans lived in communities with uncontrolled toxic waste sites.
– More than 15 million Blacks lived in communities with one or more uncontrolled toxic waste sites.
– More than 8 million Hispanics lived in communities with one or more uncontrolled toxic waste sites.
– Blacks were heavily over-represented in the populations of metropolitan areas with the largest number of uncontrolled toxic waste sites. These areas include:

Memphis, TN (173 sites)
St. Louis, MO (160 sites)
Houston, TX (151 sites)
Cleveland, OH (106 sites)
Chicago, IL (103 sites)
Atlanta, GA (94 sites)

– Los Angeles, California, had more Hispanics living in communities with uncontrolled toxic waste sites than any other metropolitan area in the United States.
– Approximately half of all Asians, Pacific Islanders and American Indians lived in communities with uncontrolled toxic waste sites.
– Overall, the presence of uncontrolled toxic waste sites was highly pervasive. More than half of the total population in the United States resided in communities with uncontrolled toxic waste sites.

MAJOR CONCLUSIONS AND RECOMMENDATIONS

The findings of the analytical study on the location of commercial hazardous waste facilities suggest the existence of clear patterns which show that communities with greater minority percentages of the population are more likely to be the sites of such facilities. The possibility that these patterns resulted by chance is virtually impossible [All of the national findings were found to be statistically significant with 99.99 percent confidence (that is, findings with a probability of less than 1 in 10,000 that they occurred by chance], strongly suggesting that some underlying factor or factors, which are related to race, played a role in the location of commercial hazardous waste facilities. Therefore, the Commission for Racial Justice concludes that, indeed, race has been a factor in the location of commercial hazardous waste facilities in the United States.

The findings of the descriptive study on the location of uncontrolled toxic waste sites suggest an inordinate concentration of such sites in Black and Hispanic communities, particularly in urban areas. This situation reveals that the issue of race is an important factor in describing the problem of uncontrolled toxic waste sites. We, therefore, conclude that the cleanup of uncontrolled toxic waste sites in Black and Hispanic communities in the United States should be given the highest possible priority.

These findings expose a serious void in present government programs addressing racial and ethnic concerns in these areas. This report, therefore, strongly urges the formation of necessary offices and task forces by federal, state and local governments to fill this void. Among the many recommendations of this report, we call special attention to the following:

– We urge the President of the United States to issue an executive order mandating federal agencies to consider the impact of current policies and regulations on racial and ethnic communities.
– We urge the formation of an Office of Hazardous Wastes and Racial and Ethnic Affairs by the U.S. Environmental Protection Agency. This office should insure that racial and ethnic concerns regarding hazardous wastes, such as the cleanup of uncontrolled sites, are adequately addressed. In addition, we urge the EPA to establish a National Advisory Council on Racial and Ethnic Concerns.
– We urge state governments to evaluate and make appropriate revisions in their criteria for the siting of new hazardous waste facilities to adequately take into account the racial and socioeconomic characteristics of potential host communities.
– We urge the U.S. Conference of Mayors, the National Conference of Black Mayors and the National League of Cities to convene a national conference to address these issues from a municipal perspective.
– We urge civil rights and political organizations to gear up voter registration campaigns as a means to further empower racial and ethnic communities

to effectively respond to hazardous waste issues and to place hazardous wastes in racial and ethnic communities at the top of state and national legislative agendas.

– We urge local communities to initiate education and action programs around racial and ethnic concerns regarding hazardous wastes.

We also call for a series of additional actions. Of paramount importance are further epidemiological and demographic research and the provision of information on hazardous wastes to racial and ethnic communities.

This report firmly concludes that hazardous wastes in Black, Hispanic and other racial and ethnic communities should be made a priority issue at all levels of government. This issue is not currently at the forefront of the nation's attention. Therefore, concerned citizens and policy-makers, who are cognizant of this growing national problem, must make this a priority concern.

Source: Reproduced from *Toxic Wastes and Race in the United States: A National Report on the Racial and Socio-Economic Characteristics of Communities with Hazardous Waste Sites.* Preface, pp. ix–x; Executive Summary, pp. xi–xvi; and Chapter 1, "A Context for Examining Toxic Wastes and Race," pp. 1–8. Copyright © 1987 United Church of Christ. All rights reserved. Reprinted with permission.

3 Jesse Jackson Rouses the Democratic National Convention, Atlanta, GA, July 19, 1988

"Keep hope alive"

A military veteran and a student at North Carolina A & T, the Rev. Jesse Jackson (b. 1941) had participated in the sit-in movement in Greensboro, North Carolina, in February 1960. He marched at Selma with the Rev. Dr. Martin Luther King, Jr., and headed Operation Breadbasket, a poverty project of SCLC. He was among those gathered at the Lorraine Hotel in Memphis the evening King was assassinated in 1968. During the year following, Jackson began work as a community organizer in Chicago. Espousing core values he absorbed in civil rights activism, Jackson emerged as an internationally prominent advocate for social justice. He ran for President of the United States in 1984, carrying 17 percent of the primary vote. With a rousing speech at the convention, Jackson enlivened Democratic forces disheartened by the nation's turn to the right. The Democrats nominated Walter Mondale, who lost to Ronald Reagan. In the 1988 Democratic primary Jackson carried a third of the total vote, placing second,

but conceded at the national convention to Michael Dukakis. The speech
excerpted below, a rallying call to Democrats, brought the floor to its feet
eighteen times.

... When I look out at this convention, I see the face of America: Red, Yellow, Brown, Black and White. We're all precious in God's sight – the real rainbow coalition.

All of us – All of us who are here think that we are seated. But we're really standing on someone's shoulders.

...

My right and my privilege to stand here before you has been won, won in my lifetime, by the blood and the sweat of the innocent.

Twenty-four years ago, the late Fannie Lou Hamer and Aaron Henry – who sits here tonight from Mississippi – were locked out onto the streets in Atlantic City....

But tonight, a Black and White delegation from Mississippi is headed by Ed Cole, a Black man from Mississippi; twenty-four years later.

Many were lost in the struggle for the right to vote: Jimmy Lee Jackson, a young student, gave his life; Viola Liuzzo, a White mother from Detroit, called "nigger lover," [had her] brains blown out at point blank range; [Michael] Schwerner, [Andrew] Goodman and [James] Chaney – two Jews and a Black – found in a common grave, bodies riddled with bullets in Mississippi; the four darling little girls in a church in Birmingham, Alabama. They died that we might have a right to live.

Dr. Martin Luther King Jr. lies only a few miles from us tonight. Tonight he must feel good as he looks down upon us. We sit here together, a rainbow, a coalition – the sons and daughters of slavemasters and the sons and daughters of slaves, sitting together around a common table, to decide the direction of our party and our country. His heart would be full tonight.

As a testament to the struggles of those who have gone before; as a legacy for those who will come after; as a tribute to the endurance, the patience, the courage of our forefathers and mothers; as an assurance that their prayers are being answered, that their work has not been in vain, and, that hope is eternal, tomorrow night my name will go into nomination for the Presidency of the United States of America.

We meet tonight at the crossroads, a point of decision. Shall we expand, be inclusive, find unity and power; or suffer division and impotence?

We've come to Atlanta, the cradle of the Old South, the crucible of the New South. Tonight, there is a sense of celebration, because we are moved,

fundamentally moved from racial battlegrounds by law, to economic common ground. Tomorrow we'll challenge to move to higher ground.
...

Today we debated, differed, deliberated, agreed to agree, agreed to disagree, when we had the good judgment to argue a case and then not self-destruct ...

The good of our Nation is at stake. Its commitment to working men and women, to the poor and the vulnerable, to the many in the world.

With so many guided missiles, and so much misguided leadership, the stakes are exceedingly high. Our choice? Full participation in a democratic government, or more abandonment and neglect. And so this night, we choose not a false sense of independence, not our capacity to survive and endure. Tonight we choose interdependency, and our capacity to act and unite for the greater good.

Common good is finding commitment to new priorities to expansion and inclusion. A commitment to expanded participation in the Democratic Party at every level. A commitment to a shared national campaign strategy and involvement at every level.

A commitment to new priorities that insure that hope will be kept alive. A common ground commitment to a legislative agenda for empowerment, for the John Conyers bill – universal, on-site, same-day registration everywhere. A commitment to D.C. statehood and empowerment – D.C. deserves statehood. A commitment to economic set-asides, commitment to the Dellums bill for comprehensive sanctions against South Africa. A shared commitment to a common direction.

Common ground.

Easier said than done. Where do you find common ground? At the point of challenge. This campaign has shown that politics need not be marketed by politicians, packaged by pollsters and pundits. Politics can be a moral arena where people come together to find common ground.

We find common ground at the plant gate that closes on workers without notice. We find common ground at the farm auction, where a good farmer loses his or her land to bad loans or diminishing markets. Common ground at the school yard where teachers cannot get adequate pay, and students cannot get a scholarship, and can't make a loan. Common ground at the hospital admitting room, where somebody tonight is dying because they cannot afford to go upstairs to a bed that's empty waiting for someone with insurance to get sick. We are a better nation than that. We must do better.

Common ground. What is leadership, if not to present help in a time of crisis? And so I met you at the point of challenge. In Jay, Maine, where paper workers were striking for fair wages; in Greenville, Iowa, where family farmers struggle for a fair price; in Cleveland, Ohio, where working women seek comparable worth; in McFarland, California, where the children of Hispanic farm workers may be dying from poisoned land, dying in clusters with cancer; in an AIDS hospice in Houston, Texas, where the sick support one another, too often rejected by their own parents and friends.

Common ground. America is not a blanket woven from one thread, one color, one cloth. When I was a child growing up in Greenville, South Carolina and grandmamma could not afford a blanket, she didn't complain and we did not freeze. Instead she took pieces of old cloth – patches, wool, silk, gabardine, crockersack – only patches, barely good enough to wipe off your shoes with. But they didn't stay that way very long. With sturdy hands and a strong cord, she sewed them together into a quilt, a thing of beauty and power and culture. Now, Democrats, we must build such a quilt.

Farmers, you seek fair prices and you are right – but you cannot stand alone. Your patch is not big enough.

Workers, you fight for fair wages, you are right – but your patch labor is not big enough.

Women, you seek comparable worth and pay equity, you are right – but your patch is not big enough.

Women, mothers, who seek Head Start, and day care and prenatal care on the front side of life, relevant jail care and welfare on the back side of life, you are right – but your patch is not big enough.

Students, you seek scholarships, you are right – but your patch is not big enough.

Blacks and Hispanics, when we fight for civil rights, we are right – but our patch is not big enough.

Gays and lesbians, when you fight against discrimination and a cure for AIDS, you are right – but your patch is not big enough.

Conservatives and progressives, when you fight for what you believe, right wing, left wing, hawk, dove, you are right from your point of view, but your point of view is not enough.

But don't despair. Be as wise as my grandmamma. Pull the patches and the pieces together, bound by a common thread. When we form a great quilt of unity and common ground, we'll have the power to bring about health care and housing and jobs and education and hope to our Nation.

We, the people, can win.

We stand at the end of a long dark night of reaction. We stand tonight united in the commitment to a new direction. For almost eight years we've been led by those who view social good coming from private interest, who view public life as a means to increase private wealth. They have been prepared to sacrifice the common good of the many to satisfy the private interests and the wealth of a few.

We believe in a government that's a tool of our democracy in service to the public, not an instrument of the aristocracy in search of private wealth. We believe in government with the consent of the governed, "of, for and by the people." We must now emerge into a new day with a new direction.

Reaganomics: Based on the belief that the rich had too little money and the poor had too much. That's classic Reaganomics. They believe that the poor had too much money and the rich had too little money, – so they engaged in reverse Robin Hood – took from the poor, gave to the rich, paid for by the middle class. We cannot stand four more years of Reaganomics in any version, in any disguise.

How do I document that case? Seven years later, the richest 1 percent of our society pays 20 percent less in taxes. The poorest 10 percent pay 20 percent more: Reaganomics.

Reagan gave the rich and the powerful a multibillion-dollar party. Now the party is over. He expects the people to pay for the damage. I take this principal position, convention, let us not raise taxes on the poor and the middle-class, but those who had the party, the rich and the powerful, must pay for the party.

...

Leadership must meet the moral challenge of its day. What's the moral challenge of our day? We have public accommodations. We have the right to vote. We have open housing. What's the fundamental challenge of our day? It is to end economic violence. Plant closings without notice – economic violence. Even the greedy do not profit long from greed – economic violence.

Most poor people are not lazy. They are not black. They are not brown. They are mostly White and female and young. But whether White, Black or Brown, a hungry baby's belly turned inside out is the same color – color it pain; color it hurt; color it agony.

Most poor people are not on welfare. Some of them are illiterate and can't read the want-ad sections. And when they can, they can't find a job that matches the address. They work hard everyday.

I know. I live amongst them. I'm one of them. I know they work. I'm a witness. They catch the early bus. They work every day.

They raise other people's children. They work everyday.

They clean the streets. They work everyday. They drive dangerous cabs. They work everyday. They change the beds you slept in in these hotels last night and can't get a union contract. They work everyday.

No, no, they are not lazy! Someone must defend them because it's right, and they cannot speak for themselves. ...

We are a better Nation than that. We are a better Nation than that.

We need a real war on drugs. You can't "just say no." It's deeper than that. You can't just get a palm reader or an astrologer. It's more profound than that.

...

I met the children in Watts, who, unfortunately, in their despair, their grapes of hope have become raisins of despair, and they're turning on each other and they're self-destructing.

...

They said, "Jesse Jackson, as you challenge us to say no to drugs, you're right; and to not sell them, you're right; and not use these guns, you're right." ... [But] "We have neither jobs nor houses nor services nor training – no way out. Some of us take drugs as anesthesia for our pain. Some take drugs as a way of pleasure, good short-term pleasure and long-term pain. Some sell drugs to make money. It's wrong, we know, but you need to know that we know. We can go and buy the drugs by the boxes at the port. If we can buy the drugs at the port, don't you believe the Federal government can stop it if they want to?"

They say, "We don't have Saturday night specials anymore." They say, "We buy AK47's and Uzi's, the latest make of weapons. We buy them along these boulevards."

You cannot fight a war on drugs unless and until you're going to challenge the bankers and the gun sellers and those who grow them. Don't just focus on the children; let's stop drugs at the level of supply and demand. We must end the scourge on the American Culture.

Leadership. What difference will we make? Leadership. Cannot just go along to get along. We must do more than change Presidents. We must change direction.

Leadership must face the moral challenge of our day. The nuclear war build-up is irrational. Strong leadership cannot desire to look tough and let that stand in the way of the pursuit of peace. Leadership must reverse the arms race. At least we should pledge no first use. Why? Because first use begets first retaliation. And that's mutual annihilation. That's not a rational way out.

...

Most people in the world today are Yellow or Brown or Black, non-Christian, poor, female, young and don't speak English in the real world.

This generation must offer leadership to the real world. We're losing ground in Latin America, Middle East, South Africa because we're not focusing on the real world. That's the real world. We must use basic principles – support international law. We stand the most to gain from it. Support human rights – we believe in that. Support self-determination – we're built on that. Support economic development – you know it's right. Be consistent and gain our moral authority in the world. I challenge you tonight, my friends, let's be bigger and better as a Nation and as a Party.

We have basic challenges – freedom in South Africa. We've already agreed as Democrats to declare South Africa to be a terrorist state. But don't just stop there. Get South Africa out of Angola; free Namibia; support the front line states. We must have a new humane human rights consistent policy in Africa.

I'm often asked, "Jesse, why do you take on these tough issues? They're not very political. We can't win that way."

If an issue is morally right, it will eventually be political. It may be political and never be right. Fannie Lou Hamer didn't have the most votes in Atlantic City, but her principles have outlasted every delegate who voted to lock her out. Rosa Parks did not have the most votes, but she was morally right. Dr. King didn't have the most votes about the Vietnam War, but he was morally right. If we are principled first, our politics will fall in place.

...

And then for our children. Young America, hold your head high now. We can win. We must not lose you to drugs and violence, premature pregnancy, suicide, cynicism, pessimism and despair. We can win. Wherever you are tonight, I challenge you to hope and to dream. ...

You must never stop dreaming. Face reality, yes, but don't stop with the way things are. Dream of things as they ought to be. Dream. Face pain, but love, hope, faith and dreams will help you rise above the pain. Use hope and imagination as weapons of survival and progress, but you keep on dreaming, young America. Dream of peace. Peace is rational and reasonable. War is irrational in this age, and unwinnable.

Dream of teachers who teach for life and not for a living. Dream of doctors who are concerned more about public health than private wealth. Dream of lawyers more concerned about justice than a judgeship. Dream of preachers who are concerned more about prophecy than profiteering. Dream on the high road with sound values.

And then America, as we go forth to September, October, November and then beyond, America must never surrender to a high moral challenge....

America must never surrender to malnutrition. We can feed the hungry and clothe the naked. We must never surrender. We must go forward.

We must never surrender to illiteracy. Invest in our children. Never surrender; and go forward. We must never surrender to inequality. Women cannot compromise ERA or comparable worth. Women are making 60 cents on the dollar to what a man makes. Women cannot buy meat cheaper.

Women cannot buy bread cheaper. Women cannot buy milk cheaper. Women deserve to get paid for the work that you do. It's right! And it's fair.

Don't surrender, my friends. Those who have AIDS tonight, you deserve our compassion. Even with AIDS you must not surrender.

...

But even in your wheelchairs, don't you give up. We cannot forget 50 years ago when our backs were against the wall, Roosevelt was in a wheelchair. I would rather have Roosevelt in a wheelchair than Reagan and Bush on a horse. Don't you surrender and don't you give up. Don't surrender and don't give up!

[People] wonder, "Why does Jesse run?" because they see me running for the White House. They don't see the house I'm running from. ... I was born in the slum, but the slum was not born in me. And it wasn't born in you, and you can make it.

...

We must never surrender!! America will get better and better.

Keep hope alive. Keep hope alive! Keep hope alive! On tomorrow night and beyond, keep hope alive!

...

Source: Jesse Jackson, Speech to the Democratic National Convention, Atlanta, GA, July 19, 1988.

4 African American Women in Defense of Ourselves, 1991

"we cannot tolerate this type of dismissal of any one Black woman's experience or this attack upon our collective character without protest, outrage and resistance"

To replace Thurgood Marshall on the Supreme Court in 1991, President George H. W. Bush nominated Clarence Thomas (b. 1948). Thomas' inexperience as a constitutional scholar caused some reservations among African Americans. In addition, on the United States Court of Appeals, as Assistant Secretary of Civil Rights at the Department of Education, and as Chair of the Equal Employment Opportunity Commission, Thomas left a record of conservatism that flew in the face of black freedom struggles and his personal experience. But it was his personal conduct that generated the clearest doubts about his qualifications for the Court. During televised confirmation hearings, Professor Anita F. Hill (b. 1956), an assistant to Thomas at DoE and the EEOC, testified that she had been subject to a

pattern of sexual misconduct and harassment on the part of Thomas.
Feminists and African American women in particular were enraged not only
by Senators' trivialization of the charges and their public denigration of the
dignified Hill, but also by Thomas' use of the term "high-tech lynching" to
shelter himself from Hill's accusation. Following the hearings 1,600 African
American women scholars, organized by Elsa Barkley Brown, Deborah King,
and Barbara Ransby, contributed $50,000 to produce the following
statement. It appeared as a full-page ad in The Sunday New York Times
in December 1991.

"African American Women in Defense of Ourselves"

As women of African descent, we are deeply troubled by the recent nomination, confirmation and seating of Clarence Thomas as an Associate Justice
of the U.S. Supreme Court. We know that the presence of Clarence Thomas
on the Court will be continually used to divert attention from the historic
struggles for social justice through suggestions that the presence of a Black
man on the Supreme Court constitutes an assurance that the rights of
African Americans will be protected. Clarence Thomas' public record is
ample evidence this will not be true. Further, the consolidation of a conservative majority on the Supreme Court seriously endangers the rights of all
women, poor and working-class people and the elderly. The seating of
Clarence Thomas is an affront not only to African American women and
men, but to all people concerned with social justice.

We are particularly outraged by the racist and sexist treatment of
Professor Anita Hill, an African-American woman who was maligned and
castigated for daring to speak publicly of her own experience of sexual
abuse. The malicious defamation of Professor Hill insulted all women of
African descent and sent a dangerous message to any woman who might
contemplate a sexual harassment complaint.

We speak here because we recognize that the media are not portraying
the Black community as prepared to tolerate both the dismantling of
affirmative action and the evil of sexual harassment in order to have any
Black man on the Supreme Court. We want to make clear that the
media have ignored or distorted many African-American voices. We will
not be silenced.

Many have erroneously portrayed the allegation against Clarence Thomas
as an issue of either gender or race. As women of African descent, we understand sexual harassment as both. We further understand that Clarence
Thomas outrageously manipulated the legacy of lynching in order to shelter

himself from Anita Hill's allegations. To deflect attention away from the reality of sexual abuse in African-American women's lives, he trivialized and misrepresented this painful part of African American people's history. This country, which has a long legacy of racism and sexism, has never taken the sexual abuse of Black women seriously. Throughout U.S. history Black women have been sexually stereotyped as immoral, insatiable, perverse; the initiators of all sexual contact – abusive or otherwise. The common assumption in legal proceedings as well as in the larger society has been that Black women cannot be raped or otherwise sexually abused. As Anita Hill's experience demonstrates, Black women who speak of these matters are not likely to be believed.

In 1991, we cannot tolerate this type of dismissal of any one Black woman's experience or this attack upon our collective character without protest, outrage, and resistance. As women of African descent, we express our vehement opposition to the policies represented by the placement of Clarence Thomas on the Supreme Court. The [George H. W.] Bush administration, having obstructed passage of civil rights legislation, impeded the extension of unemployment compensation, cut student aid, and dismantled social welfare programs, has continually demonstrated that it is not operating in our best interests. Nor is this appointee. We pledge ourselves to continue to speak out in defense of one another, in defense of the African-American community and against those who are hostile to social justice no matter what color they are. No one will speak for us but ourselves.

Source: Joy James, "African American Women in Defense of Ourselves," published in *The Black Scholar*, 22, Nos. 1 & 2 (1992): 155. Reprinted with permission.

5 Maxine Waters Explains the Causes of Urban Crises to Congress, 1992

"We have created in many areas of this country a breeding ground for hopelessness, anger and despair"

In 1991, seven police in Los Angeles beat black citizen Rodney King (1965–2012) after a traffic stop. The cops contended that King resisted arrest, but a widely aired videotape of the beating contradicted that assertion. When a jury failed to hold the officers accountable for their actions, LA broke into riots. The King incident and the verdict were not the only issues that had evoked their frustration. Rather, the insurrection represented broader disillusionments with quotidian injustice: high unemployment, failing schools, police abuse, and poverty that plagued people of color

disproportionately. When the House of Representatives held hearings to
investigate the rising crisis in urban areas, Congressperson Maxine Waters
(D-CA; b. 1938) offered a more complex explanation for the unrest.

The riots in Los Angeles and in other cities shocked the world. They shouldn't have. Many of us have watched our country – including our government – neglect the problems, indeed the people, of our inner-cities for years – even as matters reached a crisis stage.

The verdict in the Rodney King case did not cause what happened in Los Angeles. It was only the most recent injustice – piled upon many other injustices – suffered by the poor, minorities and the hopeless people living in this nation's cities. For years, they have been crying out for help. For years, their cries have not been heard.

I recently came across a statement made more than 25 years ago by Robert Kennedy, just two months before his violent death. He was talking about the violence that had erupted in cities across America. His words were wise and thoughtful:

"There is another kind of violence in America, slower but just as deadly, destructive as the shot or bomb in the night.... This is the violence of institutions; indifference and inaction and slow decay. This is the violence that afflicts the poor, that poisons relations between men and women because their skin is different colors. This is the slow destruction of a child by hunger, and schools without books and homes without heat in winter."

What a tragedy it is that America has still, in 1992, not learned such an important lesson.

I have represented the people of South Central Los Angeles in the U.S. Congress and the California State Assembly for close to 20 years. I have seen our community continually and systematically ravaged by banks who would not lend to us, by governments which abandoned us or punished us for our poverty, and by big businesses who exported our jobs to Third-World countries for cheap labor.

Conditions in South-Central Los Angeles and in many other cities around the country are severe. In Los Angeles, between 40 and 50 percent of all African-American men are unemployed. The poverty rate is 32.9 percent. According to the most recent census, 40,000 teenagers – that is 20 percent of the city's 16 to 19 year olds – are both out of school and unemployed. ...

We have created in many areas of this country a breeding ground for hopelessness, anger and despair. All the traditional mechanisms for empowerment, opportunity and self-improvement have been closed.

We are in the midst of a grand economic experiment that suggests if we "get the government off people's backs," and let the economy grow, everyone, including the poor, will somehow be better off.... The results of this experiment have been devastating. Today, more than 12 million children live in poverty, despite a decade of "economic growth," the precise mechanism we were told would reduce poverty. Today, one in five children in America lives in poverty....

The number of children in poverty increased by 2.2 million from 1979 to 1989. This was true for every subgroup of America's children. White children's poverty increased from 11.8 percent to 14.8 percent. Latino child poverty went from 28 percent to 36.2 percent. And black child poverty increased from 41.2 percent up to 43.7 percent.

While the budget cuts of the eighties were literally forcing millions of Americans into poverty, there were other social and economic trends destroying inner-city communities at the same time.

I'm sure everyone in this room has read the results of the Federal Reserve Board's study on mortgage discrimination that demonstrates African Americans and Latinos are twice as likely as whites of the same income to be denied mortgages. ...

In law enforcement, the problems are longstanding and well documented as well. In a system where judges and lawyers remain overwhelmingly white, blacks account for a share of the prison population that far outstrips their presence in the population.

Is it any wonder our children have no hope? The systems are failing us ... We simply cannot afford the continued terror and oppression of benign neglect that has characterized the federal government's response to the cities since the late 1970s.

...

Source: Statement of Maxine Waters, member, House of Representatives, from the State of California, Fiscal, Economic, and Social Crises Confronting American Cities, Committee on Banking, Housing, and Urban Affairs, Senate S Hearings 102–992, Congressional Session: 102–2 (1992), pp. 259–274.

6 The Million Man March, 1995

"I will strive to love my brother as I love myself"

With a crowd estimated at 500,000 to 1.2 million attendees, the 1995 Million Man March was the largest gathering of African Americans in one place in the history of the United States. Organized by a coalition of black

*organizations – sacred and secular, political and cultural – participants
collected on the National Mall in Washington, DC to engender a moment
of unity among a diverse people. Billed as a meeting of black men, the
March also garnered families and prioritized several goals: to raise black
consciousness; to generate spirituality and a sense of community; to
engage in self-reflection; and to return black issues to the national agenda.
More than a dozen presenters, among them Rosa Parks, Ben Chavis, and
Jesse Jackson, spoke of accountability and a responsibility and need to
move from articulation to action. Led by Minister Louis Farrakhan (b.
1933) of the Nation of Islam, attendees took the pledge printed below.
The Million Man March spurred other such gatherings, including the
Million Family March (also organized by Farrakhan), the Million Woman
March of African American women, and a Million Mom March against
guns and violence.*

I pledge that from this day forward I will strive to love my brother as I love myself. I, from this day forward, will strive to improve myself spiritually, morally, mentally, socially, politically and economically for the benefit of myself, my family and my people. I pledge that I will strive to build business, build houses, build hospitals, build factories and enter into international trade for the good of myself, my family and my people.

I pledge that from this day forward I will never raise my hand with a knife or a gun to beat, cut, or shoot any member of my family or any human being except in self-defense. I pledge from this day forward I will never abuse my wife by striking her, disrespecting her, for she is the mother of my children and the producer of my future. I pledge that from this day forward I will never engage in the abuse of children, little boys or little girls for sexual gratification. For I will let them grow in peace to be strong men and women for the future of our people.

I will never again use the 'B word' to describe any female. But particularly my own black sister. I pledge from this day forward that I will not poison my body with drugs or that which is destructive to my health and my well-being. I pledge from this day forward I will support black newspapers, black radio, black television. I will support black artists who clean up their acts to show respect for themselves and respect for their people and respect for the ears of the human family. I will do all of this so help me God.

Source: Text of the pledge that Minister Louis Farrakhan asked black men to take on October 16, 1995, during the Million Man March on Washington, DC.

7 Angela Davis Describes the Prison Industrial Complex, 1995

"prisons do not disappear problems, they disappear human beings"

Entangled herself in the early 1970s by a law enforcement system seeking to undermine black radicalism, scholar and activist Angela Y. Davis has made it a life's work to speak out about the criminal justice system. Historically, blacks and other minorities have been plagued by racialized patterns of police intimidation and violence, and subjected to harsher punishments than whites for the same and similar offenses. In the 1990s, as states began to relinquish responsibilities for prisons to private corporations, such institutions no longer addressed rehabilitation. Rather, they became storage facilities – places to "disappear" social problems – and, worse, a source of private profit for prison investors. In this 1995 article for Color Lines, a daily online news site, Davis explains how, fed by a biased criminal justice system, the prison industrial complex has become a place of racial exploitation.

"Masked Racism: Reflections on the Prison Industrial Complex"

Imprisonment has become the response of first resort to far too many of the social problems that burden people who are ensconced in poverty. These problems often are veiled by being conveniently grouped together under the category "crime" and by the automatic attribution of criminal behavior to people of color. Homelessness, unemployment, drug addiction, mental illness, and illiteracy are only a few of the problems that disappear from public view when the human beings contending with them are relegated to cages.

Prisons thus perform a feat of magic. Or rather the people who continually vote in new prison bonds and tacitly assent to a proliferating network of prisons and jails have been tricked into believing in the magic of imprisonment. But prisons do not disappear problems, they disappear human beings. And the practice of disappearing vast numbers of people from poor, immigrant, and racially marginalized communities has literally become big business.

The seeming effortlessness of magic always conceals an enormous amount of behind-the-scenes work. When prisons disappear human beings in order to convey the illusion of solving social problems, penal infrastructures must be created to accommodate a rapidly swelling population of caged people. Goods and services must be provided to keep imprisoned populations alive. Sometimes these populations must be kept busy and at other times – particularly in repressive super-maximum prisons and in INS detention centers – they must be deprived of virtually all meaningful activity. Vast numbers of handcuffed and shackled people are moved across state borders as they are transferred from one state or federal prison to another.

All this work, which used to be the primary province of government, is now also performed by private corporations, whose links to government in the field of what is euphemistically called "corrections" resonate dangerously with the military industrial complex. The dividends that accrue from investment in the punishment industry, like those that accrue from investment in weapons production, only amount to social destruction. Taking into account the structural similarities and profitability of business – government linkages in the realms of military production and public punishment, the expanding penal system can now be characterized as a "prison industrial complex."

The Color of Imprisonment

Almost two million people are currently locked up in the immense network of U.S. prisons and jails. More than 70 percent of the imprisoned population are people of color. It is rarely acknowledged that the fastest growing group of prisoners are black women and that Native American prisoners are the largest group per capita. Approximately five million people – including those on probation and parole – are directly under the surveillance of the criminal justice system.

Three decades ago, the imprisoned population was approximately one-eighth its current size. While women still constitute a relatively small percentage of people behind bars, today the number of incarcerated women in California alone is almost twice what the nationwide women's prison population was in 1970. According to Elliott Currie, "[t]he prison has become a looming presence in our society to an extent unparalleled in our history – or that of any other industrial democracy. Short of major wars, mass incarceration has been the most thoroughly implemented government social program of our time."

To deliver up bodies destined for profitable punishment, the political economy of prisons relies on racialized assumptions of criminality – such as images of black welfare mothers reproducing criminal children – and on racist practices in arrest, conviction, and sentencing patterns. Colored bodies constitute the main human raw material in this vast experiment to disappear the major social problems of our time. Once the aura of magic is stripped away from the imprisonment solution, what is revealed is racism, class bias, and the parasitic seduction of capitalist profit. The prison industrial system materially and morally impoverishes its inhabitants and devours the social wealth needed to address the very problems that have led to spiraling numbers of prisoners.

As prisons take up more and more space on the social landscape, other government programs that have previously sought to respond to social needs – such as Temporary Assistance to Needy Families – are being squeezed out of existence. The deterioration of public education, including prioritizing discipline and security over learning in public schools located in poor communities, is directly related to the prison "solution."

Profiting from Prisoners

As prisons proliferate in U.S. society, private capital has become enmeshed in the punishment industry. And precisely because of their profit potential, prisons are becoming increasingly important to the U.S. economy. If the notion of punishment as a source of potentially stupendous profits is disturbing by itself, then the strategic dependence on racist structures and ideologies to render mass punishment palatable and profitable is even more troubling.

Prison privatization is the most obvious instance of capital's current movement toward the prison industry. While government-run prisons are often in gross violation of international human rights standards, private prisons are even less accountable. In March of this year [1995], the Corrections Corporation of America (CCA), the largest U.S. private prison company, claimed 54,944 beds in 68 facilities under contract or development in the U.S., Puerto Rico, the United Kingdom, and Australia. Following the global trend of subjecting more women to public punishment, CCA recently opened a women's prison outside Melbourne. The company recently identified California as its "new frontier."

Wackenhut Corrections Corporation (WCC), the second largest U.S. prison company, claimed contracts and awards to manage 46 facilities in North America, U.K., and Australia. It boasts a total of 30,424 beds as well as contracts for prisoner health care services, transportation, and security.

Currently, the stocks of both CCA and WCC are doing extremely well. Between 1996 and 1997, CCA's revenues increased by 58 percent, from $293 million to $462 million. Its net profit grew from $30.9 million to $53.9 million. WCC raised its revenues from $138 million in 1996 to $210 million in 1997. Unlike public correctional facilities, the vast profits of these private facilities rely on the employment of non-union labor.

The Prison Industrial Complex

But private prison companies are only the most visible component of the increasing corporatization of punishment. Government contracts to build prisons have bolstered the construction industry. The architectural community has identified prison design as a major new niche. Technology developed for the military by companies like Westinghouse are being marketed for use in law enforcement and punishment.

Moreover, corporations that appear to be far removed from the business of punishment are intimately involved in the expansion of the prison industrial complex. Prison construction bonds are one of the many sources of profitable investment for leading financiers such as Merrill Lynch. MCI charges prisoners and their families outrageous prices for the precious telephone calls which are often the only contact prisoners have with the free world.

Many corporations whose products we consume on a daily basis have learned that prison labor power can be as profitable as third world labor power exploited by U.S.-based global corporations. Both relegate formerly unionized workers to joblessness and many even wind up in prison. Some of the companies that use prison labor are IBM, Motorola, Compaq, Texas Instruments, Honeywell, Microsoft, and Boeing. But it is not only the hi-tech industries that reap the profits of prison labor. Nordstrom department stores sell jeans that are marketed as "Prison Blues," as well as t-shirts and jackets made in Oregon prisons. The advertising slogan for these clothes is "made on the inside to be worn on the outside." Maryland prisoners inspect glass bottles and jars used by Revlon and Pierre Cardin, and schools throughout the world buy graduation caps and gowns made by South Carolina prisoners.

"For private business," write Eve Goldberg and Linda Evans (a political prisoner inside the Federal Correctional Institution at Dublin, California) "prison labor is like a pot of gold. No strikes. No union organizing. No health benefits, unemployment insurance, or workers' compensation to pay. No language barriers, as in foreign countries. New leviathan prisons are being built on thousands of eerie acres of factories inside the walls. Prisoners do data entry for Chevron, make telephone reservations for TWA, raise hogs, shovel manure, make circuit boards, limousines, waterbeds, and lingerie for Victoria's Secret – all at a fraction of the cost of 'free labor.'"

Devouring the Social Wealth

Although prison labor – which ultimately is compensated at a rate far below the minimum wage – is hugely profitable for the private companies that use it, the penal system as a whole does not produce wealth. It devours the social wealth that could be used to subsidize housing for the homeless, to ameliorate public education for poor and racially marginalized communities, to open free drug rehabilitation programs for people who wish to kick their habits, to create a national health care system, to expand programs to combat HIV, to eradicate domestic abuse – and, in the process, to create well-paying jobs for the unemployed.

Since 1984 more than twenty new prisons have opened in California, while only one new campus was added to the California State University system and none to the University of California system. In 1996–97, higher education received only 8.7 percent of the State's General Fund while corrections received 9.6 percent. Now that affirmative action has been declared illegal in California, it is obvious that education is increasingly reserved for certain people, while prisons are reserved for others. [...] This new segregation has dangerous implications for the entire country.

By segregating people labeled as criminals, prison simultaneously fortifies and conceals the structural racism of the U.S. economy. Claims of low unemployment rates – even in black communities – make sense only if one assumes that the vast numbers of people in prison have really disappeared and thus have no legitimate claims to jobs. The numbers of black and Latino men currently incarcerated amount to two percent of the male labor force. According to criminologist David Downes, "[t]reating incarceration as a type of hidden unemployment may raise the jobless rate for men by about one-third, to 8 percent. The effect on the black labor force is greater still, raising the [black] male unemployment rate from 11 percent to 19 percent."

Hidden Agenda

Mass incarceration is not a solution to unemployment, nor is it a solution to the vast array of social problems that are hidden away in a rapidly growing network of prisons and jails. However, the great majority of people have been tricked into believing in the efficacy of imprisonment, even though the historical record clearly demonstrates that prisons do not work. Racism has undermined our ability to create a popular critical discourse to contest the ideological trickery that posits imprisonment as key to public safety. The focus of state policy is rapidly shifting from social welfare to social control.

Black, Latino, Native American, and many Asian youth are portrayed as the purveyors of violence, traffickers of drugs, and as envious of commodities that they have no right to possess. Young black and Latina women are represented as sexually promiscuous and as indiscriminately propagating babies and poverty. Criminality and deviance are racialized. Surveillance is thus focused on communities of color, immigrants, the unemployed, the undereducated, the homeless, and in general on those who have a diminishing claim to social resources. Their claim to social resources continues to diminish in large part because law enforcement and penal measures increasingly devour these resources. The prison industrial complex has thus created a vicious cycle of punishment which only further impoverishes those whose impoverishment is supposedly "solved" by imprisonment.

Therefore, as the emphasis of government policy shifts from social welfare to crime control, racism sinks more deeply into the economic and ideological structures of U.S. society. Meanwhile, conservative crusaders against affirmative action and bilingual education proclaim the end of racism, while their opponents suggest that racism's remnants can be dispelled through dialogue and conversation. But conversations about "race relations" will hardly dismantle a prison industrial complex that thrives on and nourishes the racism hidden within the deep structures of our society.

The emergence of a U.S. prison industrial complex within a context of cascading conservatism marks a new historical moment, whose dangers are unprecedented. But so are its opportunities. Considering the impressive number of grassroots projects that continue to resist the expansion of the punishment industry, it ought to be possible to bring these efforts together to create radical and nationally visible movements that can legitimize anti-capitalist critiques of the prison industrial complex. It ought to be possible to build movements in defense of prisoners' human rights and movements that persuasively argue that what we need is not new prisons, but new health care, housing, education, drug programs, jobs, and education. To safeguard a democratic future, it is possible and necessary to weave together the many and increasing strands of resistance to the prison industrial complex into a powerful movement for social transformation.

Source: Angela Y. Davis, "Masked Racism: Reflections on the Prison Industrial Complex," *ColorLines*, Fall 1998. Reprinted with permission.

8 The Hip-Hop Summit Action Network, 2001

"We want the progressive transformation of American society"

A fierce statement of insurgency, hip-hop proactively critiqued the persistence of poverty in an age of plenty, questioned racial segregation in an era of globalization, explored the shifting role of sexuality, religion, and culture, and rearticulated a set of human rights: access to food and shelter, education and health care, employment and aspirations. Its politics responded to the paradox of the millennium: how did some African Americans attain such heights while most endured such lows? These reflected global perspectives. By the end of the twentieth century hip-hop had garnered an international contingent of performers and audiences, venerating the diversity of Africana.

Like previous black art formats – jazz, rhythm and blues, soul,
disco – hip-hop searched for black authenticity: what did it mean to be black
in the United States? What did it mean to be American? The question had
vexed Du Bois: "One ever feels his two-ness ..." At the same time,
commercialism narrowed some elements of hip-hop. Media images subsumed
politics to celebrations of violence, misogyny, drugs, and conspicuous
consumption (but made white suburban males its largest audience). In this
way, hip-hop generated a moral panic, as though the form itself created the
conditions about which it spoke. Proponents struggled among themselves,
with the mainstream media, and with their audiences to reclaim its political
intents, seeking and building alliances.

Led by black entrepreneur Russell Simmons (b. 1947) and civil rights
activist Dr. Benjamin Chavis, the Hip-Hop Summit Action Network
(HSAN) proffered one of many venues through which "Hip-Hop artists,
entertainment industry leaders, education advocates, civil rights
proponents, and youth leaders" might seek ways to make hip-hop an
"agent for social change." The document below is HSAN's initial mission
statement.

Mission Statement:

Founded in 2001, the Hip-Hop Summit Action Network (HSAN) is dedicated to harnessing the cultural relevance of Hip-Hop music to serve as a catalyst for education advocacy and other societal concerns fundamental to the empowerment of youth. HSAN is a non-profit, non-partisan national coalition of Hip-Hop artists, entertainment industry leaders, education advocates, civil rights proponents, and youth leaders united in the belief that Hip-Hop is an enormously influential agent for social change which must be responsibly and proactively utilized to fight the war on poverty and injustice.

What We Want

1. We want freedom and the social, political and economic development and empowerment of our families and communities; and for all women, men and children throughout the world.
2. We want equal justice for all without discrimination based on race, color, ethnicity, nationality, gender, sexual orientation, age, creed or class.
3. We want the total elimination of poverty.

4. We want the highest quality public education equally for all.
5. We want the total elimination of racism and racial profiling, violence, hatred and bigotry.
6. We want universal access and delivery of the highest quality health care for all.
7. We want the total elimination of police brutality and the unjust incarceration of people of color and all others.
8. We want the end and repeal of all repressive legislations, laws, regulations and ordinances such as "three strikes" laws; federal and state mandatory minimum sentencing; trying and sentencing juveniles as adults; sentencing disparities between crack and powdered cocaine use; capitol punishment; the Media Marketing Accountability Act; and hip-hop censorship fines by the FCC.
9. We want reparations to help repair the lingering vestiges; damages and suffering of African Americans as a result of the brutal enslavement of generations of Africans in America.
10. We want the progressive transformation of American society into a Nu America as a result of organizing and mobilizing the energy, activism and resources of the hip-hop community at the grassroots level throughout the United States.
11. We want greater unity, mutual dialogue, program development and a prioritizing of national issues for collective action within the hip-hop community through summits, conferences, workshops, issue task force and joint projects.
12. We want advocacy of public policies that are in the interests of hip-hop before Congress, state legislatures, municipal governments, the media and the entertainment industry.
13. We want the recertification and restoration of voting rights for the 10 million persons who have lost their right to vote as a result of a felony conviction. Although these persons have served time in prison, their voting rights have not been restored in 40 states in the U.S.
14. We want to tremendously increase public awareness and education on the pandemic of HIV/AIDS.
15. We want a clean environment and an end to communities in which poor and minorities residents are being deliberately targeted for toxic waste dumps, facilities and other environmental hazards.

Source: Hip-Hop Social Action Network Statement 2001, http://www.hsan.org (accessed April 2012; link no longer active).

Questions for Consideration

In what ways do political activists of the 1980s and 1990s draw on the legacies of earlier eras?
What possibilities and pitfalls do coalitions bring? Why is coalition building such an important topic for activists at this time?
The problems confronting American cities became increasingly associated with minority populations in the late twentieth century. What kinds of crises did urban areas face, and what did black leaders propose as solutions?
How is inequality economically profitable, according to some activists?
In what ways did the accomplishments of some black political leaders, celebrities, and businesspeople challenge efforts to create and sustain larger movements for black progress?

Bibliography

Alexander, Michelle. *The New Jim Crow: Mass Incarceration in the Age of Colorblindness*. New York: New Press, 2010.
Bell, Derrick. *And We Are Not Saved: The Elusive Quest for Racial Justice*. New York: Basic Books, 1993.
Chang, Jeff. *Can't Stop, Won't Stop: A History of the Hip-Hop Generation*. London: Ebury Press, 2005.
Coburn, David R., and Jeffrey S. Adler. *African American Mayors: Race, Politics, and the American City*. Urbana: University of Illinois Press, 2001.
Irons, Peter. *Jim Crow's Children: The Broken Promise of the Brown Decision*. New York: Viking, 2002.
Jaynes, Gerald David, and Robin M . Williams. *A Common Destiny: Blacks and American Society*. Washington, DC: National Research Society and National Academies Press, 1990.
MacLean, Nancy. *Freedom is Not Enough: The Opening of the American Workplace*. New York: Russell Sage Foundation and Cambridge, MA: Harvard University Press, 2008.
Massey, Douglas S., and Nancy Denton. *American Apartheid: Segregation and the Making of the Underclass*. Cambridge, MA: Harvard University Press, 1993.
Nesbitt, Francis Njubi. *Race for Sanctions: African Americans Against Apartheid, 1946–1994*. Bloomington: University of Indiana Press, 2004.
Patterson, Orlando. *The Ordeal of Integration: Progress and Resentment in America's "Racial" Crisis*. New York: Basic Civitas Books, 1998.
Springer, Kimberly, ed. *Still Lifting, Still Climbing: Contemporary African American Women's Activism*. New York: New York University Press, 1999.

Chapter 12   Paradox, 2005–Present

This morning I woke up
Feeling brand new I jumped up
Feeling my highs and my lows
In my soul and my goals

From "Get By" (2002) by Talib Kweli

In August of 2005 two deadly hurricanes struck the Gulf Coast of the
United States, affecting vast stretches of the region. The first, Katrina,
reached only a category 3 before landfall, but the aftermath of the storm –
when the surrounding levees failed – destroyed New Orleans. Eighty percent
of the city flooded, with a disastrous impact, and the city's black population,
its majority, suffered unduly. The loss of life was extensive. People died
in their homes, in public hospitals, on city rooftops, and in the streets; others
died by violence, including police assaults. Those who could made their way
to the Superdome and the Convention Center, as instructed, to wait for
assistance. Meanwhile media coverage revealed immediately a link between
the race of those left behind and the lethargy of federal response. The lingering damage to community infrastructure – homes, schools, and whole
neighborhoods destroyed – raised further questions about whether the race
of the residents mattered in terms of the government's and the private
sector's willingness to invest in New Orleans' recovery.

African American Voices: A Documentary Reader from Emancipation to the Present,
First Edition. Edited by Leslie Brown.

The racial issues raised by the Katrina disaster were still on the minds of Americans in 2008 when Illinois Senator Barack Obama ran for president. "[T]he son of a black man from Kenya and a white woman from Kansas," Obama possessed truncated roots in black America's history of slavery and Jim Crow. Still, his experience as a Chicago organizer, as a law professor, and a law maker suggested that his presidency potentially merged integrationist, nationalist, and internationalist crosscurrents for social justice that ran through African American history with the progressive agenda of white liberals in education, government, and business. Pundits wondered aloud if his victory signaled that finally the United States had reached a post-racial era. Did Obama's victory prove that racism had been left behind, Du Bois' problem of the twentieth century but not ours in the twenty-first?

Certainly, Obama's candidacy set a precedent: an African American not only seized the Democratic nomination, but also won election. As a black man, however, he was a lightning rod for racial tensions on the political landscape. His campaign's racial crises were many. A video surfaced of Rev. Jeremiah Wright – a black Marine veteran, civil rights activist, and minister of Obama's church – preaching a rhetoric that out of context seemed anti-American. "Birthers" claimed he was not born in the United States (he was born in Hawaii), while conservative contingents charged that he was Muslim (he embraced Christianity). At rallies supporters of the Tea Party displayed his images in racist caricature. Indeed, the hostility heaped upon his candidacy evidenced increasing rather than decreasing animosities.

Against a rising tide of near-hysteria, youths, college students, liberals, progressives, intellectuals, Leftists, senior citizens, blacks, Latinos, and average middle Americans synergized into an army of optimists who believed in the Obama campaign theme, "Yes, We Can." Could "hope," the spirit he preached, bring about the "change" Barack Obama promised?

Instead of a post-racial America, Barack Obama engendered enormous backlash. In 2008 it became clear that economic policies of the George W. Bush administration – massive spending on wars in the Middle East coupled with extensive tax cuts for the wealthy – had left behind a nation on the verge of economic collapse, without the resources to mount a progressive agenda on health care, education, job creation, infrastructure, or technology that the new president had pledged to secure. A Republican-led Congress, openly committed to a failed Obama presidency, stalled on economic fixes and deployed regressive social policies. Black unemployment soared beyond the national average, while community resources dissipated. At the same time, racial violence increased, educational options contracted, prison populations grew, and segregation expanded. And in time for the 2012 presidential election, Republican-led states unleashed a flurry of voter restrictions that defied the 1965 Voting Rights Act to intentionally limit suffrage for people of color, senior citizens, and young people. The Supreme Court gutted one of the most essential parts of the Act in 2012.

In the early 2010s, as the nation acknowledged the 150th anniversary of the Civil War and the 50th of the modern civil rights movement, we are left to ponder the nation's history of racism and the meaning of freedom and justice once more.

1 New Orleans Mayor Ray Nagin Addresses His City on Martin Luther King Day, 2006

"Chocolate City"

Before the levees broke in the wake of Katrina the New Orleans-born Mayor, Clarence Raymond Nagin, Jr. (b. 1956), was a popular politician who had gathered a crossover constituency. In the aftermath of Katrina he and the ill-resourced black population of New Orleans were isolated, abandoned, and left to bear the brunt of not only the criticism, but also the city's recovery. Nagin began calling New Orleans "Chocolate City." In its original context, the 1970s black arts movement, the term was an optimistic refrain about black-controlled urban centers that remained after white flight. Ironically, following the Katrina disaster, it was the city's black residents who had been scattered across the United States. If New Orleans and New Orleanians were going to survive, it would be by dint of their will and efforts. In some ways, then, Chocolate City was a call to home. But it was a home of frustration where neglect and corruption had bred disillusionment.

Nagin delivered this speech at City Hall on Martin Luther King, Jr., Day in January 2006, five months after the storm. In it he makes the "Chocolate City" reference again. Reflecting on what King might have thought of the situation, the Mayor appealed to his black constituency to address their problems, to do what blacks had done historically: abandoned or ignored by a schema that refused to protect them, to struggle by themselves for themselves.

I greet you all in the spirit of peace this morning. I greet you all in the spirit of love this morning, and more importantly, I greet you all in the spirit of unity. Because if we're unified, there's nothing we cannot do.

Now, I'm supposed to give some remarks this morning and talk about the great Dr. Martin Luther King Jr. You know when I woke up early this morning, and I was reflecting upon what I could say that could be meaningful for this grand occasion. And then I decided to talk directly to Dr. King.

Now you might think that's one Katrina post-stress disorder. But I was talking to him and I just wanted to know what would he think if he looked down today at this celebration. What would he think about Katrina? What would he think about all the people who were stuck in the Superdome and Convention Center and we couldn't get the state and the federal government to come do something about it? And he said, "I wouldn't like that."

And then I went on to ask him, I said, "Mr. King, when they were marching across the Mississippi River bridge, some of the folks that were stuck in the Convention Center, that were tired of waiting for food and tired of waiting on buses to come rescue them, what would he say as they marched across that bridge? And they were met at the parish line with attack dogs and machine guns firing shots over their heads?" He said, "I wouldn't like that either."

Then I asked him to analyze the state of black America and black New Orleans today and to give me a critique of black leadership today. And I asked him what does he think about black leaders always or most of the time tearing each other down publicly for the delight of many? And he said, "I really don't like that either."

And then finally, I said, "Dr. King, everybody in New Orleans is dispersed over 44 different states. We're debating whether we should open this or close that. We're debating whether property rights should trump everything or not. We're debating how should we rebuild one of the greatest cultural cities the world has ever seen. And yet still yesterday we have a second-line [a New Orleans tradition of following and enjoying an organized celebration] and everybody comes together from around this and that and they have a good time for the most part, and then knuckleheads pull out some guns and start firing into the crowd and they injure three people." He said, "I definitely wouldn't like that."

And then I asked him, I said, "What is it going to take for us to move and live your dream and make it a reality?" He said, "I don't think we need to pay attention anymore as much about the other folk and racists on the other side." He said the thing we need to focus on as a community, black folks I'm talking to, is ourselves.

What are we doing? Why is black-on-black crime such an issue? Why do our young men hate each other so much that they look their brother in the face and they will take a gun and kill him in cold blood? He said we as a people need to fix ourselves first. He said the lack of love is killing us. And it's time, ladies and gentlemen.

Dr. King, if he was here today, he would be talking to us about this problem, about the problem we have among ourselves. And as we think about rebuilding New Orleans, surely God is mad at America, he's sending hurricane after hurricane after hurricane and it's destroying and putting stress on this country. Surely he's not approving of us being in Iraq under false pretense. But surely he's upset at black America, also. We're not taking care of ourselves. We're not taking care of our women. And we're not taking care of our children when you have a community where 70 percent of its children are being born to one parent.

We ask black people: it's time. It's time for us to come together. It's time for us to rebuild a New Orleans, the one that should be a chocolate New Orleans. And I don't care what people are saying Uptown or wherever they are. This city will be chocolate at the end of the day.

This city will be a majority African-American city. It's the way God wants it to be. You can't have New Orleans no other way; it wouldn't be New Orleans. So before I get into too much more trouble, I'm just going to tell you in my closing conversation with Dr. King, he said, "I never worried about the bad people who were doing all the violence during civil rights time." He said, "I worried about the good folks that didn't say anything or didn't do anything when they knew what they had to do."

It's time for all of us good folk to stand up and say "We're tired of the violence. We're tired of black folks killing each other. And when we come together for a second-line, we're not going to tolerate any violence." Martin Luther King would've wanted it that way, and we should.

Source: Mayor Ray Nagin, "Martin Luther King Day Address," 2006.

2 Barack Obama Believes in "A More Perfect Union," 2008

"to continue the long march of those who came before us, a march for a more just, more equal, more free, more caring, and more prosperous America"

When the memorial to Martin Luther King, Jr., was dedicated on the National Mall in Washington, DC, in 2011, President Barack Obama (b. 1961) placed two speeches in the vault, one accepting his party's nomination and the other his inaugural address. They marked officially the ascendancy of the first African American to the Presidency of the United States. But other more moving speeches had paved his way to popularity. His address to

the 2004 Democratic National Convention, for instance, made him a
national political star. When he won the 2008 Democratic primaries in New
Hampshire and Iowa, his speeches used historical references to forge a new
campaign theme: "Yes, We Can." Rewritten by hip-hop artist will.i.am and
performed by a coterie of pop culture icons, "Yes, We Can" became the most
popular political video on YouTube.

It is at moments of crisis, however, that candidates define – or redefine –
themselves. In the speech excerpted below, Obama used the racial crisis
surrounding his candidacy to link his personal history to that of the nation.

"We the people, in order to form a more perfect union." Two hundred and twenty one years ago, in a hall that still stands across the street, a group of men gathered and, with these simple words, launched America's improbable experiment in democracy. Farmers and scholars, statesmen and patriots who had traveled across the ocean to escape tyranny and persecution finally made real their Declaration of Independence at a Philadelphia convention that lasted through the spring of 1787.

The document they produced was eventually signed, but ultimately unfinished. It was stained by this nation's original sin of slavery, a question that divided the colonies and brought the convention to a stalemate until the founders chose to allow the slave trade to continue for at least 20 more years, and to leave any final resolution to future generations. Of course, the answer to the slavery question was already embedded within our Constitution – a Constitution that had at its very core the ideal of equal citizenship under the law; a Constitution that promised its people liberty and justice, and a union that could be and should be perfected over time.

And yet words on a parchment would not be enough to deliver slaves from bondage, or provide men and women of every color and creed their full rights and obligations as citizens of the United States. What would be needed were Americans in successive generations who were willing to do their part – through protests and struggles, on the streets and in the courts, through a civil war and civil disobedience, and always at great risk – to narrow that gap between the promise of our ideals and the reality of their time.

This was one of the tasks we set forth at the beginning of this presidential campaign: to continue the long march of those who came before us, a march for a more just, more equal, more free, more caring, and more prosperous America. I chose to run for President at this moment in history because I believe deeply that we cannot solve the challenges of our time unless we solve them together, unless we perfect our union by understanding that we may have different stories, but we hold common hopes; that we may not look the same and may not have come from the same place, but we all want to move in the same direction: towards a better future for our children and our grandchildren. And this belief comes from my unyielding faith in the decency and generosity of the American people. But it also comes from my own story.

I'm the son of a black man from Kenya and a white woman from Kansas. I was raised with the help of a white grandfather who survived a Depression to serve in Patton's army during World War II, and a white grandmother who worked on a bomber assembly line at Fort Leavenworth while he was overseas. I've gone to some of the best schools in America and I've lived in one of the world's poorest nations. I am married to a black American who carries within her the blood of slaves and slave owners, an inheritance we pass on to our two precious daughters. I have brothers, sisters, nieces, nephews, uncles, and cousins of every race and every hue scattered across three continents. And for as long as I live, I will never forget that in no other country on earth is my story even possible. It's a story that hasn't made me the most conventional of candidates. But it is a story that has seared into my genetic makeup the idea that this nation is more than the sum of its parts – that out of many, we are truly one.

Now throughout the first year of this campaign, against all predictions to the contrary, we saw how hungry the American people were for this message of unity. Despite the temptation to view my candidacy through a purely racial lens, we won commanding victories in states with some of the whitest populations in the country. In South Carolina, where the Confederate flag still flies, we built a powerful coalition of African Americans and white Americans. This is not to say that race has not been an issue in this campaign. At various stages in the campaign, some commentators have deemed me either "too black" or "not black enough." We saw racial tensions bubble to the surface during the week before the South Carolina primary. The press has scoured every single exit poll for the latest evidence of racial polarization, not just in terms of white and black, but black and brown as well.

And yet, it's only been in the last couple of weeks that the discussion of race in this campaign has taken a particularly divisive turn. On one end of the spectrum, we've heard the implication that my candidacy is somehow an exercise in affirmative action; that it's based solely on the desire of wild and wide-eyed liberals to purchase racial reconciliation on the cheap. On the other end, we've heard my former pastor, Jeremiah Wright, use incendiary language to express views that have the potential not only to widen the racial divide, but views that denigrate both the greatness and the goodness of our nation and that rightly offend white and black alike.

Now I've already condemned, in unequivocal terms, the statements of Reverend Wright that have caused such controversy, and in some cases, pain. For some, nagging questions remain: Did I know him to be an occasionally fierce critic of American domestic and foreign policy? Of course. Did I ever hear him make remarks that could be considered controversial while I sat in the church? Yes. Did I strongly disagree with many of his political views? Absolutely, just as I'm sure many of you have heard remarks from your pastors, priests, or rabbis with which you strongly disagree.

But the remarks that have caused this recent firestorm weren't simply controversial. They weren't simply a religious leader's efforts to speak out against perceived injustice. Instead, they expressed a profoundly distorted view of this country, a view that sees white racism as endemic and that elevates what is wrong with America above all that we know is right with America; a view that sees the conflicts in the Middle East as rooted primarily in the actions of stalwart allies like Israel instead of emanating from the perverse and hateful ideologies of radical Islam.

As such, Reverend Wright's comments were not only wrong but divisive, divisive at a time when we need unity; racially charged at a time when we need to come together to solve a set of monumental problems: two wars, a terrorist threat, a falling economy, a chronic health care crisis, and potentially devastating climate change – problems that are neither black or white or Latino or Asian, but rather problems that confront us all.

Given my background, my politics, and my professed values and ideals, there will no doubt be those for whom my statements of condemnation are not enough. Why associate myself with Reverend Wright in the first place, they may ask? Why not join another church? And I confess that if all that I knew of Reverend Wright were the snippets of those sermons that have run in an endless loop on the television sets and YouTube, if Trinity United Church of Christ conformed to the caricatures being peddled by some commentators, there is no doubt that I would react in much the same way.

But the truth is, that isn't all that I know of the man. The man I met more than twenty years ago is a man who helped introduce me to my Christian faith, a man who spoke to me about our obligations to love one another, to care for the sick and lift up the poor. He is a man who served his country as a United States Marine, and who has studied and lectured at some of the finest universities and seminaries in the country, and who over 30 years has led a church that serves the community by doing God's work here on Earth – by housing the homeless, ministering to the needy, providing day care services and scholarships and prison ministries, and reaching out to those suffering from HIV/AIDS.

In my first book, *Dreams From My Father*, I described the experience of my first service at Trinity, and it goes as follows:

> People began to shout, to rise from their seats and clap and cry out, a forceful wind carrying the reverend's voice up to the rafters.
>
> And in that single note – hope – I heard something else; at the foot of that cross, inside the thousands of churches across the city, I imagined the stories of ordinary black people merging with the stories of David and Goliath, Moses and Pharaoh, the Christians in the lion's den, Ezekiel's field of dry bones.
>
> Those stories of survival and freedom and hope became our stories, my story. The blood that spilled was our blood; the tears our tears; until this black church, on this bright day, seemed once more a vessel carrying the story of a people into future generations and into a larger world. Our trials and triumphs became at once unique and universal, black and more than black. In chronicling our journey, the stories and songs gave us a meaning to reclaim memories that we didn't need to feel shame about – memories that all people might study and cherish and with which we could start to rebuild.

That has been my experience at Trinity. Like other predominantly black churches across the country, Trinity embodies the black community in its entirety – the doctor and the welfare mom, the model student and the former gang-banger. Like other black churches, Trinity's services are full of raucous laughter and sometimes bawdy humor. They are full of dancing and clapping and screaming and shouting that may seem jarring to the untrained ear. The church contains in full the kindness and cruelty, the fierce intelligence and the shocking ignorance, the struggles and successes, the love and, yes, the bitterness and biases that make up the black experience in America.

And this helps explain, perhaps, my relationship with Reverend Wright. As imperfect as he may be, he has been like family to me. He strengthens my faith, officiated my wedding, and baptized my children. Not once in my conversations with him have I heard him talk about any ethnic group in derogatory terms or treat whites with whom he interacted with anything but courtesy and respect. He contains within him the contradictions – the good and the bad – of the community that he has served diligently for so many years.

I can no more disown him than I can disown the black community. I can no more disown him than I can disown my white grandmother, a woman who helped raise me, a woman who sacrificed again and again for me, a woman who loves me as much as she loves anything in this world, but a woman who once confessed her fear of black men who passed her by on the street, and who on more than one occasion has uttered racial or ethnic stereotypes that made me cringe.

These people are part of me. And they are part of America, this country that I love.

Now, some will see this as an attempt to justify or excuse comments that are simply inexcusable. I can assure you it is not. And I suppose the politically safe thing to do would be to move on from this episode and just hope that it fades into the woodwork. We can dismiss Reverend Wright as a crank or a demagogue …

But race is an issue that I believe this nation cannot afford to ignore right now. We would be making the same mistake that Reverend Wright made in his offending sermons about America: to simplify and stereotype and amplify the negative to the point that it distorts reality. The fact is that the comments that have been made and the issues that have surfaced over the last few weeks reflect the complexities of race in this country that we've never really worked through, a part of our union that we have not yet made perfect. And if we walk away now, if we simply retreat into our respective corners, we will never be able to come together and solve challenges like health care or education or the need to find good jobs for every American.

Understanding – Understanding this reality requires a reminder of how we arrived at this point. As William Faulkner once wrote, "The past isn't dead and buried. In fact, it isn't even past." We do not need to recite here the history of racial injustice in this country. But we do need to remind ourselves that so many of the disparities that exist between the African-American community and the larger American community today can be traced directly to inequalities passed on from an earlier generation that suffered under the brutal legacy of slavery and Jim Crow. Segregated schools were, and are, inferior schools. We still haven't fixed them, 50 years after *Brown versus Board of Education*. And the inferior education they provided, then and now, helps explain the pervasive achievement gap between today's black and white students.

Legalized discrimination, where blacks were prevented, often through violence, from owning property, or loans were not granted to African-American business owners, or black homeowners could not access FHA mortgages, or blacks were excluded from unions, or the police force, or the fire department meant that black families could not amass any meaningful wealth to bequeath to future generations. That history helps explain the wealth and income gap between blacks and whites and the concentrated pockets of poverty that persist in so many of today's urban and rural communities. A lack of economic opportunity among black men and the shame and frustration that came from not being able to provide for one's family contributed to the erosion of black families, a problem that welfare policies for many years may have worsened. And the lack of basic services in so many urban black neighborhoods – parks for kids to play in, police walking the beat, regular garbage pick-up, building code enforcement – all helped create a cycle of violence, blight, and neglect that continues to haunt us.

This is the reality in which Reverend Wright and other African-Americans of his generation grew up. They came of age in the late '50s and early '60s, a time when segregation was still the law of the land and opportunity was systematically constricted. What's remarkable is not how many failed in the face of discrimination, but how many men and women overcame the odds, how many were able to make a way out of no way for those like me who would come after them.

But for all those who scratched and clawed their way to get a piece of the American Dream, there were many who didn't make it – those who were ultimately defeated, in one way or another, by discrimination. That legacy of defeat was passed on to future generations – those young men and increasingly young women who we see standing on street corners or languishing in our prisons, without hope or prospects for the future. Even for those blacks who did make it, questions of race, and racism, continue to define their world view in fundamental ways. For the men and women of Reverend Wright's generation, the memories of humiliation and doubt and fear have not gone away, nor has the anger and the bitterness of those years.

That anger may not get expressed in public, in front of white co-workers or white friends, but it does find voice in the barbershop or the beauty shop or around the kitchen table. At times, that anger is exploited by politicians to gin up votes along racial lines or to make up for a politician's own failings. And occasionally it finds voice in the church on Sunday morning, in the pulpit and in the pews. The fact that so many people are surprised to hear that anger in some of Reverend Wright's sermons simply reminds us of that old truism that the most segregated hour of American life occurs on Sunday morning.

That – That anger is not always productive. Indeed, all too often it distracts attention from solving real problems. It keeps us from squarely facing our own complicity within the African-American community in our own condition. It prevents the African-American community from forging the alliances it needs to bring about real change. But the anger is real; it is powerful, and to simply wish it away, to condemn it without understanding its roots only serves to widen the chasm of misunderstanding that exists between the races.

In fact, a similar anger exists within segments of the white community. Most working and middle-class white Americans don't feel that they've been particularly privileged by their race. Their experience is the immigrant experience. As far as they're concerned, no one handed them anything; they built it from scratch. They've worked hard all their lives, many times only to see their jobs shipped overseas or their pensions dumped after a lifetime of labor. They are anxious about their futures, and they feel their dreams slipping away. And in an era of stagnant wages and global competition, opportunity comes to be seen as a zero sum game, in which your dreams come at my expense. So when they are told to bus their children to a school across town, when they hear that an African American is getting an advantage in landing a good job or a spot in a good college because of an injustice that they themselves never committed, when they're told that their fears about crime in urban neighborhoods are somehow prejudice, resentment builds over time.

Like the anger within the black community, these resentments aren't always expressed in polite company. But they have helped shape the political landscape for at least a generation. Anger over welfare and affirmative action helped forge the Reagan Coalition. Politicians routinely exploited fears of crime for their own electoral ends. Talk show hosts and conservative commentators built entire careers unmasking bogus claims of racism while dismissing legitimate discussions of racial injustice and inequality as mere political correctness or reverse racism. And just as black anger often proved counterproductive, so have these white resentments distracted attention from the real culprits of the middle class squeeze: a corporate culture rife with inside dealing, questionable accounting practices, and short-term greed; a Washington dominated by lobbyists and special interests; economic policies that favor the few over the many. And yet, to wish away the resentments of white Americans, to label them as misguided or even racist without recognizing they are grounded in legitimate concerns, this, too, widens the racial divide and blocks the path to understanding.

This is where we are right now.

It's a racial stalemate we've been stuck in for years. And contrary to the claims of some of my critics, black and white, I have never been so naive as to believe that we can get beyond our racial divisions in a single election cycle or with a single candidate, particularly – particularly a candidacy as imperfect as my own. But I have asserted a firm conviction, a conviction rooted in my faith in God and my faith in the American people, that, working together, we can move beyond some of our old racial wounds and that, in fact, we have no choice – we have no choice if we are to continue on the path of a more perfect union.

For the African-American community, that path means embracing the burdens of our past without becoming victims of our past. It means continuing to insist on a full measure of justice in every aspect of American life. But it also means binding our particular grievances, for better health care and better schools and better jobs, to the larger aspirations of all Americans – the white woman struggling to break the glass ceiling, the white man who's been laid off, the immigrant trying to feed his family. And it means also taking full responsibility for our own lives – by demanding more from our fathers, and spending more time with our children, and reading to them, and teaching them that while they may face challenges and discrimination in their own lives, they must never succumb to despair or cynicism. They must always believe – They must always believe that they can write their own destiny.

Ironically, this quintessentially American – and, yes, conservative – notion of self-help found frequent expression in Reverend Wright's sermons. But what my former pastor too often failed to understand is that embarking on a program of self-help also requires a belief that society can change. The profound mistake of Reverend Wright's sermons is not that he spoke about racism in our society. It's that he spoke as if our society was static, as if no progress had been made, as if this country – a country that has made it possible for one of his own members to run for the highest office in the land and build a coalition of white and black, Latino, Asian, rich, poor, young and old – is still irrevocably bound to a tragic past. What we know, what we have seen, is that America can change. That is true genius of this nation. What we have already achieved gives us hope – the audacity to hope – for what we can and must achieve tomorrow.

Now, in the white community, the path to a more perfect union means acknowledging that what ails the African-American community does not just exist in the minds of black people; that the legacy of discrimination – and current incidents of discrimination, while less overt than in the past – that these things are real and must be addressed. Not just with words, but with deeds – by investing in our schools and our communities; by enforcing our civil rights laws and ensuring fairness in our criminal justice system; by providing this generation with ladders of opportunity that were unavailable for previous generations. It requires all Americans to realize that your dreams do not have to come at the expense of my dreams, that investing in the health, welfare, and education of black and brown and white children will ultimately help all of America prosper.

In the end, then, what is called for is nothing more and nothing less than what all the world's great religions demand: that we do unto others as we would have them do unto us. Let us be our brother's keeper, Scripture tells us. Let us be our sister's keeper. Let us find that common stake we all have in one another, and let our politics reflect that spirit as well.

For we have a choice in this country. We can accept a politics that breeds division and conflict and cynicism. We can tackle race only as spectacle, as we did in the O. J. trial; or in the wake of tragedy, as we did in the aftermath of Katrina; or as fodder for the nightly news. We can play Reverend Wright's sermons on every channel every day and talk about them from now until the election, and make the only question in this campaign whether or not the American people think that I somehow believe or sympathize with his most offensive words. We can pounce on some gaffe by a Hillary supporter as evidence that she's playing the race card; or we can speculate on whether white men will all flock to John McCain in the general election regardless of his policies. We can do that. But if we do, I can tell you that in the next election, we'll be talking about some other distraction, and then another one, and then another one. And nothing will change.

That is one option.

Or, at this moment, in this election, we can come together and say, "Not this time." This time we want to talk about the crumbling schools that are stealing the future of black children and white children and Asian children and Hispanic children and Native-American children. This time we want to reject the cynicism that tells us that these kids can't learn; that those kids who don't look like us are somebody else's problem. The children of America are not "those kids," – they are our kids, and we will not let them fall behind in a 21st-century economy. Not this time. This time we want to talk about how the lines in the emergency room are filled with whites and blacks and Hispanics who do not have health care, who don't have the power on their own to overcome the special interests in Washington, but who can take them on if we do it together.

This time we want to talk about the shuttered mills that once provided a decent life for men and women of every race, and the homes for sale that once belonged to Americans from every religion, every region, every walk of life. This time we want to talk about the fact that the real problem is not that someone who doesn't look like you might take your job; it's that the corporation you work for will ship it overseas for nothing more than a profit. This time – This time we want to talk about the men and women of every color and creed who serve together, and fight together, and bleed together under the same proud flag. We want to talk about how to bring them home from a war that should've never been authorized and should've never been waged. And we want to talk about how we'll show our patriotism by caring for them, and their families, and giving them the benefits that they have earned.

I would not be running for President if I didn't believe with all my heart that this is what the vast majority of Americans want for this country. This union may never be perfect, but generation after generation has shown that it can always be perfected. And today, whenever I find myself feeling doubtful or cynical about this possibility, what gives me the most hope is the next generation – the young people whose attitudes and beliefs and openness to change have already made history in this election.

...

Source: Barack Obama, "A More Perfect Union," March 18, 2008.

3 Julian Bond Reflects on Race and History in America, 2011

"Those who say that 'race is history' have it exactly backward – history is race"

The grandson of a slave, Julian Bond (b. 1940) has spent a life fighting for social justice. Among the participants at the 1960 conference called by Ella Baker, where SNCC was founded, he became its director of communications. Three times he won election to the Georgia House, which refused to seat him, allegedly because of his opposition to the war in Southeast Asia. He co-chaired the Georgia Loyal National Delegation to the Democratic National Convention, the state's freedom Democrats who successfully unseated regular delegates in 1968. That year Bond was nominated for the vice presidency of the United States, but had to withdraw his name. He was too young to serve. Chairperson emeritus of the NAACP (he served from 1998 to 2010), he has been a proponent of broad civil rights, not only for African Americans but also for immigrants, women, Latino-, Asian-, and Arab-Americans, and gays. In the speech excerpted below, delivered in 2011 at the National Underground Railroad Museum, Bond acknowledges changes that have occurred, but dispels the notion of a post-racial America.

For most of my adult life, I have been engaged in what once was called "race work" – fighting to make justice and fairness a reality for everyone. The racial picture in America has improved remarkably in my lifetime, so much so that a Black man has been elected President of the United States, an unthinkable development just a few years ago. But paradoxically, Barack Obama's victory in 2008 has convinced many that all racial barriers and restrictions have been vanquished and we have entered racial nirvana across the land. I am here to dispel that notion and, in the process, discuss the challenges that we face in the area of civil rights.

Those who say that "race is history" have it exactly backward – history is race. America is race – from its symbolism to its substance, from its founding by slaveholders to its rending by the Civil War, from Johnnie Reb to Jim Crow, from the Ku Klux Klan to Katrina and Jena.

...

We look back on the years between Montgomery in 1955 and the passage of the Voting Rights Act in 1965 with some pride. Those were the days when politicians from both parties supported the struggle for civil rights. Now they struggle to be civil. Those were the days when banks loaned money to people, and not like these days when the people lend money to banks. Those were the days when we were powered by our values, and not valued for our power. Those were the days when good music was popular and popular music was good. Those were the days when the President picked the Supreme Court and not the other way around. Those were the days when we had a war on poverty, not a war on the poor. Those were the days when the news media really was "fair and balanced" and not just mouthpieces for the misinformed.

But those were not "the good old days."

In those days, the law, the courts, the schools, and almost every institution ... favored Whites. When the Supreme Court announced in May, 1955, in the second Brown decision, that the White South could make haste slowly in dismantling segregated schools, I was a year older than Emmett Till. His death three months after the second Brown decision was more immediate to me than the Court's pronouncements had been. We were nearly the same age when he was murdered, in Money, Mississippi, for whistling at a White woman. Emmett Till's death terrified me.

But in the fall of 1957, a group of Black teenagers encouraged me to put that fear aside. These young people – the nine young women and men who integrated Little Rock's Central High School – set a high standard of grace and courage under fire as they dared the mobs who surrounded their school. Here, I thought, is what I hope I can be, if ever the chance comes my way. The chance to test and prove myself did come my way in 1960, as it came to thousands of other Black high school and college students across the South, in a mobilization of young Black people not duplicated before or since. First through the sit-ins, then in Freedom Rides, and then in voter registration and political organizing drives in the rural South, we joined an old movement against White supremacy that had deep, strong roots.

King was the most famous and best known of the modern movement's personalities, but it was a people's movement. It saw wrong and acted against it; it saw evil and brought it down. Many stand now in reflection of that earlier movement's successes, including the election of Barack

Obama, confused about what the next steps should be. The task ahead is enormous – equal to if not greater than the job already done.

Today we are four decades past the second Reconstruction, the modern movement for civil rights that eliminated legal segregation in the United States, and 14 decades past the first Reconstruction, the single period in American history in which the national government used armed might to enforce the civil rights of Black Americans.

One hundred and fifteen years ago, Black Americans faced prospects eerily similar to those we face today. Then it was 30 years after Civil War and the first Reconstruction, the 19th Century was winding down, and White America was growing weary of worrying about the welfare of the newly freed slaves, tired of fighting to secure their right to vote and to attend a public school. Then, as now, a race-weary nation decided these problems could be best solved if left to the individual states. Then, as now, racist demagogues walked the land. Then, as now, minorities and immigrants became scapegoats for real and imagined economic distress. Then a reign of state sanctioned and private terror, including ritual human sacrifice, swept across the South to reinforce White supremacy. [T]he heavy hand of racial segregation ... separated Blacks from education, from opportunity, but not from hope.

As we recall the struggles of the recent past, many of us are confused about what the movement's aims and goals were, what it accomplished and where it failed, and what our responsibilities are to complete its unfinished business today. Looking back [historically] at that movement from today, we now see a very different view of the events and personalities of the period.

Instead of the towering figures of Kings and Kennedys standing alone, we now also see an army of anonymous women and men. Instead of famous orations made to multitudes, we now also see the planning and work that preceded the triumphant speech. Instead of a series of well-publicized marches and protests, we now also see long organizing campaigns and brave and lonely soldiers often working in near solitude. Instead of prayerful petitions for government's deliverance, we now see aggressive demands and the ethic of self-reliance and self-help.

We now realize our view of the movement's goals was narrow too. Seeking more than the removal of racial segregation, the movement did not want to be integrated into a burning house; rather, it wanted to build a better house for everyone. It marched on Washington for freedom and jobs, not for abstract freedom alone. And instead of a sudden and unanticipated upsurge in Black activism in Montgomery in 1955, we now see a long and unceasing history of aggressive challenges to White supremacy that began as long ago as slavery time. And instead of a movement that ended in 1968 with the death of Martin Luther King, we now see continued movement stretching from the ancient past until this moment, with different forms and personalities, in many places and locales, with differing methods and techniques, whose central goal has always been the elimination of strictures based on race.

The NAACP's founding in 1909 gave the movement an organized base. It soon developed an aggressive strategy of litigation aimed at striking down racial restrictions enshrined in law, triumphing in 1954 with *Brown v. Board of Education*, ending legal segregation in public schools. That decision effectively ended segregation's legality; it also gave a nonviolent army license to challenge segregation's morality as well. From *Brown* in 1954 forward, the movement expanded its targets, tactics and techniques. Organizations and leadership expanded as well.

...

That movement then was a second Reconstruction, whose ripples were felt far beyond the southern states and whose victories benefited more than Blacks. Like the first Reconstruction, it saw gains for Blacks extended to greater protections for others. Like the first Reconstruction, it gave new life to other movements of disadvantaged Americans. And like the first Reconstruction, the second ended when the national purpose wavered and reaction swept the land. But before it slowed, it changed our country forever. A voteless people voted with their bodies and their feet and paved the way for other social protest. The anti-war movement of the 1960s drew its earliest soldiers from the southern freedom army. The reborn movement for women's rights took many of its cues and much of its momentum from the southern movement for civil rights.

The movement's origins were in a bitter struggle for elemental civil rights, but it largely became, in the post-segregation era, a movement for political and economic power. And today Black women and men hold office and wield power in numbers we only dreamed of before. Despite impressive increases in the numbers of Black people holding public office; despite our ability to sit and eat and ride and vote and attend school and live in places; including the White House, that used to bar Black faces; in some important ways non-white Americans face problems more difficult to attack today than in the years that went before. Black and Hispanic schoolchildren today are more separate from white children than when Martin Luther King was killed, the result of a systematic neglect of civil rights policy ... for decades, including fair housing laws. School re-segregation also means that the average Black and Latino student now is in a school where 60 percent of their classmates are poor.

I believe in an integrated America – integrated jobs, homes, and schools. I believe in it enough to have spent most of my life in its elusive pursuit. I think it is a legal, moral and political imperative for America – a matter of elemental justice, simple right waged against historical wrong.

We are such a young nation so recently removed from slavery that only my father's generation stands between Julian Bond and human bondage. Like many others, I am the grandson of a slave. My grandfather, James Bond, was born in 1863, in Kentucky; freedom didn't come for him until the 13th Amendment was ratified in 1865. He and his mother were property, like a horse or a chair. As a young girl, she had been given away as a wedding present to a new bride. And when that bride became pregnant, her husband – that's my great-grandmother's owner and master – exercised his right to take his wife's slave as his mistress. That union produced two children, one of them my grandfather ...

My grandfather belonged to a transcendent generation of Black Americans, a generation born into slavery, freed by the Civil War, determined to make their way as free women and men. Martin Luther King belonged to another transcendent generation of Black Americans, a generation born into segregation, freed from racism's constraints by their own efforts, determined to make their way in freedom ...

While we struggle toward greater efforts and grander victories, we are still being tested by hardships and adversity. The rich have been sitting at the banquet table, and the rest of us have been on the menu. So the gap has grown between the haves, the have-mores and the have-nots. Between 1996 and 2006, CEO pay rose by 45 percent, while worker[s'] pay rose a mere 7 percent. The top 300,000 Americans collectively now have almost as much income as the bottom 150 million Americans. The top 20 percent of earners take over half the national income, while the bottom 20 percent gets just 3.4 percent.

Black Americans, of course, are more likely to be poor than rich, and they are worse off than their White counterparts. Almost every social indicator, from birth to death, reflects Black–White disparities. Infant mortality rates are 146 percent higher for Blacks; chances of imprisonment are 447 percent higher; rate of death from homicide 521 percent higher; lack of health insurance 42 percent more likely; the proportion with a college degree 60 percent lower. And the average White American will live five and a half years longer than the average Black American. The fragility of middle class life for Black Americans is illustrated by their downward mobility. Nearly half of Blacks born into the middle class 40 years ago have descended into poverty or near poverty as adults compared to only 16 percent of Whites. White unemployment is high enough at 9 percent, but Black unemployment is even higher at 15.7 percent.

Homeownership rates for Blacks, already low, have been sinking under the weight of the sub-prime mortgage crisis, which stands to likely be the largest loss of African-American wealth that we have ever seen, wiping out a generation of home wealth building. Blacks were three times more likely to have sub-prime loans than Whites, with such loans accounting for 55 percent of loans to Blacks and only 17 percent of loans to Whites. This has not happened by accident. There is evidence that [minority] neighborhoods were actually targeted – that lenders have gone after people whom they think are less sophisticated borrowers. ...

The capture of the Republican Party by the Tea Party has disastrous consequences for all who care about progressive politics and the plight of the poor. Today, the marginal has become mainstream and the whackos have won election – to the Senate, the House, and the Statehouse. The right rejects rationality reflexively. They are mean to Main Street and protective of profiteers – who are also their puppeteers. The Republicans came to office saying they were concerned about jobs, but the only jobs they seem to care for are their own. In the three months they have controlled the House, they've not passed a single job creation bill; instead, they have curtailed abortion rights, they've defunded Planned Parenthood, they've defunded NPR, and they've investigated American Muslims. Displaying real political courage, they've declared English America's official language, and they've reaffirmed "In God We Trust" as America's motto.

...

Just as President Obama's victory did not herald a post-civil rights America or mean that race had been vanquished, it could not and did not end structural inequality or racist attitudes. Indeed, there is evidence that it fomented them. President Obama is to the Tea Party as the moon is to werewolves. The real issue for many opponents today is that we now have a President who they believe is guilty of governing while Black.

The Tea Baggers are 99 percent White. Fifty two percent of them – twice as many as the rest of the population – believe that too much attention has been paid to Black people. Sixty-two percent of them – more than twice the percentage of White Democrats – think discrimination against Whites is as big a problem as discrimination against minorities. They see the nation's demographics turning them into a minority, and they don't like it. They say they want their country back, and we ask, what was that country like? In their country, I couldn't eat at a lunch counter or cast a vote. I couldn't attend the University of Virginia, let alone teach there. Those weren't the good old days for me. If Obama represents the end of the America they knew, I say, "Good!"

Tea Partiers rail against deficits that were largely created by Bush and Reagan tax cuts for the rich. They are furious about taxes – when, with the exception of a brief period two decades ago, top rates are lower than at any time since World War II. And they purport to see constitutional violations about which they had no concern a few years ago. You tell me what has changed that has made them so angry.

The Civil War that freed my grandfather was fought over whether Blacks and Whites shared a common humanity. Less than 10 years after it ended, the nation chose sides with the losers and agreed to continue Black repression for almost 100 years. The freed slaves found that their former masters once again controlled their fate. American slavery was a human horror of staggering dimensions, a crime against humanity. The profits it produced endowed great fortunes and enriched generations, and its dreadful legacy embraces all of us today. Two hundred and forty-six years of slavery were followed by 100 years of state-sanctioned discrimination, reinforced by public and private terror, ending only after a protracted struggle in 1965, two years after Barack Obama was born.

If you are 45 years old or older, it is only in your lifetime that racial equality before the law became a reality, not before. For only 45 years have all Black Americans been granted the full rights of citizens, only 45 years since legal segregation was ended nationwide, only 45 years since the right to register and vote was universally guaranteed, only 45 years since the protections of the law and Constitution were officially extended to all. We are now asked to believe that 200 years of being someone's property, followed by 100 years of legal oppression in the South and discrimination in the North can be wiped away by four-and-a-half decades of half-hearted remediation and one presidential election. We are now asked to believe that no permanent damage was done to the oppressors or the oppressed. We are asked to believe that we Americans are now a healed and whole people.

The truth is that Jim Crow may be dead, but racism is alive and well. That is the central fact of life for every non-White American, including the President of the United States, eclipsing income, position, and education. Race trumps them all. So we have work to do – none of it easy, but we have never wished our way to freedom. Instead, we have always worked our way.

...

There needs to be a constantly growing and always reviving progressive movement across America if we are going to maintain and expand victories such as reforming health care.

We must not forget that Martin Luther King stood before and with thousands, the people who made the mighty movement what it was. From Jamestown's slave pens to Montgomery's boycotted busses, these ordinary men and women labored in obscurity, and from Montgomery forward they provided the foot soldiers of the freedom army. They shared, with King, an abiding faith in America. They walked in dignity, rather than ride in shame. They faced bombs in Birmingham and mobs in Mississippi. They sat down at lunch counters so others could stand up. They marched – and they organized. King didn't march from Selma to Montgomery by himself. He didn't speak to an empty field at the March on Washington. There were thousands marching with him, and before him, and thousands more who did the dirty work that preceded the triumphal march.

The successful strategies of the modern movement for civil rights were litigation, organization, mobilization and coalition, all aimed at creating a national constituency for civil rights. Sometimes the simplest of deeds – sitting at a lunch counter, going to a new school, applying for a marriage license, casting a vote – can challenge the way we think and act. We have a long and honorable tradition of social justice in this country. It still sends forth the message that when we act together we can overcome. By the year 2050, blacks and Hispanics together will be 40 percent of the nation's population. The growth in immigration and the emergence of new and vibrant populations of people of color hold great promise and great peril. The promise is that the coalition for justice has grown larger and stronger, as new allies join the fight. The peril comes from real fears that our common foes will find ways to separate and divide us. It doesn't make sense if Blacks and Latinos fight over which group has less power; together we can constitute a mighty force for right.

Racial justice, economic equality, and world peace – these were the themes that occupied Martin King's life; they ought to occupy ours today.

Source: Reprinted in *The Cincinnati Herald*, April 16, 2011.

Questions for Consideration

Obama and Bond both turn to the history of the United States to understand the political challenges of the twenty-first century. Where in that past do they see promises? And where do they see dreams deferred?

How, according to the authors in this chapter, are the issues facing African Americans unique and how are they shared by other racial and ethnic groups?

In 1903, W. E. B. Du Bois wrote that the color line was the defining problem of the twentieth century for America. What does the color line look like in the twenty-first century? Does it remain an American problem?

Is a "post-racial America" possible? Is it something for which these authors strive?

Bibliography

Brinkley, Douglas. *The Great Deluge: Hurricane Katrina, New Orleans, and the Mississippi Gulf Coast.* New York: Harper Perennial Books, 2007.
Cobb, William Jelani. *Barack Obama and the Paradox of Progress.* New York: Walker and Company, 2010.

Dyson, Michael Eric. *Come Hell or High Water: Hurricane Katrina and the Color of Disaster*. New York: Basic Civitas Books, 2007.

Ifill, Gwen. *Breakthrough: Politics and Race in the Age of Obama*. New York: Doubleday Press, 2009.

Obama, Barack. *Dreams From My Father: A Story of Race and Inheritance*. New York: Three Rivers Press, 2004.

Obama, Barack. *The Audacity of Hope: Thoughts on Reclaiming the American Dream*. Reprint. New York: Vintage Press, 2008.

Penner, D'Ann R. *Overcoming Katrina: African American Voices from the Crescent City and Beyond*. New York: Palgrave Macmillan, 2009.

West, Cornell, and Tavis Smiley. *The Rich and the Rest of Us: A Poverty Manifesto*. New York: Smiley Books, 2012.

Index

Page entries in italic refer to illustrations in the text.

Printed in Australia
06 Jun 2023
LP015906